The United States and Turkey's Path to Europe

Turkey's relations with the European Union is one of the most enigmatic topics in the European Studies literature. This country, kept at bay by Europeans for centuries, once came unexpectedly close to full-membership. The progress Turkey recorded in its European quest is difficult to account for with either Turkey's performance or the positive attitude of the Europeans towards Turkey.

In this book, Armağan Emre Çakır chronicles over six decades of US involvement in EU–Turkey relations. Shedding new light on the reasons, characteristics, transformation, and relative importance of the US influence on Turkey–EU relations, he argues that Turkey's quest for EU membership would not have advanced this far without the support from the US. Çakır's hypotheses and findings are grounded in original research that, among other things, includes archival material, newspaper articles and interviews conducted on both sides of the Atlantic with key players.

The valuable insights presented in this book make for a much needed alternative history of this volatile relationship.

Armağan Emre Çakır is an associate professor at the European Union Institute of Marmara University, Turkey. His research focuses on theories of European integration, and EU–Turkey relations.

Routledge Advances in International Relations and Global Politics

1 **Foreign Policy and Discourse Analysis**
France, Britain and Europe
Henrik Larsen

2 **Agency, Structure and International Politics**
From ontology to empirical enquiry
Gil Friedman and Harvey Starr

3 **The Political Economy of Regional Co-operation in the Middle East**
Ali Carkoglu, Mine Eder, Kemal Kirisci

4 **Peace Maintenance**
The evolution of international political authority
Jarat Chopra

5 **International Relations and Historical Sociology**
Breaking down boundaries
Stephen Hobden

6 **Equivalence in Comparative Politics**
Edited by Jan W. van Deth

7 **The Politics of Central Banks**
Robert Elgie and Helen Thompson

8 **Politics and Globalisation**
Knowledge, ethics and agency
Martin Shaw

9 **History and International Relations**
Thomas W. Smith

10 **Idealism and Realism in International Relations**
Robert M.A. Crawford

11 **National and International Conflicts, 1945–1995**
New empirical and theoretical approaches.
Frank Pfetsch and Christoph Rohloff

12 **Party Systems and Voter Alignments Revisited**
Edited by Lauri Karvonen and Stein Kuhnle

13 **Ethics, Justice & International Relations**
Constructing an international community
Peter Sutch

14 **Capturing Globalization**
Edited by James H. Mittelman and Norani Othman

15 **Uncertain Europe**
Building a new European security order?
Edited by Martin A. Smith and Graham Timmins

16 **Power, Postcolonialism and International Relations**
Reading race, gender and class
Edited by Geeta Chowdhry and Sheila Nair

17 **Constituting Human Rights**
Global civil society and the society of democratic states
Mervyn Frost

18 **US Economic Statecraft for Survival 1933–1991**
Of sanctions, embargoes and economic warfare
Alan P. Dobson

19 **The EU and NATO Enlargement**
Richard McAllister and Roland Dannreuther

20 **Spatializing International Politics**
Analysing activism on the internet
Jayne Rodgers

21 **Ethnonationalism in the Contemporary World**
Walker Connor and the study of Nationalism
Edited by Daniele Conversi

22 **Meaning and International Relations**
Edited by Peter Mandaville and Andrew Williams

23 **Political Loyalty and the Nation-State**
Edited by Michael Waller and Andrew Linklater

24 **Russian Foreign Policy and the CIS**
Theories, debates and actions
Nicole J. Jackson

25 **Asia and Europe**
Development and different dimensions of ASEM
Yeo Lay Hwee

26 **Global Instability and Strategic Crisis**
Neville Brown

27 **Africa in International Politics**
External involvement on the continent
Edited by Ian Taylor and Paul Williams

28 **Global Governmentality**
Governing international spaces
Edited by Wendy Larner and William Walters

29 **Political Learning and Citizenship Education Under Conflict**
The political socialization of Israeli and Palestinian youngsters
Orit Ichilov

30 **Gender and Civil Society**
Transcending boundaries
Edited by Jude Howell and Diane Mulligan

31 **State Crises, Globalisation and National Movements in North-East Africa**
The horn's dilemma
Edited by Asafa Jalata

32 **Diplomacy and Developing Nations**
Post-Cold War foreign policy-making structures and processes
Edited by Justin Robertson and Maurice A. East

33 **Autonomy, Self-governance and Conflict Resolution**
Innovative approaches to institutional design in divided societies
Edited by Marc Weller and Stefan Wolff

34 **Mediating International Crises**
Jonathan Wilkenfeld, Kathleen J. Young, David M. Quinn and Victor Asal

35 **Postcolonial Politics, the Internet and Everyday Life: Pacific Traversals Online**
M.I. Franklin

36 **Reconstituting the Global Liberal Order**
Legitimacy and regulation
Kanishka Jayasuriya

37 **International Relations, Security and Jeremy Bentham**
Gunhild Hoogensen

38 **Interregionalism and International Relations**
Edited by Heiner Hänggi, Ralf Roloff and Jürgen Rüland

39 **The International Criminal Court**
A global civil society achievement
Marlies Glasius

40 **A Human Security Doctrine for Europe**
Project, principles, practicalities
Edited by Marlies Glasius and Mary Kaldor

41 **The History and Politics of UN Security Council Reform**
Dimitris Bourantonis

42 **Russia and NATO Since 1991**
From cold war through cold peace to partnership?
Martin A. Smith

43 **The Politics of Protection**
Sites of insecurity and political agency
Edited by Jef Huysmans, Andrew Dobson and Raia Prokhovnik

44 **International Relations in Europe**
Traditions, perspectives and destinations
Edited by Knud Erik Jørgensen and Tonny Brems Knudsen

45 **The Empire of Security and the Safety of the People**
Edited by William Bain

46 **Globalization and Religious Nationalism in India**
The search for ontological security
Catrina Kinnvall

47 **Culture and International Relations**
Narratives, natives and tourists
Julie Reeves

48 **Global Civil Society**
Contested futures
Edited by Gideon Baker and David Chandler

49 **Rethinking Ethical Foreign Policy**
Pitfalls, possibilities and paradoxes
Edited by David Chandler and Volker Heins

50 **International Cooperation and Arctic Governance**
Regime effectiveness and northern region building
Edited by Olav Schram Stokke and Geir Hønneland

51 **Human Security**
Concepts and implications
Shahrbanou Tadjbakhsh and Anuradha Chenoy

52 **International Relations and Security in the Digital Age**
Edited by Johan Eriksson and Giampiero Giacomello

53 **State-Building**
Theory and practice
Edited by Aidan Hehir and Neil Robinson

54 **Violence and Non-Violence in Africa**
Edited by Pal Ahluwalia, Louise Bethlehem and Ruth Ginio

55 **Developing Countries and Global Trade Negotiations**
Edited by Larry Crump and S. Javed Maswood

56 **Civil Society, Religion and Global Governance**
Paradigms of power and persuasion
Edited by Helen James

57 **War, Peace and Hegemony in a Globalized World**
The changing balance of power in the 21st century
Edited by Chandra Chari

58 **Economic Globalisation as Religious War**
Tragic convergence
Michael McKinley

59 **Globalization, Prostitution and Sex-Trafficking**
Corporeal politics
Elina Penttinen

60 **Peacebuilding**
Women in international perspective
Elisabeth Porter

61 **Ethics, Liberalism and Realism in International Relations**
Mark D. Gismondi

62 **Law and Legalization in Transnational Relations**
Edited by Christian Brütsch and Dirk Lehmkuhl

63 **Fighting Terrorism and Drugs**
Europe and international police cooperation
Jörg Friedrichs

64 **Identity Politics in the Age of Genocide**
The Holocaust and historical representation
David B. MacDonald

65 **Globalisation, Public Opinion and the State**
Western Europe and East and Southeast Asia
Edited by Takashi Inoguchi and Ian Marsh

66 **Urbicide**
The politics of urban destruction
Martin Coward

67 **Transnational Activism in the UN and the EU**
A comparative study
Jutta Joachim and Birgit Locher

68 **Gender Inclusive**
Essays on violence, men and feminist international relations
Adam Jones

69 **Capitalism, Democracy and the Prevention of War and Poverty**
Edited by Peter Graeff and Guido Mehlkop

70 **Environmental Change and Foreign Policy**
Theory and practice
Edited by Paul G. Harris

71 **Climate Change and Foreign Policy**
Case studies from East to West
Edited by Paul G. Harris

72 **Securitizations of Citizenship**
Edited by Peter Nyers

73 **The Power of Ideology**
From the Roman Empire to Al-Qaeda
Alex Roberto Hybel

74 **The Securitization of Humanitarian Migration**
Digging moats and sinking boats
Scott D. Watson

75 **Mediation in the Asia-Pacific Region**
Transforming conflicts and building peace
Edited by Dale Bagshaw and Elisabeth Porter

76 **United Nations Reform**
Heading North or South?
Spencer Zifcak

77 **New Norms and Knowledge in World Politics**
Protecting people, intellectual property and the environment
Preslava Stoeva

78 **Power, Resistance and Conflict in the Contemporary World**
Social movements, networks and hierarchies
Athina Karatzogianni and Andrew Robinson

79 **World-Regional Social Policy and Global Governance**
New research and policy agendas in Africa, Asia, Europe and Latin America
Edited by Bob Deacon, Maria Cristina Macovei, Luk Van Langenhove and Nicola Yeates

80 **International Relations Theory and Philosophy**
Interpretive dialogues
Edited by Cerwyn Moore and Chris Farrands

81 **Superpower Rivalry and Conflict**
The long shadow of the Cold War on the twenty-first century
Edited by Chandra Chari

82 **Coping and Conformity in World Politics**
Hugh C. Dyer

83 **Defining and Defying Organized Crime**
Discourse, perception and reality
Edited by Felia Allum, Francesca Longo, Daniela Irrera and Panos A. Kostakos

84 **Federalism in Asia**
India, Pakistan and Malaysia
Harihar Bhattacharyya

85 **The World Bank and HIV/AIDS**
Setting a global agenda
Sophie Harman

86 **The "War on Terror" and the Growth of Executive Power?**
A comparative analysis
Edited by John E. Owens and Riccardo Pelizzo

87 **The Contested Politics of Mobility**
Borderzones and irregularity
Edited by Vicki Squires

88 **Human Security, Law and the prevention of Terrorism**
Andrej Zwitter

89 **Multilayered Migration Governance**
The promise of partnership
Edited by Rahel Kunz, Sandra Lavenex and Marion Panizzon

90 **Role Theory in International Relations**
Approaches and analyses
Edited by Sebastian Harnisch, Cornelia Frank & Hanns W. Maull

91 **Issue Salience in International Relations**
Edited by Kai Oppermann and Henrike Viehrig

92 **Corporate Risk and National Security Redefined**
Karen Lund Petersen

93 **Interrogating Democracy in World Politics**
Edited by Joe Hoover, Meera Sabaratnam and Laust Schouenborg

94 **Globalizing Resistance against War**
Theories of resistance and the new Anti-War Movement
Tiina Seppälä

95 **The Politics of Self-Determination**
Beyond the decolonisation process
Kristina Roepstorff

96 **Sovereignty and the Responsibility to Protect**
The power of norms and the norms of the powerful
Theresa Reinold

97 **Anglo-American Relations**
Contemporary perspectives
Edited by Alan P. Dobson and Steve Marsh

98 **The Emerging Politics of Antarctica**
Edited by Anne-Marie Brady

99 **Genocide, Ethnonationalism, and the United Nations**
Exploring the causes of mass killing since 1945
Hannibal Travis

100 **Caribbean Sovereignty, Development and Democracy in an Age of Globalization**
Edited by Linden Lewis

101 **Rethinking Foreign Policy**
Edited by Fredrik Bynander and Stefano Guzzini

102 **The Promise and Perils of Transnationalization**
NGO activism and the socialization of women's human rights in Egypt and Iran
Benjamin Stachursky

103 **Peacebuilding and International Administration**
The cases of Bosnia and Herzegovina and Kosovo
Niels van Willigen

104 **The Politics of the Globalization of Law**
Getting from rights to justice
Edited by Alison Brysk

105 **The Arctic in International Politics**
Coming in from the cold
Peter Hough

106 **Understanding Transatlantic Relations**
Whither the West?
Serena Simoni

107 **India in South Asia**
Domestic identity politics and foreign policy from Nehru to the BJP
Sinderpal Singh

108 **A Strategic Understanding of UN Economic Sanctions**
International relations, law and development
Golnoosh Hakimdavar

109 **Politics and the Bomb**
The role of experts in the creation of cooperative Nuclear Non-Proliferation Agreements
Sara Z. Kutchesfahani

110 **Interpreting Global Security**
Mark Bevir, Oliver Daddow and Ian Hall

111 **Foreign Policy, Domestic Politics and International Relations**
The case of Italy
Elisabetta Brighi

112 **The Scourge of Genocide**
Essays and reflections
Adam Jones

113 **Authority, Ascendancy, and Supremacy**
China, Russia, and the United States' pursuit of relevancy and power
Gregory O. Hall

114 **The Politics of Arctic Sovereignty**
Oil, ice and Inuit governance
Jessica M. Shadian

115 **Small States and International Security**
Europe and beyond
Edited by Clive Archer, Alyson J. K. Bailes and Anders Wivel

116 **Networked Governance and Transatlantic Relations**
Building bridges through science diplomacy
Gabriella Paár-Jákli

117 **The Role, Position and Agency of Cusp States in International Relations**
Edited by Marc Herzog and Philip Robins

118 **The Politics of Conflict Economies**
Miners, merchants and warriors in the African borderland
Morten Bøås

119 **Exercising Human Rights**
Gender, agency, and practice
Robin Redhead

120 **State Responses to International Law**
Who complies?
Kendall Stiles

121 **Regional Integration and Democratic Conditionality**
How democracy clauses help democratic consolidation and deepening
Gaspare M. Genna and Taeko Hiroi

122 **Profits, Security and Human Rights in Developing Countries**
Global lessons from Canada's extractive sector in Colombia
Edited by James Rochlin

123 **The Politics of Place and the Limits to Redistribution**
Melissa Ziegler Rogers

124 **Apology and Reconciliation in International Relations**
The importance of being sorry
Edited by Christopher Daase, Stefan Engert, Michel-André Horelt, Judith Renner, Renate Strassner

125 **The United States and Turkey's Path to Europe**
Hands across the table
Armağan Emre Çakır

126 **Western Muslim Reactions to Conflicts Abroad**
Conflict spillovers to diasporas
Juris Pupcenoks

Working lunch between President Clinton and Chancellor Kohl at Filomena Ristorante in Washington, DC on 31 January 1994. Credit: Filomena Ristorante, Washington, DC

The United States and Turkey's Path to Europe
Hands across the Table

Armağan Emre Çakır

LONDON AND NEW YORK

First published 2016 by Routledge

2 Park Square, Milton Park, Abingdon, Oxfordshire OX14 4RN
711 Third Avenue, New York, NY 10017

Routledge is an imprint of the Taylor & Francis Group, an informa business

First issued in paperback 2017

Copyright © 2016 Taylor & Francis

The right of Armağan Emre Çakır to be identified as author of this work has been asserted by him in accordance with sections 77 and 78 of the Copyright, Designs and Patents Act 1988.

All rights reserved. No part of this book may be reprinted or reproduced or utilised in any form or by any electronic, mechanical, or other means, now known or hereafter invented, including photocopying and recording, or in any information storage or retrieval system, without permission in writing from the publishers.

Notice:
Product or corporate names may be trademarks or registered trademarks, and are used only for identification and explanation without intent to infringe.

Library of Congress Cataloging-in-Publication Data
A catalog record for this title has been requested

ISBN: 978-1-138-18685-9 (hbk)
ISBN: 978-0-8153-7060-4 (pbk)

Typeset in Bembo
by Apex CoVantage, LLC

Contents

Acknowledgments xvii
Abbreviations xix

Introduction 1

1 The Eisenhower Administration (1953–1961):
  A Promising Start 10

2 The Kennedy Administration (1961–1963): Trade
  Winds Start Blowing 29

3 The Johnson Administration (1963–1969): EEC
  Falls Off the Agenda 41

4 The Nixon Administration (1969–1974): Zigzags 49

5 The Ford Administration (1974–1977): Cyprus 60

6 The Carter Administration (1977–1981):
  Turkey–US Relations Improve 69

7 The Reagan Administration (1981–1989): The US
  Involvement Commences 80

8 The (George H.W.) Bush Administration (1989–1993):
  The US Support Becomes Public 91

9 The Clinton Administration (1993–2001):
  Deux ex Machina 107

10	The (George W.) Bush Administration (2001–2009): An Underestimated Effort	162
11	The First Obama Administration (2009–2013): Decline	225
	Conclusion	255
	Index	279

Acknowledgments

This book was made possible by a Fulbright Grant. I especially thank Ersin Onulduran, the former Executive Director of the Turkish Fulbright Commission, and David C. Cuthell, Jr., the former Executive Director of the Institute of Turkish Studies of Georgetown University, my host institution.

I am grateful to former National Security Advisor Brent Scowcroft, former Speaker of the US House of Representatives Dennis Hastert, former US Ambassadors to Turkey Morton Abramowitz, Marc Grossman, and Ross Wilson, former US Ambassador to Greece Thomas Miller, and former Deputy Chief of Mission in the US Embassy in Turkey and the President of the American-Turkish Council James Howard Holmes. I am impressed with their accessibility and the absence of haughtiness in their demeanor.

Members of the Turkish Embassy in Washington demonstrated their courtesy and finesse by providing me with some valuable information while taking care of the confidentiality of the issues in question. Former President of the Assembly of Turkish American Associations Günay Evinch, Vice President of the Turkish Coalition of America Başak Kızıldemir, former President of TÜSİAD's Washington Representative Office Abdullah Akyüz, and Member of the Board of Trustees of the Assembly of Turkish American Associations Oya Bain shared with me their invaluable experience in and knowledge on Turkey–US relations. Likewise, I am thankful to Vice President of the Atlantic Council Frances G. Burwell, and the Director of the Turkish Research Program at the Washington Institute Soner Çağaptay for their insightful ideas.

I appreciate the friendly approach of David Zierler from the Office of the Historian of the Department of State. He made possible my access to some declassified but unpublished official documents.

David Robert Bowe, a former Member of the European Parliament, was kind enough to recount his memories and to recommend me the names of some of his former colleagues.

I feel indebted to several members of the corps diplomatique of European states in the US who preferred to remain anonymous, for sharing with me their opinion—and some confidential information too—sometimes transcending the confines of their professional position.

In Turkey, I conducted interviews with former Deputy PM of Turkey Ali Bozer, former Turkish FMs İlter Türkmen, Hikmet Çetin, Murat Karayalçın, Emre Gönensay, and Şükrü Sina Gürel, former Minister of State Tayyibe Gülek, former Ministerial Counselor at the Turkish Foreign Ministry Onur Öymen, former Ministerial Counselor at the Turkish Foreign Ministry and former Representative of Turkey to the EU Nihat Akyol, former Turkish Ambassador to the US Şükrü Elekdağ, former Secretary-General for EU Affairs Volkan Vural, former Chairman of the Foreign Affairs Commission of the Turkish Parliament Mehmet Dülger, Deputy Under Secretary of Ministry of the EU Affairs Burak Erdemir, and Permanent Representative of the Turkish Textile and Apparel Exporters' Association in Brussels M. Haluk Özelçi. I left each of those interviews with a little treasure chest filled with little-known tidbits and comments distilled through years of experience.

The insatiable thirst of the text for resources could not have been quenched without the benevolent help of the following people: Türkan Ertuna Legrand from the European Parliament in Brussels, Jan Majaniemi from the Archive and Documentation Centre of the European Parliament in Luxembourg, the staff of various presidential libraries and museums in the US including the Library of Congress, and the Joseph Mark Lauinger Library of Georgetown University (especially Brenda Bickett), the staff of the newspaper archives of the Taksim Atatürk Library in Istanbul, Vanessa Mazzucchelli from the Italian Oggi magazine, Ferai Tınç and Faruk Bildirici from Turkish daily Hürriyet, Sinem User Kara and members of the staff of the archives of Cumhuriyet, another Turkish daily, and Burcu Orhan Akgün from TÜSİAD.

My thanks extend to Birol Yeşilada from Portland State University and an anonymous reviewer for their constructive criticisms of the draft text. Yeşilada kindly provided a detailed critique of the text.

Last but not least, I am in debt to my wife Pembe for her loving patience and support.

Armağan Emre Çakır
Strasbourg, July 2015

Abbreviations

AC	Association Council
AJC	American Jewish Committee
AKP	Adalet ve Kalkınma Partisi (Justice and Development Party)
APD	Accession Partnership Document
ASSTSECDEF	Assistant Secretary of Defense
ASSTSECSTATE	Assistant Secretary of State
BMENA	Broader Middle East and North Africa
CAP	Common Agricultural Policy
CCT	Common Customs Tariff
CDA	Christen-Democratisch Appèl (Christian Democratic Appeal)
CDU	Christlich-Demokratische Union (Christian Democratic Union)
CEECs	Central and Eastern European countries
CENTO	Central Treaty Organization
CFSP	Common Foreign and Security Policy
CFT	Conservative Friends of Turkey
CHP	Cumhuriyet Halk Partisi (Republican People's Party)
CIR	Committee on International Relations
COEU	Council of the European Union
COFA	Committee on Foreign Affairs
COFR	Committee on Foreign Relations
COM	Council of Ministers
CRS	Congressional Research Service
CSCE	Conference on Security and Cooperation in Europe
CSU	Christlich-Soziale Union (Christian Social Union)
CU	Customs Union
D-8	Developing Eight
DCM	Deputy Chief of Mission
DEPSECDEF	Deputy Secretary of Defense
DEPSECSTATE	Deputy Secretary of State
DF	Domestic factor

DHKP-C	Devrimci Halk Kurtuluş Partisi-Cephesi (Revolutionary People's Liberation Party-Front)
DOA	Department of Agriculture
DOD	Department of Defense
DOS	Department of State
EC	European Community/ies
ECON	Bureau of Economic Affairs
ECPC	Economic Cooperation Partnership Council
EEC	European Economic Community
EFTA	European Free-Trade Association
EP	European Parliament
EPU	European Payments Union
ESDI	European Security and Defense Identity
EU	European Union
EUR	Bureau of European Affairs (1949–1983), Bureau of European and Canadian Affairs (1983–1999), Bureau of European Affairs (1999–2001), and Bureau of European and Eurasian Affairs (since 2001)
EURATOM	European Atomic Energy Community
FDP	Freie Demokratische Partei (Free Democratic Party)
FIR	Flight information region
FM	Foreign Minister
FP	Foreign policy
FRUS	Foreign Relations of the United States
FS	Foreign Secretary
FT	*Financial Times*
FTA	Free-trade area
G7	Group of Seven
G8	Group of Eight
G20	Group of Twenty
GAER	General Affairs and External Relations
GATT	General Agreement on Tariffs and Trade
GMFUS	German Marshall Fund of the United States
GOT	Government of Turkey
GSP	Generalized System of Preferences
GTI	Office of Greek, Turkish and Iranian Affairs
HDN	*Hürriyet Daily News*
HOR	House of Representatives
HR	Human rights
ICJ	International Court of Justice
IISS	International Institute for Strategic Studies
IMF	International Monetary Fund
INF	Intermediate-Range Nuclear Forces
ISAF	International Security Assistance Force

LAT	*Los Angeles Times*
LDCs	Less-developed countries
MEP	Member of the European Parliament
MS	Member state
NAC	North Atlantic Council
NAFTA	North American Free-Trade Agreement
NATO	North Atlantic Treaty Organization
NEA	Bureau of Near Eastern and South Asian Affairs
NIE	National Intelligence Estimate
NRA	Neorealist assumption
NSA	National Security Advisor
NSC	National Security Council
NYT	*New York Times*
OCB	Operations Coordinating Board
OECD	Organization for Economic Cooperation and Development
OEEC	Organization for European Economic Cooperation
OJ	Official Journal
OSCE	Organization for Security and Cooperation in Europe
PKK	Partiya Karkerên Kurdistan (The Kurdistan Workers' Party)
PL	Presidential Library
PM	Prime Minister
PPPUS	Public Papers of the Presidents of the United States
PRC	Policy Review Committee
PSC	Political and Security Committee
PTA	Preferential trade agreement
QIZ	Qualifying industrial zone
RRF	Rapid Reaction Force
SACEUR	Supreme Allied Commander Europe
SECDEF	Secretary of Defense
SECI	Southeast Cooperation Initiative
SECSTATE	Secretary of State
SLG	Senior Level Group
SPD	Sozialdemokratische Partei Deutschlands (Social Democratic Party of Germany)
TDN	*Turkish Daily News*
TMFA	Turkish Ministry of Foreign Affairs
TRNC	Turkish Republic of Northern Cyprus
TRT	Türkiye Radyo Televizyon Kurumu (Turkish Radio and Television Corporation)
TÜSİAD	Türk Sanayicileri ve İşadamları Derneği (Turkish Industrialists' and Businessmen's Association)
TZ	*Today's Zaman*
UN	United Nations

USAMB	United States Ambassador
USD(P)	Under Secretary of Defense for Policy
USDEL	United States Delegation
USEU	United States Mission to the European Union
USG	United States Government
USGPO	United States Government Printing Office
WEU	Western European Union
WG	Working group
WINEP	Washington Institute for Near East Policy
WSJ	*Wall Street Journal*
WT	*Washington Times*

Introduction

Aristotle, one of the earliest empiricists, made curious contributions to natural history based on experience and evidence: to discover the secrets of living organisms, he dissected octopuses or broke open chicken eggs. Some of his findings are considered accurate by modern biology.[1] However, at times, he relied on his assumptions in presenting 'facts,' which lead to grotesque mistakes such as that "(m)ales have more teeth than females in the case of men, sheep, goats, and swine."[2]

> [He] could have avoided the mistake of thinking that women have fewer teeth than men, by the simple device of asking Mrs. Aristotle to keep her mouth open while he counted. He did not do so because he thought he knew. Thinking that you know when in fact you don't is a fatal mistake, to which we are all prone. I believe myself that hedgehogs eat black beetles, because I have been told that they do; but if I were writing a book on the habits of hedgehogs, I should not commit myself until I had seen one enjoying this unappetizing dish.[3]

Aristotle's statement about the teeth of females is an example of what Roy Bhaskar calls 'epistemic fallacy,' "the reduction of being to knowledge,"[4] or in simpler terms, theorizing in advance of facts. The present book sets out to correct two fallacies of this kind:

1. A majority of the works on the enlargement of the European Union (EU) consider this enlargement as a bilateral relationship. In their conception, enlargement occurs between the country acceding to the EU on the one hand, and the EU and/or its member states (MSs) on the other. They expect this relationship to proceed in accordance with the decisions of the parties and in proportion to the acceding country's success in its domestic reforms. Thus, in these works the EU's enlargement

is examined in isolation by disregarding the external factors—especially the effect of third actors:

> The literature on EU enlargement has focused primarily on three dimensions of enlargement which all concern the process leading to enlargement, or to decisions on formal acts of horizontal institutionalization. These dimensions could be labelled respectively as: (1) applicants' enlargement politics; (2) member state enlargement politics; and (3) EU enlargement politics.[5]

2. The remaining minority does acknowledge the effect of the third actors—particularly the US—on EU enlargement, but these works are under the misconception that

   a. The US has always supported Turkey's accession to—or at least close relations with—the EU, and
   b. This support was provided mainly on the basis of geostrategic calculations.

In this book, the EU enlargement is regarded as a process open to the effect of third actors. In particular, the book traces the fingerprints of the US on Turkey–EU relations. It employs the following model where Turkey's prospects for EU membership are taken as a function of Turkey's relations with the US and with the members of the EU:

Turkey's EU prospects = f[(Turkey's relations with the members[6] of the EU) + (Turkey's relations with the US)] + other important factors[7]

To avoid the epistemic fallacy, every chapter first presents a detailed account of Turkey's relations with the US and EU in a presidential era and, then, in its Conclusion, it deduces the influence of Turkey–US relations on Turkey–EU relations. The main Conclusion section of the book is where the material presented in the chapters is distilled into the following two deductive and complementary hypotheses:

1. Turkey-US relations have always been a key variable in Turkey–EU relations.
2. In the Cold War era, Turkey and the US missed a large window of opportunity where Turkey's membership to the European Economic Community (EEC) could have become reality with US help.

The leftovers of this distillation, the residue that remains after this hypothesization process, are presented as 'findings' after the hypotheses.

The theoretical backbone of the book is Waltzian neorealism. Neorealism is a systemic theory of international politics. It explains the foreign policy (FP) choices of a given state with reference to systemic factors and intentionally leaves the effect of domestic factors out of account; neorealists posit that "a state's foreign policy is determined by hundreds of highly variable and idiosyncratic [domestic] factors that lie outside the ken of sparse structural theory."[8]

The pertinent assumptions of neorealism are as follows:

NRA1: *International political system is characterized by anarchy.*[9]

Anarchy refers to the absence of a higher authority over the units of the international system, namely states, and implies the sameness of these units.

NRA2: *The state is the only actor in international politics.*[10]

For neorealists, either the effect of non-state actors is insignificant in international political system or these actors are controlled by great powers. In domestic politics, the ordering principle is hierarchy.

NRA3: *Survival is the ground of action for states.*[11]

Beyond the survival motive, the aims of states may vary—including economic aims.

NRA4: *States refrain from becoming dependent on each other economically*[12] *or militarily.*[13]

"(D)ependent parties conform their behavior to the preferences of those they depend on." States may make use of favorable economic position to support national political ends.[14] In this context, power is defined in terms of distribution of—economic and political—capabilities.[15]

> **NRA5:** *States choose relative over absolute gains.*[16]

States are not simply concerned with whether they can gain by cooperation; they are concerned with who gains most. Power relations in international politics are based on zero-sum games.

> **NRA6:** *States tend to form balances of power whether or not they wish to.*[17]

Maintenance or reformation of balance of power may be a motive for some states[18] who, for this purpose, exert either internal (such as increasing its economic capability and/or military strength) or external (such as strengthening and enlarging its own alliance and/or weakening and shrinking an opposing one) moves.[19] "The game of power politics [. . .] presses the players into two rival camps."[20] Eventually a bipolar international system emerges where the two great powers are capable of acting on a world scale.[21] When one side of the balance of power looks like the winner, most states bandwagon with the winner.[22]

> **NRA7:** *"In bipolar as in multipolar worlds, alliance leaders may try to elicit maximum contributions from their associates.*[23]

Nevertheless, alliance leader determine their policies and strategies on the basis of their own calculations and interests.

> **NRA8:** *Ideology is subordinated to interest.*[24]

Interest is the main concern for states in, among other actions, entering into and leaving an alliance.

The discussions in the Conclusion section of the chapters are grounded in the assumptions presented above. Throughout the text each assumption is referred to with its respective abbreviation (such as '[NRA1]') whereas the idiosyncratic domestic factors left unaccounted for by neorealism are also identified and related to the assumptions of neorealism as much as possible in the case of the EU MSs, the US and Turkey. These factors are marked with '(DF).'

★★★

The inspiration to write this book came from the visit of a Turkish politician to the US. Recep Tayyip Erdoğan, the leader of the Justice and Development Party (AKP),[25] was received at the White House on 10 December 2002. An interesting detail from this visit found its way to newspapers: "'In today's discussion, I proposed to President Bush that they take us into NAFTA' said Mr. Erdoğan."[26] NAFTA (North American Free-Trade Agreement) was a regional agreement between Canada, Mexico, and the US, and it was difficult to conceive Turkey as a party to it. We do not know Bush's reply, but we have enough evidence to infer that by some circles in the US, Erdoğan's unusual NAFTA proposal was received as a feasible complement or even an alternative to the long-standing US support to Turkey's membership bid to join the EU. The same *Wall Street Journal* (*WSJ*) editorial that reported Erdoğan's words extolled this proposal:

> We think it's a brilliant idea. In the global economy, physical proximity matters little. And if the European Union leaders meeting today in Copenhagen won't give Turkey a firm date for membership talks, the U.S. should assume responsibility for further anchoring Turkey to the West.

In January 2003, Fred E. Foldvary argued for the idea under the title "Let Turkey Join NAFTA."[27] Friedman had a more ambitious proposal:

> I think Turkey's membership in the EU is so important that the US should consider subsidizing the EU to make it easier for Turkey to be admitted. If that fails, we should offer to bring Turkey into NAFTA, even though it would be very complicated.[28]

Mark Kirk, a Republican member of the US House of Representatives (HOR), proposed that the US offer Turkey a bilateral free-trade agreement as a trump card against the EU.[29]

It was as if the US had reached the limits of its opportunities to champion Turkey's EU membership and was now stretching its imagination to go further. It seems plausible to assume that Erdoğan's proposal was based on his confidence in the incessant US efforts in mending Turkey's broken heart in its extended affair with the EU.

For how long had the US been involved in the game between Turkey and the EU? Had the US always supported Turkey this strongly? What were the motives behind this support? These and similar questions prompted the writing of this book.

One may think that the massive US involvement in Turkey–EU relations can easily be unearthed with the help of the data available in the literature and the mass media. Yet the writing process of the book revealed that this was not the case: in the literature, this was an under-researched topic. The only comprehensive work available on the topic was Nathalie Tocci's book entitled *Turkey's European Future: Behind the Scenes of America's Influence on EU-Turkey Relations*[30] and published in 2011. In the book, both direct and indirect (through Turkey) US influence on Turkey–EU relations were examined and the US power that underlay this influence was analyzed on material, ideational, and discursive grounds. A year later, Tocci published an article entitled "Let's Talk Turkey! US Influence on EU-Turkey Relations"[31] on the same theme with an emphasis on broad policy suggestions for the US in this regard.[32]

Two articles that predated Tocci's works, one published by Sabri Sayarı in 2003 (perhaps the earliest academic work on the subject) and entitled "The United States and Turkey's Membership in the European Union"[33] and the other published by Ziya Öniş and Şuhnaz Yılmaz in 2005 and entitled "The Turkey-EU-US Triangle in Perspective"[34] were rather small-scale historical overviews. In his chapter entitled "The US and Turkey's Quest for EU Membership" and published in an edited book in 2006,[35] Ömer Taşpınar discussed the context and conditions of the US support to Turkey in the post-Cold War era. In 2011, Sayarı published another article entitled "Challenges of Triangular Relations: The US, the EU, and Turkish Accession,"[36] which, unlike the other works, included a—short—account of US initiatives in favor of Turkey and their consequences.

Besides these works dedicated to the US influence on Turkey–EU relations, some others written on relevant themes had references to the topic. In their chapter entitled "The Strategic Implications of Turkey's Integration in the European Union,"[37] and published in an edited volume in 2005, Henri Barkey and Anne-Marie Le Gloannec allocated a few paragraphs to discuss the mentality of the US support for Turkey's EU bid after the EU's 1997 Luxembourg Council. A similarly titled chapter, "The Strategic Implications of Turkey's EU Membership"[38] by Constantinos Koliopoulos, published in an edited volume in 2008, elaborated on the same subject this time in the context of the post-Cold War period. In the chapter he entitled "Turkish-American Relations in the post-Cold War Era: Issues of Convergence and Divergence"[39] published in an edited volume in 2004, Sayarı dedicated a title to discuss the US efforts for Turkey's EU membership. Birol Yeşilada's book entitled *EU-Turkey Relations in the 21st Century*[40] and published in 2013, contained sections examining the US factor in the lead-up to the signing of the Customs Union (CU) decision[41] and to the Conclusions of the 2002 Copenhagen European Council.[42]

As valuable and interesting contributions to the literature as they were, these sources had four shortcomings in common. They were

1 focused on the post-Cold War period, neglecting the Cold War era,
2 trying to discover the reasons behind the US support, but disregarding the modus operandi of this support mechanism,
3 contented with little historical evidence to buttress their arguments, and
4 relying on the unsubstantiated assumption that the US had always firmly supported Turkey's accession to the EU.

Our book set out to redress these shortcomings. Although information from behind closed doors was required to perform this task in a conclusive and convincing manner, going beyond publicly available knowledge proved to be an arduous challenge. The first words of a retired American diplomat in our interview were indicative of how meager the present book's prospects were without journalistic wizardry, pushing-and-prodding, and serendipity: "I do not think you will find fingerprints on a concrete event" he commented. Another one opined that there was not enough material on this topic to warrant a book; "are you going to write a treatise?" he asked. Nevertheless, like reconstructing a broken ancient pottery from a couple of original shards by using a generous amount of plaster-filling between them, the text was brought into being with a few pieces of concrete information and documentary evidence connected to each other by the cement of inference and extrapolation.

The book covers the period that starts with the Eisenhower era in which Turkey established its initial contacts with the EEC and ends with the conclusion of the Obama administration's first term in which the US involvement in Turkey–EU relations died out. In each chapter, there is a section explaining the mentality of the respective administration in its approach to Turkey–EU relations. From the Reagan era onwards, the US made its presence felt in Turkey–EU relations, while certain EU and non-EU states cooperated with the US in this endeavor. Therefore, the chapter on the Reagan administration and the ones following it have a section on the US involvement in Turkey–EU relations and another one on 'the collaborators' of the US in helping Turkey.

Every chapter of the text opens with a meal—sometimes a stately event, and sometimes a modest collation. As much as being a reflection of the subconscious of an author trapped between library shelves for long hours, these meals serve as metaphors referring to the informal nature of the US support for Turkey: The hand the US extended across the sea to cooperate with its allies when necessary, was also able to persuade them from across the dinner table. Whilst Sousa's magnificent *Hands across the Sea* was dedicated to the 'cooperation' dimension of the transatlantic relations, this modest book is intended to shed light on its 'persuasion' dimension.

Notes

1. Allan Gotthelf and James G. Lennox, *Philosophical Issues in Aristotle's Biology*, New York: Cambridge University Press, 1987, esp. pp. 53–4.
2. Aristotle, *Historia Animalium*, Oxford: Clarendon Press, 1910, p. 37.
3. Bertrand Russell, *Unpopular Essays*, New York, NY: Simon and Schuster, 1951, p. 103.
4. Roy Bhaskar, *Scientific Realism and Human Emancipation*, London: Routledge, 2009, p. 15.
5. Frank Schimmelfennig and Ulrich Sedelmeier, "Theorizing EU enlargement: Research focus, hypotheses, and the state of research," *Journal of European Public Policy*, Vol. 9, No. 4, 2002, 500–28, p. 504.
6. As the analyses contained in the text are grounded in Waltzian neorealism, references to the EU's actorness in international politics are minimized.
7. I am grateful to Professor Birol Yeşilada who recommended me to formalize my approach into such a model.
8. James Fearon, "Domestic politics, foreign policy, and theories of international relations," *Annual Review of Political Science*, Vol. 1, 1998, 289–313, p. 295.
9. Kenneth Waltz, *Theory of International Politics*, New York, NY: McGraw-Hill, 1979, pp. 93–5.
10. Ibid., p. 88–9.
11. p. 91–2.
12. p. 139–46.
13. p. 161–93.
14. p. 157.
15. p. 192.
16. p. 105.
17. p. 126.
18. p. 119.
19. p. 118.
20. p. 167.
21. p. 171.
22. p. 126.
23. p. 169.
24. p. 172.
25. At the time of this visit, although his party had won the November 2002 election, Erdoğan was unable to assume the post of PM due to his prior conviction for having recited a poem. He could become PM in March 2003 (See page 215 endnote 89.).
26. "Turkey for NAFTA," *WSJ*, 13 December 2002.
27. Fred E. Foldvary, "Let Turkey join NAFTA," *The Progress Report*. Available at www.progress.org/archive/fold281.htm, accessed 22 June 2009.
28. Milton Friedman, "War of ideas: Part 2," *NYT*, 11 January 2004.
29. Ümit Enginsoy, "ABD Türkiye'ye serbest ticaret anlaşması önerebilir," 17 December 2003, *NTVMSNBC*. Available at www.ntvmsnbc.com/news/248541.asp, accessed 22 June 2009.
30. New York University Press.
31. *Cambridge Review of International Affairs*, Vol. 25, No. 3, 399–416.
32. p. 399.
33. *The Turkish Yearbook of International Relations*, Vol. 34, 167–76.
34. *Middle East Journal*, Vol. 59, No. 2, 265–85.
35. Joseph S. Joseph (ed.), *Turkey and the European Union: Internal Dynamics and External Challenges*, New York, NY: Palgrave Macmillan, 191–210.
36. *South European Society and Politics*, Vol. 16, No. 2, 251–63.
37. In Ester Brimmer and Stefan Fröchlich (eds.), *The Strategic Implications of European Union Enlargement*, Washington, DC: Johns Hopkins University, 2005, 127–50.

38 In Meltem Müftüler-Baç and Yannis Stivachtis (eds.), *Turkey-European Union Relations: Dilemmas, Opportunities, and Constraints*, Lanham, MD: Lexington Books, 2008, 93–111.
39 In Mustafa Aydın and Çağrı Erhan (eds.), *Turkish-American Relations: Past, Present and Future*, New York, NY: Routledge, 91–106.
40 New York, NY: Routledge.
41 p. 12.
42 pp. 15–6.

1 The Eisenhower Administration (1953–1961)

A Promising Start

On 6 June 1958, the US Secretary of State (SECSTATE) Dulles was having dinner with West German President Heuss and Foreign Minister (FM) Brentano at the German Embassy in Washington.[1] The latter two were on a state visit. At the table, Heuss recalled Turkish President Bayar's visit to Germany and expressed his conviction that Turkey was in a desperate financial position; something had to be done to help Turkey. Dulles asked the opinion of his other host, von Brentano, because Suat Hayri Ürgüplü, the Turkish Ambassador to the US had found an opportunity to see von Brentano on the day of the dinner, and von Brentano had mentioned to Dulles about the ambassador's visit. Von Brentano confirmed Heuss's conviction. Dulles argued that "it would be a mistake if Germany should, on bilateral basis, extend financial assistance to Turkey without regard to the views of the IMF (International Monetary Fund) or the OEEC (Organization for European Economic Cooperation)." Von Brentano said he quite agreed. In Dulles's opinion, von Brentano had in his mind OEEC rather than the IMF.[2]

This small talk contained some themes that would reappear in the coming decades in Turkey's relations with the US and European countries:

1. Turkey, experiencing severe economic problems and continuously looking for aid from "the West" without differentiating between the US and European countries,
2. The US and Germany being attentive to Turkey's condition,
3. The US, trying to restrict the bilateral relations between Turkey and European countries and to channel these relations into organizational settings that the US dominated, and
4. Germany, admitting the US dominance but trying to limit it.

1 Integrating Turkey into the Western Alliance

The main reason behind the American and German empathy with Turkey was the escalating tensions from the Cold War. For the US, Turkey was more important than it was for Germany. In March 1947, President Truman had declared that the US would provide political, military, and economic assistance to all democratic nations (particularly Greece and Turkey) under threat from external or internal authoritarian forces (meaning the USSR and communism). Since 1947, the US had been following the 'containment policy.' In 1954, Dulles announced that this policy would thenceforth be based on 'massive retaliation' with greater reliance on nuclear weapons.[3] Turkey was expected to have a major role in this policy. This role of Turkey was emphasized in a National Security Council (NSC) report from 28 February 1955. The report recommended a number or 'courses of action' in this regard. The first three of these were as follows:

14   Encourage such continued development of democratic ideas and institutions in Turkey as would help to insure Turkey's identification of interest with the western European and other free nations of the world.
15   Cooperate with Turkey as a full and equal member of the western European alliance of free peoples.
16   Encourage Turkey to participate in appropriate regional security agreements, so as to bring selected neighboring states into regional defense pacts aimed at resisting communist penetration of the area.[4]

1.1 The Eisenhower Doctrine

On 5 January 1957, Eisenhower declared his doctrine, which promised American economic assistance and/or aid to any country in the Middle East that felt threatened by another country controlled by international communism. Turkey was one of the countries to benefit from this assistance. In an Operations Coordinating Board[5] (OCB) report published in November 1958, an 'operations plan for Turkey' was presented. The first four objectives set out by the plan were "[c]ontinuance of Turkey's independence, territorial integrity, identification with the Free World, and will and ability to resist Communist invasion or subversion."[6]

Turkey was already with 'the Free World.' Eisenhower's presidential term (1953–1961) was in overlap with Menderes's term in office (1950–1960). Menderes was considered a pro-American Prime Minister (PM) in Turkey. Of all the 54 bilateral agreements between Turkey and the US, three were signed before 1950, 31 in the 1950–1960 period, and 20 after 1960.[7] It was also in the Eisenhower period that Turkey sent troops to Korea in 1950 and—mainly thanks to this—became a NATO member in 1952. The following expression from a National Intelligence Estimate (NIE) document dated 30 December 1958 shows how assured the US was of Turkey's friendship:

> Turkey remains the strongest friend of the US in the Middle East. Its firm anti-Soviet policies enjoy wide domestic support, and there is little likelihood that Soviet gestures will weaken the Turks' basic distrust of the USSR or their policy of alliance with the West.[8]

Similarly, the memorandum of Eisenhower's meeting with the Turkish President, PM, and FM contained the following sentence: "Since no other country is so much 'in line' with the United States, as is Turkey, there is really very little to talk about."[9]

The Eisenhower administration was aware of Turks' concerns about the USSR and aspirations to have 'approved' their belonging to the West:

> Turkey is of great importance in the US effort to build a position of strength in the Middle East. Throughout modern history the Turks have had an unwavering desire to be accepted by Western Europe (and more lately the United States) as a member of the Western community. Strategically located astride the Bosphorus-Dardanelles water passage from the Black Sea to the Mediterranean, Turkey has contiguous land frontiers with the Union of Soviet Socialist Republics and Bulgaria, and historically has been at odds with Russia. Since World War II, concern over Soviet pressure on the area has caused Turkey to maintain a staunch pro-Western, anti-Soviet foreign policy.[10]

On its part, Turkey knew how to please the US, and to keep the American apprehensions about the Soviets intact. The following is an extract from the minutes of a meeting in Washington on 10 September 1958 between Owen T. Jones, Director of the Office of Greek, Turkish and Iranian Affairs (GTI) of the Department of State (DOS), and some members of the government of Turkey (GOT) including Hasan Polatkan, Minister of Finance:

> Mr. Polatkan [. . .] thanked the Secretary for the financial assistance recently arranged for Turkey in Paris [. . .]. The Minister commented particularly on the assistance and cooperation of the American officials in Paris. This, he said, represented an example of United States efforts to raise the standard of living of countries such as Turkey and proved wrong the Russian propaganda that the United States was not prepared to help its friends.[11]

For the US, what remained to be done was to extend further military, political, and economic assistance to this aspiring and promising ally.

1.2 Low Expectations of the US from the EEC

An OCB report[12] from 1957 set 'achieving a stable Turkish economy' a target. A subsequent report[13] issued in 1958 stated that "[i]n military and political matters there was continuing progress towards meeting [. . .] major objectives [of the US], [but] in economic matters there was little progress towards the achievement of the stable Turkish economy [set as a target by the

1957 report]." As explained above, the US had certain international institutions/organizations such as IMF or OEEC in mind that could help Turkey financially, and the EEC was not among them.[14] A telegram sent by Dulles to the US Embassy in Turkey contained the following:

> U.S. considers approach by Turkey to both IMF and EPU[15]-OEEC most effective method exploring possibility help from Western European creditors and international institutions on assumption there will be fully adequate Turkish stabilization program.[16]

This position of the US may be attributed to three reasons:

1. The US policy towards the EEC was in the process of formation. Eisenhower advocated the idea of a unified Europe. He "repeatedly talked about Western Europe as a 'third force.'"[17] Nonetheless, the EEC had been established in 1957, and when the OCB reports quoted above were being written, it was a fledgling organization. For the Eisenhower administration, the importance of the EEC in comparison to the European Atomic Energy Community (EURATOM)—an organization that would, in fact, soon fall into oblivion—was low. In a telegram he sent to the US Embassy in Belgium in 1956, Dulles had written the following:

> United States does not attach to common market proposals same immediate security and political significance as we do to EURATOM. However, we believe that a common market which results in a general reduction of international trade barriers could contribute constructively to European integration.[18]

Thus, it was too early to see the EEC as a source of financial relief to Turkey.

Within a few years, the US developed a more positive attitude towards the EEC but remained confused and uninformed. The following circular written in 'diplomatic shorthand,' dated 27 June 1959 and sent to the US diplomatic missions in Europe and Canada stated that there was a "positive political ground for US support" for the EEC. Yet the DOS was unable to locate the EEC in a context together with the free-trade area (FTA) plans of the Outer Seven,[19] and to evaluate Turkey's place in this picture. Rather than giving directions and information, the DOS was demanding "information and field views":

> Dept[20] considering possible political and economic advantages and disadvantages limited FTA and has not made final assessment pending receipt additional information and field views. Do not see same positive political grounds for US support nor comparable elements economic integration as in EEC. [. . .] Following are examples main questions

which occur to us and Dept will welcome any further views from missions on these or other aspects:

A   Will outer seven FTA serve to improve chances for mutual accommodation between Common Market and other OEEC countries or is result apt to be divisive?
B   What will be likely economic and political effects on countries not included in limited FTA; e.g. Turkey, Iceland, and Finland? For info addressees who not informed Dept has learned in confidence of recent Greek initiative[21] to seek association with EEC.[22]

Americans were also concerned about Germany's possible dominance in Europe,[23] and refrained from encouraging Turkey for an EEC over which the US control was not substantial.

2   In those days, Turkey was not seen fully European by the US geographically. In evaluating Turkey, an OCB report,[24] dated 16 December 1959, summarized Turkey's 'area relations.' This summary had no reference to Turkey's relations with European countries except the infamous Turkish–Greek dispute. It was focused on the country's dealings with Egypt, the USSR, Iraq, and Iran. Moreover, Turkey and Greece were outside the responsibility of the European Bureau (EUR) of the DOS.

[These two countries] remained instead the responsibility of State's Bureau of Near Eastern and South Asian Affairs (known as NEA) [. . .]. For much of that period, the Greek and Turkish desks belonged to the Office of Greek, Turkish and Iranian Affairs (whose acronym was GTI) [of NEA]. These three countries had little in common except their ancient hostilities, a modern history of internal instability, and their proximity to the Soviet bloc.[25]

3   Turks themselves were undecided between the EEC and the Outer Seven.[26] The UK who was leading the establishment process of EFTA by the Outer Seven was sympathetic to Turkey's inclusion in their project.[27] There also was a lesser-known proposal by the three Benelux countries who, on 15 March 1959, announced a plan to bring the Six and 11 other nations including Turkey together to form a 'European Free Market.'[28]

In criticizing the FP orientation of the—Republican—Eisenhower administration, Chester Bowles, a—Democrat—member of the HOR, underlined the indeterminacy and inconsistency of the US policies towards Europe. His recommendations included a reference to Turkey:

Precisely because American military policy is and must remain identified strongly with NATO it is essential that we encourage this other unifying movement[29] to play an active political and economic role in softening, not hardening, the present military dividing line from the Baltic to the Black Sea. Let us hope that it may develop in a way that will enable it to offer a continuing invitation to the rest of Europe including the satellite countries to associate themselves with the integration of Europe however tentative or timid the initial steps. Associate membership in the Common Market for Greece and Turkey, for instance, could conceivably lead to future association of a similar kind for Yugoslavia.[30]

1.3 Bilateral Aid Schemes Frustrate Turkey

Turks were going through dire times. They experienced an acute economic crisis in 1958. The value of the US dollar increased from 2.8 to 9 Turkish liras (the highest devaluation rate in the history of Turkey). The government declared a moratorium.[31]

The plan forged at the dinner on 6 June was put into practice in less than two months. On 26 July, Dulles came to Bonn and had talks with Adenauer, the German Chancellor. The following day, Turkish PM Menderes and FM Zorlu, too, came to Bonn.[32] On 29 July, Turkish newspapers announced that Germany would give a special long-term credit to Turkey. The amount of the credit was 50 million dollars, and as requested by Dulles at the dinner, this credit would not be paid on bilateral basis: A portion of the balance standing to Germany's credit at the EPU would be transferred to Turkey.[33]

For Turks, international organizations were settings where they—and any other members—could receive aid regardless to the objectives of the organization in question. The NSC report mentioned above propounded that within Central Treaty Organization (CENTO) Turkey was urging increased US assistance to Iran in particular, and together with other regional members was demanding increased US and UK assistance to CENTO in general.[34] Below, we will also see that Turkey was discontented with that the North Atlantic Treaty did not qualify its signatories for intra-alliance financial aid.

Paradoxically, Turks had a historical discomfort with receiving foreign aid, due to their past experience with capitulations.[35] On 8–10 October, a conference was held in Paris, where representatives of the European countries that had contributed to the Turkish stabilization loan came together with US and Turkish representatives to work out a repayment schedule and an interest rate. At the conference "Turkish sensitiveness was excited by a French idea for a set-aside of a percentage from Turkish exports to meet scheduled indebtedness. Turks [. . .] made invidious comparisons of this idea to the Ottoman Debt Commission."[36] When, in February 1959, Germany made the payment of the second half of the aforementioned 50 million dollars conditional to the return of the German movable and immovable properties confiscated in the pre-war period and to the transport of half of the German aid by German ships, the fear of revival of capitulations haunted the Turks.[37]

In a telegram signed by Dulles and sent from the DOS to the US Embassy in Turkey on 7 March 1958, it was indicated that the US was "prepared to consider any assistance" and to coordinate the European aid to Turkey as long as the GOT prepared a program that satisfied the EPU and the OEEC.[38] A cooperation agreement in the field of defense was signed between Turkey and the US on 5 March 1959.[39] Art. 2 of this agreement rendered economic assistance complementary to defense aid.

The signals from individual European countries were not promising. The German Minister for Economic Affairs Ludwig Erhard visited Turkey on 17 August 1959. He declared his government's full support for Turkey's associate membership to the EEC.[40] Nevertheless, he added, no financial aid would be extended without concrete projects.[41]

Under these conditions, Turks were attracted to the EEC's funds and to the fact that the internal relations within the Community were based more on a sui generis legal order than bilateral debt schemes. Americans were supportive of Turkey's inclusion in European economic integration projects that would alleviate their economic burden of helping this country. As long as this inclusion was not solely predicated on aid schemes . . . A circular dated 20 March 1958 and sent from the DOS to certain diplomatic missions contained the following paragraph:

> US has therefore supported and continues support negotiation of Free Trade Area arrangements which mutually acceptable Europeans and which would [. . .] embrace on equitable basis Greece, Turkey and other less-developed OEEC countries while providing for assumption progressively of FTA membership obligations by LDCs.[42]

2 Turkey Applies for Associate Membership

On 31 July 1959, Turkey submitted its associate membership application to the EEC. Turkish FM Zorlu had had the application file prepared in only two weeks and gotten the approval of PM Menderes and President Bayar quickly. Before bringing the file to the cabinet's attention, the US ambassador (USAMB) Fletcher Warren was summoned to the Turkish Ministry of Foreign Affairs (TMFA) and asked what Washington's reaction to Turkey's application would be. The reply came three days later: "In principle, Washington would be glad with reinforcement of Turkey's relations with Western Europe; it has no objections."[43] Declassified official documents of the DOS or the news reports by the American media from the period do not contain noteworthy references to Turkey's application. Hence, it is difficult to corroborate the claim that Turkey's application was *cum permissio*.

The official documentation of a conversation between Dillon and Robert Marjolin, Vice President of the EEC Commission, on 30 September 1959 shows that 'pleasing the Americans' was an important—or if we are to take

Marjolin's words literally, 'the only'—factor in the Europeans' acceptance of Turkey's application:

> At the conclusion [of the conversation] there was a brief discussion of Greek and Turkish association with the Common Market. Mr. Marjolin said that the only real justification for an association of these countries with the European Community would be as a device to provide substantial aid, thereby reducing the burden on the U.S.[44]

On 10 August 1959, *La Libre Belgique*, a Belgian newspaper, wrote that although Turkey and Greece knew they were not eligible for EEC membership, they were contemplating to apply, because they were counting on the US patronage.[45]

3 For a Fistful of Wheat

Turks had to wait to reap the benefits of their application to the EEC. For Turkey to become an associate member, an agreement had to be drafted, signed, and ratified. Considering the sensitivities of the parties, it was obvious that this process would take long. While waiting, Turkey had to seek urgent aid.

3.1 Menderes Appeals for Wheat—and for Intervention

On 5 October 1959, Menderes went to the US for CENTO meetings. He extended his stay until 16 October to elicit economic aid from Eisenhower; a year's supply of wheat, at least, would be enough. Eisenhower maintained that such financial aid would require the approval of the Congress, which would take time. This was a negative reply cast in a politically correct mold.[46] Yet FM Zorlu and Minister of Finance Polatkan who accompanied Menderes were able to secure an 80-million-dollar aid package after their talks with Dillon, the Under SECSTATE for Economic Affairs, and with Erhard.[47] Turks also requested that the US convince the Germans to help Turkey financially, thereby breaking the 'collusion' within the OEEC. Dillon said they would speak to the Germans via the US Embassy in Bonn.[48] This was one of the earliest requests of the Turks from the Americans to intervene to convince the Europeans for financial aid.

In this process, Turkey had to maintain good relations with the US. With an agreement they signed on 28 October, Turkey gave its consent to the installation of 15 Jupiter missiles on its soil.[49]

3.2 The EEC Keeps the US Updated

Following Turkey's application to the EEC, Americans kept a watchful eye on Turkey–EEC relations. In November 1959, Walter Hallstein, President of the EEC Commission, came to Washington for a conference of NATO parliamentarians.[50] He met with Christian Herter, the new US SECSTATE. Herter inquired about other European countries joining the EEC. Hallstein professed that this issue occupied much of the Commission's time and cited Greece and Turkey as two special cases of association under consideration.[51]

On 10 December, some key members of the EEC Commission held a meeting with Dillon in Brussels, where Jean Rey, European Commissioner for External Relations, told Dillon that "the talks with Greece and Turkey on their proposed association with the EEC were parallel, although in point of time the discussions with Greece were further advanced." Rey said he believed that the Commission would be able to submit a draft agreement of association for Greece and Turkey to the Ministers of the Six by Easter. Dillon welcomed this statement. Rey also shared the details about the respective CUs Greece and Turkey were expected to establish with the EEC, and the demands of these two countries for financial assistance from the EEC.[52]

3.3 Eisenhower Expresses His Support and Sells Wheat

On 6 December 1959, Eisenhower came to Ankara for a two-day informal visit as a part of an 11-nation good-will tour.[53] On the first day of the visit, a conference was held with the presence of Turkish President Bayar, PM Menderes, FM Zorlu, President Eisenhower, and the USAMB Warren.[54] In his speech, Zorlu denoted that through an economic conference in Berne, Turkey had found short-term credits that were not of much help. Germany[55] and Italy had expressed willingness to assist Turkey, but they had not taken any concrete steps yet. He said that some elements in NATO were conservative[56] and added that "[t]he Marshall Plan would never have been implemented if it had been left up to the bankers." Any dissonance among allies, he asserted, encouraged the USSR. Zorlu requested US help in convincing European governments to extend economic assistance to Turkey. He emphasized that for Turkey, EEC membership was an economic alternative to borrowing from private bankers. He asked for help for this membership. This appeal is the earliest documented case where Turkey brought its relations with the EEC to the attention of the US and asked for assistance in this regard.

Zorlu's speech contained clues about his view of Turkey's relations with the EEC and US:

a   Firefighting with the budget deficit was the first priority for him. International organizations—even NATO—were potential sources of financial help, and the EEC was not an exception, although Zorlu was well aware of the historic significance of Turkey's accession to the EEC; and
b   He was asking for US support for Turkey's EEC membership in an enticing package: such a support would make Turkey stronger against the Soviets and lessen the burden of the US in assisting Turkey financially.

In response, Eisenhower said he "recognized the need" and promised to talk with Adenauer to secure economic aid to Turkey.[57] He added that Randall[58] was studying the problem. He had brought with him something that may or may not be considered as 'economic assistance': a proposal to sell Turkey wheat worth 38 million dollars.[59] Based on this proposal, Turkey would buy wheat from the US in June 1960 and make the payment in chrome.[60]

Eisenhower's visit was concluded with a joint Turkish–US communiqué that included the following sentence: "The initiative of Turkey to be an associate member of the European Common Market was also examined and the hope expressed that such association would foster solidarity among these countries.[61]"

3.4 "No" from Randall and "Yes" from Adenauer

Given hope by Eisenhower's words, Turks were waiting for good news from Randall and/or Adenauer. Randall's study did not yield the results they hoped for; he advised that Turkey resort to private capital. Turks turned their face to Adenauer.

On 11 December 1959, Dillon had a talk with Adenauer in Bonn and drew his attention to the need for continued assistance to Greece and Turkey. Adenauer assured Dillon that Germany would cooperate in the extension of such aid.[62]

A summit of Western heads of government would convene in Paris on 19–21 December. Before the summit, at the 89th sitting of the German Cabinet on 16 December 1959, Adenauer informed the Cabinet of that Zorlu intended to address him at this summit about the issue of German economic aid to Turkey. He stated that without advisers he did not want to negotiate this affair with Zorlu. The Federal Minister of Economic Affairs declared that the American representative to the OEEC was against this plan and was of the opinion of requesting the Turkish investment plan first. The Minister suggested that the Federal Chancellor propose the US President in Paris that the US, Canada, and Germany make available an interim credit amounting up to 30 million dollars. Adenauer agreed to this proposal and requested that the Minister inform Turkish Ambassador İksel accordingly; he also discussed the matter with Eisenhower and Zorlu on the fringe of the summit in Paris. It was agreed that a German and an American representative would negotiate about urgent financial aid to Turkey.[63] On 10 March 1960, Rolf Otto Lahr, German ambassador to the EEC and EURATOM, visited Turkey.[64] The amount Turks requested from him was 250 million German marks. Although the discussions in Ankara took as long as nine days, no agreement could be reached. The parties came to Istanbul to resume their talks. Finally, Germany agreed to pay 147 million German marks. Later in June, at the German *Bundestag*, Adenauer was criticized for this credit.[65] Nevertheless, "on recommendations from the US" Adenauer spoke with İksel in Bonn in September 1960 and told him that Germany would extend this financial aid to Turkey.[66]

4 Turks Play 'the Red' Card

Towards the end of 1960, American demands for German financial assistance to several schemes increased. In November, Dillon came to Bonn and convinced Germans to extend aid to underdeveloped countries.[67] On 6 February 1961, Bonn announced that it would pay its war debt to the US before its due date and even extend direct financial assistance to the US. Germans agreed to contribute to American aid to Greece and Turkey unless it was military aid.[68]

Unsatisfied with the financial assistance it received from 'the West,' the GOT was trying to make the Americans and Europeans believe that Turkey was now turning its face to 'the East.' Through various channels, the Turkish PM made it known to the Soviets that a rapprochement between the two countries could be possible. The Soviets quickly reciprocated and declared that a development credit could be extended to Turkey. The Turkish Minister of Health visited Moscow, and on 11 April 1960, a forthcoming exchange of visits between Menderes and Khrushchev was announced.[69]

5 Coup d'État in Turkey

A few weeks later, on 27 May 1960, the GOT was overthrown by a military coup, which made Menderes's visit to Khrushchev scheduled for 12 July 1960 impossible. We have no convincing evidence that Americans had a hand in the coup, but we do know that they established contacts with the provisional junta government immediately. Only a day after the coup, General Cemal Gürsel, the leader of the junta, was visited by the USAMB Warren and Sarper, the new FM of Turkey. They had come in Warren's car. Warren recounts their talk as follows:

> [Gürsel] said previous administration for which he not responsible left junta [country?][70] in awful financial mess. He had asked Under Secretary Finance how much money he needed on June 1. He replied he had 23 million lira available but needed 180 million lira to meet civil and other payrolls. Gursel said I need not tell you how important it is for new government meet that first payroll. [. . .] I said "Sir, I think I fully realize how important it is for military junta or provisional government be able pay those first salary checks. I must tell you, however, that certain things remain to be cleared up before question of financial assistance can be considered. (I had in mind, of course, question of recognition.)[71]

A Special NIE dated 19 July was trying to guess the FP orientation of the junta:

> Immediately after the coup, the provisional government gave assurances that it would honor Turkey's international commitments and that no

change in Turkish foreign policy was contemplated. In general, we think this is likely to be the case. Turkish participation in NATO and CENTO councils has continued without interruption and with no discernible change in tactics or purpose.[72]

The fear of losing Turkey to the Soviets, which occupied Warren's mind since the last months of the Menderes government, was difficult to dislodge. His letter to the G. Lewis Jones, the head of the NEA, dated 11 August 1960 contained the following passage:

> If the Gursel Government finds, as I am afraid it will, that it must have more aid than we are prepared to give, what can it do? We know that the Soviet Government is ready to supply and is urging the Gursel Government to accept as much as 500 million dollars at three percent interest per year. How long can a Provisional Government whose origin is a coup d'état, a Government feeling the stresses and strains that exist in the Turkish economy today, resist the tempting offer of the Soviets. We know from experience that, once it does accept such aid, the bars will be down. The United States and the Western World will have suffered a major and tragic defeat.
> [. . .]
> We must bear with this Government, try to see that it doesn't succumb to Commie blandishments and that it remains loyal to the United States, to CENTO, to NATO.[73]

The Eisenhower administration was following the developments in the EEC and drawing inferences from them for Turkey. A dispatch sent from the US mission at the EEC to the DOS on 27 July 1960 contained the following:

> Greek association with the Common Market is still a major objective of Community officials, second only to the year-end move toward the common external tariff. [. . .] Aside from its importance per se, the terms of the Greek association are significant for the precedents they may set for Turkey and ultimately for countries such as Tunisia which might seek association with the Common Market.[74]

6 The US Clarifies Its Policy towards Turkey's Association

In these circumstances, the Eisenhower administration felt a need to draw up a more methodical strategy towards Turkey. This strategy would be based on developing the Turkish economy and strengthening Turkey's political ties with the West. The Turkey–EEC association would serve both of these purposes. Eventually, an NSC Report[75] from 5 October 1960 drew up an elaborate and reasoned policy. This policy would be based on advocating Turkey's association on the following grounds:

1. Turkey's close relations with the EEC would have a catalyzing effect on the rapprochement between Greece and Turkey;
2. The Common Market would constitute an outlet for Turkish exports and divert Turkish trade from the Soviet Bloc to the EEC;
3. With Turkey's association, the EEC countries would have cooperate with the US in assisting Turkey's economic and political development; and
4. Association with the EEC would anchor Turkey to the market system of the 'Free World.' This would expand the sphere of dominance of the US economy. To this aim, the US should

> (e)ncourage and support the GOT's efforts to strengthen Turkey's economic ties with the Free World, including association with the EEC in an arrangement which would be compatible with U.S. national trade policy and interests.[76]

7 Mentality of the Eisenhower Administration

The Eisenhower era was a period when the US had to develop a policy towards Turkey–EEC relations as well as the EEC itself. The US supported Turkey's association from the beginning. Initially, this support was indistinct and lacking substance; it was based on the assumption that the EEC was just another tie that would connect Turkey to the West. In its last years, the Eisenhower administration substantiated this policy; the US got convinced that Turkey's association would have positive effects on Greek–Turkish relations, create a market for Turkey's exports leaving no need for Turks to seek trade with the Soviets, strengthen Turkey economically and politically making further US aid unnecessary, and integrate Turkey's economic and political system to the West.

8 Conclusion

Turkey lodged its application for associate membership of the EEC towards the end of the Eisenhower era. This was a period of transition and tribulation for everyone: The anarchy characteristic, assumed to be inherent in international politics by neorealists (NRA1) was palpable: The Cold War was escalating; and Eisenhower's term (1953–1961) was in overlap with that of Khrushchev (1955–1964), one of the most 'hawkish' of the Soviet leaders. At the time of Turkey's application, it had been only a few years since Khrushchev made the following threat:

> About the capitalist states, it doesn't depend on you whether or not we exist. If you don't like us, don't accept our invitations, and don't invite

us to come to see you. Whether you like it or not, history is on our side. We will bury you!⁷⁷

Faced with this outright menace, Eisenhower was expecting Western Europe to emerge as a 'third force,' a power bloc acting with the rest of the 'free world.'⁷⁸ SECSTATE Dulles initiated a 'New Look' for the containment policy calling for a greater reliance on nuclear weapons (NRA7).

In this general picture, the role expected from Turkey was bigger than it had been in the past. Turkey was seen as a 'Near Eastern' country but was expected to act together with 'the West' against the Soviets. With this approach, the Eisenhower administration was hoping to reform the current balance of power (NRA6) by trying to strengthen the Western alliance with the emergence of Europe as a third force and to enlarge it with Turkey's incorporation into this alliance.

The pro-American stance of the Menderes government in Turkey and Turkey's economic problems, two major domestic factors (DF) that affected the US approach to Turkey's relations with Europe, were consistent with the expectations of the US. The Eisenhower administration knew Turkey needed financial aid. For both the Americans[79] and Turks, the aid schemes implemented by such organizations as the IMF or OEEC were preferable to bilateral aid arrangements. The preference of the Americans was grounded in their dominance in these organizations (NRA4), while the Turks had an apprehension of a 'capitulation' element they believed to be hidden in bilateral arrangements. However, in many cases Turks had no other option than seeking bilateral aid especially from Germans with whom they had close relations.

The heavy insecurity atmosphere of the Cold War and their grave economic problems were making the Turks anxious about their survival (NRA3). Preoccupied with their fate, they loosened their ideological attachment to the West (NRA8), and approached the Soviets to receive financial assistance and/or to attract the attention of the Americans and Europeans. This plan paid off: The Soviets declared their readiness to help the Turks, while the Americans formulated a strategy to integrate Turkey into the Western bloc, which included the Turkey–EEC association.

The Turks—especially the far-sighted FM Zorlu—were aware of the potential benefits and difficulties of the associate membership of the EEC, but for them any international organization was a source of economic assistance in the short term, and, in their opinion, as an alliance leader (NRA6), the US had considerable influence over the EEC (NRA2). They not only asked for American support in their relations with the EEC, but if Birand's claim is correct, they even felt a need to get the permission of the US before their associate membership application. A week after they lodged their application, Zorlu requested Eisenhower's backing for full-membership.

The first contacts of the Americans with the Europeans for Turkey were to secure financial aid for this needy ally, but this potential contribution of the Europeans was not indispensable for the Americans (NRA7). In the issue of Turkey's association, rather than to put pressure on the Europeans, Americans chose to remain in touch with, be informed by, and perhaps make a few recommendations to them. Europeans were willing to exchange information with the US about Turkey and were regarding Turkey's association as an initiative that would please the US by reinforcing Turkey's ties with the West and sharing the burden of helping Turkey financially.

Certain EEC members, particularly Germany and Italy looked disposed to extend financial assistance to Turkey, but their capabilities were limited in this regard.

Notes

1 John Foster Dulles, "Memorandum of conversation," 6 June 1958, in Ronald Landa et al. (eds.), *Foreign Relations of the United States (FRUS), 1958–1960, Vol. X, Part 2*, Washington: US Government Printing Office (USGPO), 1993, p. 751.
2 On 4 August 1958, a stabilization program was announced for Turkey. Within this program, Turkey would receive support from the OEEC and IMF. (Source: Editorial note in Ronald Landa et al. [eds.], *FRUS, 1958–1960, Vol. X, Part 2*, Washington: USGPO, 1993, 755–6.)
3 David MacIsaac, "Strategy: Nuclear warfare strategy and war plans" in John Whiteclay Chambers (ed.), *The Oxford Companion to American Military History*, New York, NY: OUP, 1999, 691–5, p. 693.
4 James S. Lay, "Statement of policy on Turkey (Enclosure to NSC Report NSC 5510/1)," 28 February 1955, in Ronald Landa et al.(eds.), FRUS, 1955–1957, Vol. XXIV, Washington: USGPO, 1989, 620–8, p. 626.
5 OCB was established by Eisenhower in 1953 to integrate the implementation of national security policies across several agencies. It was abolished by Kennedy in 1961.
6 "OCB report: Operations plan for Turkey," 19 November 1958, in Ronald Landa et al. (eds.), *FRUS, 1958–1960, Vol. X, Part 2*, Washington: USGPO, 1993, 772–84, p. 772.
7 Mehmet Gönlübol et al., *Olaylarla Türk Dış Politikası, 1919–1995*, Ankara: Siyasal Kitabevi, 1996, pp. 235–6.
8 "National Intelligence Estimate: Prospects for Turkey," 30 December 1958, Ronald Landa et al. (eds.), *FRUS, 1958–1960, Vol. X, Part 2*, Washington: USGPO, 1993, 784–6, p. 784.
9 John S.D. Eisenhower, "Memorandum of conference with President Eisenhower," 6 December 1959, in Ronald Landa et al. (eds.), *FRUS, 1958–196, Vol. X, Part 2*, Washington: USGPO, 1993, 820–4, p. 824.
10 "National Security Council Report: Statement of U.S. Policy towards Turkey," 5 October 1960, Ronald Landa et al. (eds.), *FRUS, 1958–1960, Vol. X, Part 2*, Washington: USGPO, 1993, 888–9, p. 888.
11 "Memorandum of conversation," 10 September 1958, in Ronald Landa et al. (eds.), *FRUS, 1958–1960, Vol. X, Part 2*, Washington: USGPO, 1993, 757–8, p. 757.
12 "OCB report: Report on Turkey," 29 June 1957, in Ronald Landa et al. (eds.), *FRUS, 1955–1957, Vol. XXIV*, Washington: USGPO, 1989, 720–7.
13 "OCB report: Report on Turkey," 29 January 1958, in Ronald Landa et al. (eds.), *FRUS, 1958–1960, Vol. X, Part 2*, Washington: USGPO, 1993, 741–4, p. 741.
14 IMF, OEEC, and the EEC were not mutually exclusive alternatives for Turkey. John F. Cahan, the Deputy Secretary-General of the OEEC, visited Turkey and Greece, and

encouraged these countries towards EEC membership. (Source: Hikmet Saim, "Türkiye ile her mevzuda mutabakata varılmıştır," *Zafer*, 2 July 1959. See also "Organization for European Economic Cooperation," *International Organization*, Vol. 12, No. 3, 1958, 408–15.)
15 European Payments Union.
16 "Telegram from the Department of State to the Embassy in Turkey," 7 March 1958, in Ronald Landa et al. (eds.), *FRUS, 1958–1960*, Vol. X, Part 2, Washington: USGPO, 1993, 744–5, p. 745.
17 Geir Lundestad, *The United States and Western Europe since 1945: From 'Empire' by Invitation to Transatlantic Drift*, New York, NY: OUP, 2003, p. 86.
18 "Telegram from the Secretary of State to the Embassy in Belgium," 26 January 1956, in Nancy Johnson et al.(eds.) *FRUS, 1955–1957*, Vol. IV, Washington: USGPO, 1988, 399–400, p. 400.
19 The OEEC members originally proposed an OEEC-wide FTA to which countries not wishing to join the EEC could belong, and in which the EEC would function as one unit. After this proposal failed in November 1958, the 'outside' group, then composed of Austria, Denmark, Norway, Portugal, Sweden, Switzerland, and the UK (later known as the Outer Seven) established the European Free-Trade Association (EFTA) on 3 May 1960.
20 The Department of State.
21 Greece submitted its associate membership application to the EEC on 8 June 1959. Interestingly, the DOS was informing its missions of this application 20 days later.
22 C. Douglas Dillon, "Circular telegram from the Department of State to certain diplomatic missions," 27 June 1959, in Ronald Landa et al.(eds.), *FRUS*, 1958–1960, Vol. VII, Part I, Washington: USGPO, 1993, 138–9, p. 139.
23 Geir Lundestad, *The United States and Western Europe since 1945: From 'Empire' by Invitation to Transatlantic Drift*, New York, NY: OUP, 2003, pp. 77–8.
24 "National Security Council Report: Report on Turkey," in Ronald Landa et al. (eds.), *FRUS, 1958–1960*, Vol. X, Part 2, Washington: USGPO, 1993, 825–9.
25 Monteagle Stearns, *Entangled Allies: U.S. Policy Toward Greece, Turkey, and Cyprus*, New York, NY: Council on Foreign Relations, 1992, pp. 8–9. For the establishment of NEA and GTI, see Bruce Robellet Kuniholm, *The Origins of the Cold War in the Near East: Great Power Conflict and Diplomacy in Iran, Turkey, and Greece*, Princeton, NJ: Princeton University Press, 1980, pp. 238–9 and 433.
26 Armağan Emre Çakır, "Political dimension: Always in the list of 'also-ran': Turkey's rivals in EU-Turkey relations," Armağan Emre Çakır (ed.), *Fifty Years of EU-Turkey Relations: A Sisyphean Story*, London: Routledge, 2011, 10–45, p. 12.
27 "British hopes of agreement between 'Outer Seven,'" *The Manchester Guardian*, 2 May 1959.
28 "Benelux trio backing new trade plan," *WP*, 17 March 1959; "New trade parley is urged in Europe," *NYT*, 17 March 1959; and "Europe market tie asked," *Christian Science Monitor*, 17 March 1959.
29 The EEC.
30 Chester Bowles, "A new foreign policy for new conditions," *NYT*, 20 December 1959.
31 Yakup Kepenek and Nurhan Yentürk, *Türkiye Ekonomisi*, Istanbul: Remzi Kitabevi 1995, p. 96–7.
32 "Başvekil uçakla Bonn'a hareket etti," *Milliyet*, 27 July 1958.
33 "Alman kredisi: 50 milyom dolar," *Milliyet*, 29 July 1958.
34 "National Security Council Report: Report on Turkey," in Ronald Landa et al. (eds.), *FRUS, 1958–1960*, Vol. X, Part 2, Washington: USGPO, 1993, p. 825–9.
35 Capitulations were treaties whereby Ottomans permitted European rulers to exercise extraterritorial jurisdiction over European nationals within Ottoman Empire. In the case of early capitulations, powerful Turkish sultans were not anxious about their sovereignty since they were motivated only by a desire to avoid the burden of

administering justice to foreign merchants. As the Ottoman Empire declined, capitulations resulted from military pressure by European states and came to be regarded as contemptuous derogations.
36 "Memorandum for the Files: Review of Turkish Debt Conference," in Ronald Landa et al. (eds.), *FRUS, 1958–1960, Vol. X, Part 2*, Washington: USGPO, 1993, 763–6, p. 765. An NSC report (6015/1) warned that "[t]heir centuries of experience under the Capitulations have caused the Turkish people to be especially sensitive to any inference that foreigners in Turkey enjoy privileged status. In consequence, in connection with our efforts to cooperate with Turkey, special attention has been devoted by all US agencies to the development and strengthening of programs designed to promote conduct and attitudes among US personnel conducive to good will and mutual understanding" (p. 889).
37 "Alman yardımı ile ilgili açıklama," *Milliyet*, 7 February 1959.
38 "Telegram from the Department of State to the Embassy in Turkey," 7 March 1958, in Ronald Landa, et al.(eds.), *FRUS*, 1958–1960, Vol. VII, Part I, Washington: USGPO, 1993, 744–5, p. 745.
39 "Agreement of Cooperation between the Government of the United States of America and the Government of the Republic of Turkey," *United States Treaties and Other International Agreements*, Vol. 10, Part 1, Washington: USGPO, 1959, 320–2.
40 "Resmi tebliğ," *Milliyet*, 23 August 1959; "Erhard leaves for Turkey," *NYT*, 18 August 1959; and "Erhard off to Turkey," *WP*, 18 August 1959.
41 Mehmet Ali Birand, *Bir Pazar Hikayesi: Türkiye-AET İlişkileri*, Istanbul: Milliyet Yayınları, 1978, p. 32.
42 Less-developed countries. (Source: "Circular instruction from the Department of State to certain diplomatic missions," 20 March 1958, in Ronald Landa et al.[eds.], *FRUS*, 1958–1960, Vol. VII, Part I, Washington: USGPO, 1993, 20–3, p. 20.)
43 Mehmet Ali Birand, *Türkiye'nin Ortak Pazar Macerası*, Istanbul: Milliyet Yayınları, 1990, p. 73. Author's translation. Birand does not reveal the source of this information.
44 "Memorandum of conversation," 30 September 1959, in Ronald Landa et al.(eds.), *FRUS*, 1958–1960, Vol. VII, Part I, Washington: USGPO, 1993, 152–5, pp. 154–5.
45 Mehmet Ali Birand, *Türkiye'nin Ortak Pazar Macerası*, Istanbul: Milliyet Yayınları, 1990, p. 81.
46 For details of this visit, see *Prime Minister Adnan Menderes in the United States*, New York, NY: Turkish Information Office, 1959; Avni Özgürel, "Menderes'in ABD ümidi," *Radikal*, 20 January 2002; and Orhan Karaveli, *Bir Gazetecinin Sıradışı Anıları*, Istanbul: Doğan Kitapçılık, 2010.
47 Abdi İpekçi, "Amerika bize 80 milyon dolar veriyor," *Milliyet*, 6 October 1959.
48 "Memorandum of Conversation," 7 October 1959, in Ronald Landa et al. (eds.), *FRUS, 1958–1960, Vol. X, Part 2*, Washington: USGPO, 1993, 814–6, p. 816. The editors state that no message to Bonn has been found in the archives.
49 Ayşegül Sever, "Yeni bulgular ışığında Türkiye ve 1962 Küba krizi," *Siyasal Bilgiler Fakültesi Dergisi*, Vol. 52, No. 1–4, 1997, 647–60, p. 648.
50 The first of these conferences convened in 1955. These conferences were transformed into the North Atlantic Assembly in 1966. For the conference in 1959, see "Washington Conference of NATO Parliamentarians," *External Affairs*, Vol. 12, No. 2, 1960, 516–9.
51 "Memorandum of Conversation," 18 November 1959, in Ronald Landa et al.(eds.), *FRUS, 1958–1960, Vol. VII, Part I*, Washington: USGPO, 1993, 168–72, p. 170. The editors erroneously state that Turkey's application for associate membership was submitted on 31 October. As noted above, this application was submitted on 31 July. See also Michael Geary, "A public courtship: The European Commission and the United States" in Catherine Hynes and Sandra Scanlon (eds.), *Reform and Renewal: Transatlantic Relations during the 1960s and 1970s*, Newcastle upon Tyne: Cambridge Scholars Publishing, 2009, 43–58, p. 49.

52 "Memorandum of Conversation," 10 December 1959, in Ronald Landa et al.(eds.), *FRUS, 1958–1960*, Vol. VII, Part I, Washington: USGPO, 1993, 186–94, p. 190.
53 "Editorial note," in Ronald Landa et al. (eds.), *FRUS, 1958–1960, Vol. X, Part 2*, Washington: USGPO, 1993, 819.
54 Unless stated otherwise, the account of the conference is based on "Memorandum of Conference with President Eisenhower," 6 December 1959, in Ronald Landa et al. (eds.), *FRUS, 1958–1960, Vol. X, Part 2*, Washington: USGPO, 1993, 820–4, pp. 822–4.
55 In October 1959, the GOT solicited 67 million dollars bilateral loan from Germany. Germany declined the request and directed Turkey to the World Bank and the OEEC who also refused further credit actions in view of the total indebtedness of Turkey. On 11 December 1959, Turkish Ambassador Settar İksel made a representation to Adenauer. On 16 December 1959, the GOT contacted Adenauer again over İksel. (Source: Josef Henke and Uta Rössel [eds.], *Die Kabinettsprotokolle der Bundesregierung, Band 12, 1959*, Munich: R. Oldenbourg Wissenschaftsverlag, 1982, p. 427.)
56 The North Atlantic Treaty is composed of 14 articles all of which aim at creating a collective defense system; it contains no provision about the financial dimension. Yet, in the Eisenhower era, for Turks, NATO members, if not NATO itself, were potential sources to get financial aid.
57 In his written account of his father's talk with Zorlu, John S.D. Eisenhower, the President's son and an Assistant Staff Secretary in the White House, states that "[s]ome people feel that economic aid is injurious to an alliance. The Turks do not agree with this and are willing to accept aid from the NATO allies." (Source: "Memorandum of conference with President Eisenhower," 6 December 1959, in Ronald Landa et al. (eds.), *FRUS, 1958–1960, Vol. X, Part 2*, Washington: USGPO, 1993, 820–4, p. 824.)
58 Clarence B. Randall was a participant in the Foreign Operations Administration and the Chairman of Private Investment Mission to Turkey in 1953. Between 1954 and 1956, he was a Special Consultant to President Eisenhower on Foreign Economic Policy and in 1956 he served as the Representative of the US in the Special Economic Mission to Turkey. At the time of Eisenhower's visit, he was the chairperson of the Council on Foreign Economic Policy.
59 Avni Özgürel, "Menderes'in ABD ümidi," *Radikal*, 20 January 2002.
60 "Amerika'dan bir milyon kile buğday satın aldık," *Milliyet*, 16 June 1960.
61 "U.S.-Turkish Communiqué," *NYT*, 7 December 1959.
62 "Memorandum of Conversation," 11 December 1959, in Ronald Landa et al.(eds.), *FRUS, 1958–1960*, Vol. VII, Part I, Washington: USGPO, 1993, 196–200, pp. 197–8.
63 Josef Henke and Uta Rössel (eds.) with the collaboration of Ralf Behrendt et al., *Die Kabinettsprotokolle der Bundesregierung, Band 12, 1959*, Munich: R. Oldenbourg Wissenschaftsverlag, 1982, p. 427.
64 "Batı Almanya ile kredi görüşmesi başlıyor," *Milliyet*, 10 March 1960. Birand wrongly claims that Adenauer was with Lahr. Mehmet Ali Birand, *Bir Pazar Hikayesi: Türkiye-AET İlişkileri*, Istanbul: Milliyet Yayınları, 1978, p. 47.
65 "Menderes'e kredi açtığı için Adenauer dün sert tenkitlere maruz kaldı," *Milliyet*, 26 June 1960.
66 "Almanya bize yardım yapacak," *Milliyet*, 1 October 1960.
67 "Almanya iktisadi yardım yapacak," *Milliyet*, 24 November 1960.
68 "Almanya, Türkiye'ye askeri yardıma iştirak etmeyi reddetti," *Milliyet*, 7 February 1961.
69 Avni Özgürel, "Menderes'in ABD ümidi," *Radikal*, 20 January 2002 (Özgürel's text contains some chronological mistakes); Walter Laqueur, *The Struggle for the Middle East: The Soviet Union and the Middle East, 1958–70*, Harmondsworth, Middlesex: Penguin, 1972, p. 30; and Yaacov Ro'i, *From Encroachment to Involvement: A Documentary Study of Soviet Policy in the Middle East, 1945–1973*, New York, NY: John Wiley and Sons, 1974, p. 330.

70 The editors' brackets.
71 "Telegram from the Embassy in Turkey to the Department of State," 28 May 1960, in Ronald Landa et al. (eds.), *FRUS, 1958–1960, Vol. X, Part 2*, Washington: USGPO, 1993, 845–8, pp. 847–8.
72 "Special National Intelligence Estimate: Short-term prospects for Turkey," 19 July 1960, in Ronald Landa et al. (eds.), *FRUS, 1958–1960, Vol. X, Part 2*, Washington: USGPO, 1993, 857–62, p. 858.
73 "Letter From the Ambassador to Turkey (Warren) to the Assistant Secretary of State for Near Eastern and South Asian Affairs (Jones)," 11 August 1960, in Ronald Landa et al. (eds.), *FRUS, 1958–1960, Vol. X, Part 2*, Washington: USGPO, 1993, 869–78, pp. 875 and 878.
74 "Despatch from the mission at the European Communities to the Department of State," 27 July 1960, in Ronald Landa et al.(eds.), *FRUS, 1958–1960, Vol. VII, Part I*, Washington: USGPO, 1993, 290–3, p. 293. Indeed, Tunisia would sign an association agreement with the EU, albeit at a much later date, in 1995.
75 "National Security Council Report: Statement of U.S. policy toward Turkey," 5 October 1960, in Ronald Landa et al. (eds.), *FRUS, 1958–1960, Vol. X, Part 2*, Washington: USGPO, 1993, 888–99.
76 p. 898.
77 "We will bury you!" *Time*, 26 November 1956, p. 24.
78 Geir Lundestad, *The United States and Western Europe since 1945: From 'Empire' by Invitation to Transatlantic Drift*, New York, NY: OUP, 2003, p. 86.
79 In Harris's opinion, the US preference for international organizations was based on their avoidance of "ruffling Turkish feelings." (Source: George Harris, *Troubled Alliance: Turkish-American Problems in Historical Perspective, 1945–1971*, Washington: American Enterprise Institute of Public Policy Research, 1972, p. 75.)

2 The Kennedy Administration (1961–1963)
Trade Winds Start Blowing

History repeats itself. At least it did so in the successive terms of office of Eisenhower and Kennedy. The deities governing Turkey–EEC relations once again started the plot with a meal in Washington. One with a lower profile than the dinner of the Dulles, Heuss, and Brentano trio though . . .

İlter Türkmen, a counselor at the Turkish Embassy in his early thirties, had invited an official from the DOS to lunch.[1] This official was not high-ranking but instrumental in shaping the views of the DOS in the field of international trade. The official was against the conclusion of an association agreement between Turkey and the EEC. In his opinion, the text of the agreement was contrary to the principles of the General Agreement on Tariffs and Trade (GATT) and detrimental to American interests, because whereas the Athens Agreement Greece had concluded with the EEC would create mutual obligations for the parties from the beginning, according to the Ankara Agreement, Turkey would assume no obligations in the preparatory stage.[2] Despite several démarches of the newly appointed Turkish ambassador Turgut Menemencioğlu, the DOS upheld the view of the official in question. Türkmen was hoping to change the mind of this official.

The lunch was Türkmen's idea, but he was not self-appointed in this venture. He had gotten the approval of Menemencioğlu. At the lunch, Türkmen performed a zealous monologue on why Turkey was unable to undertake as many responsibilities as Greece could, comparing Turkey and Greece with an emphasis on the larger amount of funds the latter had received from the EEC, and the larger population of Turkey. The official listened to him attentively, and while they were leaving the restaurant, said that he would ponder about those points.

A few days later, on one of the stagnant Saturdays of the Embassy Row of Washington, Türkmen happened to come to his office. Menemencioğlu was not at the building; he was enjoying the weekend hunting for collectibles in the historic Georgetown area. The Embassy's phone rang—which was a miraculous event per se on a weekend. What was more astonishing was that on the other end of the line was the superior of the official with whom Türkmen had had lunch. He was saying that his office at the Department was not against the conclusion of the association agreement anymore. Türkmen was choked up with happiness. After hanging up the phone, he started formulating a telegram to Ankara to inform them about the good news. Before he finished the message, Menemencioğlu came to the Embassy, and with a victorious smile on his face, started talking about the game he caught in his antiques hunt. Türkmen was impatiently waiting for him to finish his talk. "By the way" Menemencioğlu finally changed the subject "we have not heard from the Department of State since your lunch, have we?" Now it was Türkmen's turn to tell about what *he* had caught.

1 Changing Parameters

In the Kennedy period, the US became more cautious towards the EEC, Turkey, and the relations between these two. This had a number of reasons:

1. De Gaulle, the President of France since 1959, was advocating his *l'Europe des patries* model based on intergovernmentalism and independence from US influence. Such a Europe would not be the 'third force' the US had in mind.

   Thus, Secretary of State Dean Rusk told French ambassador Herve Alphand that the "third force" issue touched a very sensitive nerve. "The concept that Europe could be the arbiter between the US and the Soviets was basically fallacious. Europe was the key issue outstanding between the US and USSR." Rusk even vaguely threatened that if Europe ever decided to play an independent role, "issues between the US and the USSR would be greatly reduced." If Europe did not behave, Rusk thus threatened to reach some sort of deal with Moscow.[3]

   When de Gaulle had all the references to NATO deleted in the Fouchet Plan[4] and vetoed the accession of the UK to the EEC on 14 January 1963, Kennedy concluded that it was impossible to establish a good rapport with the EEC as a bloc.

2. Relations of the third countries with the EEC were distracting the US from focusing on Turkey-EEC relations. On 9 August 1961, the UK submitted its membership application to the EEC. With a National Security Action Memorandum dated 20 August, Kennedy made his concerns and confusion known to George Ball, Under SECSTATE for Economic and Agricultural Affairs:

   I am concerned about what will be the economic effect upon the United States if England joins the common market. [. . .] I have been informed that the effect will be extremely serious. Could you consider the matter and talk to me about it and suggest what action we should properly take. We have been in the position, of course, of encouraging the expansion of the common market for political reasons. If it should have an extremely adverse effect upon us a good deal of responsibility would be laid upon our doorstep.[5]

The application of the UK had a negative bearing on Turkey for two reasons: First, now, the US was concerned that its commercial interests could be harmed by the entry of the UK to the EEC and, ergo, would try to prevent further harm that could come from Turkey's association; and second, Turkey would have to share with the UK the support it was hoping to elicit from the US against Europeans.

Interests of several other countries than the UK also started to cast their shadow over those of Turkey. Robert W. Komer,[6] a senior staff member of the NSC between 1961 and 1965, recounts how confused and busy they were in those days:

> The Indians, the Paks and all the other LDCs [. . .] that thought they would be adversely affected by the Common Market would come around to try and get us to intercede for them. We were much more interested in getting the Common Market going and getting Britain in than were in interceding for all these other countries—I might add, including Australia. [. . .] The African bureau (Bureau of African Affairs) was constantly arguing that the Common Market should be influenced to be more reasonable for the developing African countries. And then EUR [. . .] and ECON (Bureau of Economic Affairs) would come in and say, "Christ, getting the Common Market is much more important."[7]

3   The discomfort of the US with the protectionism of the EEC was on the rise. Whereas with the help of the Marshall Plan, Europe had largely recovered from the devastation of the war, the US was suffering from slow rate of growth and balance of payments deficit. The Common Agricultural Policy (CAP) and Common Customs Tariff (CCT) of the EEC were fortifications that limited the access of US exporters to the European market. The strong agriculture lobby in the US was unhappy with the protectionist nature of the Common Market. For a long time, Douglas Dillon, the Under SECSTATE for Economic Affairs in the Eisenhower's cabinet and the Secretary of the Treasury in that of Kennedy, had been trying to ensure the access of American exports to European market in more liberal terms. The so-called 'Dillon round' of negotiations within the GATT took longer than usual (May 1961–January 1962): While, for the EEC, a continuous process of consultations among the MSs was necessary to reach a common position, in the case of the US, the presidential mandate to negotiate was handicapped by the Congress and the Department of Agriculture (DOA). This frustration brought about Kennedy's Trade Expansion Act[8] in 1962.[9] Before this act, trade policy was under the responsibility of the DOS that would give concessions on this policy relatively easily.

> With this act, the DOS lost its powers in this area. The act called for the President to appoint a Special Representative for Trade Negotiations and established an interagency trade organization to make recommendations to the President.[10]

The discord between the US and EEC culminated with the so-called 'Chicken War' that 'erupted' over the issue of inexpensive frozen chicken exported from the US to Europe.

> The Dutch accused the U.S. of dumping chickens in Europe at prices below cost of production. In Bavaria and Westphalia, protectionist German farmers' associations stormed that U.S. chickens are artificially fattened with arsenic and should be banned. The French government did ban U.S. chickens, using the excuse that they are fattened with estrogen. With typical Gallic concern, Frenchmen hinted that such hormones could have catastrophic effects on male virility.[11]

The American Farm Bureau Federation, who wanted more than the services already provided by the Foreign Agricultural Service, authorized an affiliate corporation to open an office in Rotterdam to sell American farm products in Europe.[12]

In July 1962, the EEC raised the protective barriers of the CAP with a regulation. In September 1963, the sides agreed to submit the matter to a special GATT tribunal. The tribunal found US claims to be justified, estimating, however, the losses of the US only about half as high as the Kennedy administration had argued.[13]

4   The US was disturbed by the association agreements the EEC was about to conclude with Greece and Turkey. The contracting parties presented these agreements to GATT under Art. XXIV that contained exceptions for CUs and FTAs. GATT working parties reported inconclusively and the agreements were neither approved nor rejected formally within GATT,[14] leaving the so-called 'GATT conformity' of the agreements unauthenticated. For the US, this situation left room for political maneuver. The source of the discomfort of the US was the possible access of certain agricultural products of Greece and Turkey to the Common Market in privileged terms. For instance, these two countries were competing with the US in the European tobacco market. As the first country that established an association relation with the EEC, Greece had encountered the initial shockwave of the US pressure. On 9 December 1960, almost a month before Kennedy was sworn in as the President, Ellis O. Briggs, the USAMB to Greece, warned Greeks not to insist on their demands regarding the tariffs on tobacco in negotiations with the EEC. Failing that, he added, Greece would have to face the gravest economic consequences.[15]

After Greece, Turkey faced a similar but less intimidating reaction from the US. In those days, agricultural products constituted 87 percent of Turkey's exports. In the preparatory negotiations with the EEC on 2–4 December 1959, Turkey asked for a special status for its cotton and tobacco exports to Europe.[16] In 1961, the *New York Times* (*NYT*) published an alarmist article that drew attention to the increase in Turkey's cotton exports to the EEC and the threat this situation posed for American cotton exporters.[17] Turkey had not even signed its association agreement yet.

5   A fifth factor was

> the movement in the terms of world trade against primary commodities which began in 1957. Many countries in which the United States ha[d] a special interest—especially in Latin America—[were] almost entirely dependent for their livelihood on the export of one or more such commodities. The possibility that the Common Market tariff might also discriminate against them and give preference to the produce of the European Community's African associates ha[d] raised fears for the stability of the countries concerned.[18]

The privileged status Turkey was demanding for its exports would be prejudicial to the interests of those "countries in which the United States ha[d] a special interest."

From the beginning of 1962 till the signing of the association agreement, the US objected to the quotas to be opened to Turkish tobacco. Rusk and Ball sent protest telegrams, and the US Mission to the EEC made démarches. The Council of Ministers (COM) of the EEC gave assurances to the US. On 30 September 1962, when in New York to attend a General Assembly meeting of the UN, Turkish FM Erkin talked with Rusk and informed him of the EEC–Turkey negotiations. Rusk was not contented. In December, he summoned the ambassadors of the Six and told them that the US would prevent the approval of the agreement with Turkey. Inclusion, in the agreement, of clauses giving Turkey a prospect for full-membership and stipulation of the gradual establishment of a CU between Turkey and the EEC put the preferential treatment of Turkey by the EEC into a context and thus undermined the substance of the Americans' arguments if not lessened their worries. Erkin had to talk with Kennedy, Erhard—who was now the German Chancellor—and the PMs and FMs of the MSs of NATO. Kennedy told Erkin that he was uneasy with the thriving Common Market. Erkin explained him how vital the EEC was for Turkey as an export outlet and as a source of relief to compete with Greece. Kennedy was unconvinced but consented nonetheless.[19]

6   The Cold War was escalating. With an ultimatum, the Soviets demanded the withdrawal of Western armed forces from West Berlin, which led to

the Berlin crisis in 1961. In October 1962, a confrontation, known as the Cuban missile crisis, erupted between the US and the USSR over Soviet ballistic missiles deployed in Cuba.

2 Turkey Is Pushed towards the USSR

Although concerned by the possible negative trade implications of Turkey's association, the US was cognizant of Turkey's increasing geopolitical value. As noted above, in 1959 Turkey had given its consent to the installation of 15 Jupiter missiles on its soil. In April 1962, these missiles became operational.[20] The Jupiters were withdrawn from Turkey in October in accordance with an agreement between the US and the USSR,[21] but the escalating tension between the two blocs continued to cement Turkey's strategic importance.

On 8 January 1963, a telegram, signed by Rusk, was sent from the DOS to the US Embassy in Turkey. This telegram contained the following passage:

> USG[22] is reviewing current policy affecting following bilateral problems having connection with Turkish defense and Turkey's status as US ally:
>
> 1. Soviet chrome ore shipments to US
> 2. US support of Turkish consortium
> 3. Interpretation of Status of Forces Agreement
> 4. US attitude toward Turkish association with EEC[23]

This passage denotes that as of January 1963, the Kennedy administration

1. had not clarified its view on the association agreement the EEC was planning to sign with Turkey, and
2. was evaluating Turkey's association with reference to some other economic and military issues.

Turks were in need of US help against the EEC that was procrastinating over the process of formulation the association agreement. On 27 April 1963, Rusk spent a day in Ankara on his way to Karachi. In his talk with Turkish authorities, which was focused on security issues, Turks demanded support for their association.[24]

2.1 Financial Aid Continues

Despite its confusion, the Kennedy administration would continue to assist Turkey financially, and Germany would maintain its collaboration with the US in this endeavor. At the 8–10 May 1963 meeting of the COM of the EEC, Germans advocated an extension in the aid to be given to Turkey in the preparatory stage of the planned association relationship.[25] To the initially proposed 125 million dollars, the Council added

50 million dollars.[26] Besides, a consortium, mentioned in Rusk's telegram, was established on 31 July 1962 by 11 OECD countries to help Turks. In July 1963, this consortium agreed to give 250 million dollars to Turkey. The US and Germany were again the main contributors.[27] The other contributors had agreed to take part in the consortium due to American and German pressure.[28]

2.2 Turkey Starts Flirting with the USSR Again

Turks were unsatisfied with these aid schemes, and disappointed to see that Americans and Europeans were trying to formulate an association agreement that would limit Turkish agricultural exports to Europe and delay Turkey's association. For them, approaching the Soviets was a feasible alternative once again after three years. An article written by a Turkish journalist in February 1963 discussed this option:

> Turkish economists forecast an expansion of "bilateral trade agreements" with other countries if Turkish tobacco, figs, and raisins cannot enter the Common Market area.
>
> "Bilateral trade agreements" mean in effect an expansion of trade with the Communist bloc.
>
> At present Turkish trade with the Communist bloc accounts for 13 percent of Turkey's overall trade. Some observers say an expansion of trade with the Communist countries could lead to a lessening of ties between Turkey and Western Europe.[29]

In the same month, a visit of a Turkish parliamentary delegation to the USSR was scheduled for May 1963. This delegation would be authorized to discuss economic matters. Russians had been offering long-term credits to Turkey anyway. In February, after announcing this visit, the *Washington Post* (*WP*) established a connection with this visit and "the continued refusal, or at least postponement, of [Turkey's] application to join the Common Market." This, WP continued, was "a question of which people in the West, amid the din about Britain's entry into the Common Market and other matters, [were] hardly aware, but which might well be of great importance."[30] On 29 May, the delegation went to the USSR,[31] and stayed there for 17 days. This visit bore no concrete results.[32]

2.3 Yaoundé Convention

On 20 July 1963, the EEC signed an association agreement, known as the Yaoundé Convention, with 18 African ex-colonies. With this agreement, the Yaoundé countries would be able to export the small amount of industrial goods they manufactured to the Community with zero-tariff for most items. For their agricultural exports, they would enjoy less preference. In technical terms, this Convention did not pose a serious competitive threat for Turkey's exports to the EEC, but it affected Turkey-EEC relations in three ways:

1. Turks felt the EEC was 'flirtatious' in nature. To them, a little matchmaking from the US seemed necessary to keep the attention of the Europeans on Turkey;
2. The privileged status of the Yaoundé countries would soon disturb the US; and
3. The Yaoundé Convention added to the disillusionment of the Turks with the West and made them keep 'the Soviets' option in mind.

3 The Ankara Agreement Is Signed

Forty days before the Kennedy assassination, on 12 September 1963, Turkey signed the Ankara Agreement,[33] and became an associate member of the EEC. The aim of the agreement was

> to promote the continuous and balanced strengthening of trade and economic relations between the Parties, while taking full account of the need to ensure an accelerated development of the Turkish economy and to improve the level of employment and living conditions of the Turkish people.[34]

The agreement was giving Turkey a prospect—but not a guarantee—of full-membership:

> As soon as the operation of this Agreement has advanced far enough to justify envisaging full acceptance by Turkey of the obligations arising out of the Treaty establishing the Community, the Contracting Parties shall examine the possibility of the accession of Turkey to the Community.[35]

The association process would comprise three stages:[36]

1. a preparatory stage
2. a transitional stage
3. a final stage

In the preparatory stage, all Turkey would have to do was "with aid from the Community, [to] strengthen its economy so as to enable it to fulfill the obligations which [would] devolve upon it during the transitional and final stages."[37] In this stage, the Community would concede annual tariff quotas with low customs tariff rates for certain agricultural imports originating in and coming from Turkey.[38] In particular, on 31 December 1967, the customs tariff applicable to tobacco would be abolished within the limits of the relevant quota. This quota was reduced later in 1964 and 1965 with the respective decisions (4/64 and 2/65) of the Association Council (AC).[39]

In the transitional stage, Turkey and the EEC would progressively establish a CU and align their economic policies. The conditions, detailed rules, and timetables for the implementation of the transitional stage would be laid down in an additional protocol to be prepared four years after the entry into force of the Ankara Agreement.[40]

The final stage would be based on the CU and shall entail closer coordination of the economic policies of Turkey and the EEC.[41]

The signing of this agreement was a milestone in Turkey–EEC relations. The agreement was anchoring Turkey, a critical ally of the US, to Europe. However, in the US, the press and the official documents had only passing references to this event. Less than three weeks after the signing of the agreement, Kennedy, accompanied by some US officials, had a conversation with the Turkish Deputy PM and the Finance Minister. Turkey's association agreement was not a subject they discussed.[42]

4 Mentality of the Kennedy Administration

The initial positive attitude of the US in the Eisenhower period towards European integration and to Turkey–EEC relations was almost reversed with the Kennedy administration. This administration was not fundamentally against the association agreement to be signed between the EEC and Turkey, thinking that this agreement would reinforce the Western bloc. Nevertheless, until early 1963, it maintained strong reservations about the privileged status Turkish agricultural exports to the EEC would enjoy, which might prejudice the commercial interests of the US and of the Latin American countries the US favored.

5 Conclusion

The Kennedy era was a transition process in the history of the US involvement in Turkey–EEC relations. Although the US was still positive towards Turkey's associate membership, and despite the Berlin crisis and the Cuban missile crisis both of which underlined Turkey's geopolitical importance (NRA6 and 7), a number of critical changes were at work against Turkey's interests:

1   Turkey's geopolitical importance was temporarily overshadowed by the commercial interests of the US. While the US tried to prevent Turkish agricultural exports to Europe from gaining a privileged status, Turkey did its best to secure such a status. The relative distribution of economic capabilities had become more important than of military capabilities (NR4, 5, and 8). The US and Turkey were competing for economic power in the European market, thereby reducing the meaning of Turkey's association to commercial interests. Until the Nixon era, the US would maintain this sensitivity.
2   Lobbies—especially the agriculture lobby—emerged as important actors that shaped the US policy towards European integration (DF). Turkey got its fair share of this challenge.

3   It was in this term that Turkey started competing with the UK and some LDCs to secure US backing against the EEC (NRA5).

Turkey once again approached the USSR (NRA8). This move did not have a considerable impact on the US attitude towards Turkey–EEC relations.

One important constant the Kennedy administration inherited from the Eisenhower era was Germany's collaboration in helping Turkey financially. In accordance with the preferences of the US and Turkey, German aid was extended via the EEC and OECD (NRA7)., 1961–1963, Vol. XVI, Washington: USGPO, 1994, 760–3, p. 760.

Notes

1   The exact date of this lunch is not known. It must have taken place between 24 April 1962 (the first day of Menemencioğlu in office) and 12 September 1963 (the signing of the Ankara Agreement). The narrative of the event is based on author's interview with Türkmen in Istanbul on 13 June 2008.
2   For details, see the following section on the Ankara Agreement.
3   Geir Lundestad, *The United States and Western Europe since 1945: From 'Empire' by Invitation to Transatlantic Drift*, New York, NY: OUP, 2003, p. 86.
4   This was a plan designed by France in 1961. It aimed at creating a union of states in Europe with a common foreign and security policy based on intergovernmental mechanisms. The plan did not garner enough support. The US was initially positive towards the plan.
5   John F. Kennedy, "National Security Action Memorandum No. 76: Memorandum for Under Secretary of State George Ball," 21 August 1961, in John Glennon (ed.), *FRUS, 1961–1963, Vol. XIII*, Washington: USGPO, 1994, p. 32.
6   Komer would be appointed as the USAMB to Turkey in 1968.
7   Oral history interview with Robert W. Komer, 30 January 1970, John F. Kennedy Oral History Collection, JFK #6, The John F. Kennedy Presidential Library (PL), Boston, MA.
8   Pub. L. 87–794, 76 Stat. 872, enacted October 11, 1962.
9   John Major, "President Kennedy's 'grand design': The United States and a united Europe," *The World Today*, Vol. 18, No. 9, 1962, 383–38, p. 383; and Geir Lundestad, *The United States and Western Europe since 1945: From 'Empire' by Invitation to Transatlantic Drift*, New York, NY: OUP, 2003, p. 85. See also John Conybeare, *Trade Wars: The Theory and Practice of International Commercial Rivalry*, New York: Columbia University Press, 1987, pp. 160–78; and Bruce Clubb, "Dismantling trade barriers; Implementation of the Trade Expansion Act," *University of Illinois Law Forum*, Vol. 1965, 366–98, pp. 368–76.
10 Irving Destler, *American Trade Politics*, New York: NYU Press, 1992, pp. 18–9.
11 "Western Europe: Nobody but their chickens," *Time*, 30 November 1962.
12 "Farm Bureau unit pushes U.S. items in Western Europe," *NYT*, 20 August 1961.
13 John Conybeare, *Trade Wars: The Theory and Practice of International Commercial Rivalry*, New York: Columbia University Press, 1987, pp. 161–2.
14 Richard Pomfret, *The Economics of Regional Trade Arrangements*, New York, NY: OUP, 1997, p. 349.
15 Mogens Pelt, *Tying Greece to the West: US-West German-Greek Relations, 1949–1974*, Copenhagen: Museum Tusculanum Press, 2006, p. 208.
16 Mehmet Ali Birand, *Türkiye'nin Ortak Pazar Macerası*, Istanbul: Milliyet Yayınları, 1990, pp. 87–9.

17 Kathleen McLaughlin, "Cotton imports climb in Europe," *NYT*, 22 October 1961.
18 Bruce Clubb, "Dismantling trade barriers: Implementation of the Trade Expansion Act," *University of Illinois Law Forum*, Vol. 1965, 366–98, pp. 383–84.
19 Mehmet Ali Birand, *Türkiye'nin Ortak Pazar Macerası*, Istanbul: Milliyet Yayınları, 1990, pp. 169–70; and İskender Songur, "Dean Rusk, Erkin'le özel konuşma yaptı," *Milliyet*, 1 October 1962. Birand mentions the démarches of a 'Mr. Cortney' and a 'Mr. Caro'—or 'Caron'—dated respectively 4 December 1961 and 10 December 1962. Charles Sam Courtney who worked in the US embassy in Ankara in the 1960s is the first name that Birand's 'Mr. Cortney' brings to mind. In author's correspondence with him on 8 April 2011, Mr. Courtney made it clear that he was not the one. A second possibility is Raymond F. Courtney who worked at the US embassy in London between 1961 and 1963 and for the EUR in 1963. Although, when in London, Courtney was a 'political/military officer on the staff' whose duty was related to defense issues, probably it was him who formulated this demarche. Courtney's background information is available in the Association for Diplomatic Studies and Training Foreign Affairs Oral History Project, Box: 1 Fold: 109, Georgetown University Lauinger Library, Washington. The confusion between the words 'Caro' and 'Caron' results from Birand's omission of the apostrophe necessary before the genitive suffix in Turkish grammar. It seems that no person with the name 'Caro' or 'Caron' worked for the DOS or another relevant state institution in those years. One possibility is a confusion with Giuseppe Caron who served as the European Commissioner for Internal Market between 1959 and 1963.
20 Ayşegül Sever, "Yeni bulgular ışığında Türkiye ve 1962 Küba krizi," *Siyasal Bilgiler Fakültesi Dergisi*, Vol. 52(1–4), 1997, 647–60, p. 651.
21 Jim Hershberg, "Anatomy of a controversy: Anatoly F. Dobrynin's meeting with Robert F. Kennedy, Saturday, 27 October 1962," *The Cold War International History Project Bulletin*, No. 5, Spring 1995, 75–80.
22 United States Government.
23 "Telegram from the Department of State to the Embassy in Turkey," 8 January 1963, in James Miller (ed.), *FRUS*, 1961–1963, Vol. XVI, Washington: USGPO, 1994, 745–8, pp. 748.
24 "Turks give Rusk protest on metal," *The Sun*, 28 April 1963.
25 An outline of the association agreement was already on the table in May.
26 Edward T. O'Toole, "Turkey granted 175 million aid," *NYT*, 13 May 1963.
27 "Konsorsyum yardımı arttırmayı kabul etti," *Milliyet*, 6 July 1963.
28 Mehmet Ali Birand, *Türkiye'nin Ortak Pazar Macerası*, Istanbul: Milliyet Yayınları, 1990, p. 149.
29 Hilmi Toros, "Turkey weighs EEC competition," *Christian Science Monitor*, 21 February 1963.
30 "Turkish delegation to visit Soviet in May," *WP*, 4 February 1963.
31 "Parlamento heyetimiz dün Rusya'ya gitti," *Milliyet*, 30 May 1963.
32 "Kruşçev Türk heyeti ile görüştü," *Milliyet*, 13 June 1963; and "Parlamento heyeti Rusya'dan döndü," *Milliyet*, 15 June 1963.
33 "Agreement establishing an association between the European Economic Community and Turkey (12 September 1963)," *OJ of the EEC*, 217, 29 December 1964, 3687–8.
34 Art. 2(1).
35 Art. 28.
36 Art. 2(3).
37 Art. 3(1).
38 In the Provisional Protocol to the Ankara Agreement, it was stipulated that the customs duties applicable to these agricultural products including tobacco would be the same as the ones specified in the Athens Agreement. The date when the customs tariff for tobacco would be reduced to zero is also defined with reference to the

Athens Agreement. (Source: "Accord créant une Association entre la Communauté Economique Européenne et la Grèce (9 July 1961)," *OJ of the EEC*, 26, 18 February 1963, 296–313.)

39 The AC was a body established by the Ankara Agreement. The agreement would be implemented with the decisions of this Council. The AC would consist of members of the governments of the MSs, of the Council Ministers, of the Commission, and of the GOT.

40 Art. 4 and Provisional Protocol, Art. 1.

41 Art. 5.

42 "Memorandum of conversation: President's Meeting with Deputy Prime Minister Alican of Turkey, September 30, 1963," 30 September 1963, in James Miller (ed.), *FRUS, 1961–1963, Vol. XVI*, Washington: USGPO, 1994, 760–3, p. 760.

3 The Johnson Administration (1963–1969)
EEC Falls Off the Agenda

Only one or two years after Türkmen's lunch, another one would stand out in Turkey–US relations. On 12 May 1964, Raymond A. Hare, the USAMB to Turkey, and his wife were the guests of the İnönüs[1] in Ankara. In appearance, this was an informal family event, but Hare knew it had been intended to afford occasion to discuss a hot issue: Cyprus. An intercommunal clash had been going on unabated between the Turkish and Greek populations of the island since 21 December 1963 with several people missing—and presumed dead—from both sides.[2] Turkey–US relations were also tense.[3]

In Hare's words, that day "İnönü was model of courtesy and hospitality but burden of his remarks constituted heavy fare indeed."[4] While talking about the gravity of the situation on the island, Hare proposed some solutions based on developing the dialogue between Turkey and Greece. İnönü replied that he, too, had always preferred direct talks with Athens but that Greeks were not open to discussion. Hare

> said all this seemed be getting nowhere and asked if Inonu as man of great experience could not identify certain areas where effort might be made break through present barriers. It was at this point that Inonu delivered what he apparently intended be punch-line of conversation by saying that time for persuasion now passed; no longer any role for "the old statesman," as matter now stand there are only two alternatives, either submit to Makarios or beat some sense into his head by force.[5]

At that moment, Hare was saved by the bell: The lunch was ready.

After the lunch, Hare "asked what İnönü meant by using force to bring Makarios to see reason. [İnönü] said he meant military force; it wouldn't be necessary to invade all of island, merely occupy part of it. This was the only language Makarios could understand."[6] İnönü added that Washington was not fully aware of what was happening in Cyprus and was favoring *enosis*[7] as a solution. He stated that he was prepared for the escalation of the conflict to a full-scale war between Greece and Turkey. Hare tried to pacify İnönü. He was known as 'the Silent Ambassador' for his measured and subtle style.[8] He emphasized solutions such as strengthening the peacekeeping efforts and establishing communication with Athens. After a while, İnönü showed signs of calming down. Their dialogue ended with İnönü's request from Hare "to convey to Washington Turkish despair in finding road out of Cyprus imbroglio and its determination to use force if necessary."

1 Crisis in Turkey–US Relations

During the three weeks following the lunch, the situation in Cyprus worsened while Hare did his best to maintain the communication between Ankara and Washington and to prevent a Turkish military intervention. At the height of the crisis, on 4 June, Hare paid an urgent visit to Erkin, the Turkish FM. Erkin told him that the situation on the island was critical and the Cabinet would meet at 8:30 (Turkish local time) that night to decide what to do. Hare asked whether an intervention might be decided. Erkin said it was possible. The telegram Hare immediately sent to Washington at 6:00 contained the following "Hope you or Athens can give me something urgently which I can convey to Erkin in effort deter precipitate action."[9] This message alarmed Washington. At 7:45, Rusk, the SECSTATE, phoned Menemencioğlu, the Turkish Ambassador. Rusk tried to be as clear as possible:

> We have considered we have had a flat assurance through the FM such a step would not be taken and that there would be full consultation with allies. We would find this a very very grave departure from our understandings and would have a serious effect on the problem of our security commitments with our allies. The President asked most urgently that we urge in the gravest terms that we have an opportunity for consultations on these matters.

In response, Menemencioğlu told him that it was difficult for him to get through to Ankara and asked if Rusk was also sending a message to Hare. At 8:15, Rusk instructed Hare to see İnönü immediately, "calling him out of cabinet meeting if necessary" to express US opposition to a military intervention in Cyprus and to "use all arguments in [his] arsenal to pull them back from any such decision and to insist upon consultation." The telegram received by the US Embassy in Ankara from the US Embassy in Greece at 8:30 did not change the situation. As instructed, Hare rushed to see İnönü. They talked for almost three hours until 11:00 while the cabinet waited. From the start of their conversation, İnönü made it clear that he would stick to the decision to carry out the operation. He even said that not only Cyprus but also the relationship between Turkey and the US could hinge on agreement with Turkish decision. Hare was about to lose the game. He informed the DOS about the situation:

> When Inonu made another move to join Cabinet I said was certain what I had been told would be great disappointment to President

who has stressed importance of consultation and was only being given opportunity to agree or disagree on single proposition. [. . .] I said what we needed was time make our views known. Inonu asked how much time. I said twenty-four hours in belief that request for longer delay would be refused. Inonu agreed, saying would be difficult call off plans at this stage but that he would do so. He must however stress importance of strict secrecy. This I assured. Longer tel follows but this is guts of discussion and is being sent as preliminary report so you can get wheels turning since we shall need strongest and most forthcoming assurances and arguments possible if we are to head Turks off. Although we didn't finish till eleven o'clock they asked for our reply by nine o'clock (local time) tomorrow night.[10]

The "strongest and most forthcoming assurance and argument possible" Hare invoked, came at 7:15 in the morning on 5 June. This was a long telegram from Johnson[11] addressed to İnönü and sent to the US Embassy in Turkey. The content and wording of this telegram were quite acrimonious. It reminded Turkey of its responsibilities under the Treaty of Guarantee on Cyprus and the bilateral treaty of military assistance signed between the US and Turkey, and those arising from its membership to NATO and UN. The telegram stated that the US would not agree to the use of any US-supplied military equipment for a Turkish intervention in Cyprus since this equipment had been provided under the said assistance treaty (thus, its use was subject to US approval). The telegram contained the following passage:

> Ambassador Hare has indicated that you have postponed your decision for a few hours in order to obtain my views. I put to you personally whether you really believe that it is appropriate for your Government, in effect, to present an ultimatum to an ally who has demonstrated such staunch support over the years as has the United States for Turkey. I must, therefore, first urge you to accept the responsibility for complete consultation with the United States before any such action is taken.
> [. . .]
> I must [. . .] inform you in the deepest friendship that unless I can have your assurance that you will not take such action without further and fullest consultation I cannot accept your injunction to Ambassador Hare of secrecy and must immediately ask for emergency meetings of the NATO Council and of the United Nations Security Council.[12]

Hare rushed the telegram to İnönü "who read it carefully, said disagreed with certain points which he would explain later but that he agreed with final sentence to effect that GOT would delay any action on understanding there would be full and frank discussion with a view to reaching a peaceful solution of Cyprus problem."[13]

This telegram, which came to be known as the 'Johnson letter,' would leave an indelible mark in Turkey–US relations. Those who benefited the most from this process were Greeks who continued to enjoy the liberty to run after their *enosis* plan, and Hare who, for his efforts during the crisis, received the DOS's Distinguished Service Award.[14]

Turks would play their usual trump card. On 30 October 1964, a Turkish delegation led by Erkin, visited Moscow.[15] A Soviet parliamentary delegation headed by Podgorny, the Second Secretary of the Communist Party, came to Ankara on 4 January 1965.[16] On the same day, *Pravda* wrote that Turkey was planning to withdraw from NATO.[17] On 26 February, the new PM Suat Hayri Ürgüplü announced that Turkey would continue to cooperate with its partners in the Atlantic alliance and strive to fulfill the principles governing the Turkey–EEC association, but that would pursue a more independent FP, particularly in developing better relations with the USSR.[18]

The US rose to the bait, and on 3 July 1965, declared that it would lend Turkey 40 million dollars for the Keban Dam project. France, Italy, Germany, the International Development Association, and the European Investment Bank pledged to help meet the 331 million dollars of the cost.[19]

On 10 August 1965, Ürgüplü invited Kosygin, the Soviet PM, to Turkey. Kosygin promised to deal with the fate of the Turks in Cyprus and appointed a team of technocrats to work on the Soviet financial aid planned for the Turkish Cypriots.[20]

2 EEC–US Relations Deteriorate

Americans' relations with Europeans were not better than their relations with Turks. The three problems inherited from the Kennedy period were still present:

1. De Gaulle was still seeking to 'liberate' France and Europe from American influence. In a speech he delivered on 23 July 1964, he remarked that Europe should maintain an alliance with the US, but the reasons that made this alliance a form of subordination were fading away day-by-day.[21] In 1966, French armed forces were removed from the integrated military command of NATO, and all non-French NATO troops were asked to leave France. Even a nuclear confrontation between France and the US became a possibility in 1967.[22]
2. On 10 May 1967, the UK submitted its second application to the EEC. This application was again vetoed by de Gaulle on 27 November, which was an unpleasant development for the US.[23]
3. Despite the abovementioned decision of the GATT tribunal, there still were problems in the US–EEC trade. In retaliation for the losses of US chicken farmers, Johnson imposed 20 percent tax on potato starch, dextrin, brandy, and light trucks imported from Europe.[24]

As a result, the US was now less willing and able to put pressure on the Europeans for Turkey.

3 Turkey–EEC Relations Improve

While the relations of the US with Turkey and the EEC were going through difficult times, there was a honeymoon in Turkey–EEC relations. Turkey was basking in the favor of the EEC in the preparatory stage of the association. This stage had started with the entry into force of the Ankara Agreement on 1 December 1964 and would continue until 1973.[25] As foreseen in the agreement and its protocols, in this stage Turkey had no other obligation than strengthening its economy in order to shoulder the responsibilities that would arise from the implementation of the subsequent stages. The EEC opened tariff quotas for imports of certain Turkish agricultural products and extended financial aid to Turkey. For the first—and the last—time, in its relations with the EEC, Turkey did not need US patronage.

Turks did not use this opportunity wisely. The first Five-Year Development Plan of Turkey,[26] which covered the 1963–1967 period, had no reference to the country's relations with the EEC, whilst the next one,[27] which covered the 1968–1972 period, contented itself with a four-sentence reference. The financial aid received from the Community was squandered, and no substantial reform was undertaken to prepare Turkey's economy for the subsequent stages.

4 No Reference to Turkey–EEC Relations

The deteriorating relations of the US with the EEC and Turkey affected approach of the US to Turkey–EEC relations negatively. This effect was amplified by the facts that Johnson abandoned the great designs of Kennedy, and that the US was less interventionist now. The declassified documents from the period, available in the DOS archives, are full of details about trade-related general problems or the Cyprus crisis but contain no significant reference to Turkey–EEC relations.

The US was still concerned by the competitive position of its agricultural exports to the EEC. Although this issue had been on the table since the Kennedy administration, the net effect of this situation had not clarified yet:
A study published by the US DOA in 1964 contained the following passage:

> This duty preference adversely affects US tobacco exports to the EEC countries. For the most part, tobaccos from the Unites States will be assessed 17.2 cents per pound import duty compared with zero duty on tobaccos from Greece and Turkey.[28]

Another study prepared by Lawrence B. Krause in 1968[29] was more elaborate and its findings were less alarming. Krause was an economist by training, but his study had a political dimension as well. The study, which was an analysis of the EEC–US relations, had a section entitled "The U.S. Interest in the Greek and Turkish Associations," where Krause wrote that although the potential tariff discrimination against US exports to the EEC had been widened to the advantage of Greece and Turkey due to the association agreements of these two countries, the overall competitive effect would be slight, because

1 Turkey and Greece were not major recipients of American exports; and
2 The advantageous status of the agricultural exports of these two countries to the EEC would not be at the detriment of comparable US exports. Since

   a Turkish and Greek tobacco varieties were different than the American one;
   b In the case of cotton, the applicable CCT rate of the EEC was already 'zero' for imports from the US; and
   c Turkish coarse grain exports could be a threat, but the total volume of these exports was low relative to US exports.

According to Krause, the association of Turkey and Greece with the EEC would be in the benefit of the US since the EEC would cooperate with the US in supporting these two countries financially against Soviet threat. Krause wrote that after the coming into force of the association agreement of Greece, US aid to this country began to taper off and eventually ceased by 1965. He predicted that the same would be the case for Turkey. He added that it was not a coincidence that the US economic aid program Turkey was benefiting from was expected to terminate at about the time that Turkey would enter the second stage of its association agreement.[30]

As Krause predicted, the 'Economic Support Fund/Security Support Assistance' item in the US economic aid scheme was terminated in 1964 although some other items in the scheme continued to be regularly paid until 1984.[31]

Krause was a senior staff member of the Council of Economic Advisers between 1967 and 1969,[32] and his study must have given a certain reassurance to the Johnson administration.

5 Mentality of the Johnson Administration

The decrease that started in the motivation of the US to contribute to the improvement of Turkey–EEC relations in the Kennedy era ended up with indifference—if not hostility—in the Johnson era. The following were the reasons underlying this process:

1 Despite its involvement in the Cyprus crisis, the US was now less interventionist in its FP;

2   The US commitment for European integration was less now. Europe was able to stand on its feet as a bloc and compete with the US commercially;
3   Turkey was enjoying the advantages of the preparatory stage of its association relationship and did not seem to be in need of US help;
4   Turkey's agricultural exports to the EEC was still a source of concern for the US; and
5   Turkey's insistence in launching a military intervention in Cyprus was seen unacceptable by the US.

6 Conclusion

The Johnson administration was trying to guard the economic interests of the US (NRA5) while defending the integrity of the Western bloc (NRA6). These two objectives were contradictory, and economic and political relations of the US with Europeans and Turkey deteriorated.

Turkey–EEC relations, on the other hand, improved in this era, while, for the first and perhaps the last time, these relations disappeared from US FP agenda. Thinking that Turkish economy would sufficiently benefit from the association with the EEC, the US terminated one of the main items in its aid scheme to Turkey (NRA7).

The administration never abandoned its caution about the Turkey-EEC association and passed the duty of clarifying the meaning of this association on to the Nixon administration.

Notes

1. İsmet İnönü, the PM of Turkey.
2. For a detailed account of the conflict, see *Report by the Secretary-General to the Security Council on the United Nations Operation in Cyprus, for the Period 26 April to 8 June 1964*, S/5764, 15 June 1964.
3. A month before the lunch, Mehmet Ali Kışlalı, a correspondent of *The Time* magazine in Turkey, conducted an interview with İnönü, where İnönü fulminated against the US. He said that it was as if some NATO members such as the US and the UK were in tandem with some external forces who try to destroy NATO. He added that he was doing his best to contribute to keeping the Alliance intact, but if this Alliance was to be destroyed, a new world would be established under new conditions, and Turkey would find its place in that world. *The Time* refused to publish the interview. Kışlalı had it published it in *Milliyet*, one of the major dailies in Turkey, on 16 April 1964. Today, excerpts from this interview are still quoted in nationalist and/ or anti-Western texts in Turkey. (Sources: Mehmet Ali Kışlalı, "Batı ittifakı yıkılır," *Milliyet*, 16 April 1964; and Mehmet Ali Kışlalı, "Sadece İnönü düşündü," *Radikal*, 12 January 2007.)
4. Raymond A. Hare, "Telegram from the Embassy in Turkey to the Department of State," 12 May 1964, in James Miller (ed.), *FRUS, 1964–1968, Vol. XVI*, Washington: USGPO, 2000, 90–2, p. 90.
5. Ibid., p. 90–1.
6. p. 91.

7 Enosis means 'union' in Greek. In this context, it refers to a specific movement that strives for incorporation of Cyprus into Greece.
8 Teresa Thomas, "Raymond Arthur Hare," in Cathal Nolan (ed.), *Notable US Ambassadors since 1775*, Westport, CT: Greenwood Press, 1997, 130–6, p. 134.
9 "Telegram from the Embassy in Turkey to the Department of State," 4 June 1964, in James Miller (ed.), *FRUS, 1964–1968, Vol. XVI*, Washington: USGPO, 2000, 103–4, p. 104.
10 "Telegram from the Embassy in Turkey to the Department of State," 5 June 1964, in James Miller (ed.), *FRUS, 1964–1968, Vol. XVI*, Washington: USGPO, 2000, 106–7, p. 106.
11 Later on, Dean Rusk admitted that he wrote the telegram. See: Haluk Şahin, *Gece Gelen Mektup: Türk-Amerikan İlişkilerinde Dönüm Noktası*, Istanbul: Cep Kitapları, 1987, p. 65. Rusk had been aided by Harlan Cleveland, ASSTSECSTATE and his deputy Joseph Sisco. Ball described the letter as the most brutal diplomatic note he had ever seen. (Source: George W. Ball, *The Past Has Another Pattern: Memoirs*, New York, NY: W.W. Norton & Co., 1983, p. 350.)
12 Dean Rusk, "Telegram from the Department of State to the Embassy in Turkey," 5 June 1964, in James Miller (ed.), *FRUS, 1964–1968, Vol. XVI*, Washington: USGPO, 2000, 107–10, pp. 107 and 110.
13 Raymond A. Hare, "Telegram from the Embassy in Turkey to the Department of State," 5 June 1964, in James Miller (ed.), *FRUS, 1964–1968, Vol. XVI*, Washington: USGPO, 2000, p. 111.
14 Teresa Thomas, "Raymond Arthur Hare," in Cathal Nolan (ed.), *Notable US Ambassadors since 1775*, Westport, CT: Greenwood Press, 1997, 130–6, p. 134.
15 Abdi İpekçi, "Erkin, Moskova'da," *Milliyet*, 31 October 1964.
16 "Sovyet parlamento heyeti dün geldi," *Milliyet*, 5 January 1965.
17 "Pravda: 'Türkiye NATO'dan çekilmeyi düşünüyor," *Milliyet*, 5 January 1965.
18 "Turkey will stress her links to Soviet," *NYT*, 27 February 1965.
19 Edwin Kenworthy, "U.S. to lend Turks $40 million for big Euphrates Dam project," *NYT*, 3 July 1965.
20 "Rus Başbakanı da Türkiye'ye gelecek," *Milliyet*, 11 August 1965.
21 A video and transcript of this speech are available on www.ina.fr/fresques/de-gaulle/notice/Gaulle00095/conference-de-presse-du-23-juillet-1964, accessed 3 March 2012.
22 Bernard Ledwidge, *De Gaulle*, London: Weidenfeld and Nicolson, 1982, p. 341.
23 Erin R. Mahan, *Kennedy, de Gaulle and Western Europe*, New York, NY: Palgrave Macmillan, 2002, pp. 143–4.
24 Alan Swinbank and Carolyn Tanner, *Farm Policy and Trade Conflict: The Uruguay Round and CAP Reform*, Ann Arbor: University of Michigan Press, 1997, p. 12.
25 The preparatory stage was supposed to last five years, but for several reasons it lasted nine years.
26 Available at http://ekutup.dpt.gov.tr/plan/plan1.pdf, accessed 29 October 2012.
27 Available at http://ekutup.dpt.gov.tr/plan/plan2.pdf, accessed 29 October 2012, p. 123.
28 Robert Fitzsimmonds, *Factors Affecting US Fruit Markets in Japan*, Washington: US DOA, 1964, p. xxxvi.
29 Lawrence B. Krause, *European Economic Integration and the United States*, Washington DC: Brookings Institution, 1968.
30 pp. 200–1.
31 "U.S. economic assistance," *U.S. Agency for International Development*. Available at http://gbk.eads.usaidallnet.gov/data/files/us_economic_assistance.csv, accessed 16 July 2012.
32 Krause's CV is available at http://irps.ucsd.edu/academics/f-krause-cv.php, accessed 3 August 2006.

4 The Nixon Administration (1969–1974)

Zigzags

President Nixon took office on 20 January 1969. On 1 March, he was having a lunch with President de Gaulle and French PM Couve de Murville at the Grand Trianon Palace in Versailles. The palace had been commissioned by Louis XIV in 1670 for his escapades with his mistress Madame de Montespan and renovated by de Gaulle in 1963 as a guesthouse for presidents of France and as an official presidential residence.

The lunch started with an informal dialogue between Nixon and de Gaulle.

> De Gaulle felt a prisoner in his official quarters and wanted to know what Nixon did to get away from it all. Did he go in the White House pool? The President preferred the ocean, he said, where there was wind and sun and where he could walk. They shared campaign experiences, neither being overly fond of that aspect of a politician's life.[1]

Following the lunch, some critical issues were addressed. After all, this was a meeting of the leaders of two countries that had been at odds for some time. The official American memorandum of the conversation felt a need to state that Nixon "was speaking in great confidence." He emphasized that the USG would express its views on European problems "including those of the UK," but that "things in Europe should be allowed to develop in their own way."

> Times had changed. 22 years ago Europe was prostrate economically, militarily and spiritually. [. . .] The US was still ahead in economic and military power, but the nations of Europe were stable and developed political strength and substance and in some cases nuclear capabilities. [. . .] [The US] would continue [its] role in NATO and do everything [it] could to draw the nations of Europe together. Political realities had changed and [the Americans] would expect initiatives to come from Europeans.[2]

De Gaulle said he agreed with Nixon. He emphasized that he "was not opposed to rapprochement and even union" in Europe but added that instead of resigning themselves to a subordinate position, Europeans should take over their responsibilities. In his opinion, the US could do a great deal to help. A *détente* atmosphere was palpable throughout the talk.

On 28 April, two months after the lunch, de Gaulle resigned, but the dialogue between the two countries did not stop there. Georges Pompidou became the President on 20 June. He did not even have to wait as much as Nixon did after taking the office: Only four days later, he was at the White House for a dinner given in his honor by Nixon. The following day, this time the French organized a dinner for Nixon where the two sides gave further assurances:

> President Pompidou said he would like to ask the President to say a few words about Europe. He wanted to know what importance he should give to the statements by Ambassador Schaetzel concerning the fears and even opposition to the European Common Market by the United States.[3]
>
> President Nixon replied, "None."[. . .] It [would] be increasingly competitive with the US as the UK [came] in and it [might] become a rather serious problem for [the US] in an economic sense. But the President said he took the long view that a strong productive European Community including the United Kingdom [was] in the interest of world peace and stability. The US would have to pay some costs for achieving this bigger goal and the President did not agree with those who rejected this point.[4]

We can draw two—somehow conflicting—inferences from these meals:

1. Nixon would be even less interventionist than his predecessor in European affairs.
2. As it is obvious in Ambassador Schaetzel's words, the US was still sensitive about the effect of the EEC on American commercial interests.

1 Commercial Concerns Persist

Despite the warming up between the US and the EEC, the Nixon administration had two worries about the preferential trade agreements (PTAs) and association agreements the Community had concluded with certain countries:

1. The tariff preferences the EEC applied to the exports of its underdeveloped partners would be detrimental to the comparable US exports to the EEC. For instance, American citrus growers were uncomfortable with the tariff preferences the EEC had given to the produce of some

North African countries, Spain, Israel, and Turkey. The pressure they put on the Nixon administration was transferred to the EEC. A news story from the *WP* reported that "[b]owing to U.S. pressure, the European Common Market [was] planning to lower its tariff on American citrus imports [. . .]."[5]

2   The 'reverse preferences' (tariff privileges applied by developing countries to the imports from certain developed countries) that the European exporters enjoyed would be to the disadvantage of their American competitors. *The Times* was drawing attention to this fact:

[T]he Community [has a] habit of demanding reverse preferences from the Mediterranean countries, particularly poor ones like Tunisia and Morocco, with which the EEC has trade and association agreements. [. . .]
[. . .]
What the Community is striving for is a more consistent set of arrangements than the existing hotchpotch of trade and association agreements which it has negotiated or is negotiating with Greece, Spain, Turkey, Tunisia, Morocco, Lebanon, Algeria, Malta, Israel, Egypt, Yugoslavia, and Cyprus.[6]

2 Political Considerations Outweigh Commercial Concerns

De Gaulle's replacement by Pompidou was good news for the British as much as it was for the Americans. At the Meeting of the Heads of State or Government in The Hague on 1–2 January 1969, Pompidou indicated that his government was ready to lift the French veto on Britain's EEC entry:[7]

Together with Ireland, Denmark, and Norway, Britain started its accession negotiations with the EEC on 30 June 1970. A few days later, in a National Security Decision Memorandum[8] written by Henry A. Kissinger, a National Security Advisor (NSA) under Nixon, the USG clarified its position towards this first enlargement of the EEC, which would be based on the following principles:

1   US support for expansion of the membership of the Community.
2   US willingness to accept some—but not excessive—economic costs as a result of the accession of new members to the Community. [. . .]
3   Clear indication to the countries involved that [the US expects] them to take fully into account, in their own negotiations, the rights and interests of third countries, including the US and the importance of maintaining an equitable system of multilateral trading rules.
4   Defense of [US] economic interests in specific agricultural and industrial products by appropriate means, primarily through notifying the countries involved during the course of the negotiations of [US] intention of exercising [US] rights under GATT.

Similar opinions started to be expressed for the Turkey's 'acquittal.' In December 1970, George Harris[9] prepared a lengthy report on Turkish–American relations for the DOS. Two years later, this report was published in the form of a book. In Harris's words

> Turkey's membership in the European Communities accorded with U.S. policy and over the long run would be a most important step in assuring the permanence of healthy relations between the two states.[10]

This positive outlook proved short-lived.

3 Commercial Concerns Resurface

The 'economic costs' mentioned in Kissinger's memorandum soon started to preoccupy the Nixon administration. In Turkey's case, these concerns were not unwarranted. In the preparatory stage of its association with the EEC, Turkey was enjoying an advantageous position. Between 1964 and 1971, Turkey's imports from the EEC increased by 194 percent, and in 1973, 40 percent of Turkey's exports were to the EEC. The Community had reduced the customs duties applicable to tobacco, dried fig, and hazelnut imports from Turkey,[11] and applied no customs duty to Turkish cotton. After September 1971, almost all industrial products originating from Turkey were exempt from customs duty when entering into the EEC.

The US was expected to offer trade facilitation measures to underdeveloped countries in pursuance of UNCTAD decisions. In November 1970, a high-ranking official from the DOS declared that the US would not extend this facilitation to the 18 Yaoundé countries mentioned above together with Turkey and Greece since these 20 states had an association relationship with the EEC. The official explained that, in their understanding, 'underdeveloped countries' were supposed to be those who did not extend trade concessions to industrialized countries, whereas these 20 states did give concessions to the EEC. Turks were zealously trying to change this understanding of the Nixon administration.[12]

The US was still uncertain about its policy towards the relations of the EEC with third countries. The DOA reckoned that in the case of accession of the UK, Ireland, Denmark, and Norway to the EEC, the volume of US tobacco exports would be reduced by 75 percent. The US was intending to bring a complaint to the GATT about this issue.[13] A National Security Decision Memorandum contained the following:

> The President has decided that the United States will oppose the Spain-European Community trade agreements as presently proposed, in the context of opposition to all preferential arrangements illegal under the international trading rules of the GATT.[14]

Two years later, in a memorandum from acting SECSTATE John N. Irwin to Nixon, this outlook was emphasized once again:

> We have consistently stated that we will object to any of these arrangements [of the EEC] which are inconsistent with GATT and that, where our trade interests are damaged, we will seek specific compensation. These arrangements include (1) existing ones with the EFTA non-applicants, (2) existing ones with former colonial states, (3) existing ones with Greece and *Turkey*, (4) proposed new arrangements with Mediterranean states and others, and (5) existing arrangements with Spain and Israel which are special cases.[15]

Jean Rey, President of the Commission of the EEC, was of the contrary opinion.

> [He] said 80 to 90 percent of EEC trade is in accordance with GATT regulations and that the rest is based on exceptions laid down by GATT itself.
> [. . .]
> As for preferential accords around the Mediterranean basin, these are partly imposed by circumstances, he said. Agreements with Greece and Turkey, for example stem from special ties these nations already had with Western Europe, and such agreements were not contested in Geneva.[16]

Europeans thought that Americans did not understand them. The strain between the two shores of the Atlantic was noticeable:

> Thoughtful visitors returning from the United States have remarked flatly that EEC and European problems are only known to a handful of people in New York or Washington. The return to isolationism is imminent. The idea of Atlantic Partnership is dead.[17]

4 1973: A Turning Point

In our context, 1973 was a turning point for three reasons:

1. In this year, the transitory stage of Turkey's association started. This meant the end of Turkey's honeymoon with the EEC. Once again, Turkey would need the US assistance.
2. It was also in this year that the US accepted Turkey's Europeanness and dropped its objections to Turkey's association.
3. The year 1973 was special for Kissinger. He declared it as 'the Year of Europe.'

4.1 The Transitory Stage Starts

On 1 January 1973, the preparatory stage of Turkey's associate membership ended with the entry into force of the Additional Protocol, and the transitory stage started. In the Protocol, Turkey was given two lists of goods originating from the EEC. For the goods in the first list, Turkey would gradually reduce its customs duties to zero in a period of 12 years. For the goods in the second list, Turkey would do the same in 22 years. As a result, at the end of the twenty-second year, a CU would have been established between Turkey and the EEC in practice, but the two parties would also need to sign a formal decision to initiate the CU and pass to the final stage.

Turkey was supposed to make its first reduction in the customs duties on the day of entry into force of the Protocol, and regular reductions were supposed to follow in the coming years. Turkey played a trick, and one day before the entry into force of the Protocol, increased its relevant customs duties.[18]

These mutual tariff reductions meant that a bilateral preferential trade regime was developing between Turkey and the EEC. This regime would be in conflict with US commercial interests. However, since the US had always argued that it was against the unilateral nature of the preparatory stage of Turkey's association but not this association itself, now the Nixon administration had little ground for its objections.

4.2 The Year of Europe

In 1973, Kissinger contributed to the formulation of several history-making decisions related to such issues as the Vietnam War, or the Yom Kippur War. One of these decisions was the declaration of 1973 as the Year of Europe on 23 April.[19] In doing so, he was hoping to mend the transatlantic relations. On 22 September, he was appointed as the SECSTATE while retaining his position as a NSA.

Many sources[20] concur that the Year of Europe initiative of Kissinger was not so successful. An article from *Foreign Affairs*, published in January 1974, reviewed the previous year as follows:

> Symptoms of [. . .] outburst of bad temper have included numerous attacks from American sources on the unhelpfulness of European allies at the height of the Arab-Israeli fighting. [. . .] There followed Secretary of State Kissinger's complaint to a group of parliamentarians from the European Community that Europeans had "acted as though the alliance did not exist" and his reported aside: "I do not care what happens to NATO, I am so disgusted."
>
> [. . .] Secretary of the Treasury Shultz has once again suggested that Europeans are being unhelpful about the coming trade negotiations within the framework of [. . .] GATT [. . .].[21]

Nevertheless, as we will see below, Kissinger's new European policy brought a considerable improvement to Turkey's relations with the US and with the EEC.

4.3 Turkey's Europeanness Acknowledged and EEC Association Cleared

Despite the detriment the Turkey–EEC association might pose to US commercial interests, in March 1973, William J. Casey, the Under SECSTATE for Economic Affairs, announced that the association agreements of Turkey and Greece, which, different from the agreements the EEC concluded with Spain, Israel, and African countries, had a prospect of EEC membership were more acceptable for the US but that this did not mean that the US did not have any objections to these two agreements.[22] At last, in October 1973, William D. Eberle, Nixon's trade representative, attested that the US would not object the Greek and Turkish association agreements anymore, on the ground that these agreements had been intended for the full-membership of these two countries to the EEC.[23] Nonetheless, the US retained its concerns about the full-membership itself of these two countries.

Eberle's statement was also an indirect approval of Turkey's Europeanness. Six months later, Kissinger would 'formalize' this approval: In his meeting with the Turkish FM Turan Güneş in New York on 15 April 1974, he declared his plans to transfer Turkey from the NEA to EUR:

THE SECRETARY: [. . .] Have you met Mr. Hartman?[24] You know that Turkey is moving to the European Bureau.
FOREIGN MINISTER GUNES: Yes. I have met both of these gentlemen (indicating Atherton[25] and Hartman). One Assistant Secretary will be acting for Thrace and one for Anatolia.[26]
THE SECRETARY: You will have to talk to Hartman in Istanbul, not Ankara.[27]
(Laughter)
FOREIGN MINISTER GUNES: Yes.[28]

Two and a half months later, this change materialized:

> As late as the spring of 1974, for example, 22 years after they joined NATO, Greece and Turkey had still not joined [EUR]. [. . .] If Greece and Turkey were stepchildren of [NEA], they often were treated like orphans in [EUR], which they at last joined in the summer of 1974. [On 30 June], Secretary of State Henry A. Kissinger, unfriendly to the policy recommendations he was receiving from NEA, abruptly transferred responsibility for Greek, Turkish and Cypriot affairs to EUR.[29]

By taking these steps, Kissinger was hoping to contribute the improvement of not only the transatlantic relations in general but also to Turkey–US relations. Since the Johnson letter, Turkey had been resentful to the US in the Cyprus issue, and another problem was developing between the two countries around the opium poppy issue.[30] Besides, in its association with the EEC, Turkey would have to develop friendly relations with Greece. This would ensure the strength of the southeastern flank of NATO.

In the short run, these aims proved to be difficult to attain. The summer of 1974 brought a double whammy. The crisis in Cyprus grew worse when Turkey launched a military operation on the island on 20 July 1974, and the opium poppy issue turned into a silent war between Turkey and the US.[31] In those days, the Watergate scandal was at its height. In that mayhem, Turkey–EEC relations were not among the priorities of the Nixon administration that would soon end on 9 August.

5 Mentality of the Nixon Administration

The costs and benefits of the Turkey–EEC association were still unfolding in the Nixon era. It would be difficult for any administration to assess such a large and unsteady set of variables in its entirety.

The US was apprehensive of Turkey's association because of the privileged status of Turkish agricultural exports to the Common Market. This apprehension was among the sources of its opposition to the European integration rather than being an outcome of it. Turkey was not the only country in this position; the US also frowned at the advantages Greece and the Yaoundé countries were enjoying. Even the relations with the UK, a close ally of the US, were badly affected by such concerns. This was the case, although the FP of the Nixon administration was marked by a certain degree of isolationism.[32]

On the benefits side, Turkey's association would strengthen its ties with the West and mend the rift in Turkey–US relations. Turkey would be more cooperative in the issue of Cyprus and less tolerant to opium poppy farming on its soil. This association would lead to establishment of cordial relations between Greece and Turkey, which would consolidate the southeastern flank of NATO. The EEC would share with US the burden of helping Turkey economically.

After weighing these costs and benefits, in 1973 the US declared that it was not against Turkey's association anymore. The conclusion of Turkey's preparatory stage meant the end of the privileges Turkey enjoyed unilaterally. Since these privileges had been the main basis of the US opposition to Turkey's association, now the US had less reason to object this association.

The Nixon administration knew that the association packages of Turkey and Greece contained a prospect for full-membership to the EEC, which might enable the EEC's to become a rival economic player to the US. It remained opposed to the full-membership of these two countries.

For the US, it would not be 'politically correct' to officially accept its reasoning in the dropping its objection to Turkey's association. Instead, the US justified its decision with the fact that Greek and Turkish association agreements contained full-membership prospect. This was an implicit recognition of the Europeanness of Turkey, which was corroborated by the transfer of Turkey—together with Greece and Cyprus—from NEA to EUR. This official justification—not the real reasoning—of the acquiescence to Turkey's association contained a contradiction: If this association was acceptable on the ground that it was a step towards full-membership, the Nixon administration should not have maintained its opposition to the full-membership itself.

6 Conclusion

Turkey–EEC relations re-entered onto the US FP agenda in Nixon's term. However, this was not good news for Turks, because the agriculture lobby in the US was trying to influence the FP of the Nixon administration. In Turkey's case, this influence materialized as an objection to Turkey–EEC association (DF). In line with the neorealist assumption regarding the hierarchical ordering principle in domestic politics (NRA2), the Nixon administration managed to keep immune to this influence some critical FP issues including Turkey's association (NRA6)—but remained opposed to Turkey's full-membership (NRA5).

At Kissinger's behest, Turkey was transferred to EUR of DOS, which was a paradigmatic change. Although Turkey would be considered 'second-rate' under this bureau in the coming presidential periods, that policies regarding Turkey were to be prepared in the "European" kitchen of the DOS was a significant development. This was a 'fine-tuning' in the existing balance of power in neorealist sense (NR6). The administration was trying to mend the rift within the alliance, while supporting European integration cautiously, and expecting Europeans to stand on their own feet (NRA6 and 7).

The Nixon era ended with an escalation in the opium problem between Turkey and the US, and Turkey's launching of a military operation in Cyprus. Of these two problems, the latter would continue into the Ford era—and well beyond—and have important implications regarding Turkey–EEC/EU relations.

Notes

1 Hugh Sidey, "Two ex-exiles hit it off," *Life*, Vol. 66, No. 10, 14 March 1969, p. 4.
2 "Memorandum of Conversation between the President, General de Gaulle, Prime Minister Couve de Murville, Mr. Andronikov, and MG Walters at Grand Trianon Palace, Versailles, March 1, 1969," Folder Memcons-Europe-February 23-March 2, 1969; Box 447; President's Trip; NSC Files, Nixon PL, California.
3 Robert J. Schaetzel was the USAMB to the EC between 1966 and 1972. Pompidou is probably referring to Schaetzel's speech in Bonn. Schaetzel "said, 'There is a strong feeling that Europe is insensitive to the economic problems and the political and military burdens we must carry. [. . .]' Schaetzel went on to recite chapter and verse

detail such as a 6 % annual decline in American agricultural exports to the Common Market during the last two years plus the growing web of Common Market preferential trade agreements with Israel, Spain, Austria, Sweden, the African states, Morocco, Greece, *Turkey* and others." (Source: Don Cook, "U.S., Common Market 'truce team' studied," *LAT*, 30 March 1970. Emphasis added.)

4 "Memorandum of conversation," 26 February 1970, in Bruce Duncombe (ed.), *FRUS, 1969–1976, Vol. III*, Washington: USGPO, 2002, 91–2, pp. 91–2.

5 Richard Norton-Taylor, "Commart set to lower tariff on U.S. citrus," *WP*, 5 June 1971.

6 Roger Berthoud, "US shadow over meeting of Nine," *The Times*, 6 November 1972. Emphasis added.

7 "Statement by M. Georges Pompidou: President of France," *Bulletin of the EC*, No. 1, 1970, 33–5, p. 35. See also Stephen Wall, *The Official History of Britain and the European Community, Vol. II: From Rejection to Referendum, 1963–1975*, London: Routledge, 2012, p. 393.

8 "US Policy toward the European Community," National Security Decision Memorandum 68, 3 July 1970, The NSC Institutional Files, Box H-208, Nixon PL, Yorba Linda, California.

9 In those days, Harris was a special projects officer at the Near East Division of the Office of Analysis for Near East and South Asia of the Bureau of Intelligence and Research of the DOS. (Source: www.american.edu/spa/ccps/upload/harris.pdf, accessed 19 August 2014.)

10 George Harris, *Troubled Alliance: Turkish-American Problems in Historical Perspective, 1945–1971*, Washington: American Enterprise Institute of Public Policy Research, 1972, p. 184.

11 These rates were applicable to quantities beyond the quotas specified in the Provisional Protocol of the Ankara Agreement and were changed with the subsequent decisions of the AC.

12 "ABD Ortak Pazar üyelerini gelişmiş ülke kabul ediyor," *Milliyet*, 10 November 1970.

13 "ABD'nin Ortak Pazar'a tütün ihracı azaldı," *Milliyet*, 10 November 1970.

14 "National Security Decision Memorandum from Henry Kissinger, Subject: U.S. Policy towards Spain: Proposed Spanish Trade Agreement with the European Community (45)," 2 March 1970, The NSC Institutional Files, Box H-208, Nixon PL, Yorba Linda, California.

15 John N. Irwin II, "Memorandum from Acting Secretary of State Irwin to President Nixon," 20 October 1972, in Bruce Duncombe (ed.), *FRUS, 1969–1976, Vol. III*, Washington: USGPO, 2002, 275–9, p. 275. Emphasis added.

16 Richard Neff, "U.S. Common Market to iron out problems," *Christian Science Monitor*, 5 March 1970.

17 Johannes Haubenreisser, "Atlantic partnership and the Mills Bill," *Intereconomics*, Vol. 6, No. 2, 1971, 54–7, p. 54.

18 "7/2/1967 tarih ve 828 sayılı kanunun 2nci maddesinin değiştirilmesi ve ithalde alınacak damga resmi nispetinin yeniden tespitine dair ilişik kararın yürürlüğe konulmasına dair karar (7/5554)," *T.C. Resmi Gazete*, No. 4408, 31 December 1972.

19 Henry A. Kissinger, *American Foreign Policy*, New York, NY: Norton, 1977, 99–113.

20 See, for example, Catherine Hynes, *The Year that Never Was: Heath, the Nixon Administration and The Year of Europe*, University College Dublin Press, 2009; and Alistair Horne, *Kissinger: 1973, the Crucial Year*, New York, NY: Simon & Schuster, 2009.

21 Z, "The Year of Europe," *Foreign Affairs*, January 1974, 237–48, p. 237.

22 Mehmet Ali Birand, "Amerika, AET'nin Türkiye'ye olan tavizinde değişme istiyor," *Milliyet*, 27 March 1973.

23 Mehmet Ali Birand, "ABD, Türkiye AET işlerine karışmayacak," *Milliyet*, 8 October 1973.

24 Arthur A. Hartman, ASSTSECSTATE for EUR.

25 Alfred Atherton, ASSTSECSTATE for NEA.
26 His wit refers to the fact that a part of Turkey is situated in Europe while the other part is in Asia.
27 Istanbul, the cultural and financial center of the country, is located in Europe, whereas Ankara, the capital city, is located in Asia.
28 "Memorandum of Conversation," 15 April 1974, in Laurie Van Hook (ed.), *FRUS, 1969–1976, Vol. XXX*, Washington: USGPO, 662–6, p. 663.
29 Monteagle Stearns, *Entangled Allies: U.S. Policy Toward Greece, Turkey, and Cyprus*, New York, NY: Council on Foreign Relations, 1992, pp. 8–9.
30 Anatolia has been one of the major sources of opium for the world for centuries. In dealing with the drug addiction problem, the US tried to persuade Turkey to cut down poppy cultivation. Till 1974, Turkey did not remain unresponsive to US demands. See Nasuh Uslu, *Turkish-American Relationship between 1947 and 2003: The History of a Distinctive Alliance*, New York, NY: Nova Publishers, 2003, pp. 219–52.
31 In the summer of 1974, Turkey increased from four to seven the number of the provinces where cultivation of poppy plant was authorized, and announced that it aimed at harvesting 200 ton crop as opposed to 75 tons harvested in 1972. USAMB Macomber was called back to Washington and the Congress moved to begin legislation cutting the aid to Turkey. A *New York Post* article called Turkey's move as 'an act of war' and advocated bombing of the poppy fields by the US Air Force. (Source: James W. Spain, "The United States, Turkey and the poppy," *Middle East Journal*, Vol. 29, No. 3, 1975, 295–309, p. 302. Spain was the USAMB to Turkey between 1980 and 1981.)
32 Raymond Aron, "The United States and the international system," in Yair Reiner (ed.), *The Dawn of Universal History: Selected Essays from a Witness of the Twentieth Century*, New York, NY: Basic Books, 2003, 263–404, p. 386.

5 The Ford Administration (1974–1977)

Cyprus

In the evening of 30 July 1975, Finnish President Urho Kekkonen hosted the heads of state and government of 32 other European states and of the US and Canada at a dinner. Being one of the last steps of the long process called the Conference on Security and Cooperation in Europe (CSCE) that had started in 1973, this effulgent event in Helsinki would leave its mark on the history of the Cold War.

> The Russians had been plumping for a European security conference ever since 1954. Hoping to make it the capstone of his career, Brezhnev had been anxious for it to be completed well in advance of the Soviet Party Congress next February, at which time he will probably retire. The long-ailing party chief remained fairly active throughout the week, though he left President Kekkonen's formal dinner on the first night after less than an hour. "Why does he do such things?" asked a slightly amused British diplomat. "He must know what everyone will say." The Soviets claimed that Brezhnev had simply left early so he could work on his speech.[1]

Brezhnev's early leave would be the subject of another joke at the breakfast table the following morning where President Ford, SECSTATE Kissinger, Turkish PM Demirel, and some other key figures were present. The joke was not enough to dissipate the tense atmosphere that obfuscated the conversation:

THE SECRETARY: That was certainly a strange seating arrangement at dinner last night. Mr. Prime Minister, I want to know what you had said to Brezhnev that made him leave after the first course.
DEMIREL: It wasn't anything I said. He was apparently very tired but you are right, it was a strange seating arrangement. I noticed that you, Mr. President, were next to Makarios.
THE SECRETARY: Yes, we had actually refused to talk to him because of some personal remarks he had made about the President before leaving Nicosia, but I am sure he must have asked to sit next to the President.

DEMIREL: He is now the "former" President.
THE PRESIDENT: What does that mean?
THE SECRETARY: What the Prime Minister is saying is that he is not considered to be President by Turkey.[2]

Indeed, Makarios was not considered to be the President of the Republic of Cyprus by Turkey anymore. Following Turkey's operation in July 1974, the island had been partitioned into Greek and Turkish sectors. Due to this operation, the US Congress intended to impose an embargo on Turkey. Citing the damage it would do to US interests, Ford tried in vain to have the Congress reconsider the embargo. On 5 February 1975, the embargo was put into effect

> freezing deliveries over 200 million dollars in arms purchases and grants which had been scheduled for transfer to Turkey. All military assistance, all states of defence articles and services (whether for cash or by credit, or any other means), and all licences with respect to the transformation of arms, ammunitions, and implements of war to the Turkish government were suspended. The ban included 78 million dollar worth of equipment already paid for.[3]

The embargo aroused mass indignation in Turkey. On 18 June 1975, Turkey declared that 20 US installations in Turkey would be subject to a 'special status' unless negotiations on their future were opened in 30 days.[4] Six days before Demirel's breakfast with Ford and Kissinger, on 25 July 1975, Turkey announced that the Defense Cooperation Agreement of 1969, together with all the related agreements, had lost its validity, and that the US military bases in Turkey passed under the control and custody of the Turkish armed forces. Turkey also suspended all the relevant non-NATO military activities.[5]

It was on this background that Demirel spoke as follows at the breakfast:

> [I]t has been extremely difficult to explain to Turkish public opinion why Congress did what it did. I have expressed great appreciation for what you, Mr. President, have done but it did not change the result. Our friendly relations have been spoiled. [. . .] I have tried not to create any provocations. Such provocations could easily be created.[6]

After a lengthy talk at the table, Ford signaled that the embargo could be lifted. In a—probably pre-arranged—dialogue with Kissinger in the presence of Demirel, he insinuated that he would expect some concrete steps from Turkey in the opium problem in return:

THE PRESIDENT: I have a report in this morning that the Senate will try to attach a lifting of the embargo to another bill. [. . .] Henry, why don't you explain the problem with Rangel?

THE SECRETARY: Charlie Rangel is a black Congressman who is very interested in seeing that progress is made on the opium problem. [. . .] If we could write a letter that sets out what you intend to do it would help us with Rangel and he says that he could probably get another ten votes for us.[7]

1 An Ineptly Staged Play with the Soviets

To gain the attention of the US, Turkey started flirting with the members of the socialist bloc once again.[8] Turkey and Bulgaria signed a declaration on cooperation and good neighborhood in Sofia on 3 December 1975. This was followed by another declaration to develop the relations, signed, this time, in Bulgarian President Zhivkov's visit to Turkey in June 1976.[9] Kosygin, the Soviet premier, was in Turkey between 26 and 30 December 1975.[10] He was the guest of honor in the opening ceremony of the Iskenderun iron and steel plant, one of the most strategic and expensive pieces of infrastructure in Turkey, built thanks to the financial aid extended by the Soviets.

However, it was not difficult to notice that Turkey's 'close' relations with the USSR were unfounded: Demirel did not reciprocate Kosygin's arrival speech, which was unprecedented in Turkish diplomatic history, and the Soviet flags that adorned the streets of Ankara during Kosygin's visit were collected and torn up by unknown people in the night.[11]

2 A Bag of Surprises

No matter how makeshift Turkey's move was, it seems to have brought about the intended consequences:

1   The US Congress partially lifted the arms embargo on 6 October 1975.[12]
2   The US provided customs concessions to Turkish exports and once again acknowledged that Turkey–EEC association was not harmful for US interests. The 'Trade Act of 1974' enacted on 3 January 1975 by the Congress had initiated the formulation of a Generalized System of Preferences (GSP). This was a system designed to promote economic growth in the least developed countries by lowering tariffs for their exports to the US market. The formulation of the GSP took a year. At first, it was unclear whether Turkey would be among the countries to be included in this system, because the US feared that the Ankara Agreement and the Additional Protocol Turkey signed with the EEC would be deleterious for US trade. On 25 December 1975, Turkish newspapers gave the good news: the Ford administration had concluded that the agreement and the protocol in question had not had a negative effect on US foreign trade, and that, therefore, Turkey would benefit from the GSP from 1 January 1976 onwards.[13]
3   The US dropped its objections to the full-membership of Turkey—and of Greece—to the EEC. In December 1975, officials from the US

Department of Commerce declared that, in 1974, the US and EEC had reached an agreement whereby the US gave its consent to the EEC's establishment of close relations with other European countries, its Mediterranean neighbors, and the former colonies of its members.[14] The officials remarked that considering the 'Europeanness' of Greece and Turkey, the US was not against the accession of these two countries, but that they would not accept the EEC's extension of its sphere of influence further eastward, especially to Iran.[15]

3 The EEC Gets Involved in the Cyprus Issue

After a long incubation period of nearly two decades, in the mid-1970s the EEC dared to take its first hesitant steps in international politics. The Cyprus crisis would be one of the test cases for this fledgling global actor. The announcement the French FM Jean Sauvagnargues made on the day following Turkey's operation in Cyprus included the following statement:

> The role of the United States is important. But the weight of Europe must not be underestimated. The pressing appeal we have sent out to the parties involved must cause them to reflect seriously about what could happen if it were not heeded.[16]

With their better prospects for EEC membership, Greeks were likely to pay heed to this appeal:

> The Greek leaders see that the European Community can provide a framework with a new climate for Greek-Turkish rapprochement. For Greece this would have the advantage of eliminating the prospect of recurring Turkish intimidation over bilateral problems, as well as the needless arms race that would inevitably ensue.[17]

In Turkey's case this membership was not on the cards in the near future. Turks were unhappy with the EEC paving the way for Greece's full-membership and forcing Turkey to assume a certain position in Cyprus:

> [T]he Turks maintain[ed] that while appearing to be accommodating, the Greek Government [was] merely playing for time—thus prolonging the strain in American-Turkish relations and all that entail[ed]. Similarly, it [was] believed [Turkey], Greece had been further reinforced in this policy by the EEC decision to open negotiations for her full membership of the Community.[18]

A conversation between the Turkish FM Güneş and the US SECSTATE Kissinger on 24 September 1974, at the height of the crisis, is an illustration of the increasing influence of the EEC on the Cyprus crisis. Nevertheless, both Güneş and Kissinger were inclined to take into consideration the MSs of the EEC individually and to ignore the EEC's collective identity. In this conversation, Güneş tried to attract Kissinger's attention to the involvement of the MSs of the EEC in the Cyprus issue. Kissinger, known for his disbelief in the significance of the 'corporate identity' of the EEC[19] and expecting concessions rather than complaints from Güneş, parried this move and riposted:

GUNES: I don't have the intention to make concessions but I know that everyone is beginning to get mixed into the act. Our friends in the Common Market are beginning to get involved too much in political questions. We try to say no to their pressures nicely.

We have put together a collection of little gestures.

THE SECRETARY: I understand. I do not need to know them now. We can talk about what they are later.
GUNES: I want you to understand our methods.
THE SECRETARY: What about some progress before the Greek elections?[20]

Minutes later, Güneş brought the topic to the EEC once again:

GUNES: I mentioned the Common Market countries, our allies. The British usually see things in a realistic way, but they seem a little disoriented now.
THE SECRETARY: We have had some influence with the British. They have refused to join common pressures on you.
GUNES: I wonder if the Common Market wishes to follow France.
THE SECRETARY: The British have been quite responsible and I believe they will follow our course. If you and we agree we can get the Federal Republic of Germany to support it.[21]

Neither Turkey nor the US was happy with this evolving international actorness of the EEC:

FOREIGN MINISTER GUNES: As I have said before, we don't desire differences between America and Europe. [...] We have strong ties to Western Europe through NATO. Also, we will become members of the European Economic Community. [...] We don't like artificial labels like "Nine." We want to see the western world as an entity. [...]
THE SECRETARY: Yes, we agree. The western world should be looked at as a unit. We don't want to see it consumed in internal squabbles.[22]

The US had high expectations from the UK. Kissinger was eagerly waiting for the Dutch Presidency of the COM to end and that of the British to come. Before flying to The Hague in August 1976, he said he would raise the issue of finding a peaceful solution to the conflict between Greece and Turkey, and that it was "the responsibility of Europeans as well as the United States" to avoid the conflict.[23]

On 20 October, a plan on the Cyprus issue, prepared by Europeans and Americans, was presented to the GOT. This plan could not be implemented because of the change of government in the US.[24] In November, Kissinger's assistant Hartman reminded him that the British Presidency was on the horizon:

> The European Community, and especially the British, who still retain two sovereign base areas in Cyprus, have worked closely with the United States this past year in seeking to stimulate negotiations on Cyprus. They are anxious to continue this cooperation, particularly in the first six months of 1977 when the British will rotate into the position as President of the EC[25] Council of Ministers.[26]

In Hartman's opinion, the EEC was ineffective as an international actor:

> Our friends in Western Europe have their own reasons to seek solutions and ease tensions on the southeastern flank of NATO. But the European Community mechanism is cumbersome and incapable of devising quick decisions or initiatives. Thus, we will doubtless have to formulate the new ideas and take the lead, while encouraging continued close EC support.[27]

Therefore, according to the Ford administration, the Community was nothing more than one of the ties that connected Turkey to the West and, as such, had to stand one step behind NATO in this context:

> Turkey is an associate of the EC, looking toward full membership by 1995,[28] and a member of several other European regional organizations. NATO, however, is Turkey's most important tie to the West and the Turks have taken great pride in the active role they have played in the organization.[29]

4 Turkey's EEC Prospects Deteriorate

Turkey–EEC relations were not going well. As stated above, on the date of entry into force of the Additional Protocol, Turkey made the first tariff reduction, but skipped the reductions of 1974 and 1975. The second reduction was made in 1976. On 6 January 1976, Turkish newspapers announced that Turkey's trade deficit with the EEC in the first eight months of 1975 had increased by 223 percent.[30] Even some of the staunchest advocates of Turkey's EEC membership were now cautious towards the Community that, in their opinion, was taking advantage of the feeble Turkish economy and that had sided with Greeks in the Cyprus crisis.

Towards the end of 1974, it became evident that Greece would apply for full-membership to the EEC. Despite the recommendations of such figures as Emile Noël, the Secretary-General of the EEC Commission, and of Tevfik Saraçoğlu, the Turkish Permanent Representative to the EEC, Turkey did not submit a parallel application. The Bülent Ecevit, Sadi Irmak, and Süleyman Demirel[31] governments that were in power between January 1974 and June 1977 were reluctant to work for Turkey's EEC membership.

Greece submitted its application on 12 June 1975. Regardless of the Opinion of the Commission, which, despite its positive response, recommended the institutionalization of a pre-accession transition period before full-membership, thanks to the appeal of the Greek PM Karamanlis to the EEC MSs, accession negotiations of Greece were initiated on 27 July 1976.

5 Mentality of the Ford Administration

The Ford administration preferred to see the EEC as a safe haven for Turkey in 'the West'; nothing more nothing less . . . A report forwarded to the Departments of State and Defense and the CIA on 15 December 1975 gives us an idea on the role the Ford administration envisioned for the EEC in southeastern Europe:

> Neither the European Community nor its members is going to be in a position to take over the major US stabilizing role in the Southern European area for the foreseeable future. But both the EC and its members can contribute to the orderly evolution of the area by means of the economic assistance they can provide and the political influence which, in varying degrees, they possess.[32]

The US and EEC were trying to maintain an equal distance from Turkey and from Greece. For both the US—because of the embargo—and the EEC—because of the full-membership application of Greece—this was an uneasy task.

> The market's decision to accept Greece, pending negotiations that could take several years, aggravated ancient feelings here that the West really prefers a European, Christian Greece to an Asian, Moslem Turkey. [. . .] Those feelings had already been aggravated by the [embargo] decision of the United States. The Common Market has tried to maintain a careful balance between the two countries, but, as Washington has discovered, that is difficult.[33]

6 Conclusion

In the Ford era, Turkey–US relations revolved mainly around the Cyprus crisis. When the US imposed an embargo on Turkey to rein in this 'wayward' ally (NR6), Turkey increased its control over the US bases in Turkey, used its opium farming as a trump card and established closer relations with the socialist bloc (NRA8). Turks' maneuvers did yield some benefits: They received financial assistance, the embargo was partially lifted, and the US declared that it would not object Turkey's EEC membership anymore. In the context of Cyprus crisis, two other 'firsts' occurred in the Ford era:

1. The EEC tested its potential as an international actor, by putting pressure on Turkey. Neither Turks nor Americans liked this. They addressed their displeasure to the MSs of the EEC, since, in their opinion, behind the actions of the Community were the interests of its major MSs (NRA2); and
2. Turks requested help from the US against the EEC. Before intervening, the US expected a more cooperative attitude from Turkey in the Cyprus crisis (NRA7 and 5).

The trade concessions given by the US to Turkey, Turkey's inclusion in the GSP, and the US acquiescence to Turkey's EEC membership meant that political concerns of the US prevailed over its commercial interests, and that the US regained its interest in strengthening the Western alliance (NRA6).

In this era, the UK and Germany[34] were willing to act in line with US preferences, although the US did not resort to their help much (NRA7).

After the coming into force of the Additional Protocol, Turkey faced with the real 'weight' of its association with the EEC. The unilateral nature of the preparatory stage was over, and, now, Turkey was expected to gradually lower its tariffs to the imports from the EEC. To keep pace with the 'big boys,' the Europeans, Turkey would need political resolution, economic strength . . . and US support.

Notes

1. "Diplomacy: Festive finale to the Helsinki Summit," *Time*, 11 August 1975.
2. "Memorandum of Conversation," 31 July 1975, in Laurie Van Hook (ed.), *FRUS, 1969–1976, Vol. XXX*, Washington: USGPO, 769–8, p. 769.
3. Nasuh Uslu, *The Cyprus Question as an Issue of Turkish Foreign Policy and Turkish-American Relations, 1959–2003*, New York, NY: Nova Publishers, 2003, p. 152.
4. "Üsler için Amerika'ya 30 günlük süre verdik," *Milliyet*, 18 June 1975.
5. In those days, Spain, too, was using this 'trump card' against the US to secure closer relations with NATO. (Source: "İspanya üsler için ABD ile anlaşamadı," *Milliyet*, 21 June 1975.)
6. "Memorandum of Conversation," 31 July 1975, in Laurie Van Hook (ed.), *FRUS, 1969–1976, Vol. XXX*, Washington: USGPO, 769–8, p. 771.
7. Ibid., p. 772.
8. Richard Wigg, "France developing strong friendship with Athens," *The Times*, 20 August 1974.
9. "Türk-Bulgar ilişkilerinin geliştirilmesi kararlaştırıldı," *Milliyet*, 7 June 1976.

10 "Kosigin bugün Ankara'da çok sıkı güvenlik tedbirleri altında karşılanıyor," *Milliyet*, 26 December 1975.
11 "Kosigin: 'İyi ilişki için bütün esaslar var," *Milliyet*, 27 December 1975.
12 The GOT did not restore the status of the US bases in return.
13 "ABD, Türk ihraç mallarına gümrük tavizi tanıdı," *Milliyet*, 25 December 1975.
14 It was also in 1974 that Turkey was transferred to EUR of DOS.
15 Mehmet Ali Birand, "ABD, Ankara ve Atina'nın AET üyeliğine itirazı bıraktı," *Milliyet*, 2 December 1975.
16 Charles Hargrove, "EEC show of unity and accord with US in facing crisis," *The Times*, 22 July 1974.
17 Mario Modiano, "EEC may hold the key to lasting peace in the Aegean," *The Times*, 30 August 1974.
18 Paul Martin, "Can Turkey patch up the breach with US," *The Times*, 5 March 1976.
19 Rumor has it that in 1973, to the people around him Kissinger asked the following jocular question: "When I want to call Europe, whom do I call?" However, after his conversation with Peter Rodman, a close associate of Kissinger, Lieber states that neither Rodman nor Kissinger has any recollection of Kissinger making this statement. (Source: Robert Lieber, "The European Union and the United States: Threats, interests and values," ACES Working Paper Series, Washington: American University, 2004, p. 16.)
20 "Memorandum of conversation," 24 September 1974, in Laurie Van Hook (ed.), *FRUS, 1969–1976, Vol. XXX*, Washington: USGPO, 683–9, p. 687.
21 p. 688–9.
22 p. 664
23 Bernard Gwertzman, "Kissinger in plea for peaceful Greek-Turkish solution," *NYT*, 11 August 1976.
24 Mehmet Ali Birand, *Diyet: Türkiye ve Kıbrıs Üzerine Uluslararası Pazarlıklar*, Istanbul: Milliyet Yayınları, 1986, p. 206.
25 The European Community.
26 "Action Memorandum from the Assistant Secretary of State for European Affairs (Hartman) to Secretary of State Kissinger, Subject: Future Cyprus Policy," 3 November 1976, Laurie Van Hook (ed.), *FRUS, 1969–1976, Vol. XXX*, Washington: USGPO, 643–9, p. 645.
27 p. 646.
28 The author must have confused 'the completion of Turkey-EC CU' with 'Turkey's accession to the EC.'
29 Central Intelligence Agency, "Interagency Intelligence Memorandum, Subject: Turkey after the US Arms Cutoff, (DCI/NIO 386–75)," 21 February 1975, NIC Files, Job 79-R01012A.
30 "AET ile Türkiye'nin ticaret açığı sekiz ayda % 223 arttı," *Milliyet*, 6 January 1976.
31 Demirel was sympathetic to Turkey's EEC membership, but two of his coalition partners, Alpaslan Türkeş and Necmettin Erbakan, were against the idea.
32 "Paper prepared in response to National Security Study Memorandum 222: U.S. and Allied security policy in Europe," 15 December 1975, in Laurie Van Hook (ed.), *FRUS, 1969–1976, Vol. XXX*, Washington: USGPO, 194–207, p. 206.
33 Steven Roberts, "Turkey is asking Common Market for concessions on aid, products and movement of its workers," *NYT*, 10 October 1976.
34 When, in his visit to West Germany, the Greek PM Karamanlis pressed his country's case for early full-membership of the EEC, Germans responded to his appeal positively, "but they also said the development of European unity was possible only within the framework of the alliance in Nato with the United States." (Source: Dan van der Vat, "Karamanlis appeal to W. Germany," *The Times*, 17 May 1975.)

6 The Carter Administration (1977–1981)
Turkey–US Relations Improve

The Rose Garden of the White House borders the Oval Office and the West Wing. This garden has been "an unsurpassed location for heart-warming events such as greeting returning astronauts."[1] On 29 May 1978, this time a beloved 'returning ally' would be entertained there. President Carter was hosting a dinner honoring heads of delegations to the North Atlantic Council (NAC) Meeting. Turkish PM Bülent Ecevit, the Honorary President of the Council Meeting, was being pampered as if he was the proverbial prodigal son or Peer Gynt who had come back home. The timing of this reconciliation between Turkey and the US was important since only a few weeks ago, in April, the communist People's Democratic Party had seized power in Afghanistan, and a tense period was starting in the Cold War. In his toast at the dinner, Carter addressed Ecevit as follows:

> I've enjoyed very much being with our President[2] this evening, Prime Minister Ecevit. I've learned a lot about politics from him. We have several very distinguished Members of the Congress here, and I called one over to meet him tonight, Senator Bob Morgan from North Carolina. And when he came over, Prime Minister Ecevit told him that he used to live in North Carolina and worked for the Winston-Salem newspaper, and he said, "I've even got Tar Heel[3] cuff links on." So he's taught me a great deal.[4]

Ecevit reciprocated Carter's courtesy with a speech that emphasized Turkey's allegiance to NATO, and the party proceeded to attend a performance by the New York City Ballet company.[5]

The following morning, Carter received Ecevit at the White House. They both emphasized the important place Turkey occupied in NATO and the urgent need to consolidate the Alliance's southern flank and to rebuild Turkey–US relations. Ecevit stressed the significance he attached to Turkey's closer economic cooperation with the US. He denoted that a healthy economy was necessary for the maintenance of an efficient defense structure and the strengthening of democratic institutions in Turkey. Carter showed "full understanding in this respect" and assured Ecevit that "he was determined to obtain congressional approval for the repealing of the remaining arms restrictions[6] on Turkey."[7]

For a few months, Carter had been working to have the embargo repealed. According to *The Times* this meant a change in his priorities:

> Mr. Carter, who was definitely a pro-Greek presidential candidate, has now become surprisingly pro-Turkish president. He has bought, and is now trying hard to sell Congress, the stock Turkish argument that the embargo itself has become the main obstacle to a Cyprus solution.[8]

The Greek lobby in the US,[9] the Greek Cypriots,[10] the Greek government,[11] and the Greek media[12] were all disturbed by this change. In their opinion, Turkey was hoping to get concessions from the EEC; improvement of Turkey–EEC relations would make it more difficult for the US Congress to maintain the embargo.[13]

Like the Carter administration, Europeans were in favor of repeal of the embargo. Germany, France, or Belgium made their opinion known to the US. The General Affairs and External Relations (GAER) Council of the EEC discussed the issue and was determined to send a message to Carter to lift the embargo. A few days later, upon hearing that the US Congress was already discussing the issue, they abandoned the idea:[14]

> The arms embargo [. . .], coupled with Turkey's more general dissatisfaction with its treatment by the EEC, could, it is feared in Brussels, seriously weaken NATO's southern flank. [. . .]
> But the foreign ministers of the Nine seemed at a loss to identify much that could be done to improve political and economic relations with Ankara beyond granting better access to Turkish agricultural goods.[15]

Following his meeting with Ecevit, Carter accelerated his efforts to convince the Congressmen[16] and on 26 September 1978, he finally signed the legislation[17] repealing the remaining elements of the embargo.

1 No Increase in the Support for Turkey's EEC Bid

An increase in the US support for Turkey's EEC bid could have been a natural corollary to the gesture Americans did for Turkey in the embargo issue in 1978. Exigencies of the conjuncture also necessitated such an increase: Iran was in disarray, which would end up with the 1979 revolution, and a war was brewing in Afghanistan. At least two key members of Carter's staff were in favor of improving Turkey's relations with the EEC. Paul B. Henze, Deputy NSA, prepared an NSC Memorandum,[18] dated 15 December 1978, for Zbigniew Brzezinski, NSA. Entitled "Is Turkey Susceptible to the Iranian Sickness?" this was a long and insightful text that presented Turkey as "the only corner of the 'Crumbling Triangle'[19] which has not yet crumbled." Henze tried to ease the reader's mind by concluding that it was unlikely that Turkey would become another Iran. Nevertheless, he identified an "erosion of confidence in the West that infect[ed] Turkish intellectuals and youth" mainly because of the embargo. He emphasized the importance of Turkey's integration with Europe:

> The U.S. Government invests little money and even less imagination in information programs in Turkey. [. . .] To some extent, these shortcomings have been compensated for by intensified Turkish links with Europe, which have broadened both as a result of workers and technicians (of whom there are still more than half a million, mostly in Germany) but also as a result of integration of Turkey into many European institutions and activities.[20]

Brzezinski liked Henze's ideas and scribbled down a few notes on the cover of the memorandum:

1   I like it. A good job.
2   Hold a WG[21] meeting to discuss and flesh out proposals.
3   Then perhaps PRC[22] + recommendations to the P.[23]
    ZB

This positive attitude did not translate into positive actions for Turkey. This had six main reasons:

1   Carter was not as 'pro-Turkish' as Greeks assumed. His courtesy to Ecevit and the support he was trying to extend to Turkey was primarily to bolster the southeastern flank of NATO and to maintain the security of the Persian Gulf. The Carter Doctrine included the following: "An attempt by any outside force to gain control of the Persian Gulf region will be regarded as an assault on the vital interests of the United States of America, and such an assault will be repelled by any means necessary, including military force."[24] Turkey's integration to the West via closer relations with—let alone via membership to—the EEC would be a too burdensome strategy. Keeping Turkey by the side of the West via simpler means would be enough. The mind-set of the European leaders was in line with that of Carter.[25]

> 'Turkey-EEC relations' did not occupy a special place in Carter's approach to Turkey. This approach was based on a two-pronged strategy:
> a   Together with the Europeans, the US would assist Turkey financially. In 1978, Turkey's economic problems peaked once again. Prices increased by an average of 5 percent a month.

Foreign debt, both short and long term, exceeded the '10 million dollars' mark. Investment fell to its lowest rate since 1973, and industry was operating at about 55 percent of capacity.[26] On 5–6 January 1979, the US, the UK, Germany, and France held an informal summit in Guadeloupe. There, the US President Carter, the German Chancellor Schmidt, the British PM Callaghan, and the French President Giscard agreed on the need for emergency steps to halt Turkey's slide into bankruptcy. Ten days later, representatives of these four countries convened in Bonn, where they made the aid to Turkey conditional on the conclusion of an agreement between Turkey and the IMF.[27] It was only when, in April, NATO Secretary-General Joseph Luns warned that Turkey might pull out of the Alliance unless aid is extended to this country, did the US and 13 other industrial countries pledge more than 1.45 billion dollars in emergency financial assistance to Turkey. The decision on the release of this assistance package was signed on 30 May.[28]

The lifting of the embargo and the Guadeloupe financial assistance were also consolatory gestures to Turkey. On 28 May 1979, two days before the financial assistance decision was secured in writing, the accession treaty of Greece, Turkey's arch-rival, had been signed.

In April 1980, 15 OECD countries and the EEC agreed to provide Turkey with a loan package of 1.160 million dollars. The main contributors to the package were the US and Germany.[29]

b   Problems between Turkey and Greece had to be solved, and Europeans had to help here too. A presidential memorandum prepared by Brzezinski states that Carter had directed that the Policy Review Committee (PRC) undertake an evaluation of the Cyprus issue and of the situation in the Aegean, which would, *inter alia*, "[r]eview the possibilities for involving our European allies in the process of settling the disputes, including assessments of various forms of U.S.-European cooperation and/or types of negotiation forums."[30]

When in the US, Ecevit had complained about "Greek intentions to carry the quarrel with Turkey into the EEC, of the Aegean 12-mile territorial limit and FIR[31] issues."[32] Despite Ecevit's plea, two years later, Henze recommended the following: "We should not get ourselves into the middle of the Cyprus situation at this late stage, having avoided for so long [. . .]. But we might, as a tactic and as a way of trying something different from the lackadaisical UN effort, consider appointment of a European mediator."[33]

2   Progressing with the timetable foreseen in the Ankara Agreement was not among Turkey's priorities anymore. In Carter's term, quite a few governments[34] came to power in Turkey. For these governments, Turkey's obligations in the transitory stage were a burden, and a 'revision' of Turkey–EEC relations was included in the program of almost all of them. For example, the program of the Fifth Demirel Government (which was a coalition) included the following sentence: "We deem it imperative to handle and revise our relations with the European Economic Community in such a way as to serve the development and strengthening of our national industry, to provide market for our exports and to protect our national interests."[35]

> On 9 October 1978, Turkey requested its obligations be frozen for five years, which was accepted by the EEC. The relations would remain dormant more than five years. Until Turkey submitted its application for full-membership on 14 April 1987. . .
>
> As stated above, Demirel was a proponent of Turkish membership in the EEC. In February 1980, Hayrettin Erkmen, FM in Demirel's cabinet, made an announcement that Turkey would lodge its full-membership application. His main aim was to guarantee Turkey's membership before Greece became a member and gained veto power. A motion of censure was brought against him by some nationalist and conservative groups in the Turkish parliament on the ground of incompatibility of his action with national interests, and he was removed from the office on 5 September.[36]

3   Ecevit's premiership in two of the GOTs in the Carter era was not conducive to US support for Turkey against the EEC for two reasons:

   a   Carter administration had a question mark over Ecevit. Ecevit had been educated in an American school in Istanbul and, then, studied and worked in the UK and US. He was well-versed in Western literature and arts. Nevertheless, his political stance was shaped by the Republican/Kemalist ideology that attributed importance to Western culture but recommended an arm's length political relationship with the West itself. He was an admirer of Norway, a NATO ally that refused to allow nuclear weapons or foreign troops on its soil.[37] On one occasion he said "We do not intend to leave NATO even if the American arms embargo is not lifted. But we can no longer rely on NATO alone for our national security."[38] Four days before his dinner at the White House, he visited Brussels—not to keenly negotiate for Turkey–EEC relations but—to ask for financial aid and to confer with NATO officials before the approaching Council Meeting he would preside.[39] In his talk with Roy Jenkins, President of the EEC Commission, he claimed that, Turkey's problems with the West were of economic nature only. Jenkins, who probably recalled Turkey's *political* problems with the US, interjected: "Do you make a distinction between the West and the US?" Ecevit's reply was more of a criticism than an answer: "Is the West anything more than the US? Just like NATO . . ." In Ecevit's opinion, the American and German influence on certain international bodies such as IMF, OECD, and the EEC was increasing.[40] He was questioning the fundamentals of NATO. He once said that he had suggested that Turkey's economic problems be taken up with its defence problems. These had brought to the surface some basic deficiencies within Nato. If one member (the United States) was unable to fulfil its commitments then the others were inclined to take a resigned attitude and say they were unable to fill the gap.[41]

He argued for a new Turkish defense policy "that would depend to some degree on the cooperation shown by Turkey's European partners in joint production of military equipment,"[42] and in supporting the country's economy, but that would also be compatible with Turkey's continued membership in NATO.[43] Even a special declaration of faith in the future of NATO to be signed at the NAC meeting mentioned above was likely to be postponed for 12 months since Turkey had refused to take part.[44]

Towards the end of 1978, Ecevit made an appeal to NATO to obtain funds. His request was based on the argument that half of Turkey's budget was consumed by the military. On 9 October, he made another appeal for financial help to the EEC on the ground of Turkey's potential candidacy, asked for 8 billion dollars but was given 1 billion dollars instead. As indicated above, Ecevit also requested from the EEC Turkey's obligations be frozen for five years.

In his talk with a group of Turkish businessmen in Washington in 1979, Brzezinski's words about Ecevit were stern: "With this man Turkey cannot get anywhere."[45] Ecevit resigned in October 1979. In a memorandum Henze prepared for Brzezinski, the following paragraph took place:

The President was disappointed in Ecevit because he sensed him to be a kindred soul and expected him to accommodate us because of shared idealism. But, like Carter, he was constrained by the hard realities of national interests and domestic politics. [. . .] The new Demirel government offers the best prospect in more than five dismal years for a solid improvement in U.S. relations.[46]

b   Although he denied this in a few occasions[47] and would strive for Turkey's EU membership in the 1990s, some still believe that on ideological grounds Ecevit was against Turkey's EEC membership in the 1970s.[48]

4   The US argued for Turkey's getting closer to Europe. However, the EEC did not have a special importance for the US in this context. In his memorandum, Henze talked about "integration of Turkey into many European institutions and activities," but there was no mention of the EEC in this ten-page document. As an international actor, the EEC had not come of age in the eyes of the Americans yet.
5   Europeans were not so open to US interventions anymore.
6   The US knew that, in technical terms, Turkey had a long way to join the EEC. A report prepared by two experts from the Library of Congress for the Committee on Foreign Affairs (COFA) of the HOR noted that "[f]ull integration [of Turkey] into the EC [would] not take place until 1995 at the earliest."[49] The report ended up with a two-page list of recommendations. Support for Turkey's bid for the EEC was not among them.

2 Turks in Search of Alternatives

Turkey was still making advances to the USSR and trying to develop its relations with Muslim countries. On 21 June 1978, the day Ecevit went to Moscow, Carter was discussing the repeal of the embargo with the 70 guests at a dinner he hosted.[50] In this visit, Ecevit signed four agreements on the continental shelf in the Black Sea, Cyprus, economic aid, and trade.[51] The amount of Soviet military aid Turkey received increased from 650 million dollars in 1975 to 800 million dollars in 1978, making it the number-one Soviet foreign aid recipient in the world then.[52] This predilection was not limited to the Ecevit Governments. For example, in the Fourth Demirel Government, FM Çağlayangil visited Moscow on 13 March 1977.[53]

An insightful interpretation of this situation appeared in an editorial published in a Finnish newspaper, *Helsingin Sanomat*. Finland, itself was a country that remained neutral in the Cold War era by trying to keep an equal distance from the US and the USSR. The editorial concluded that Turkey's close relations with the USSR did not mean a dramatic ideological change; as one of the most dependable members of NATO, Turkey was still willing to improve its relations with the EEC that had deteriorated in the past few years.[54]

3 Coup d'État in Turkey

Towards the end of Carter's term, the domestic turbulence caused by armed conflicts, economic problems, and unstable governments in Turkey led to a coup d'état (the third in the history of the republic) on 12 September 1980. In the speech he delivered on the day of the coup, General Kenan Evren, the leader of the junta, reaffirmed Turkey's loyalty to NATO.[55] An evaluation of the coup drawn up on the same day by Henze for Brzezinski contained some clues about the priorities of the US pertaining to Turkey in the immediate period after the coup. Henze's evaluation was also an assurance that

Turkey's geopolitical importance was still significant for the US. After all, Henze was an expert on Turkish politics:[56]

> [The Turkish military's] first priority is restoring domestic tranquility to Turkey, keeping the economy functioning well and setting a constitutional reform process in motion. These should be our priorities too—for it is only by accomplishment of these objectives that Turkey can be secured as a valuable ally and effective member of NATO and rebuilt as a bastion of strength in the Middle East.[57]

The EEC was undetermined about the coup at first. The junta government declared its determination to bring back democracy as soon as possible. This assurance and the stable atmosphere that prevailed in the country garnered relatively positive remarks from the EEC. The GAER Council announced that Turkey–EEC relations would continue as before.[58] Gaston Thorn who presided the Council stated that instead of undermining the assurances given by the Turkish army, the EEC would assume an encouraging posture.[59] However, after a few weeks, Europeans started exerting pressure on Turks to return to democracy as soon as possible.

For the US, a reasonable amount of pressure by the Europeans on the junta government was acceptable. In his dialogue with the US SECSTATE Edmund Muskie, Türkmen, now the FM of the government established by the military, complained about that the Europeans undervalued Turkey's efforts on democratization. Muskie replied that his administration was "aware of the commitment to democracy of the Turkish military. But it was understandable that there would be outside pressure for a return to democracy."[60]

4 Mentality of the Carter Administration

Carter looked positively towards Turkey's close relations with Europeans. By establishing closer relations with Turkey, Europeans could keep Turkey aligned with the West, take on some responsibility in assisting Turkey financially, and contribute to the solution of the problems between Turkey and Greece. This strategy was in line with the Carter Doctrine, which emphasized the importance of protecting the US interests in the Persian Gulf; a Turkey that flirted with the Soviets or caught 'the Iranian sickness' would be prejudicial to US interests in this region.

5 Conclusion

After the troubled Ford period, in Carter's term, Turkey–US relations improved in a process triggered by the lifting of the embargo. To keep Turkey together with the West (NRA6), to reduce the cost of supporting Turkey financially (NRA7), to reinforce the southeastern flank of NATO by reconciling Turkey and Greece (NRA6), and to safeguard the US interests in the

Middle East (NRA6 and 7), the Carter administration lifted the embargo and developed a favorable outlook towards Turkey–EEC relations. Notwithstanding, Carter was unwilling to exert much effort for Turkey's EEC bid, because the EEC did not have a special importance for him (NRA2). Also, the members of the EEC—especially Greeks with whom Carter had close relations—would not tolerate an intensive meddling from him, as they were less dependent on the US now (NRA4). Above all, Turks themselves were not ready and willing for EEC membership.

In 1976, Turkey stopped the gradual reduction in customs tariffs applicable to the goods originating from the EEC. Almost every GOT in the Carter period aimed at revising Turkey's relations with the EEC to minimize Turkey's burden (NRA5), and, finally, Ecevit shot the ailing relationship in 1978 by freezing Turkey's obligations. Under these circumstances, all the US did was to convince certain European leaders in Guadeloupe to extend financial aid to Turkey while paying attention to keep this aid under the control of IMF (NRA7), which was reminiscent of the policy pursued by the Eisenhower administration.

In Turkey, domestic problems led to a coup in 1980 (DF). The Americans and Europeans reacted to the coup with a cautious approval. In the case of the Europeans, this approval was shaped rather by their national interests than the founding principles of the EEC, which entail intolerance of overthrow of democratically elected governments (NRA8): In the insecurity atmosphere of the Cold War, the Europeans were taking care not to offend Turkey, which had a central role in NATO.

The standstill in Turkey–EEC relations, together with the cessation of the domestic turmoil in Turkey after the coup meant a blank page in Turkey's relations with the US and with the EEC. This blank page was what Carter would bequeath to Reagan.

Notes

1 Stephen Bauer, *At Ease in the White House: Social Life as Seen by a Presidential Military Aide*, Lanham, MD: Taylor Trade Publications, 2004, p. 73. Bauer was an *aide-de-camp* who assisted President Nixon, Ford, and Carter.
2 Ioannides, who quotes this paragraph in his book, marks the word "President" with a "[*sic*]." However, as indicated above, Ecevit's presidency here refers to the Honorary Presidency of the NAC that rotates in alphabetical order. See Chris P. Ioannides, *Realpolitik in the Eastern Mediterranean: From Kissinger and the Cyprus Crisis to Carter and the Lifting of the Turkish Arms Embargo*, New York, NY: Pella Publishers, 2001, p. 228.
3 'Tar Heel' is a nickname used for the state and citizens of North Carolina.
4 "North Atlantic Summit: Toast of the President at the Dinner Honoring the Heads of Delegation, March 30, 1978" *Presidential Papers: Carter, Book 1: January 1 to June 30*, National Archives and Records Service, Office of the Federal Register, 1979, p. 1016.
5 *The Daily Diary of President Jimmy Carter*, May 30, 1978. Available at the Jimmy Carter Library, Atlanta, Georgia.
6 Read 'the embargo.' As indicated above, some elements of the embargo had been lifted by the Ford administration on 6 October 1975.

7 "Meeting with Prime Minister Bulent Ecevit of Turkey: White House Statement," *Presidential Papers: Carter, Book 1: January 1 to June 30*, National Archives and Records Service, Office of the Federal Register, 1979, p. 1017; and Mehmet Ali Birand, *Diyet: Türkiye ve Kıbrıs Üzerine Uluslararası Pazarlıklar*, Istanbul: Milliyet Yayınları, 1986, pp. 314–8.
8 "The Cypriot labyrinth," *The Times*, 26 June 1978.
9 Saynur Gören, "Carter bizi hayal kırıklığına uğrattı," *Milliyet*, 23 June 1978.
10 Mustafa Gürsel, "Atina, Türk-Yunan görüşmelerini erteledi," *Milliyet*, 12 April 1978.
11 Mustafa Gürsel, "Yunan hükümetinin ambargoya ilişkin tutumu 'sert' bulundu," *Milliyet*, 9 April 1978.
12 Michael Hornsby, "Why Mr. Karamanlis pins his hopes on the EEC," *The Times*, 1 June 1978.
13 John Palmer, "Greece and Turkey jostle over EEC," *The Guardian*, 25 May 1978.
14 Nusret Özgül, "ABD Senatosu'nun kararı NATO ve AET'de 'ferahlık' yarattı," *Milliyet*, 27 July 1978; and *The American Arms Embargo against Turkey: A Historical Review*, Nicosia: Public Information Office, 1979, p. 17.
15 Michael Hornsby, "EEC seeks ways to soothe Turks," *The Times*, 22 May 1978.
16 David Cross, "President Carter tries to persuade Congress to end the Turkish arms sales embargo," *The Times*, 9 June 1978; Mehmet Ali Birand, "Carter 16 temsilciyle ambargoyu görüştü," *Milliyet*, 2 June 1978; "Carter, Kongre üyelerinden ambargonun kaldırılması için olumlu oy vermelerini istedi," *Milliyet*, 16 June 1978; Saynur Gören, "Carter dün de Beyaz Saray'da verdiği akşam yemeğinde 70 kişiyle ambargoyu görüştü," *Milliyet*, 22 June 1978; and Mehmet Ali Birand, "Carter, yeterli oyu sağlayamayacağını anlayınca, erteleme yolunu seçti," *Milliyet*, 20 July 1978.
17 S. 3075, Public Law 95–384.
18 "National Security Council Memorandum from Paul B. Henze to Zbigniew Brzezinski, Subject: Is Turkey Susceptible to the Iranian Sickness? (No. 7597)," 15 December 1978. After preparing the text, Henze needed to put a second cover page on the memorandum with another title: "Whither Turkey?—and What Can We Do?"
19 Henze refers to the following article published in *The Economist* a few days before: "The Crumbling Triangle," *The Economist*, 9 December 1978, p. 12.
20 p. 8–9.
21 Working group.
22 NSC Policy Review Committee.
23 The President.
24 Robert P. Watson, Charles Gleek, Michael Grillo, *Presidential Doctrines: National Security from Woodrow Wilson to George W. Bush*, New York, NY: Nova Publishers, 2003, p. 86.
25 "Times: Kıbrıs giderek karmaşık bir nitelik alıyor," *Milliyet*, 27 June 1978; and "The Cypriot labyrinth," *The Times*, 26 June 1978.
26 Andrew Borowiec, "Turkey looks to US to help resolve economic crisis," *NYT*, 6 January 1979.
27 Mehmet Ali Birand, *12 Eylül Saat 04.00*, Karacan Yayınları, 1985, p. 72; and *Diyet: Türkiye ve Kıbrıs Üzerine Uluslararası Pazarlıklar*, Istanbul: Milliyet Yayınları, 1986, p. 395.
28 Paul Lewis, "Industrial allies offer Turkey $1.45 billion," *NYT*, 31 May 1979.
29 Ian Murray, "Turkey given $1,160m international loan," *The Times*, 16 April 1980.
30 "National Security Council, Presidential Review Memorandum from Zbigniew Brzezinski, Subject: Cyprus/Aegean, (NSC 5)," 21 January 1977.
31 Flight Information Region.
32 "The White House Memorandum of Conversation, Subject: Summary of the President's Meeting with Prime Minister Ecevit of Turkey," 31 May 1978 (declassified but unpublished document).
33 "National Security Council Memorandum from Paul B. Henze to Zbigniew Brzezinski, Subject: Greece-Turkey-Cyprus, (2072)," 4 April 1979 (declassified but unpublished document).

34 The Fourth Demirel Government, the Second Ecevit Government, the Fifth Demirel Government, the Third Ecevit Government, the Sixth Demirel Government, and the Ulusu Government.
35 Programs of the GOTs available at www.tbmm.gov.tr/hukumetler/hukumetler.htm, accessed 5 May 2012. Author's translation.
36 Mehmet Ali Birand, *Türkiye'nin Ortak Pazar Macerası*, Istanbul: Milliyet Yayınları, 1990, pp. 403–4. See also Edward Mortimer, "Mr. Demirel determined to bind Turkey more closely to the West," *The Times*, 11 February 1980.
37 Steven V. Roberts, "Greece and Turkey seeking more equality in U.S. ties," *NYT*, 18 August 1975; and "Ecevit, örnek gösterdiği Norveç'te," *Radikal*, 5 June 2000.
38 Mario Modiano, "Why Turkey will not be wooed," *The Times*, 5 May 1978.
39 "Turkish premier visiting Brussels," *NYT*, 25 May 1978.
40 Mehmet Ali Birand, *Türkiye'nin Ortak Pazar Macerası*, Istanbul: Milliyet Yayınları, 1990, pp. 381–2 and 393.
41 "Turkey turns to EEC and the European Nato nations for economic and defence aid," *The Times*, 27 May 1978.
42 Henry Stanhope, "Turkey may change relationship with NATO," *The Times*, 16 May 1978.
43 Mario Modiano, "Why Turkey will not be wooed," *The Times*, 5 May 1978.
44 Henry Stanhope, "Turks force delay in signing of Nato pledge," *The Times*, 18 May 1978.
45 Mehmet Ali Birand, *12 Eylül Saat 04.00*, Karacan Yayınları, 1985, p. 99.
46 "National Security Council Memorandum from Paul B. Henze to Zbigniew Brzezinski, Subject: The U.S. and Turkey (No. 67)," 27 November 1979.
47 Haluk Özdalga, *Kötü Yönetilen Türkiye: Örnek Vaka DSP*, Istanbul: Kitap Yayınevi, 2005, p. 219.
48 Yalım Eralp, "Ortak Pazar'a ideolojik ret," *Milliyet*, 11 October 2000.
49 Richard F. Grimmett and Ellen B. Laipson, *Turkey's Problems and Prospects: Implications for U.S. Interests: Report*, Washington: USGPO, 1980, p. 31. The year 1995 was when Turkey's CU with the EC would be completed.
50 Saynur Gören, "Carter dun de Beyaz Saray'da verdiği akşam yemeğinde 70 kişiyle ambargoyu görüştü," *Milliyet*, 22 June 1978.
51 "Moskova'da bugün dört anlaşma imzalanıyor," *Milliyet*, 23 June 1978.
52 Jon Kofas, *Under the Eagle's Claw: Exceptionalism in Post-war US-Greek Relations*, Westport, CT: Greenwood Publishing Group, 2003, p. 164.
53 "Çağlayangil'i Moskova'da Gromiko karşıladı," *Milliyet*, 14 March 1977.
54 Erdinç Ekim, "Türklerin Batı endüstrisine olan bağlılığı azalacak," *Milliyet*, 4 January 1976.
55 Frederick Bonnart, "Coup leader pledges Turkey's continued loyalty to Nato," *The Times*, 13 September 1980.
56 Henze was the CIA station chief in Turkey between 1974 and 1977 and the CIA representative to the NSC between 1977 and 1980. He was frequently accused of having instigated much of the political violence in the years before the coup and, then, having contributed to the staging of the coup.
57 "National Security Council Memorandum from Paul B. Henze to Zbigniew Brzezinski, Subject: Significance of the Turkish Military Takeover for Greek and Cypriot Issues (No. 5082)," 12 September 1980 (declassified but unpublished document).
58 Frederick Bonnart, "Coup leader pledges Turkey's continued loyalty to Nato," *The Times*, 13 September 1980; and Nusret Özgül, "Türkiye ile AET ilişkileri eskisi gibi sürecek," *Milliyet*, 17 September 1980.
59 "Evren, demokrasiye dönüleceğini dünyaya ilan etti," *Milliyet*, 18 September 1980.
60 "NAC Ministerials: Secretary's bilateral meeting with Turkish Foreign Minister Turkmen," Cable from USDEL Secretary in Brussels to SECSTATE and a number of US Embassies, 1 January 1980 (declassified but unpublished document).

7 The Reagan Administration (1981–1989)
The US Involvement Commences

On 27 June 1988, the Rose Garden of the White House was once again the venue for an important event: a dinner in honor of the Turkish President Kenan Evren who was on a state visit. The garden had been more modestly decorated and more dimly lit compared to ten years earlier when President Carter hosted the dinner honoring Ecevit and the other heads of delegation to the NAC meeting. The littleleaf lindens and crabapple trees surrounding the garden were covered with faint netlights. Each of the 13 tables had a small electric candelabrum. In the background was the Washington Monument lighted in pale blue, and this crepuscular atmosphere was completed by a full moon.[1] The exchange of toasts between Reagan and Evren was insipid and stereotypical. Reagan started with a reference to a worn-out Turkish proverb on Turkish coffee:

> Ladies and gentlemen, I've been told of a Turkish proverb that states: "A cup of coffee will bear the fruit of 40 years of friendship." Well, my sense of this expression is that in the give and take of conversation over coffee people establish the sense of caring and loyalty, and of shared hopes and expectations, that define friendship.
>
> Now, Americans and Turks sitting here will soon be sharing a cup of coffee.[2]

He called attention to the support the US had extended to Turkey since 1947, emphasized how important Turkey was for NATO, and flattered the Turks' pride by mentioning the blood they shed with Americans in Korea.

In return, Evren spoke in "careful English"[3] based on a text. His speech was different from that of Ecevit, which was improvised and fluent. Into his short speech of 500 words, Evren had managed to squeeze three wishes from the US:

1   Recognition of Turkey's success in "establishing a democracy with all its institutions based on respect for human rights" after the 1980 coup and of "Turkey's position as an island of peace and stability in a region in turmoil,"

2   Continuation of the US–USSR negotiations over disarmament after the conclusion of the Intermediate-Range Nuclear Forces (INF) Treaty on 8 December 1987, without neglecting Turkey's defense requirements, and
3   Consideration of the economic dimension of the US–Turkey relations as integral to the "traditional friendship and security partnership" between the two countries.[4]

These three wishes had not been scribbled down just before the dinner but were a pensive summary of Turkey's expectations under Evren's presidency whose term of office (1980–1989) overlapped with that of Reagan (1981–1989). 'Support for Turkey's EEC bid' was not among these wishes. The reasons behind this particular set of preferences of Turkey lay in the peculiar conditions of the period explained below.

1 The EEC Turns Away from Turkey

After the 1980 coup, Turkey was governed by the junta led by General Evren until 7 November 1982 when a new constitution was accepted in a referendum. On 9 November, Evren was appointed President for the next seven years. The first general election after the coup was held on 6 November 1983. The leader of the Motherland Party, Turgut Özal was the winner of the election. He established a one-party government. Özal won the next general election too and remained the PM until 1989.

In the first few years after the coup, Turkey's priorities were to restore the democracy, revitalize the economy, and open up the economy to foreign competition and investment in accordance with the neoliberal program of the Özal government.

Only a few months after the coup, on 25 March 1981, a meeting presided by Evren was held in Ankara to discuss the future of Turkey–EEC relations that remained inactive since 1978. Evren listened to the views of the bureaucrats most of whom were in favor of resuming relations with the EEC and working towards full-membership. Evren instructed some of those present to implement the required reforms.

Initially, Europeans were relatively tolerant towards the junta government. However, their dissatisfaction with Turkey's slow progress in the democratization process grew quickly. Especially the European Parliament (EP) found the methods of the junta harsh and saw Özal as not pro-European enough. With an initiative of the EP, the EEC suspended its relations with Turkey on 22 January 1982. The Fourth Financial Protocol[5] that envisaged a financial aid totaling 600 million ECUs to Turkey was suspended; the regular meetings of the AC were not held; the Turkey–EEC Joint Parliamentary Committee was disintegrated; and the free movement of Turkish workers that was supposed to be gradually made possible between 1976 and 1986 was put aside. The AC could convene as late as September 1986.[6]

2 Turkey Decides to Apply for Full Membership

In 1981, Greece, and in 1986, Spain and Portugal became EEC members. Turkey concluded that it would be wise not to waste any more time and submitted its membership application on 14 April 1987. This was an early application, made when Turkey was in the second (the transitory stage) of the three stages envisaged in the Ankara Agreement. The Community's response to this application would come nearly three years later on 18 December 1989.[7] Two months after Turkey's application, the EP took another step and, on 18 June 1987, adopted a resolution[8] asking the Council to secure from the GOT an acknowledgment of the alleged Armenian genocide of 1915–1917. Turks, for whom this was a very sensitive issue, reacted to this resolution fervently. Turkish President Evren said if the EEC was this much inimical to Turkey, Turkey should rethink about its existence in NATO.[9] The UK, Germany, and Belgium declared that they did not agree with the EP.[10]

3 The US Front

Compared to the Europeans, the Americans were more tolerant to the coup and more optimistic about the process of restoration of democracy in Turkey. "[T]he United States government is confident that the Turkish government is moving in good faith to implement its schedule for a return to stable parliamentary democracy and full constitutional freedoms," declared the Reagan administration. Whereas the EEC suspended the abovementioned aid package to Turkey, the US Foreign Assistance Act provided 400 million dollars for foreign military sales credits and 300 million dollars for economic assistance funds, with a pending bill that asked for increases for the following year.[11] Despite this relatively positive approach, the Reagan administration could not pen anything down on the blank page inherited from the Carter administration in the name of supporting Turkey against the EEC, because of the following reasons:

1. A thaw was developing between the USA and the USSR in the second half of the 1980s. The Soviet leader Gorbachev's commitment to his reforms was appreciated by the Americans. The INF Treaty, signed in 1987, marked an important step in the ending of the Cold War. Now, integrating Turkey to the West and bolstering the southeastern flank of NATO were less urgent needs. As his White House speech revealed, Evren was aware of this fact.
2. In the early 1980s, Turkey had other priorities in its FP than the EEC. In a two-hour talk between FM İlter Türkmen, and his American counterpart Alexander Haig, the topics covered included military and economic assistance to Turkey, problems related to the Middle East, Greco-Turkish disputes, international terrorism, Afghanistan, Iran-Iraq war, and Poland[12] but not Turkey–EEC relations. In the same vein, the two sets of written

questions submitted by Turkish daily *Hürriyet* to Reagan, one in 1985 and the other only five days before Evren's abovementioned dinner with Reagan in 1988, did not include any question about Turkey–EEC relations.[13]

3   Turgut Özal was not pro-European in his early years in office. After he won the 1983 election, he said if the burden would be high, Turkey could abandon the idea of applying for EEC membership.[14] In his first visit to the US between 27 March and 5 April 1985, Özal delivered 18 speeches, made 22 official contacts, and gave 12 interviews.[15] On these occasions, numerous issues were discussed such as the US proposal to construct antennae towers in Turkey for anti-communist radio broadcast[16] or the establishment of a Turkish-American Business Council,[17] but it seems that 'Turkey–EEC relations' was not included on Özal's agenda. Şükrü Elekdağ, the Turkish ambassador to the US between 1979 and 1989, confirms this.[18]

Özal's next visit to the US was in February 1987, almost two months prior to Turkey's submission of its application for full-membership to the EEC. By that time, there had been a radical change[19] in Özal's standpoint towards the EEC. He was now more positive to Turkey's membership, and this time, he did solicit help against the Europeans. Reagan promised support but did not make a specific commitment.[20] Probably, this was the second time Turks were asking for US backing for full-membership years after Zorlu first did so in December 1959.

4   Americans and Turks did not want to annoy the Europeans. Turks were apprehensive that US intervention would do more harm than good, and Americans were observing closely the negative reaction of Europeans to the coup in Turkey. According to the Europeans, after the coup

   a   The US was too tolerant towards the junta and Özal governments,
   b   The US was trying to fill in the gap left in Turkey's FP by the suspension of Turkey–EEC relations; and
   c   There was a secret deal between Turkey and the US by which Turkey gave some concessions to the US to secure its friendship.[21]

5   Turks doubted the willingness of the US to exert influence over Europeans, and the actual effectiveness of such an influence;[22] the so-called Mersin crisis was a test case for them:

> In January 1989, in the mandate for the negotiations leading to the Treaty on Conventional Armed Forces in Europe, Turkey and Greece had a disagreement over whether the Mersin port in southern Turkey would be in or out of the area of application of the Treaty.[23] European powers sided with Greece. Özal asked George P. Schultz, the US SECSTATE, to use his influence on the Europeans, but the US position remained parallel to that of the European powers. Although the status of Mersin was left

ambiguous in the final text of the Treaty, which was a relatively satisfactory solution for Turkey, what Turks deduced from this process was that in their relations with Europeans, they should not expect much from the Americans.[24]

6   As explained previously, in the 1980s, the EP emerged as an important determinant in Turkey–EEC relations by initiating a process that ended up with the suspension of the EEC's relations with Turkey and by keeping the process of restoration of democracy in Turkey under constant observation. It was technically difficult for the US to have an influence over the Parliament for two reasons:

   a   Before 1979, members of the EP (MEPs) were drawn from the national parliaments. Then, it would have been easier for the US to affect the MEPs via national governments. However, in 1979, the first direct election for the EP was held, to be repeated every five years. From then on, the MEPs were less subject—and less attentive—to instructions from national governments.
   b   The EP was a large (414 MEPs in the 1981–1986 period, and 518 MEPs in the 1986–1994 period) and complex (MEPs were organized into parliamentary groups, not according to their nationality) organization.

7   Robert Strausz-Hupe, the USAMB to Turkey between 1981 and 1989, was an unpopular figure among Turks. Especially towards to end of his long incumbency, his meddling in the domestic politics of Turkey and his critical comments about the country caused dissatisfaction among Turkish public,[25] and prevented him from becoming an emergency button in Turkey–EEC relations.

4 US Involvement in Turkey–EEC Relations

In the first years of the Reagan administration, the EEC was an insignificant item in Turkey–US relations. In the later years, this situation changed. It was with the Reagan administration that the US got actively involved in Turkey–EEC relations. This involvement took three forms:

1   The US acted as a mediator in the immediate period after the 1980 coup where the dialogue was cut off between the EEC and Turkey: For both the EEC and Turkey, Haig, the US SECSTATE, was the ideal person for this job. When in Brussels for NATO meetings, he had talks with Gaston Thorn, President of the Commission of the European Communities. To Thorn, Haig's message was that it would be better not to freeze the credits to Turkey. Thorn replied that the EEC would not change its position at that stage. Haig also conferred with Hans-Dietrich Genscher, German FM (their half-an-hour talk was devoted solely to Turkey–EEC relations), and some other politicians

from the MSs. Haig's message to them was that the developments around Turkey increased its strategic importance, that, therefore, Europeans had to be more forbearing while waiting for the restoration of democracy in Turkey, and that Turkey should be backed up financially. Their reply was that they, too, were willing to provide credit to Turkey but were misunderstood by Turks. It was their expectation that Haig would convey their message to Turks correctly.[26]

In November 1982, Chancellor Kohl visited the US. He and Reagan "were in complete agreement on the requirement for special attention to Alliance needs on the Southern Flank. They emphasized [. . .] their resolve to support the Turkish Government in its efforts to lead Turkey back to democracy."[27] However, Germans were apprehensive of Turkey's EEC membership and were impatient to see concrete results in the democratization process. It was difficult to find a common ground beyond the NATO context.

2   The US 'guaranteed' to Turkey that after Greece's accession to the EEC, Greece would not put obstacles in front of Turkey in the Community: To protest NATO's attitude in the Cyprus crisis, Greece had left the integrated military structure of the Alliance on 14 August 1974. In June 1977, Greece declared its intention to return.[28] Turkey maintained its veto right against Greece and, in 1978, rejected a plan devised for Greece's readmission. A subsequent plan drawn up taking Turks' preferences into consideration was this time rejected by Greeks in May 1979. For Turks, this veto right was a trump card that would be used in the future to facilitate Turkey's accession to the EEC. Meanwhile, General Bernard W. Rogers, the Supreme Allied Commander Europe (SACEUR), and Evren, the leader of the junta government in Turkey, agreed on a plan at the end of the four talks held between 12 September and 16 October 1980. Their plan was acceptable to Greece too. The plan was put into action, and Greece returned to the integrated military structure of NATO on 20 October. With this plan Turkey and Greece gave mutual concessions over the Aegean airspace. The subject-matter of the Evren–Rogers negotiations was not made public in those days.[29] Later, Evren professed that Rogers had verbally ensured him that in return for Turkey's lifting its veto on readmission of Greece to NATO's military structure, a guarantee would be given to Turkey that Greece would not create any problems for Turkey in the EEC.[30] It was this accord that gave rise to abovementioned accusation of a 'secret deal' between the US and Turkey.[31]

Rogers's proposal was in line with a recommendation Henze had made to Brzezinski ten months earlier:

> We need to talk to the Turks pragmatically, show understanding for their problems and explain ours clearly to them. Instead of pouting about

their disappointing our expectations, we need to bargain with them cleverly to get them to make concessions on Greek NATO re-entry and even, perhaps, Cyprus.[32]

The main reasons behind the concession Evren gave were to get the approval of Carter for the coup,[33] and to appease Carter's general disappointment with Turkey. Almost a year before the coup, Evren had requested from Spiers, the USAMB to Turkey, a "strong signal" that the US would stand by Turkey against the USSR and asked for more military hardware. Upon reading Spiers's account of that conversation, Carter spoke as follows: "Turkey needs to reciprocate. They have been consistently negative."[34]

For a year, the Reagan administration remained to be bound by this promise made to Turkey three months before Reagan's inauguration. Andreas Papandreou who became the PM of Greece on 21 October 1981 declared that he did not recognize the deal negotiated by his predecessor George Rallis. Rogers apologized to Evren for being unable to do much to make the Greeks keep their promise.[35] Turks had wasted their trump card.

3   The US revealed that it was in favor of Turkey's full-membership application but added that it would refrain from taking any direct initiatives in this direction: As noted above, in February 1987, Reagan told Özal that he supported Turkey's application. In April, the Reagan administration confirmed its position and emphasized that it would support Turkey's application 'silently'; there would be no lobbying for Turkey. The administration stated that since the US was not an EEC member, it was unable to 'twist the arm' of the Europeans.[36]

5 Collaborators of the US

From the 1980s onwards, the US collaborated with certain EEC and non-EEC countries in backing Turkey against the EEC. The UK was the first and most perseverant of these countries.

In the Reagan era, the three successive British ambassadors in Turkey, Sir Peter Laurence (1980–1983), Sir Mark Russel (1983–1986), and Sir Timothy Daunt (1986–1992) actively argued for Turkey in matters relevant to the EEC. Turkish politicians and public were sympathetic towards these names. Laurence was a close figure to Türkmen and Özal.[37] On various occasions, Russel declared that the EEC's treatment of Turkey was unfair,[38] and gave recommendations to Turks to develop their relations with the EEC.[39]

Margaret Thatcher, the British PM, was positive towards Turkey's EEC membership, but, in her opinion, it would be wiser for Turkey to continue with its reforms for another ten years before launching its application. When Britain was holding the Presidency of the COM in the second half of 1986, British Foreign Secretary (FS) Geoffrey Howe played a vital role in the resumption of Turkey–EEC relations: In September, the Turkey–EEC AC meeting was held at the level of FMs after an interruption of six years. When the Greek FM Pangalos addressed his Turkish counterpart Halefoğlu with criticisms at the meeting, Howe cut in and said that bilateral problems between the two countries could be discussed in other fora. While 11 MSs agreed to start a political dialogue with Turkey and to exchange the technical files, Greece objected. Despite the objection of Greece, Howe convened a press conference after the meeting as a fait accompli and announced these two points as the decisions taken at the meeting.[40]

As noted above, the UK was also one of the three MSs who declared that they did not agree with the EP's Armenian resolution in 1987.

6 Mentality of the Reagan Administration

In the 1980s, Turkey was still important for the US geopolitically. British journalist Edward Mortimer expressed this importance as follows:

> Turkey is our ally, and those who think strategically see it as a rather important one. This is not because of its military strength—considerable in manpower terms but at present very poorly equipped and largely untested—but because of its position. Turkey lies between the Soviet Union and the eastern Mediterranean, bordering both Iran and Iraq and within an hour or so's flying time of the Gulf.[41]

Turkey's ties with the West had to be fastened. Turkey's accession to, or at least close relations with, the EEC, would serve this purpose. Not to annoy the Europeans, however, the US preferred not to put pressure on them.

The US response to the 1980 coup in Turkey was more lenient than that of the EU. As Uslu stated in another context, "[u]nlike the United States, European states seemed to give priority to the democratization before the stability."[42]

To reinforce the southeastern flank of NATO, the Reagan administration strived to enable Greece to return to the integrated military structure of the Alliance. To this aim, the administration took advantage of Turkey's EEC ambitions.

7 Conclusion

In the Reagan era, Turkey was going through a restructuration and recuperation process. After the 1980 coup, it took some time for Turkey to put its domestic politics and economy in order. Until 1987, the country did not take a significant step in its relations with the EEC. Thus, there was no reason for a substantial US intervention. In these years, the Reagan administration tried to prevent crises in Turkey–EEC relations (NRA6) and to convince certain European states to extend financial help to Turkey (NRA7).

In 1987, Turkey submitted its full-membership application to the EEC. Two months before this application, Turks requested US support. The response of the Reagan administration was positive, but no concrete action was taken in this direction. A few days after Turkey submitted its application, the administration declared that it would silently support Turkey's application.

In this era, while patronizing Turkey, the US sustained its first rebuffs from the EEC. For example, when Haig tried to make sure that the EEC would not freeze credits to Turkey, Thorn closed the door without ifs, ands, or buts (NRA4). This situation led Turkey to believe that the US did not have much influence on Europe, while the Mersin crisis made the willingness of the Reagan administration to support Turkey also questionable. Meanwhile, Europeans were accusing Americans of trying to fill in the void left by the EEC in Turkey's FP (NRA5).

The Reagan administration convinced Turks to lift their veto on the readmission of Greece to the integrated military structure of NATO (NRA6 and 7). In return, among other things, the US assured Turkey that Greece would not create problems for Turkey in the EEC—especially in the issue of Turkey's accession. This soon proved to be an empty promise when Greeks declared that they did not recognize this deal.

The EEC was aspiring to become a global—normative—power and, as such, trying to assume a critical stance towards the junta government in Turkey. The criticism of the Community could not go beyond the walls of the EP; there was a radical difference of opinion over Turkey among the MSs. The pro-American and pro-Turkish policy of the UK was especially salient (NRA2).

Germany, who had acted together with the US in the issue of Turkey–EEC relations until then, started to follow a path still parallel to yet apart from that of the US (NRA4). Germans were agreeable to the idea of extending financial assistance to Turkey but displeased by the possibility of Turkey's EEC membership.

Notes

1 The physical description of the event is based on a photograph (C48058–22A) of the event available at the Reagan PL in Simi Valley, California.
2 Office of the Federal Register, National Archives and Records Service, General Services Administration, *Weekly Compilation of Presidential Documents*, Vol. 24, Nos. 26–38, 1988, p. 871.
3 Jacqueline Trescott and Donnie Radcliffe, "The Turks' night in the garden: A state dinner under the stars," *WP*, 28 June 1988.
4 Office of the Federal Register, National Archives and Records Service, General Services Administration, *Weekly Compilation of Presidential Documents*, Vol. 24, Nos. 26–38, 1988, p. 872.
5 This protocol had been initialed in July 1980.
6 Semih Günver, "Ortaklık başvurusu yapılmalı," *Milliyet*, 7 October 1986.

7   This response is discussed in the George H.W. Bush era below.
8   "Resolution on a political solution to the Armenian question (18 June 1987)," *OJ of the EC*, 20 July 1987, No C 190, pp. 119–21.
9   Kemal Saydamer, Oktay Ensari and Sirer Doğan, "Evren:"NATO gözden geçirilmeli," *Hürriyet*, 23 June 1987.
10 "AET'yi bağlamaz," *Milliyet*, 19 September 1987.
11 Jeri Laber, "Our blind spot on Turkey alienates European allies," *LAT*, 11 October 1982.
12 Saynur Gören, "Türk-ABD görüşmelerinde uyum sağlandı," *Milliyet*, 3 April 1981.
13 "Written responses to questions submitted by Hurriyet of Turkey," *Ronald Reagan: Vol. 1, 1985*, Office of the Federal Register, National Archives and Records Service, General Services Administration, 1985, p. 374; and "Written responses to questions submitted by Hurriyet of Turkey," *Weekly Compilation of Presidential Documents*, Vol. 24, Nos. 26–38, Office of the Federal Register, National Archives and Records Service, General Services Administration, 1988, p. 867.
14 Edward Mortimer, "Özal indicates change of policy on applying for EEC membership," *The Times*, 12 November 1983.
15 "HP'li Karakaş'a kızan Özal TBMM salonunu terketti," *Milliyet*, 10 April 1985.
16 "Türkiye'de ABD radyo antenine 'hayır' dedik," *Milliyet*, 30 March 1985; "Amerika ile üç pürüz," *Milliyet*, 7 April 1985.
17 Çetin Emeç and Mehmet Ali Birand, "Reagan: 'Türkiye'ye geleceğim," *Milliyet*, 4 April 1985.
18 Interview with Şükrü Elekdağ, Istanbul, 9 August 2011.
19 Birand attributes this change to the influence of his advisors Gündüz Aktan, Cem Duna and Özden Sanberk. Mehmet Ali Birand, *31 Temmuz 1959'dan 17 Aralık 2004'e Türkiye'nin Büyük Avrupa Kavgası*, Istanbul: Doğan Kitapçılık, 2005, p. 322.
20 Turan Yavuz, "'Ben kurtardım,'" *Milliyet*, 6 February 1987.
21 Mehmet Ali Birand, "Türkmen: ABD'ye ödün verilmiyor," *Milliyet*, 13 December 1981. The basis of this accusation is explained in endnote 352.
22 Interview with Şükrü Elekdağ, Istanbul, 9 August 2011.
23 Thomas Graham and Damien J. LaVera, *Cornerstones of Security: Arms Control Treaties in the Nuclear Era*, University of Washington Press, 2003, pp. 593 and 597. Mersin's status was important for Greece, because Mersin was the port from which Turkey had launched the military operations targeting Cyprus in 1974.
24 Derya Sazak, "Koordinasyon sorunu," *Milliyet*, 17 January 1989.
25 Nur Batur, "İki elçi başağrısı," *Milliyet*, 7 February 1989.
26 Mehmet Ali Birand, "Türkmen: ABD'ye ödün verilmiyor," *Milliyet*, 13 December 1981; and "Haig, Türkiye gerçeğini herkesten daha açık anlattı," *Milliyet*, 14 January 1982.
27 "Joint Statement Following Discussions With Chancellor Helmut Kohl of the Federal Republic of Germany," 15 November 1982, DOS, Office of the Historian, *Documents on Germany, 1944–1985*, USGPO, 1985, p. 1362.
28 "Yunanistan, Brüksel'de yapılacak NATO manevrasına katılacak," *Milliyet*, 12 May 1977.
29 "Rogers'in Ankara'yı ziyareti gizliliğini koruyor," *Milliyet*, 8 October 1980.
30 Yasemin Çongar, "Biz vetodan vazgeçtik, onlar da sözlerinden," *Milliyet*, 25 December 1994; and "İş 1979'da bitmişti," *Milliyet*, 26 December 1994.
31 On 10 December 1979, a similar proposal had been made to Turkish FM Hayrettin Erkmen by the Secretary-General of NATO Joseph Luns who said the West attributed great importance to Greece's return to NATO; like Israel and Egypt both of whom had been awarded by the US millions of dollars for their consent to the Camp David Accords, a sacrifice by Turkey in this matter would not remain unrequited. (Source: Mehmet Ali Birand, "Yunanistan'a hayır deme vakti geldi," *Milliyet*, 17 October 1980.)

32 "National Security Council Memorandum from Paul B. Henze to Zbigniew Brzezinski, Subject: The U.S. and Turkey (No. 67)," 27 November 1979.
33 Yasemin Çongar, "Rogers'i 12 Eylül rahatlattı," *Milliyet*, 21 December 1994.
34 The White House Memorandum from Zbigniew Brzezinski to the SECSTATE, Subject: Turkish Security, 26 November 1979 (declassified but unpublished document).
35 Yasemin Çongar, "Biz vetodan vazgeçtik, onlar da sözlerinden," *Milliyet*, 25 December 1994; and "İş 1979'da bitmişti," *Milliyet*, 26 December 1994.
36 Turan Yavuz, "ABD'den sessiz destek," *Milliyet*, 27 April 1987.
37 "[W]ithin a few months of [Laurence's] arrival [to Ankara as the British ambassador] a coup brought the Turkish generals to power. Mercifully they picked as foreign minister one who proved congenial to Laurence." (Sources: Richard Eyre, "Obituary: Sir Peter Laurence," *The Guardian*, 7 January 2008 and author's interview with Türkmen in Istanbul on 13 June 2008.)
38 Zeynep Göğüş, "İngiltere'den tam destek," *Milliyet*, 30 January 1986.
39 Nilüfer Yalçın, "İyimserlikte acele etmeyin," *Milliyet*, 20 September 1986.
40 Semih Günver, "Ortaklık başvurusu yapılmalı," *Milliyet*, 7 October 1986; Mehmet Ali Birand, "Yunanistan yalnız kaldı," *Milliyet*, 17 September 1986.
41 Edward Mortimer. "Can Turks be good Europeans?" *The Times*, 26 July 1985.
42 Nasuh Uslu, *Turkish-American Relationship between 1947 and 2003: The History of a Distinctive Alliance*, New York, NY: Nova Publishers, 2003, p. 275.

8 The (George H.W.) Bush Administration (1989–1993)
The US Support Becomes Public

Dolmabahçe Palace, situated on the shore of the Bosphorus Strait in Istanbul, was home to six sultans from 1856 until 1924. In the republican period, numerous banquets were held here in the Entrance Hall under the world-famous gigantic Baccarat chandelier, in honor of such names as King Faisal of Iraq or General de Gaulle of France. One of the most sumptuous of these events was the banquet given for President George H.W. Bush by President Özal on 21 July 1991. At the banquet, in front of each of the 150 guests there was a gold plate. This set of plates was from the Ottoman period and had been personally bought by the Turkish first lady, Semra Özal, from France especially for Bush's visit.[1] Delectable specialties of the Turkish cuisine were prepared by 15 cooks and served by 60 waiters. The event was broadcast live by TRT, the national broadcaster of Turkey, and seven international channels.[2] The Bushes and the Özals were seated at a table positioned in such a way that all the other guests—and the cameras—could see them. The intimacy between Bush and Özal was marked in their stagey gestures. During the dinner, Bush said, "[t]here has been no country as resolute as Turkey and no ally like President Ozal." He mentioned Turkey as his 'second home.'[3] He expressed his support for Turkey's European aspirations as follows:

> A decade of free government and free enterprise have [sic] made Turkey a rising star of Europe. Politically and economically, Turkey is today a nation transformed. There should be no question that Turkey deserves entry into the European Community and the Western European Union, and Turkey can count on America's strong support.[4]

Bush reiterated this line of thought on some other occasions during his stay in Turkey between 20 and 22 July 1991, such as his talk with Mesut Yılmaz, the Turkish PM.[5] As Morton Abramowitz, the USAMB to Turkey at the time, notes, this was the first time that the US was publicly speaking in favor of Turkey's accession to the EC.[6] Considering the hesitant efforts of the US in the Reagan period, Bush's words were a harbinger of a change, and his visit was a milestone. Even Abramowitz could not have imagined that such a visit would take place: "In my first year as ambassador in Ankara in 1989, I had to fight to get even an Assistant Secretary of State to come to Turkey"[7] Abramowitz complained.

This proactive and positive attitude of the US toward Turkey's EC membership was as disturbing for the nationalistically inclined intellectuals as it was comforting for the GOT. Three months after Bush's visit, Ali Sait Yüksel, a university professor and an occasional columnist, wrote as follows:

> It is not possible to become a member of the EC by sacrificing national prestige in various ways disproportionately, struggling in defiance of the EC, or accusing certain members of the EC in front of the world public. Above all, hoping to accede to the EC with the help of the USA or any other super power signifies ignorance of the realities of the EC.[8]

1 Background Conditions

The US support for Turkey's European vocation was easy to identify but difficult to explain, because it was the net result of a number of positive and negative developments that were complex in themselves:

1. The most important development in this period was the collapse of communism. The Warsaw Pact ceased to exist on 31 March 1991. The engine of the communist bloc, the USSR, was officially dissolved on 26 December. In the same month, the Russian President sent a letter to NATO headquarters and signaled Russia's goal of becoming a full-member of the Alliance. In January 1992, Andrey Kozyrev, Russian FM, called for assistance of the EEC "to set [Russia] on [its] feet and become a normal member of the European Community." Russia started negotiations with the Community for a new 'partnership agreement' that, by some commentators, was seen as a first step towards full-membership.[9] A few Central and Eastern European countries (CEECs) such as Poland and Hungary expressed their readiness to become members of NATO.

    For some, NATO would lose much of its value and rigor,[10] and perhaps this systemic change would lessen the US support for Turkey for two reasons:

    a. For the US, Turkey, the proud outpost of the southeastern flank of NATO, would be less worthy of assisting.
    b. Europeans' need for the US would be less now, and, thus, they would be less tolerant to US intervention on Turkey's behalf.

    As explained below, there were times in the Bush era, when the US did stay away from Turkey–EEC relations, and the two arguments above may explain those instances. However, for the most of the Bush era, the collapse of communism seems to have reinstated Turkey's geopolitical importance for the US and emphasized the need for increased US support against the EEC for the following reasons:

a   In this period, the Alliance remained "the leading security organization in Europe."[11] In his speech on 18 October 1990, Manfred Wörner, the Secretary-General of NATO, emphasized the enduring need for NATO and Turkey's importance in the Alliance.[12] He added that the Gulf War (see below) once again demonstrated the need for NATO and Turkey.[13]

As a self-fulfilling prophecy, between 1992 and 2004 NATO would also play an active role in Bosnia for the establishment and maintenance of peace.

b   Whereas in the Cold War period Turkey–EEC relations had been based more on cooperation, in the post-Cold War era these relations were of confrontational nature. This would purport a greater need for US leverage against Europeans, and the US was aware of this. A report prepared by the Congressional Research Service (CRS) contended that with the weakening of NATO, Turkey would find it more difficult to develop its relations with the EEC and, therefore, prefer to establish closer relations with the US.[14]

2   In the early years of the Bush administration, the EEC–US relations saw a marked improvement.

Bush [. . .] met European Commission President Jacques Delors five times during 1989, the Commission's Delegation to Washington was upgraded to full diplomatic status, and in December 1989 Secretary of State James Baker called for a 'New Atlanticism.' On 20 November 1990 the Declaration on EC-US Relations was concluded [. . .].[15]

The US could employ this improved channel of communication for Turkey's interests.

3   The Gulf War began on 2 August 1990 with the invasion, and then annexation, of Kuwait by Iraqi troops. An economic embargo followed by an operation of a coalition force of 34 nations led by the US ensued. To please the US and/or to gain a higher international profile, Turkey left its traditional posture of neutrality towards the conflicts in the Middle East. It closed the Kirkuk-Yumurtalık pipeline, which was one of the main outlets of Iraqi oil, suspended all other commercial links with Iraq, and allowed the use of İncirlik Air Base by the coalition forces.[16] These moves contributed to the economic and military subjugation of

Iraq. This war affected the US involvement in Turkey–EEC relations in a few ways:

a The war showed that the US acknowledged Turkey's new role as an active regional power and was ready to assist Turkey. The war brought some severe economic costs for Turkey. Allowing for the loss of exports to Iraq and Kuwait, and also of invisible exports and pipeline royalties, the direct costs to the Turkish balance of payments probably ran at the rate of around $2.0 billion to $2.5 billion per year (Turkish government spokespersons claimed a far higher figure).[17]

For the first time in years, voices in favor of Turkey were heard at the US Congress,[18] which, mainly under the influence of the Greek and Armenian lobbies, had usually been critical towards Turkey. The Bush administration provided emergency economic and military aid to Turkey during the war and tried to increase the proportion of the aid Turkey received relative to the aid extended to Greece.[19] Getting US support for Turkey's EEC membership was one of Özal's expectations in siding with Bush.[20]

b The war evidenced that the EEC did not appreciate Turkey's new role. Turkish President Özal complained that his government's determined attitude in the case of the sanctions applied to Iraq could not increase Turkey's chances of EEC membership.[21] A source from the period identifies the reasons as follows:

> First, EU officials continue to compartmentalize security, politics and economics, in spite of the Maastricht commitment to give the EU responsibility in all three issue areas. Second, the nations of Western Europe are still guided by the logic of 'civilian power Europe' which encourages EU governments to accord a much higher priority to issues of economic self-interest than to issues of regional security.[22]

c The war demonstrated that Turkey needed US help against Germany and that Germany was not at the beck and call of the US to help Turkey anymore. Due to the negative opinion of the German public towards the involvement of the country in the Gulf War, its economic problems and the limitations dictated by its constitution, Germany sided with the US-led coalition half-heartedly. Turks were trying to make sure that in case of an attack initiated by Iraq, the other allies would come to assist in accordance with Art. 5 of the North Atlantic Treaty. This assurance was given to Turkey at the NATO Summit on 11 August 1990. Then,

> Turkey officially asked for the defensive deployment of NATO air forces on 30 November, and on 2 January 1991 it was

announced that Germany, Italy and Belgium would be sending 40 aircraft as part of an allied mobile force. However, most of the planes sent were obsolescent F-104 and Alpha-Jet aircraft. The move also triggered off complaints in Germany, where there was strong opposition to any military involvement in the Middle East. This, in turn, provoked some sharp attacks by Özal on the Germans as unreliable allies.[23]

Americans were equally frustrated with "Germany's failure to show early and full support for the coalition in other areas and its open debate over whether an attack on Turkish bases hosting NATO planes would require German support of Turkey."[24]

4   Turkey emerged as an important player in geopolitics of energy. Between 27 April and 2 May 1992, Turkish PM called on Central Asian countries and Azerbaijan to export their energy resources through Turkey.[25] Azerbaijan approached this proposal positively and talks between the two countries started. This increased Turkey's value for the US and EEC.

5   In 1990, two developments stirred public resentment in Turkey against the US. On 20 April, George Bush released a statement[26] on the observance of 24 April as the seventy-fifth anniversary of the aforementioned 1915–1923 events, which Armenians called as genocide. Bush did not use the word 'genocide' but referred to the events as 'terrible massacres.'

The other sensitive development occurred on 8 July. That day, the US and Greece signed a defense treaty. The treaty allowed two major US military bases to remain in Greece for at least eight more years and guaranteed defense of Greece's territory against any hostile country, including Turkey.[27]

Some interpreted these developments as a sign that the US was ready to sacrifice Turkey.[28]

6   Turkey improved its relations with Israel. One of the factors in this improvement was the urgent need to lobby the US Senate to defeat a draft resolution on the alleged Armenian genocide. Richard Perle[29] who had served as the Assistant Secretary of Defense (ASSTSECDEF) in the Reagan administration encouraged his former intern Douglas Feith to establish a lobbying firm in 1989 to serve Turkey. Perle became a highly paid consultant for this firm called International Advisers, Inc.[30] Feith hired Morris J. Amitay,[31] the former executive director of the American Israel Public Affairs Committee[32] and the founder of the Washington Political Action Committee. The volume of trade between Turkey and Israel expanded from 91.4 million dollars in 1989 to 202 million dollars in 1993.[33] In December 1991, the two countries upgraded their diplomatic relations to ambassadorial level. Several high-level visits and

cooperation agreements ensued. Israel and the Jewish lobby in the US did not take any concrete action for the development of Turkey–EEC relations, but for Turkey this was an investment for the future.

7   After the collapse of the USSR, many circles in the US and in Turkey believed that as a secular and democratic country with a predominantly Muslim population, Turkey might serve as a model for the newly independent Turkic states of the Caucasus and Central Asia. This belief made Turkey more valuable for the US, but it gradually faded by the end of 1993.[34]

8   The security dimension of European integration became the focus of discussions:

   a   With the Maastricht Treaty signed on 7 February 1992,[35] the EU was established. Together with the European Coal and Steel Community and EURATOM, the EEC became the first pillar of the Union, the other two being the Common Foreign and Security Policy (CFSP) pillar and the Justice and Home Affairs pillar.
   b   In 1990, some key names such as Gianni de Michelis, FM of Italy and President of the COM of the EEC, or Mark Eyskens, FM of Belgium, and some MSs such as Greece were of the opinion that the Western European Union (WEU) be incorporated into the EEC. Wörner criticized the EEC of trying to capture the role of NATO. In his opinion, the Community could not act alone in the field of security and defense; such a venture would lead the US to withdraw its forces from Europe.[36]

Some Turkish newspapers claimed that Turkey and the US were being excluded from European security and that, in the near future, becoming a member of the WEU would only be possible via becoming an EEC member; it was likely that Turkey would be offered solely an associate membership status in the WEU.[37]

Turks' fears came to be justified. On 9–10 December 1991, the European Council drafted the Maastricht Treaty. The 'Declaration on Western European Union' in the Treaty invited those NATO members who were not an EU member to become an *associate* member of the WEU. On 20 November 1992, Iceland, Norway, and Turkey signed their respective documents of associate membership.[38]

9   During the George H.W. Bush presidency, four governments came to power in Turkey. The PMs of these governments (Turgut Özal, Yıldırım Akbulut, Mesut Yılmaz, and Süleyman Demirel) were all dedicated to Turkey's EEC membership. Özal, who became the President of Turkey less than a year after the inauguration of Bush, was pro-European now. He established close relations with the Bush administration. Morton

Abramowitz, the USAMB to Turkey between 1989 and 1991, remembers that Özal and Bush talked 30 or 40 times on the phone during the Gulf War.[39] President Özal's dominance over FP and security issues was so heavily felt that it led to the resignations of FM Mesut Yılmaz (in February 1990), FM Ali Bozer (in October 1990), and Chief of the General Staff, General Necip Torumtay (in December 1990).[40]

10 After waiting nearly three years, Turkey received an answer to the full-membership application it had submitted to the EEC in 1987. The Commission issued its opinion on 18 December 1989,[41] which was endorsed by the COM on 5 February 1990.[42] The answer was negative.[43]

2 New Parameters

When evaluated altogether, the ten factors above suggest that the positive side of the ledger outweighed the negative in the Bush era.

Although Turkey's valuable geopolitical position defined in Cold War terms lost its basis in this period, the country regained its prominence in the geopolitical equation with a new parameter: proximity to the Balkans, the Gulf region, and the energy resources in the Middle East and Caspian region. Turkey also proved to be a cooperative partner in the Gulf War, and a model for the Turkic republics. Its governments and its president were pro-European and pro-American.

For Turkey, in its relations with the EEC, US patronage was more possible and necessary than ever. According to some prominent Turkish political analysts, it would be an exaggeration to say that the US had turned its back to Turkey with the US–Greek Defense Treaty or with Bush's statement about Armenians.[44] 'The new world order' was the 'buzzword' of the day, and to many, including Turks, this term was synonymous with *Pax Americana*. Turkey's membership application to the EEC had been refused. Turks were resentful of being marginalized in the new security setting of Europe. Their efforts in the Gulf War had not been appreciated by Europeans. Germany, in particular, was not willing to cooperate with the US anymore to help Turkey, and was critical of the human rights (HR) situation in Turkey.[45] The UK—who had already been furthering Turkey's interests in the EEC—and Israel were ready to take this role over.

Now let us see the breadth and depth of the actual US involvement in Turkey–EEC relations under these conditions.

3 US Involvement in Turkey–EEC Relations

Following Bush's inauguration on 20 January 1989, within almost a year Americans made it clear to the Turks that they were willing to make an effort for Turkey's EEC bid. The intensity of this effort increased towards the end of the Bush era, while new actors such as the US Congress or Cyprus joined in the process. The following are the developments related to the involvement of the US in Turkey–EEC relations in the Bush era:

1. The Bush administration informed the Turks that it was willing and ready to talk to the Europeans to try to elicit a positive decision on Turkey's full-membership application. As explained above, the relations of the US with the Commission of the EEC were developing rapidly in 1989. As the Commission was the 'kitchen' where the decision of the EEC on Turkey's application would be prepared, an intervention by the Bush administration could have been timely and effective. However, Turks decided not to use that opportunity. Ali Bozer, the Minister Responsible for EEC Affairs between 1986 and 1989, remembers that they appreciated but rejected this offer of the US since they surmised that a US intervention might further disturb the Europeans.[46] Abramowitz speaks about this offer as follows: "I think, I actually asked Mr. Özal. I don't recall. So, I can't say with certainty."[47] If Abramowitz's recollection is accurate, this proposal must have been made between 1 August (the day Abramowitz presented his letter of confidence to President Evren[48]) and 18 December 1989 (the day Turkey received the Community's response). In any case, the proposal may not have been made before 30 March, the date Bozer assumed the office. In this period, Özal was the PM until 31 October and the President afterwards.

2. On several occasions Bush expressed his support to Turks in private. In Özal's ten-day visit to the US, Bush welcomed him at the White House on 25 September 1990.[49] In their talk, Bush declared his determination to use his influence on Brussels for Turkey, but only minutes after Bush made this promise and even before Özal's limousine brought him to his hotel, a high-ranking US official gave a press briefing and said that the applications of several countries, including that of Turkey, to the EEC were being kept suspended. European leaders were trying to establish the so-called Common European Home, the official maintained, and these applications would not be considered before 1992. A Turkish daily presented this story with the title "Empty Promises from the US" and questioned the sincerity of Bush's commitment in this matter.[50]

The EEC looked askance at the news about Bush's intention to intervene on Turkey's behalf. European officials and politicians, who preferred to remain anonymous, said that the US had no right to interfere and that the US was behaving as if it was still the Cold War period. They were displeased with the publicized image of a Europe manipulated by the US.[51] A Greek MEP, Sotiris Kostopoulos, brought the issue onto the agenda of the EP. On 30 April 1991, he submitted a Parliamentary question on the "unwarranted interference by the United States in EC internal affairs on behalf of Turkey." His question was as follows:

> The President of the United States, Mr. George Bush, recently called for the immediate accession of Turkey to the European Community, at a time when Turkey is disregarding resolutions by the EC and other bodies on human rights, the situation in Cyprus, etc.
> Is European Political Cooperation[52] willing to accept such recommendations by the United States, thereby disrupting the planned timetable and strategy for the accession of other countries to the Community, and does it consider that reservations about Turkish accession to the EC [. . .] are no longer justified?[53]

His question was answered by Jacques Poos, FM of Luxembourg and President of the COM:

> [T]he honourable member is clearly aware that the procedures followed in regard to requests for accession do not take account of the opinion of third country authorities, although they are free to express their views.[54]

3 The US Congress got involved in Turkey–EEC relations. Whereas the aforementioned report prepared for the Subcommittee on Europe and the Middle East of the COFA in 1980 had no reference to Turkey–EEC relations, now the Subcommittee was recommending that the US support Turkey's full-membership to the EEC and WEU.[55] Moreover, a resolution[56] urging the Congress to back "Turkey's inclusion in the full range of political, economic, and military institutions in Europe, including the European Community and the Western European Union" was introduced on 18 April 1991. This resolution, sponsored by Representative Stephen Solarz and co-sponsored by Representative Dan Burton, was the first attempt to get the support of the Congress to improve Turkey's relations with Europe. The resolution was calling upon the President to "do everything possible to support Turkey's inclusion in the full range of political, economic, and military institutions in Europe, including the European Community and the Western European Union." The resolution was emphasizing Turkey's importance as "a valued friend and ally of the US" and "the key to the defense of the southern flank of the NATO alliance," detailing the sacrifices Turkey had made during the Gulf War, and underlining the "crucial role" Turkey played "as a link between Islamic and Western societies."

However, the critical stance towards Turkey of such influential figures in the Congress as Claiborne Pell, the Chairman of the Senate Committee on Foreign Relations (COFR), or Paul Sarbanes, a senator of Greek origin, together with the unabating opposition the of the Greek and Armenian lobbies prevented the Congress from leaving its reserved attitude towards Turkey. The resolution could not make it beyond the relevant subcommittees of the COFA of the HOR.

4   Before the Gulf War, SECSTATE James Baker visited Turkey three times. In August 1990, he was in Ankara to get Özal's permission to use the US bases in Turkey against Iraq. Later on, Özal implied that in this visit Baker had pledged that a second full-membership application to the EEC, after the one submitted in 1987, would be supported by the US.[57] Baker had already started working for Turkey. Before coming to Ankara, around July 1990, he had sent a letter to the FMs of the 12 MSs of the EEC emphasizing the potential benefits of Turkey's EEC membership and stating that this membership would be welcome by the US. The repercussions of Baker's efforts varied across European capitals. In Germany, while *Frankfurter Rundschau* wrote that the US was about to start actively working to facilitate Turkey's EEC membership,[58] *Übersee Rundschau* predicted that if Turkey acceded to the EEC, it would be the European branch office of the US.[59] Italian FM Gianni de Michelis expressed his contentment with Baker's visit and letter. De Michelis added that he had always been in favor of closer relations between Turkey and the EEC. Now, he said, the crisis in the Gulf was proving him right.[60]

5   Morton Abramowitz said[61] that his own first statements backing Turkey's admission to the EEC were in 1990 and 1991. He was hoping that his statements would increase the willingness of the Turkish public to side with the US in the Gulf War, and strengthen Özal's hand in domestic politics. This, Abramowitz adds, was done against the negative views of the EUR[62] of the DOS. The bureau's view was that US intervention for Turkey would antagonize Europeans. To circumvent the EUR, Abramowitz had gotten in touch with Robert Zoellick, the Counselor to DOS. Zoellick was the most senior among Baker's aides and 'the gatekeeper' to Baker.[63]

6   In his visit to the US in 1990, Özal declared Turkey's intention to sign a free-trade agreement with the US, and despite Baker's initial hesitation, he and the US Trade Representative Carla Anderson Hills agreed that experts from both sides start working on the project.[64] This agreement would not replace Turkey's agreement with the EEC but constitute an alternative to it. The project could not be implemented since Bush could not obtain authorization from the Senate to conclude the planned 17 free-trade agreements (including that of Turkey).[65] A few months later, the Bush administration got convinced that such an agreement with Turkey might offend the Europeans.[66] It was also claimed that this agreement would not be possible technically due to Turkey's contractual commitment to become a part of the CU of the EEC. Officials from the EEC stated that they could not understand the aim behind this project,

while some Turkish columnists speculated that the sole aim behind this project was to show the EEC that Turkey had alternatives.⁶⁷

7 Cyprus became an important determinant in the US involvement in Turkey–EEC relations once again. Over Cyprus, the US influenced these relations both positively and negatively.

   a On the positive side, the US tried to appease Turkey that unless the Cyprus talks were concluded with an agreement, Cyprus would not be admitted to the EEC.⁶⁸ 'The Republic of Cyprus' had submitted its full-membership application on 4 July 1990. The government of the Turkish Republic of Northern Cyprus (TRNC) was uncomfortable with the idea of Cyprus being represented by the Greek side and admitted to the EEC as such.
   b On the negative side, for the Greek lobby in the US Congress, the Cyprus problem became a channel through which they tried to manipulate the approach of the US to Turkey–EEC relations. In the process of his appointment to Turkey as the USAMB, Morton Abramowitz was questioned by Pell and Sarbanes at the COFR. Sarbanes asked Abramowitz if he believed the Cyprus problem was an obstacle for Turkey's accession to the EEC. Abramowitz answered the question affirmatively but added that he believed Turks were willing to solve the problem.⁶⁹

4 Collaborators of the US

The normalization of Turkey Israel relations in this term did not bring about immediate results in Turkey–EEC relations, but Israel emerged as a potential collaborator of the US. This potential would be tapped in the Clinton period. Nonetheless, this normalization yielded other indirect positive results in Turkey–EEC relations:

1 By establishing close relations with Israel and the Jewish lobby, Turkey corroborated its secular image, thereby emphasizing its European credentials; and
2 With the help of Israel and the Jewish lobby in Washington, Turkey strengthened its position against the Greek and Armenian lobbies in the Congress.

The approach of the UK to Turkey–EEC relations was well-matched to that of the US. However, it was only in the last six months of Bush's presidency that the British took concrete steps in this direction. The UK assumed the Presidency of the Council in the second half of 1992. British FS Douglas Hurd promised assistance to Turkey 'in every field.' He said he would work to make the completion of the CU possible, to improve the financial and industrial cooperation and to start the political dialogue between Turkey and the EEC. He added that he would try to make the release of the Fourth Financial Protocol—that had remained suspended because of the Greek veto—possible.[70] Hurd could not overcome the Greek veto on the Protocol, but at the Turkey–EEC AC meeting on 9 November 1992, he was instrumental in convincing the Greek representative to start the political dialogue with Turkey.[71]

5 Mentality of the (George H.W.) Bush Administration

The Bush administration preferred to support Turkey's EEC membership, because Turkey

1. was exerting considerable effort in the Gulf War;
2. had an important role as an energy corridor; and
3. was a role model for the Turkic republics.

The main characteristics of this support were as follows:

1. It was still based on geopolitical calculations. However, now Turkey was seen as a Middle Eastern country neighboring Iraq and the Central Asia, not as a country located in the southeastern corner of Europe. As Lesser noted, "the notion of Turkey as a key Middle Eastern ally was always an uncomfortable fit with Ankara's European aspirations."[72]
2. The Eastern element in Turkey's identity was seen more essential, and instances where Turkey's Europeanness was emphasized were infrequent.
3. The US support was not an item of bargaining. It was

    a   a gesture in exchange for which the US was expecting Turkey's cooperation in the Gulf War (when Baker came to Ankara for the US bases in Turkey, the US campaign for Turkey had already been going on),

    b   a reward given to Turkey during and after the Gulf War in appreciation of its efforts for the Gulf War, and

    c   a move supposed to reinforce Özal's position in domestic politics that was damaged by his pro-American strategy in the Gulf War.

4. This support contained a contradiction:

    On the one hand, the United States has interests that argue for strong U.S. support of Turkish goals of increased integration in European political, economic, and security organizations. On the other, strong U.S. support of Turkish initiatives to facilitate increased integration with Europe could alienate other U.S. European allies who may hesitate to grant Turkey increased access to European institutions.[73]

5. Bush's support to Turkey lacked historical depth. Remembering the following sentence from his remarks at the Dolmabahçe Palace quoted

above will suffice to evidence the point: "A decade of free government and free enterprise has made Turkey a rising star of Europe."

6 Conclusion

The US efforts for Turkey's EEC ambitions were meagre in the early years of the Bush administration. The interest of the Turkey-watchers in the subject was equally low. In a detailed report[74] on Turkey written by Henze (he was now a resident consultant at the RAND Corporation) and published in 1992, there were only a few cursory references to the EEC.

It was around 1990 or 1991 that Bush, and the USAMB to Turkey, Abramowitz, started publicly advocating Turkey's EEC membership. Marc Grossman, the USAMB to Turkey between 1994 and 1997, confirms that it was in the first years of the 1990s that the US started actively championing of Turkey's quest for the EEC.[75] The following three factors triggered this change:

1 The Gulf War appeared on the horizon (NRA7).
2 Turkey regained an interest in the EEC. During Bush's presidency, pro-European governments came to power in Turkey (DF).
3 Europeans lost their interest in Turkey—if they had had any. The country's application for full-membership to the Community was refused within the first year of Bush's term. Turkey was also being pushed out of the emerging security architecture of Europe (NRA6 and 4). Especially Germans were antagonistic towards Turks. The US backing in the EEC proved to be more necessary than ever.

In line with the 'hierarchy in domestic politics' assumption of neorealists (NRA2), sometimes the support of the Bush administration was extended in defiance of the disapproval of certain segments of the USG (primarily the EUR of the DOS). Despite such attempts as the Solarz-Burton bill, because of the powerful Greek and Armenian lobbies, the Congress distanced itself from this issue.

The administration preferred to be in contact with the EEC MSs rather than the EEC itself (NRA2). Britain, Germany, and to some extent France decided to act in harmony with the US; they preferred bandwagoning to balancing.[76]

The Reagan administration had not established a connection between the Cyprus issue and Turkey–EEC relations. In the Bush era, the Cyprus issue re-emerged in Turkey–EEC relations.

Israel emerged as a potential collaborator of the US in supporting Turkey, but this potential could not be tapped in the Bush era. The UK was willing to cooperate with the US. Towards the end of Bush's term, the UK took over the Presidency of the COM and contributed to the start of the political dialogue between Turkey and the EEC (NRA2).

Notes

1 Barbara Bush, *Barbara Bush: A Memoir*, New York NY: Simon and Schuster, 2003, p. 424.
2 Mücahit Büber, "Bush'a istim kebabı," *Milliyet*, 19 July 1991.
3 Human Rights Watch, *Human Rights Watch World Report 1992*, New York NY: 1992, p. 581.
4 George H.W. Bush, "Remarks at Dolmabahce Palace, Istanbul, Turkey, July 21, 1991," *Dispatch*, the US DOS, Vol. 2, No. 31, 5 August 1991; and "Türkiye AT'a girmeyi hak etti," *Milliyet*, 22 July 1991.
5 "Her alanda destek sürdürülecek," *Milliyet*, 21 July 1991.
6 Morton Abramowitz, "An American perspective on Turkey and the EU," *Today's Zaman (TZ)*, 13 December 2004.
7 Morton Abramowitz, "Springtime in Turkish-American relations?" *The Century Foundation*, 5 April 2009. Available at http://tcf.org/commentary/2009/nc2268, accessed 25 June 2012.
8 Ali Sait Yüksel, "AT ilişkileri nereye," *Milliyet*, 20 October 1991. Author's translation.
9 Maurizio Massari, "Russia and Europe after the Cold War: The unfinished agenda," Working Paper 98–16, Weatherhead Center for International Affairs, Harvard University, 1998, p. 2.
10 For instance, in 1990 Mearsheimer claimed that without the threat the USSR posed, NATO would lose its efficiency. In the same year, in his testimony before the Foreign Relations Committee of the US Senate, Waltz contended that NATO was a disappearing thing. (Sources: John J. Mearsheimer, "Back to the future: Instability in Europe after the cold war," *International Security*, Vol. 15, No. 1, 1990, 5–56, p. 52; and Kenneth Waltz, "Relations in a multipolar world," Hearings before the Senate Committee on Foreign Relations, US Congress, 102nd Cong., 1st sess., 26, 28, and 30 November 1990, Washington: USGPO, 1991, p. 210.)
11 John S. Duffield, "NATO and alliance theory," paper presented at the annual meeting of the International Studies Association, 21–25 February 1995, Chicago, p. 763.
12 "JFC Naples/AFSOUTH, 1951–2009: Over fifty years working for peace and stability," *NATO*. Available at www.afsouth.nato.int/JFCN_Factsheets/JFC_Naples_history.html, accessed 17 August 2011.
13 "Wörner'a protestolu doktora," *Milliyet*, 19 October 1990. NATO was not involved in the Gulf War. However, this war triggered a series of discussions on the need for 'out-of-area' operations of the Alliance.
14 Turan Yavuz, "Türkiye'nin tek yolu ABD," *Milliyet*, 24 May 1990. CRS does not provide direct public access to its reports and requires citizens to request them from their Member of Congress.
15 Alan P. Dobson and Steve Marsh, *US Foreign Policy since 1945*, New York, NY: Routledge, 2001, p. 145.
16 For the initial demands of the US, see Morton Abramowitz, "The complexities of American policymaking on Turkey," *Insight Turkey*, Vol. 2, No. 4, 2000, 3–35, p. 5.
17 William Hale, "Turkey, the Middle East and the Gulf Crisis," *International Affairs*, Vol. 68, No. 4, 1992, 679–92, p. 684.
18 Turan Yavuz, "'Kıbrıs'ta ödün verin,'" *Milliyet*, 19 September 1990.
19 Douglas T. Stuart, *Can Europe Survive Maastricht*, Carlisle, PA: Strategic Studies Institute, 1994, p. 19.
20 William Hale, *Turkey, the US and Iraq*, London: The London Middle East Institute, 2007, p. 38 and 57.
21 "Zararımızı karşılayın," *Milliyet*, 22 August 1990.
22 Douglas T. Stuart, *Can Europe Survive Maastricht?* Carlisle, PA: Strategic Studies Institute, 1994, p. 19.

23 William Hale, "Turkey, the Middle East and the Gulf Crisis," *International Affairs*, Vol. 68, No. 4, 1992, 679–92, p. 685.
24 Diana Jean Schemo, "Germany's lukewarm support of Gulf war leaves its allies cold," *The Baltimore Sun*, 13 March 1991.
25 "Timeline of the Baku-Tbilisi-Ceyhan pipeline," *Turkish Daily News (TDN)*, 13 July 2006.
26 "Statement on the observance of the 75th anniversary of the Armenian Massacres." Available at http://bushlibrary.tamu.edu/research/public_papers.php?id=1782&year=1990&month=4, accessed 16 September 2011.
27 "U.S., Greece sign 8-year pact on military bases," *LAT*, 9 July 1990.
28 Nur Batur, "Türkiye gözden mi çıkıyor?" *Milliyet*, 23 April 1990; and Sami Kohen, "O kadar da değil," *Milliyet*, 19 July 1990.
29 Later, in 1996, a study group led by Richard Perle would prepare a policy document for Benjamin Netanyahu, the PM of Israel. The document, entitled "A Clean Break: A New Strategy for Securing the Realm," suggested Israel to improve its relations with Turkey. For the text of the document see Grant F. Smith, *Deadly Dogma: How Neoconservatives Broke the Law to Deceive America*, Washington: Institute for Research-Middle Eastern Policy, 2006, pp. 225–32.
30 Janine R. Wedel, *Shadow Elite: How The World's New Power Brokers Undermine Democracy, Government, and the Free Market*, New York, NY: Basic Books, 2009, p. 149.
31 Michael Bobelian, *Children of Armenia: A Forgotten Genocide and the Century-Long Struggle for Justice*, New York: Simon and Schuster, 2009, p. 181.
32 For the influence of Amitay and of the Committee, see John J. Mearsheimer and Stephen M. Walt, *The Israel Lobby and U.S. Foreign Policy*, New York, NY: Farrar, Straus and Giroux, 2007, pp. 152–62.
33 Meliha Altunışık, "The Turkish-Israeli rapprochement in the post-Cold War era," *Middle Eastern Studies*, Vol. 38, No. 2, 2000, 172–91, p. 175 and 176.
34 Turan Yavuz, "ABD'den Türkiye'ye iki rol," *Milliyet*, 22 January 1992; and İdris Bal, *Turkey's Relations with the West and the Turkic Republics: The Rise and Fall of the 'Turkish Model,'* Aldershot: Ashgate, 2000.
35 The Treaty entered into force on 1 November 1993, almost a year after the H.W. Bush administration ended.
36 Peter Thompson, "EC must strengthen institutions," *Europe*, December 1990, 37–8, p. 38; and Ahmet Sever, "NATO ile AT kapışıyor," *Milliyet*, 22 September 1990.
37 For example, Ahmet Sever, "Türkiye dışlanıyor," *Milliyet*, 29 March 1991.
38 The associate membership status of these three countries would be effective from 6 March 1995.
39 Interview with Morton Abramowitz, Washington, 7 May 2010.
40 William Hale, "Turkey, the Middle East and the Gulf Crisis," *International Affairs*, Vol. 68, No. 4, 1992, 679–92, pp. 685–6.
41 "Commission Opinion on Turkey's Request for Accession to the Community," Commission of the EC, Brussels, 20 December 1989, SEC(89) 2290 Final.
42 Conclusions of the Council (General Affairs) of 5 February 1990, *Bulletin of the EC*, 1/2–1990, Part 2.2.37.
43 p. 5.
44 For example, Sami Kohen, "O kadar da değil," *Milliyet*, 19 July 1990.
45 Morton Abramowitz, "Dateline Ankara: Turkey after Ozal," *Foreign Policy*, No. 91, 1993, 164–81, pp. 166–7 and 179–80.
46 Interview with Ali Bozer, Ankara, 20 December 2009.
47 Interview with Morton Abramowitz, Washington, 7 May 2010.
48 "Abramowitz'ten güven mektubu," *Milliyet*, 2 August 1989.
49 "Visits by foreign leaders of Turkey," US DOS. Available at http://history.state.gov/departmenthistory/visits/turkey, accessed 6 August 2012.
50 "ABD'den kuru vaatler," *Milliyet*, 27 September 1990.

51 Mehmet Ali Birand, "Özal'ın ABD gezisine AT'ın bakışı," *Milliyet*, 7 October 1990.
52 European Political Cooperation was the FP coordination practice within the EC before the introduction of the CFSP.
53 Question No 26 by Mr Kostopoulos (H-0375/91) to European Political Cooperation: "Unwarranted interference by the United States in EC internal affairs on behalf of Turkey," *Debates of the European Parliament*, No. 3–405, 15 May 1991, p. 201.
54 Joint Answer (991H0431), *Debates of the European Parliament*, No. 3–405, 15 May 1991, p. 202.
55 Turan Yavuz, "ABD'den yardıma çengel," *Milliyet*, 19 April 1991.
56 102d Congress, H. Con. Res. 132.
57 Temuçin Tüzecan, "AT üyeliğimize destek sözü," *Milliyet*, 14 August 1990.
58 "ABD, Avrupa'yı sıkıştırıyor," *Milliyet*, 12 August 1990.
59 "ABD'nin Avrupa şubesi Türkiye olacak," *Milliyet*, 13 December 1990.
60 Pino Aprile, "Faremo ogni sforzo per scongiurare la guerra," *Oggi*, No. 36, 5 September 1990, 6–9, p. 8. Author's translation.
61 Interview with Morton Abramowitz, Washington, 7 May 2010.
62 Abramowitz states that during his tenure in Ankara as ambassador, Turkey issues were largely handled by EUR. (Source: Morton Abramowitz, "The complexities of American policymaking on Turkey," *Insight Turkey*, Vol. 2, No. 4, 2000, 3–35, p. 27.)
63 Philip Zelikow and Condoleezza Rice, *Germany Unified and Europe Transformed: A Study in Statecraft*, Cambridge, MA: Harvard University Press, 1995, p. 23.
64 Turan Yavuz, "Özal, Irak'ı gözden çıkardı," *Milliyet*, 28 September 1990.
65 "ABD ile serbest ticaret suya düşüyor," *Milliyet*, 16 May 1991. See also Matthew Baldwin, John Peterson, and Bruce Stokes, "Trade and economic relations," in John Peterson and Mark A. Pollack (eds.) *Europe, America, Bush: Transatlantic Relations in the Twenty-First Century*, London: Routledge, 2003, 29–46, p. 44.
66 Yasemin Çongar, "ABD ile serbest ticaret," *Milliyet*, 18 August 1997.
67 Mehmet Ali Birand, "Özal'ın ABD gezisine AT'ın bakışı," *Milliyet*, 7 October 1990.
68 Turan Yavuz, "Kıbrıs'ta ödün verin," *Milliyet*, 19 September 1990.
69 Turan Yavuz, "Türkiye'ye teşvik gerek," *Milliyet*, 10 June 1989.
70 Temuçin Tüzecan, "Ankara'ya her konuda destek," *Milliyet*, 18 April 1992. For the Fourth Financial Protocol, see page 81.
71 Ahmet Sever, "Türkiye-AT ilişkilerinde önemli gelişme," *Milliyet*, 11 November 1992.
72 Ian Lesser, "Turkey, the United States and the delusion of geopolitics," *Survival*, Vol. 48, No. 3, Autumn 2006, 83–96, p. 84.
73 William Johnsen, "Turkey and Europe: Expectations and complications," in Stephen Blank, William Johnsen, and Stephen Pelletière (eds.) *Turkey's Strategic Position at the Crossroads of World Affairs*, Carlisle, PA: Strategic Studies Institute, 1993, p. 10.
74 Paul B. Henze, *Turkey: Toward the Twenty-First Century*, Santa Monica, CA: RAND, 1992.
75 Interview with Marc Grossman, Washington, 11 May 2010.
76 For a different perspective, see Douglas Lemke, "Great powers in the post-Cold War world: A power transition perspective," in Tharza Varkey Paul et al. (eds.), *Balance of Power: Theory and Practice in the 21st Century*, Stanford: Stanford University Press, 2004, 52–75, pp. 58–65.

9 The Clinton Administration (1993–2001)

Deux ex Machina

In November 1999, a handful of officials from the Ministry of Public Works in Ankara were stressed out to complete an important project in time: the construction of a new reception hall within the presidential compound. The old reception hall was considered inadequate in terms of its size and facilities, and the new one had been in construction since 1997. The deadline was 14 November, the arrival date of President Clinton for a five-day visit. As this date approached, it became obvious that an extra week would be needed to make the hall ready to host the prestigious guest. This was bad news for Turks who had never looked forward to hosting a US President as much as they did Clinton. The good old reception hall would have to be called into emergency duty for a last time before it retired.[1]

The long-awaited guest arrived at Ankara at 23.45 on the day expected, accompanied by his family and a high-level delegation, which included Madeleine Albright, the SECSTATE. They would stay in Turkey until 19 November and participate in the Istanbul Summit of the Organization for Security and Cooperation in Europe (OSCE) on the last two days of their visit. Less than 24 hours later, a dinner would be held in Clinton's honor. The chocolate and chestnut cake to be served after the dinner had been ordered to a famous patisserie in Ankara and prepared under the close scrutiny of the CIA agents who 'camped' in the kitchen of the shop for a week. The plates on which the cake was going to be served had been decorated with Turkish and American flags made of sugar.[2]

The following day, the old reception hall was ready for its 500 invitees. American guests came at around 19.30 and were warmly welcomed at the door by President Demirel. A candid atmosphere was apparent from the beginning. First, Clinton received the Order of the State of the Turkish Republic Award. Then, the party proceeded to the dinner.[3] Clinton was cheerful at the table. He tried to draw everyone into the conversation. When the cake was served, he asked whether the flags on the plate were edible. A few second later, the stars, the stripes, and the crescent were all intertwining in his mouth.[4] The laughter emanating from this corner of the table overshadowed an embarrassing event occurring in another. In accordance with protocol rules, Albright was supposed to be seated next to Ahmet

Necdet Sezer, the Chief Justice of the Turkish Constitutional Court. Sezer had not arrived yet, and Albright asked if she could be seated next to İsmail Cem, the Turkish FM, sitting at the far end of the table; she had some issues to discuss with Cem. So, Sezer's place-card was swapped with Cem's. When Sezer arrived at the hall and saw his place-card relegated to a remote corner, he left the event instantly in resentment. Later, he sent a letter of protest to the office of the Turkish President and never took part in any of the subsequent presidential events.[5]

This dinner scene was reflective of two important features of what we may call the 'Clinton style of diplomacy':

1   Clinton's intimacy was an important determinant in the relations between the two countries. His visit to Turkey was longer than usual: Whereas Eisenhower visited Turkey for one day, and Bush came for two days, Clinton stayed for five days. He pledged 'full support' to Turkey in almost every area. He visited the earthquake-stricken regions of the country. Columnists praised him as a genuine leader who rubbed shoulders with ordinary Turks, a favor, they said, Turkish politicians refrained from bestowing upon their own people.[6] A joke circulating at that time in the US was that when Clinton left office, he could be elected Turkey's next president in a landslide.[7] In 2005, long after his presidency ended, Clinton would still appear very popular in a public opinion survey[8] where Turks ranked the US presidents in terms of their contribution to world peace and security as follows:

   a   Bill Clinton (69%)
   b   Ronald Reagan (8%)
   c   George W. Bush (3%)
   d   George H.W. Bush (1%)
   e   Don't know (19%)

2   Albright's change of seats exemplified that Clinton administration established shortcuts with certain names from Turkish politics whom they considered to be more effective and/or more prone to cooperate. Bypassing PMs Mesut Yılmaz and then Bülent Ecevit, Clinton preferred to remain in touch with President Demirel (for instance, he exchanged letters with Demirel between February and June 1998 about the Gulf crisis and Cyprus[9]). Some newspapers interpreted this new role of Demirel as 'de facto presidency.'[10]

The diplomatic style of the Clinton administration was apparent all along his visit. Five hours before President Demirel's dinner, Clinton delivered a speech at the Turkish Parliament that took nearly half an hour. In this speech, he flattered Turks' pride by emphasizing Turkey's importance and praising Turkish history. He reaffirmed the partnership between the two countries for a 'common future,' and expressed his commitment to Turkey's European aspirations.[11] Although his speech included only a few concrete promises to Turkey, coverage of this speech by the Turkish media was euphoric. Newspapers claimed that with this speech all the members of the parliament regardless of political affiliation were elated[12] and that the friendship between the two countries reached its prime.[13]

1 The Context

It would be an oversimplification to attribute the warm embrace Clinton received in Turkey only to the diplomatic savoir-faire of himself and of his cadre.

> Consider the context. [. . .] The end of the Cold War robbed [Turkey] of its iconic role as the anchor for NATO's southern flank. The breakup of the Soviet empire put at risk in places like Chechnya and Yugoslavia populations with ethnic and historic connections to Turkey. The first Gulf War had disrupted Turkey's trade with Iraq and the Gulf, fueled terror within Turkey, and created a nightmare situation next-door: a quasi-independent Kurdish statelet under U.S. protection. Turkey found itself at odds with most of its neighbors. Its economy was fragile and subject to recurrent crises. Its human rights reputation was tarnished. Europe was unresponsive to Turkey's hopes of joining former Warsaw Pact foes on the path to membership.
>
> Turkey needed a new identity. Or at least a friend. Bill Clinton's administration would eventually provide both.[14]

Yet, there also were some grave problems between the two countries:

1. Turkey's HR record had an adverse bearing on Turkey–US relations. The struggle of the GOT with the terrorist activities of the illegal Kurdistan Workers' Party (PKK) and the legal proceedings instituted against DEP (Democracy Party), the political wing of PKK, drew allegations of HR violations from the EU. On the other hand, the US had listed PKK as a terrorist organization and, on many occasions, reiterated its approval of Turkey's right to combat PKK terrorism.[15] Nevertheless, for two reasons, the Clinton administration decided to put pressure on Turkey to improve its HR record:
    a. In Clinton's opinion, Turkey's HR problems were major obstacles to the country's accession to the EU. In 2002, after his presidency ended, he was still recommending Turks to try to meet the EU's HR standards.[16]
    b. Turkey's HR problems were on the agenda of the US Congress. In 1994, a draft legislation proposed making 25 percent of the amount of assistance available to Turkey conditional on Turkey's

improvement of its HR performance and restricting the use of any American military equipment acquired through the assistance program for internal security purposes. Turks believed an arms embargo was a possibility. It was after the objections of the GOT and the personal appeal of the Turkish PM Tansu Çiller to Clinton that the final version of the legislation made only 10 percent of the aid conditional on Turkey's improvement of its policies on the Kurdish issue and Cyprus.[17] Turkey refused to use this 10 percent.[18] Later on, on the ground that Turkey was in violation of HR and of its obligations in international law, the Congress put pressure on the Clinton administration not to hold the aforementioned OSCE Summit in Istanbul.[19]

In his visit to Istanbul, Clinton brought the HR issue forward in a few of his speeches. When PM Ecevit visited the US in September 1999, Clinton emphasized the HR as one of the factors that negatively affected Turkey–EU relations.[20]

2 Developments pertaining to the power vacuum in northern Iraq and to Saddam Hussein's persecution of Kurds posed some problems in Turkey–US relations. The US and some of its allies in the Gulf War initiated a military operation named Operation Provide Comfort in 1991. The aim of this operation was to defend the Kurds in this region and provide humanitarian aid to them. After completing their missions in Kuwait, the troops included in this operation were relocated to Turkey and northern Iraq. Although initially they were supposed to stay for a limited period, their stay was extended several times with the permission of the Turkish Parliament. Shortly before Clinton's first inauguration on 20 January 1993, some circles in Turkey expressed doubts over the 'real intention' of the operation. Uğur Mumcu, an influential columnist wrote several times that the raison d'être of the Operation was to enable the establishment of a Kurdish state in northern Iraq and, then, to protect it in its fledgling period.[21] Mumcu's assassination on 24 January 1993—an incident still unsolved today—meant a shaky ground for Clinton to build his relations with Turkey on. Necmettin Erbakan, leader of the Welfare Party, claimed that the troops in the operation were made up of Jewish soldiers who could speak Kurdish. Erbakan became the PM on 28 June 1996 and, on 31 December, requested that the Operation be ended. The Clinton administration reluctantly accepted this request and replaced the Operation Provide Comfort with Operation Northern Watch that would enforce the no-fly zone above the 36th parallel in Iraq (this new operation could not remain free from criticism either).[22]

3 Turkish press published a number of allegations extending from shipment of arms by the US to Armenia, to employment of the Turkish PM Çiller by the USG as a CIA operative.[23]

In the face of these problems, some observers claimed that the coming of the Clinton administration meant the end of the warm climate created in the Bush era;[24] they were expecting an anti-climax. However, Clinton's conspicuous commitment to Turkey's European aspirations proved them wrong. Even before his inauguration, Turks had high expectations from him in their relations with Europeans.[25] It was this commitment of Clinton combined with Turks' high expectations from him, and the peculiar circumstances of the era that led to an unprecedented upsurge in the US involvement in Turkey–EU relations. What made Clinton's visit the 'climax' of Turkish–US friendship was that his visit was built on top of this mountainous involvement.

2 US Involvement in Turkey–EU Relations

In the Clinton era, the US involvement in Turkey–EU relations materialized in the following five cases:

1. establishment of the CU between Turkey and the EC,
2. recognition of Turkey's eligibility at the Luxembourg European Council of 1997,
3. approval of Turkey's candidate status at the Helsinki European Council of 1999,
4. protection of Turkey's interests in the drawing up of the Accession Partnership Document (APD), and
5. inclusion of Turkey in the new security architecture of Europe.

Let us examine these five cases in detail.

2.1 The Customs Union

Clinton administration worked hard to enable the establishment of the CU[26] between Turkey and the EC.[27] To this aim, at the end of 1994, the US launched an initiative that continued for a few months until the signing of the decision on 6 March 1995.

When Turkey's resolution to complete the CU with the EC became manifest, some MSs such as Greece, Germany, Belgium,[28] and—after becoming an EU member—Austria[29] expressed their opposition. As the resumption of the gradual reduction of customs tariffs was a technical matter, it was overseen by the Commission, and the MSs had no veto power over the tariff reduction process itself.[30] However, the final decision to officially establish the CU would be taken by the Turkey–EC AC.[31] This was an uncertainty for Turks. Another uncertainty was that the decisions of the AC would be subject to the approval of the EP. The US helped Turkey overcome these uncertainties, and endeavored to convince and encourage the Turks themselves to undertake the necessary reforms, thereby facilitating Turkey's acceptance as a CU partner. These efforts of the US are summarized under the following five titles.

2.1.1 Convincing the Greeks

Among the MSs that were against the establishment of a CU with Turkey, Greece constitutes a special case. At the 9 November 1992 meeting of the AC, the Greek representative tried to prevent the Council from assuming a 'common position' on a set of issues pertaining to the completion of the CU in particular and Turkey–EU relations in general. He could be convinced only with the inclusion of statements criticizing Turkey's policy in the Cyprus problem in the Decision of the Council.[32]

The Clinton administration contemplated a Turkish–Greek common market that, among its other benefits, would lead to lifting of the Greek objection to Turkey's EU membership. Clinton discussed this plan with the Greek PM Papandreou in April 1994.[33] The plan did not come to fruition. At the fourth Summit of the CSCE in Budapest on 5–6 December 1994, to the Turkish PM Çiller and FM Karayalçın, Clinton disclosed his dedication to Turkey's CU and determination to convince Greece.[34]

Greeks blocked another AC meeting on 19 December 1994. They declared that they would lift their veto only in return for accession of the Republic of Cyprus to the EU.[35] Probably, Greece would also stymie the critical decision on the completion of the CU to be negotiated at the AC on 6–7 March 1995.

Germans left their initial skepticism towards Turkey's CU, and, prior to the AC meeting, Germany, France, and the UK agreed to set up a consortium. This consortium would extend financial help to Turkey before the completion of the CU. To a degree, this would obviate the objections of Greece who was claiming that the financial aid Turkey would receive from the Union's budget prior to the establishment of the CU would be a burden.[36] The FMs of the three countries were hoping to convince the Greek FM Karolos Papoulias at the Council of FMs meeting to be held in Brussels on 28 November, but they could not. The Deputy FM Kranidiotis signaled the Greek veto was on the horizon because of such issues as the Kurdish and HR problems in Turkey, Turkey's textile exports to the EU (in the CU, Turkish textile exports would be a threat for the Greek textile sector), financial aid to be extended to Turkey in the context of the CU, the right to free movement that Turks would enjoy once they become an EU member, and Turkey's attitude in the Aegean.[37] German Chancellor Kohl and French President Mitterrand put pressure on Greek PM Papandreou at the Essen European Council on 9–10 December 1994,[38] but they were unable to convince him.[39] Then, Greece added even more items to its list of demands from Turks, such as handing over of a region in Cyprus by the Turkish Cypriots to Greek Cypriots, or clarification of the whereabouts of the Greeks who had been declared missing during the 1974 Cyprus operation.[40]

At this point, Richard Holbrooke, Assistant Secretary of State (ASSTSEC-STATE) for European and Canadian Affairs, came to the forefront. Justifying his nickname 'bulldozer,' Holbrooke first attempted to approach this obstacle 'head-on.' On 14 December 1994, Loucas Tsilas, the Greek ambassador to the US, was summoned to the DOS where he was informed about the discontentment of the US with the objections of Greece.[41] Greeks were unlikely to change their mind. A different strategy had to be devised and put into practice before March.

2.1.1.1 HOLBROOKE'S INVENTION

Faced with this deadlock, Holbrooke thought up a deal that would serve more than one purpose. This deal would be based on having the Greek veto on Turkey's CU lifted in exchange for receiving a date from the EU for the start of the accession negotiations of the Republic of Cyprus. As such, Holbrooke's solution would

1   pave the way for Turkey's CU,
2   make the accession of Cyprus to the EU possible, and
3   constitute a kind of deadline or a fait accompli for both Turkish and Greek Cypriots to resolve the Cyprus issue.

The deal was known even to the lower ranks of the American diplomatic corps before it was put into motion. James Howard Holmes was the Deputy Chief of Mission (DCM) in the US Embassy in Ankara between 1992 and 1995. He spoke about the deal in a hesitant manner:

> I did not witness it. I did not hear about it, I did not understand it at the time. I was aware that an arrangement was being made whereby the EU would accept the CU agreement with Turkey in return for a future—not a specific date but a future—accession of Cyprus to the EU, but it was a very general sort of understanding, not one which was outlined in any specifics or details as far as I was aware. It actually took place after I left there.[42]

Nevertheless, by its nature, this deal had to be kept confidential among the 'relevant parties.' Especially to conceal the US influence on the EU . . . The Republic of Cyprus was already being represented by the Greek administration, and after having secured the CU, perhaps the Turks would not react to the accession of Cyprus. Nevertheless, it was also possible that Turks might react for the following reasons:

1   In the EU, Cyprus would act together with Greece against Turkey's interests;
2   In their relations with the EU, Turks would have to recognize the Greek government of Cyprus as the legitimate government of the island; and

3   The fate of the Greek Cypriots who had established a separate republic (the TRNC) would be unclear.

The Americans preferred to inform the Turks about the deal and ask for their consent. In January 1995, in his talk with Emre Gönensay, a chief advisor to Turkish PM, Holbrooke disclosed the deal and requested Ankara's approval. He added that there was no reason for the Turks to be apprehensive since it was impossible for the Greek Cypriot administration to accede to the EU without the Turkish Cypriots.[43]

2.1.1.2 TURKS' REPLY

Turks' reply to this request is a contentious issue. A number of clues establish the verity of Holbrooke's deal and suggest that Tansu Çiller (the PM) and/or Murat Karayalçın (the Deputy PM and FM) consented to this deal. Şükrü Sina Gürel, who served as a state minister responsible for Cyprus and EU affairs between June 1997 and January 1999, criticized Çiller and Karayalçın of verbally assuring the Americans that Turkey would not object to the accession of Cyprus to the EU. Gürel said that in August 1997, in his talks with Holbrooke in New York and with Thomas Miller in Washington, he was reminded of the assurance given by Karayalçın and/or Çiller. Gürel's reply was that verbal promises made at dinners would not bind Turkey and that no such detail existed in the memory of the Turkish Republic.[44] A second clue is hidden in a letter sent by Clinton to Çiller on 22 February 1995 on the loss of her mother. In the letter, among other details, Clinton thanked Çiller for the help and flexibility shown by Turkey in the Cyprus problem.[45] A third clue shows that Europeans—or at least the British—were aware of the Turks' acquiescence: In 1998, British FS Robin Cook declared that in 1995 Turkey had accepted the initiation of the membership negotiations with Cyprus and this made the CU possible.[46]

Çiller and Karayalçın adamantly denied having given such an assurance. In January 1995, rumors about the deal appeared in the press. On 2 February, British FS Douglas Hurd brought together four of his counterparts at the Lancaster House in London. His guests were Alain Juppe from France, Klaus Kinkel from Germany, Susanna Agnelli from Italy, and Murat Karayalçın from Turkey. 'Turkey–EU relations' was the main item on the agenda. Karayalçın brought the rumors about Holbrooke's deal to the attention of the other participants, expressed his discomfort about them, and stated that such a deal was unacceptable. After the meeting, Karayalçın wrote a letter to Juppe in which the same points were emphasized.[47] For her part, Çiller denied the claims that she had given her implicit consent, said that consent in such a critical issue could never be implicit and maintained that such claims had no legal value.[48] Nihat Akyol, who had been the Deputy Director General for EU Affairs at the TMFA when the deal was allegedly made, also denied that there was such a deal; in his opinion, the establishment of the CU was an automatic process that did not need US help.[49]

As if the issue was not complex enough, Greece threatened that it would veto the EU's planned Eastern enlargement, unless Cyprus was included among the candidates.[50]

In February 1995, Turkish newspapers informed their readers of the 'pressure' the US put on Greece. Perhaps this claim had been intentionally leaked to the press to cover up the deal and to explain the Greeks' change of mind to be seen a few weeks later. According to the newspapers, Tsilas was once again summoned to the DOS on 16 February 1995—this time by Holbrooke himself—and Holbrooke 'warned' Tsilas that Greece should change its position in the CU issue. The news story felt a need to emphasize that in his talk with Tsilas, Holbrooke did not bring up the topic of Cyprus or talk about any sanction against Greece.[51] The same story had it that a démarche was expected to be made on the same issue by Thomas Niles, the USAMB to Greece. On 17 February, an official from the US embassy in Ankara visited the TMFA and informed them about the initiatives taken in this direction.[52]

To keep up appearances, the TMFA declared that the Republic of Cyprus had already been included in the enlargement process, that starting of the negotiations between Cyprus and the EU would not guarantee the accession of Cyprus, and that if the Republic of Cyprus was to be admitted to the Union, Turkey would annex the TRNC.[53]

2.1.1.3 CONCURRENT DECISIONS

At the meeting of the Turkey–EU AC on 6 March 1995, Greeks lifted their veto, and the decision on the establishment of the CU between Turkey and the EC as of 1 January 1996 was taken.[54] On the same day, in a package decision, the GAER approved Turkey's CU and decided that the accession negotiations of Cyprus would start six months after the conclusion of the Turin Intergovernmental Conference of 29 March 1996, taking into consideration its results.[55] The synchronicity between the two events was another token of Holbrooke's deal. At the AC meeting, Karayalçın once again emphasized that the CU and Cyprus were not related and that Turkey was against "unilateral application of the Greek Cypriot administration to the EU." He reiterated the threat the TMFA voiced two days earlier: "Turkey will be left with no option but to take steps towards achieving a similar integration with the Turkish Republic of Northern Cyprus."[56]

2.1.1.4 THE AFTERMATH

Marc Grossman, the USAMB to Turkey when the deal was made, was pleased with the result. "Turkey's entry into the CU was probably one of the greatest accomplishments of Turkish–US relations in 1995" he said.[57] In 2010, he would summarize the reasoning of the US as follows:

> What Richard Holbrooke and I both believed was that if we could figure out how to encourage Turkey, Greece and the EU to bring Cyprus into the EU as a whole, as a bizonal, federated state, that [. . .] incentive of the EU would allow Turkish Cypriots and Greek Cypriots to think more broadly about their future. And, in fact, that is almost what happened.[58]

Holbrooke was more reticent about the deal. In his book *To End a War*, he contented himself with a careful reference to the issue: "With American encouragement, the European Union approved a controversial but important Customs Union with Turkey in the spring of 1995 and moved Cyprus into the first tier of countries to be considered for future membership."[59] He would not neglect to follow up the 'Cyprus' half of the deal: In his speech at the Atlantic Council, a think-tank based in Washington, in June 1995, he expressed his hope that the Greek and Turkish communities of the island would come together as a federal state and accede to the EU as such.[60]

One of the wariest among the US diplomats who witnessed the deal was Thomas Miller. He was the DCM at the US Embassy in Athens when the deal was brokered. During the interview conducted with him for this book, Miller proved to be a mnemonist: He remembered the page number of the aforementioned reference to the deal in Holbrooke's book, but when asked about the deal itself, he said: "I do remember the discussions, I do remember talking to the Europeans about it, I do remember the elements of the deal; I don't remember the details. And I do remember that it was a deal. I . . . I . . . [a short pause] I don't want to mislead you, because my memory is not that good."[61]

Greeks were happy with the result. On 29 June 1995, the spokesperson of the Greek government told the reporters that "the lifting of the veto had been combined with the prospects of a Cyprus accession in the EU, setting of a date for negotiations for its accession and the commencement of pre-accession talks."[62]

The reaction of the Turkish media to the signing of the CU decision was ambivalent. While most of the headlines were announcing the glad tidings about the CU, for a few columnists this was a Pyrrhic victory: They blamed the US for the 'loss' of Cyprus.[63] There even were those who gave the credit for the signing of the decision to France.[64]

The GOT adopted a position of repudiation of the deal. In 1997, Şükrü Sina Gürel, the then Turkish representative at the Council of Europe, summarized this position.

> "That's a wrong impression on the part of such observers and it does not bind Turkey," Gurel said. He recalled that, back then, the TMFA had sent a letter to the EU, making Turkey's position on Cyprus very clear.[65]

2.1.2 Convincing the Other Member States

The US tried to convince the other EU members to approve the CU decision. Early in 1995, Holbrooke said the US mobilized its embassies in the EU MSs for this aim.[66] As veritable as this initiative may be, part of the logic underlying Holbrooke's statements was to claim most of the credit for the realization of Turkey's CU. With the exception of Greece and Austria, EU MSs were already agreeable to the CU. In particular, Germany and Belgium had changed their initial negative attitude and were even trying to persuade Greece.[67]

With the establishment of the CU, industrial products imported from the EU to Turkey would enjoy the same status as the equivalent Turkish exports to the EU had done since 1971, and be subject to no customs duty or quantitative restriction. This prospect was a powerful incentive for the major MSs (especially Germany). Germany held the Presidency of the Council in the July–December 1994 period. German FM Kinkel was hoping to guarantee the establishment of the CU in this period. He was planning to talk with his Greek counterpart Papoulias on 14 November and to convince him. French FM Juppe was also supposed to be present in this talk to help Kinkel. This plan could not be realized due to Kinkel's workload in Germany.[68]

Probably upon Clinton's invitation, even former President Bush got involved in this pursuit: According to Hikmet Çetin, the Turkish FM between 1991 and 1994, without any request from Turks, Bush made phone calls to the UK, France, and Germany in favor of Turkey's CU.[69]

2.1.3 Encouraging Turkey

The US tried to persuade and propel Turks for further reforms so as not to leave any pretext for the EU to delay the CU. In his testimony before the Committee on International Relations (CIR) of the HOR in July 1995, Holbrooke declared that they were encouraging the GOT to take the steps necessary to dispel the concerns of the EP in the field of HR.[70]

Grossman's recollection of the period shows the relative importance of this objective on the US FP agenda then:

> In the Customs Union period, for me—I was in Turkey at that time as ambassador—, the biggest thing was trying to get the Turkish government and the Turkish people to accept certain changes, for example, in laws, releasing a number of journalists from jail, making some changes in the economic structures of Turkey so that Turkey's entry into the Customs Union would be a compatibility question. [. . .] In the period of '93, '94 and '95, we worked very hard to encourage the Turkish government and the Turkish people to make the changes necessary to get into the Customs Union with the European Union.[71]

2.1.4 Garnering Congressional Support

From time to time, pro-Turkish members of the US Congress cared to remind their fellow members of the importance of Turkey's close relations with the EU. Congressman Ed Whitfield delivered a speech about Turkey in the Congress on 3 March 1995, three days before the signing of the CU decision. After bringing Turkey's economic and political problems to the attention of the audience, he continued as follows:

> To help solve these [. . .] problems, it is essential for Turkey's longterm stability that it be admitted to the European Union. The Clinton administration has acknowledged that they have not paid enough attention to this issue, and they are stepping up their activities.
>
> Today, southern Europe is one of the most volatile areas in the world, and it is time for the U.S. Government to step up diplomatic activities to assure admittance of our longtime ally, Turkey, into the European Union.[72]

The fact that Whitfield was a Republican whereas Clinton was a Democrat was an indication of the bipartisan consensus on the necessity of championing Turkey's EU bid.

On 20 November 1995, Amo Houghton, another Republican, delivered a similar speech that ended with the following sentence: "I hope you'll join me in urging the European Parliament to vote in favor of the Customs Union with Turkey on December 14."[73]

2.1.5 Influencing the European Parliament

For the Turkey–EC CU to come into effect, the relevant decision of the AC had to be approved by the EP. It seemed that unless Turkey improved its HR and democracy record substantially, the EP would not give such an approval.[74] The EP had already been against the meeting of the AC on 6 March let alone the signing of the decision.[75]

A high-ranking US official, who preferred to remain anonymous, declared that securing the EP's approval of the decision was made a priority item in the American FP for the year 1995.[76] For the US, this was a difficult task, because although most European leaders were rather positive to the EP's approval of the decision (as they had been of the decision itself), neither they nor Clinton had much influence on the EP. At the end of May, Clinton sent a letter to Turkish PM Çiller, in which he confirmed the continuation of the US support to get a positive result from the EP, and added that the US appreciated Turkey's democratization efforts.[77] In June, at the EU–US Summit in Washington, Turkey was one of the four items on the agenda; Clinton and the US SECSTATE Warren Christopher emphasized this issue to the two other participants, the French President Jacques Chirac, and the President of the European Commission Jacques Santer.[78] In the same month, Christopher delivered a speech in Spain. He laid emphasis on the importance of a democratic Turkey integrated to the transatlantic community and expressed his hope that the EP would approve the CU decision.[79] Meanwhile, in his abovementioned Atlantic Council speech, Holbrooke was inviting the EP to approve the decision,[80] while Stuart Eizentstat, the US Ambassador to the EU, was working "very hard" in Brussels and Strasbourg to convince the Europeans.[81] In early June, Eizenstat was in Turkey and had contacts with politicians and businessmen.[82] On 5 June, together with Grossman, he convened a press meeting in Ankara where he said the EP was expecting—not perfect but—concrete steps from Turkey.[83] In the following months, he sought talks with the chairpersons of the political groups in the EP and some officials of the European Commission.[84] In particular, he tried to convince Claudia Roth, the chairperson of the Green Group, one of the most critical MEPs of Turkey's shortcomings. The point Eizenstat accentuated was that postponing or refusing the establishment of the CU would not contribute to the democratization process in Turkey.[85]

At the historic EU–US Summit in Spain in December, where the famous New Transatlantic Agenda was accepted, Turkey was one of the key topics besides Bosnia and Russia. Spanish PM Felipe González, the President of the Council of the European Union (COEU), and Clinton agreed on the indispensability of the EP's approval of the decision. For them, this approval had to be secured before the 24 December general election in Turkey. They were apprehensive of the possibility of an Islamist and/or anti-European party coming to power.[86]

For the GOT, what the EP expected from them was an onerous task that included, among other things, release of political prisoners, lifting of the state of emergency in southeastern Turkey, and abolishing the Art. 8 of the Anti-Terror Law. Especially because of the separatist terrorist activities afflicting the country, the GOT was reluctant to take any of those steps. The state of emergency would be lifted in as late as 2002 and Art. 8 would be abolished in 2003. In the summer of 1994, the Turkish Parliament adopted a few constitutional amendments that broadened political participation, and in the fall, it amended an anti-terrorist law. Turkey's actual performance was well below the demands of the EP.

Despite this unsatisfactory performance of Turkey, the EP approved the CU decision on 13 December 1995 by a wide margin (with 343 in favor, 149 against, and 36 abstentions).

One main reason behind the MEPs' approval was their eventual conviction that Turkey's CU would be beneficial for the Common Market and that this CU would not mean a guarantee for Turkey's EU membership, but it is also difficult to deny the contribution of the US.

2.2 The Luxembourg European Council

The year 1996 passed without a remarkable development in terms of US involvement in Turkey–EU relations. Americans and Turks were resting up from the previous year's turbulence and had let the Europeans cool down. The US was maintaining a silent vigilance: Sometime between 6 March 1995 and 28 June 1996,[87] Pamela Harriman, the USAMB to France, called Emre Gönensay, the Turkish FM, and asked if the US could do anything for Turkey vis-à-vis the EU.[88]

In 1997, Turkey–EU relations returned to their usual state of chaos. At the Amsterdam European Council scheduled for June, the EU was supposed to finalize the list of the candidate states for the next enlargement round. Turkey's domestic politics and FP preferences were not encouraging for EU candidacy. The PM of the coalition government in Turkey was Erbakan, known for his Islamic, anti-American, and anti-European views. In his election campaign in 1995, he had called for a revision of the CU agreement.[89] On 4 January, under his leadership, Bangladesh, Egypt, Indonesia, Iran, Malaysia, Nigeria, and Pakistan took a decision to establish the D-8 (Developing Eight) group as an alternative to the G7 (Group of Seven) and to the EU.[90] It was thanks to the efforts of such members of the government as Çiller, now the Deputy PM and the FM, and President Demirel that Turkey's European aspirations were intact. Turkey's inclusion in the enlargement list was a crucial matter for Turks, and Americans were determined to work in this direction.[91]

2.2.1 Turkey Plays the NATO Card

On 28 January 1997, Çiller declared that as long as Turkey was excluded from the EU's enlargement process, her government would veto the enlargement of NATO.[92] The US interfered to prevent Turkey's exclusion and crippling of NATO. On the same day, US SECSTATE Albright had a talk with her Dutch counterpart Hans van Mierlo and Sir Leon Brittan, European Commissioner for External Relations and Commissioner for Trade. She emphasized that for the common security of the West, supporting Turkey's emergence as a democratic, prosperous, and tolerant country that would exert its influence on the area extending from the Balkans to the Central Asia was essential. She recommended that the EU confirm Turkey's right to full-membership and apply the Copenhagen criteria[93] not only to the CEECs but also to Turkey. On 29 January, Nicholas Burns, Spokesperson of the DOS and Acting ASSTSECSTATE for Public Affairs, called upon the EU not to make HR problems an obstacle to Turkey's membership. *Reuters* reported this news story together with an interesting comment: "The US took this position, even though the Department of State's own annual human rights report due out tomorrow will criticize Turkey's human rights record."[94]

2.2.2 Religion and Culture

In February 1997, Albright visited ten European capitals. Her agenda included convincing the Europeans to approve Turkey's candidacy.[95] At the

NATO meeting in Brussels, she confirmed the US support to Turkish PM Çiller. With the exception of Rome, all the capitals Albright visited happened to be against Turkey's membership. During these visits, she concluded that the main reason behind the EU's refusal of Turkey was economic; such factors as religion, culture, or HR were of secondary importance. She declared that, this time, convincing the Europeans was much more difficult than it had been in the case of the CU, and that an interim solution might be an option.[96]

Religion and culture were not as insignificant as Albright thought. In Turkey, on 28 February, the NSC[97] took a number of imperious decisions to secure the secular nature of the regime and forced Erbakan to sign them. On 4 March 1997, at a meeting of the European People's Party,[98] the representatives of the Christian Democrats from six countries lead by Helmut Kohl concurred that "the European Union [was] a civilization project and within this civilization project, Turkey [had] no place." Kohl made no reference to religion, though. He also complained about the US pressure for Turkey. At the meeting, it was only Romano Prodi, the Italian PM, who disagreed with the others, but his views were disregarded.[99]

Kohl's words were brought to Burns's attention in a press briefing by a journalist who, for some reason, added a 'religion' dimension to Kohl's words:

QUESTION: [. . .] President of EU, a Christian Democrat,[100] said, "The EU had cultural and Christian values different from Turkey." What is your response to this approach that EU should be a Christian club?

MR. BURNS: We don't write the bylaws of the European Union, and we don't get to decide who gets to be a member. But the United States believes that Turkey—our NATO ally—is a European country, and we don't believe that religion should have anything to do with association in NATO, certainly, and it hasn't had anything to do for 50 years.[101]

In March 1997, Burns made an announcement praising Turkey's recent reforms and declared that the USAMBs in the EU MSs had been instructed to argue for Turkey. Carey Cavanaugh, Director of Southern European Affairs and Acting Special Cyprus Coordinator, visited a few European capitals having in his briefcase files about the Aegean, Cyprus, and Turkey–EU relations.[102]

As the Amsterdam Council drew near, the US speeded its efforts up. On 21 April, Albright met with Hans van den Broek, the EU Commissioner for External Relations, in Washington. They agreed on the need to keep Turkey 'facing westward,' and to invite it to participate in various fora as a member of the West.[103] A few days later, with reference to Çiller's threat to veto NATO's enlargement, Albright said she hoped that Turks did not link their NATO membership to their relations with the EU. She added that her administration was making known to the EU the US support for

Turkey's membership.[104] On 6 May, Strobe Talbott, the Deputy Secretary of State (DEPSECSTATE), stated that Turkey had been a part of the European system since the sixteenth century, and that Turkey's democracy and HR problems would not make it less European.[105]

In June, Kohl came to Washington for the fiftieth anniversary celebrations of the Marshall Plan. On the third of the month, Clinton had a tête-à-tête dinner with him. For this event, Clinton had chosen an Italian restaurant in Georgetown that was Kohl's favorite.[106] In the relaxed atmosphere of the dinner, one of the topics Clinton shared with his guest was the importance of Turkey's inclusion in the list of candidates. Kohl listened to him tranquilly.[107]

On 15 June, the formal establishment of the D-8 group, Erbakan's brainchild, was proclaimed. For the Turkish army, this was one of the last straws that broke the camel's back: On 18 June, Erbakan had to resign because of an implicit threat of coup d'état coming from the military and the mounting pressure from the opposition. One day before his resignation, the Amsterdam Council reached an agreement on the draft Amsterdam Treaty. Turks were pleased with this draft text, because it did not specify the names of the candidate countries but referred to them as 'applicant countries' (Turkey *was* an applicant country). Also, there was not a separate section for Turkey in the text this time (for some time, Turkey had been treated as a separate case in the official texts of the EU).[108] Identification of the candidate states was postponed to the Luxembourg European Council scheduled for December.

Continuing uncertainty for Turkey's candidacy necessitated maintenance of US support. Richard Burt, who had been ASSTSECSTATE for European and Canadian Affairs and the USAMB to Germany in the Reagan period, recommended that the Clinton administration intensify its backing for Turkey.[109] In June, German FM Kinkel declared that despite the US pressure on Turkey's behalf, it was impossible for the EU to admit Turkey. He drew attention to Turkey's HR violations, the problems in Turkey's southeastern region, and the plight of the Turkish economy. He added that cultural issues did not play any role.[110] Also, for Germany, the accession of the CEECs to the EU had precedence over that of Turkey.

Turks' complacency emanating from their wishful inferences from the draft of the Amsterdam Treaty was short-lived. The Agenda 2000 document[111] the European Commission presented on 15 July 1997 contained two details that were disappointing for the Turks and challenging for the Americans:

1. The Commission recommended the accession negotiations be initiated with the Republic of Cyprus regardless to whether the Cyprus problem is solved or not; and
2. Turkey was not included among the 11 applicant countries whose preparations for accession were to be reinforced.

With these two details Holbrooke was not happy. He had been appointed as the Presidential Special Envoy for Cyprus and the Balkans in June. A few days after his appointment, he was reconsidering his deal:

> [W]e must either change the EU attitude [towards Turkey] or recognize that we were getting the component elements of the negotiation in the wrong order, trying to make progress on Cyprus itself before the Turks would be ready for it.[112]

In his column published on 22 July 1997, Altan Öymen, a prominent Turkish columnist, described the Agenda 2000 document as a bomb that undermined the ongoing talks between the sides of the Cyprus problem and asked whether this development was something the US had expected—or preferred.[113] The US *was* prepared for such a development: On the previous day, it had promised to intervene to make sure that unless the Cyprus problem was solved, the island would not become an EU member.[114] In appearance, everyone was in agreement with the US. Nevertheless, the US did not want to leave this process to chance:

> The Greeks, the EU, the UN and the Americans all hope that talks on Cyprus's future can run parallel to those on its entry to the EU. [. . .] America, too, will use all its clout to persuade Turkey to help strike a Cyprus deal. Just as well that Richard Holbrooke [. . .] will soon become actively (and no doubt militantly) engaged.[115]

A few days later, German FM Kinkel reiterated that the membership of Cyprus would not be possible until the problems were solved. He complained about the pressure the US exerted on Turkey's behalf and added that this pressure did not yield any result.[116]

2.2.3 Two Bluffs

Turkey initiated two bluffs in August 1997:

1. On 6 August, Turkey and the TRNC signed an 'association council agreement.' The aim of this agreement was to promote economic and financial integration between the parties and achieve partial integration between their foreign, defense, and security policies.[117] This was a concrete step to show that Turkey's declarations of intention to annex Cyprus were not empty threats. The US stated that this move of Turkey would preclude the solution of the Cyprus problem.[118] As indicated above, in this month, Holbrooke and Miller told Gürel that Turkey had consented to the 'CU deal.'[119]
2. The stillborn Turkish–US free-trade agreement project of 1990 was resurrected. Phil Gramm, a Republican senator, visited Turkey in August

to promote the project. In his opinion, such an agreement would be a "signal to Europe of Turkey's importance as a partner and an economic market." Turkish FM Cem's initial reaction was positive: "The world is not limited to the EU. Our ministry is seriously working on the feasibility for a free-trade agreement with the US. [. . .] The EU [is] likely to lose its position as a preferential partner in the allocation of important contracts in Turkey." However, the project was interred back for a few reasons:

a   It would not be wise to imperil the country's prospect of accession that was still the priority of the government. To this aim, Cem was about to visit a few European capitals.
b   The US did not want to give the impression it was trying to supplant the EU in Turkey's FP.
c   There were a few technical factors that precluded such a project: Legislation pertaining to industrial property rights was far from perfect in Turkey; the US was applying import quotas to certain goods (especially textiles) originating from Turkey; and the agreement Turkey and the US signed in the previous year to prevent double-taxation had still not been ratified by the Turkish Parliament and the US Congress.[120]

Towards the end of August, DOS Spokesperson James Rubin announced that if Turkey, together with Cyprus, were given a membership perspective to the EU, this would be conducive to the solution of the Cyprus problem. The EU declared that it would not change its attitude in this issue.[121]

Rauf Denktaş, leader of the TRNC, further complicated the issue: He revealed that he would resist the admission of Cyprus to the EU as a federation unless the TRNC was recognized as a political entity; as long as the Turkish entity on the island is seen as a community but not a state, the federal solution would be unfair.[122] In this process, even the application of the TRNC to the EU for membership was considered as an option.[123]

The Luxembourg Council was approaching, and Holbrooke was trying to find a practical[124] solution to the Cyprus problem, which would also increase Turkey's chances to be recognized as a candidate. For this purpose, he even mobilized the private sector and inquired about economic cooperation schemes applicable among Cyprus, Greece, and Turkey.[125]

In the first half of November, almost a month before the Luxembourg Council, Holbrooke came to Ankara. He informed the Turkish authorities that the US would strive to improve Turkey's position in Luxembourg. He had visited Rome before coming to Ankara and was planning to visit Bonn and Brussels afterwards. He recommended Turks to rethink their position on integrating the TRNC.[126]

Towards the end of November, Santer, President of the European Commission, criticized the pressure the US put on the EU for Turkey. He stated that it was normal for the US to have an opinion on this matter but that the EU would take its decisions on its own.[127]

On 5 December, Kohl and Chirac exchanged views in Bonn. They agreed that if excluded from the EU, Turkey would get closer to the US, which would not be in the benefit of Europe. They decided to find a formula that would also be acceptable for Greece.[128]

2.2.4 SECI

A few days before the Luxembourg Council, at a time when Turkey was signaling that it intended to sever its relations with the EU, Richard Schifter, a special advisor to Albright, visited Ankara.[129] Schifter was the founding father of the Southeast Cooperation Initiative (SECI). Through extensive consultations with the EU,[130] SECI had been established on 6 December 1996 to allow southeast European countries to have access to resources that would help them rebuild and stabilize. Turkey was among the initial members of the organization. One of the projects in the Initiative was about trade facilitation. The purpose of Schifter's visit was to convince the GOT to participate in this project. He said that following the last waves of enlargement of NATO and the EU, some countries in southeastern Europe felt abandoned by the West, but, he continued, the interest of the US in the region was intact. The project would be run by the USG and private sector, the World Bank, as well as the governments and the private sectors of the SECI MSs, and be sponsored by the US, Italy, Switzerland, the World Bank, and some international financial institutions. Despite Schifter's personal zeal, this project did not have a promising start.[131] Turkey was not positive to SECI in general and to the trade facilitation project in particular, because there were more than 20 of such international projects all focusing on southeast Europe. Moreover, Turkey would prefer the projects initiated by the EU, not the US.[132]

2.2.5 Turks' Disillusionment

The Luxembourg European Council was held on 12–13 December 1997. The Conclusions of the Council conceded Turkey's eligibility for membership but refused to grant the country a candidate status.[133] The Council made "strengthening of Turkey's link with the European Union" conditional on not only Turkey's fulfillment of the Copenhagen criteria[134] but also its pursuit of its reforms

> including the alignment of human rights standards and practices on those in force in the European Union; respect for and protection of minorities; the establishment of satisfactory and stable relations between Greece and Turkey; the settlement of disputes, in particular by legal process, including the International Court of Justice; and support for negotiations under the aegis of the UN on a political settlement in Cyprus.[135]

Also, the Council "decided to launch an accession process comprising the ten Central and East European applicant States and Cyprus." Turks saw a stark contrast between the Council's treatment of these 11 states and of Turkey.

Turkish PM Mesut Yılmaz received the bad news at the Brussels airport on his way to the US.[136] He announced on the spot that Turkey would not participate in the European Conference scheduled for March 1998,[137] and that if Turkey's candidacy was not approved at the Cardiff European Council in June 1998, he would withdraw Turkey's application and seek a 'strategic partnership' with the US.[138] Deputy PM Ecevit commented that the US was able to understand and interpret Turkey's importance and the state of world affairs better; if Turkey developed its relations with the US and the Far Eastern countries, it would become clear that Europe was not the only option for Turkey.[139] On 12 December 1997, Hikmet Çetin, the Chairman of the Turkish Parliament, received the USAMB Mark R. Parris. Çetin stated that the US had always supported Turkey's close relations with the EU, and announced that the agreement on the prevention of double-taxation, signed between Turkey and the US, had finally been ratified by the Turkish Parliament.[140] On 15 December, DOS Deputy Spokesperson James Foley declared that drawing irreversible conclusions from the outcomes of the Luxembourg Council would not be wise.[141]

Turks' reaction did not register with the officials of the European Commission. When a journalist asked Hans van den Broek, the Commissioner for External Relations, whether Yılmaz's words were significant, the following dialogue ensued:

VAN DEN BROEK: Listen to him once again after his return from the US.
JOURNALIST: Will he get a different message from the US?
VAN DEN BROEK: Yes.
JOURNALIST: It seems that either you have consulted with the US, or you know the Americans well.
VAN DEN BROEK: The second is true.[142]

As van den Broek guessed, Yılmaz was soothed by Clinton and Holbrooke in the US. On 19 December, Yılmaz and Clinton discussed the rebuff Turkey faced in Luxembourg. Only hours before Yılmaz's arrival, Clinton had had a conversation with Chirac on the phone and, a few days later, sent him a letter. With Chirac, Clinton agreed on the necessity of anchoring Turkey to Europe.[143] Clinton informed Yılmaz about his call to Chirac. He added that although he had done his best, he could not secure Turkey's candidacy. He recommended Yılmaz to look to the future: "Where do we go from here?" he asked. He promised to strive to change the Europeans' mind. He underlined the fact that the UK would assume the Presidency of the Council the following month and gave his word that the British would help Turkey. His recommendation to Yılmaz was not to burn the bridges with the EU.

While in the US, Yılmaz had a long and detailed talk with Albright. She shared with him her impressions of the meeting of NATO FMs held in Brussels on 16–17 December. She related that an important part of her conversations had been on Turkey's reaction to the Conclusions of the Luxembourg Council. Marc Grossman—now the ASSTSECSTATE for European Affairs—who was also present at the talk, said the Europeans were trying to find a way to rectify their mistake. Yılmaz replied that he would not burn the bridges but that he would keep insisting to secure Turkey's candidacy.[144]

This approach of the Clinton administration was endorsed by some prominent analysts. Zalmay Khalilzad from the RAND Corporation recommended that Clinton use his influence on Turks to prevent them from overreacting to the Luxembourg European Council.[145]

There was one issue, however, Yılmaz was still uncomfortable with in Turkey–US relations. In an interview conducted in this US visit, he said Turkey had been deceived in the case of Cyprus.[146]

2.2.6 Killing Two Birds with One Stone

The Clinton administration would not like to see a deterioration in Turkey–EU relations. Nonetheless, when inevitable, such a deterioration could open up some opportunities for the US. This was the case when Yılmaz was in the US:

> The first U.S. action following the Yılmaz visit was to allow American manufacturers of attack helicopters to bid on a Turkish contract for 145 choppers. Assistant secretaries of state John Shattuck and Marc Grossman, seizing the leverage afforded by Turkey's turning away from Europe and European arms makers, negotiated an agreement with Yılmaz making the helicopter sale contingent on improvements in Turkey's human rights performance. [. . .] Both officials insist that the Turkish military agreed to these conditions.
> [. . .] After the Shattuck-Grossman-Yılmaz deal was struck, a consortium of Israeli and Russian companies announced that they would also bid on the helicopter contract, possibly undercutting the U.S. position. Therefore, partial or even cosmetic compliance with the agreement's human rights provisions [might] prove to be enough for an administration that [would] be under heavy pressure from arms exporters to complete the $3 billion deal.[147]

According to Turkish newspapers Yılmaz refused to negotiate such a deal.[148] This agreement would serve two purposes: Not only would the American manufacturers have made profit but also Turkey's HR record would be improved, thereby enhancing Turkey's standing vis-à-vis the US Congress and the EU. "In the end, the Clinton administration decided to pursue the sale. The Turkish government, ironically, was not sufficiently convinced of the administration's commitment and decided to delay its decision until after the 2000 presidential election."[149]

In this visit, Yılmaz also signed a 2.5-billion-dollar deal with Boeing to buy 49 commercial 737–800 aircraft.[150]

2.3 The Helsinki European Council

The US was instrumental in the EU's change of mind regarding Turkey's candidate status in the period between the Luxembourg European Council of 1997 and the Helsinki European Council of 1999. In March 1998, Jean-Claude Juncker, the PM of Luxembourg, declared that no MS had supported Turkey at the Luxembourg Council,[151] which meant that a hard work was waiting for the US.

2.3.1 The Year 1998: Focusing on Greece and Germany

The year 1998 passed with the discussions about the operation the US was planning to conduct in Iraq. Turkey–EU relations were overshadowed by these discussions;[152] references the US policy-makers to Turkey-EU relations were few.

In March, Holbrooke said by not including Turkey among the candidate countries, the EU complicated the Cyprus problem.[153] Turks insisted that unless the existence of the TRNC was somehow reflected in the Cyprus–EU negotiations, Turkey would not resume its relations with the EU. Thomas Miller, the Special Representative of the DOS to Cyprus, came to Ankara to convince the GOT not to sever their relations with the EU.[154] In May, Holbrooke's mission as a special envoy ended. While leaving the island, he convened a press conference and said the EU was right in inviting Cyprus to accession negotiations as a whole and wrong in not doing the same thing for Turkey. He criticized the Turkish Cypriots for their insistence on the withdrawal of the membership application of Cyprus and on the recognition of the TRNC.[155] Amidst that commotion, a positive development went unnoticed: On 4 March 1998, the European Commission submitted to the Council a communication entitled "The European Strategy for Turkey: The Commission's Initial Operational Proposals to Prepare Turkey for Accession."

As envisaged by Yılmaz, Turkey declined the invitation to participate in the meetings of the European Conference in London on 12 March 1998. The accession negotiations between Cyprus and the EU were launched on 31 March. The island was represented by the Greek Cypriots.

At the end of April, Albright declared that the most serious point of disagreement between the US and Germany was Turkey. In her visit to China, she even requested help for Turkey from Jiang Zemin, the General Secretary of the Communist Party.[156] When Clinton visited Germany in May, he surprised Kohl with his speech at the official welcoming ceremony, where he said the EU should open its doors to Turkey.[157] Kohl pouted at Clinton's words.[158] After Germany, Clinton came to Birmingham for the G8 Summit. There too, Turkey–EU relations and Cyprus were on his agenda. The Clinton administration's request from the EU was that the steps Turkey took in improving its democracy and HR record be rewarded. In their opinion, the recent increase in the HR violations in Turkey was partly due to the mistreatment of the country at the Luxembourg Council; reformists had been left alone in domestic politics.[159]

This constant and conspicuous US backing for Turkey soon became a reference point. Prior to the 27 September election in Germany, SPD (*Sozialdemokratische Partei Deutschlands*—The Social Democratic Party of Germany) leader Gerhard Schröder revealed that, being in favor of Turkey's accession to the EU, his view regarding Turkey–EU relations was parallel to that of Clinton.[160] In his visit to the US, Schröder promised Clinton to do his best to prevent Turkey's exclusion.[161]

On 5 December 1998, Clinton brought together in the White House 16 leaders of the Greek lobby in the US. He told them that Turkey's EU membership was the 'primary aim' of himself and of the US policy regarding the region. This aim, he said, could be achieved in cooperation with Europeans. He added that he was also trying to solve the Cyprus problem and improve the Turkish–Greek relations altogether. He emphasized that this strategy was wholeheartedly approved by Blair. It was his hope that Schröder would cooperate with him. After Clinton, Sandy Berger, Clinton's NSA, conferred with the Greeks and explained them the details of Clinton's policy package. He told them that Turkey's EU membership would mean the end of the Turkish 'occupation' in Cyprus.[162]

2.3.2 The Year 1999: The Eve of the Grand Finale

The year 1999 started with an unpleasant surprise. The program of the Ecevit government, announced on 12 January, did not include any reference to the EU.[163] This was a warning sign for the Europeans. Nevertheless, there was some good news too. Germany, who would hold the Presidency of the Council in the January–June 1999 period, declared its intention to end Turkey's exclusion.[164] Austria, who held the Presidency in the previous term, had already made a similar declaration.[165] One of the factors behind this change was the dominance of the Social Democratic governments in Europe: In 1999, 13 out of the 15 governments in the EU were from the center left. Social Democrats had generally been more positive towards Turkey. In the notable case of Germany, following the 16 years of the Christian–Liberal coalition, a coalition was formed between the SPD and the Greens as the result of the 27 September 1998 election. SPD's Gerhard Schröder (the new chancellor), and Greens' leader Joschka Fischer (the vice-chancellor and FM) were sympathetic to Turkey's cause. In April 1999, at the German Federal Parliament, Schröder said he 'decisively' backed Turkey's bid for EU candidacy.[166] In May, Ecevit sent a letter to Schröder, where he emphasized Turkey's resolution to move forward with a series of reforms and expressed his expectation that at the Cologne European Council to be held under Germany's Presidency, Turkey would be proclaimed a candidate. In his letter of response, Schröder stated that he would do his best at the Council. Drawing on this exchange of letters, Turkish and German officials prepared a paragraph that would declare Turkey's candidacy and emphasize the resolution of the GOT to implement the necessary reforms and to find a constructive solution to the problems in its southeastern region. This paragraph would be included in the Presidency Conclusions of the Council. However, at the Council on 3–4 June 1999, this plan was thwarted by Greece who was seconded by Sweden and Italy.[167] The US believed that Schröder did his best at the Council and that there were some other MSs that hid behind Greece.[168] The replacement of Theodoros Pangalos, the Greek FM known for his uncompromising attitude towards Turkey, by George Papandreou, whom Turks regarded as a more cooperative politician, on 18 February 1999 somewhat eased the minds of Turks and Americans.

In mid-June, the US Secretary of Defense (SECDEF) William Cohen visited Turkey. He repeated that the US preferred a bizonal federation in Cyprus. Ecevit replied that Turkey was not in favor of the federation option anymore, because, he continued, after the accession of Cyprus to the EU had been made possible, it became clear that the southern part of the island would be united with Greece. Now, Turkey was arguing for two separate states in Cyprus.[169]

On 17 August 1999, a destructive earthquake occurred in Turkey. The Greek government announced that in order to help the earthquake victims it was ready to lift its veto on the provision of funds to Turkey under the 1995 CU decision. Philip T. Reeker, Deputy Spokesperson and Deputy ASSTSECSTATE, welcomed the news and announced that the total earthquake assistance the USG itself extended to Turkey had exceeded 10 million dollars.[170] Albright visited the regions devastated by the earthquake. She proposed a new bilateral trade agreement and expressed her encouragement to Turkey's efforts to join the EU.[171] When the US and Europeans were at the height of their sympathy for Turks, Turkish FM Cem delivered a threat of *coup de grâce* to Turkey–EU relations: "If its candidacy is not approved at the Helsinki European Council" he said "Turkey will take the candidacy issue out of its agenda."[172] Whilst these words must have been a piece of good news to the ears of certain EU MSs, they presumably were alarming for the US.

In the first half of September, there were strong signals from all the MSs, except Greece, that Turkey's candidacy would be approved at the Helsinki Council.[173] Thus, in Ecevit's official visit to the US between 26 September and 1 October, 'Turkey–EU relations' was not an item on his agenda.[174] To Ecevit, Clinton reiterated his determination to champion Turkey's EU vocation.[175] Mainly due to the Greek lobby in the US, he was unable to offer a substantial economic aid package,[176] but he promised his backing for the Baku-Tbilisi-Ceyhan pipeline project and in Turkey's negotiations with the IMF. He said he would try to increase the quota the US was applying to textile imports from Turkey.[177] He assured Ecevit that going back to the pre-1974 period in Cyprus would be impossible.[178]

In his speech at the press conference he convened upon his return, Ecevit sounded as if he had come from Belgium. He stated that the EU's doors were still closed to Turkey because of Greece but that he was satisfied with his visit in general.[179] Meanwhile, the Greek government took a positively surprising step for Turks and announced that it could lift its veto, if the following two conditions were fulfilled:

1   A roadmap—which would also include Greek demands—should be drawn up for Turkey's accession process, and Turkey should be urged to follow it; and
2   The EU should declare at the Helsinki Council that the accession process of Cyprus would not be hindered even if the Cyprus problem was not solved.[180]

2.3.3 Turkey's Homework or in Search of Lost Time

In parallel to these diplomatic maneuvers, Turkey was striving to meet the Copenhagen political criteria. In the 1998–1999 period, the GOT introduced some legal reforms regarding such issues as torture, civil servants, HR, or organized crime. These reforms were far from satisfactory, which would make the job of the Clinton administration more difficult. These reforms were brought to the attention of the Clinton administration by Ecevit in September 1999.[181] In November, Albright announced that she appreciated the reforms, said that whenever she met one of her colleagues from "the EU cabinet," she would tell him that Turkey was eligible for candidacy and heralded that there were important developments concerning Turkey.[182]

On 13 October 1999, the European Commission published its Regular Report for Turkey. This report did not proclaim Turkey's candidacy in formal terms, but Turkey's inclusion in some processes and programs of the Union together with other candidate countries was interpreted as an indirect and unofficial recognition of Turkey's candidacy.[183] The DOS announced that it was pleased with the report.[184]

2.3.4 Clinton's Visit to Turkey

It was following this long and toilsome period that Clinton paid the aforementioned visit to Turkey in November 1999. The waters were calm now, and apparently the European leaders—including that of Greece—would recognize Turkey's candidacy at Helsinki. Clinton and his team had a right to expect to be welcome in Turkey, and Turks did their best to fulfill this expectation.

During his five-day visit, Clinton continued to reiterate his commitment to Turkey's European prospects on every occasion, such as his speech at the US Embassy in Ankara[185] or the speech he delivered to American and Turkish business leaders.[186] At the press conference convened before the dinner on 15 November, he spoke as follows:

> I think if you [. . .] were to go home tonight and make a list of the big problems you think the world could face in the next 10 or 20 years, every one of them would be strengthened if Turkey were a full partner in a Europe that respected religious and cultural diversity and shared devotion to democracy and human rights.
>
> [. . .]
>
> I will continue to talk to the leaders of Europe. [. . .] I feel very strongly that one of the four or five key questions to the future of this whole part of the world is whether Turkey is a full partner with the European Union.[187]

Clinton recommended Ecevit to reciprocate the gesture of Greeks who, for the first time, supported Turkey's close relations with the EU: "If it will not have a great cost for you, could you possibly make a goodwill gesture? If you do, this will also help me in my effort to defend you before Athens, the European Union and Congress" he said. In his opinion, reopening of the Theological School of Halki in Turkey would be a good idea.[188] Ecevit listened to him silently. After Clinton's visit, in reply to a question, Ecevit declared that Clinton had "said nothing that could be interpreted as a deal."[189]

Some Greek newspapers wrote that Clinton was like a Turkish ambassador in the EU.[190] After leaving Turkey, Clinton flew to Athens "to face the fury of tens of thousands of leftwing demonstrators in what is proving to be his most controversial visit yet to a Nato member state."[191] Greek PM Simitis and his FM Papandreou told Clinton that they were in favor of Turkey's candidacy in principle, but in the face of the negative attitude of the Greek public, Turkey had to take some steps to have its candidacy approved by the Greek government. Among their demands were Turkey's recanting its claim that if Greece was to extend its territorial waters to 12 nautical miles, this would be regarded as a casus belli, accepting the jurisdiction of the International Court of Justice (ICJ) over Aegean disputes, and declaring in writing that Turkey had no designs on Greek soil. Simitis and Papandreou were expecting to get—at least an implicit—approval of these points from their guest.[192] As if he was representing Turkey . . .

As the Helsinki Council approached, the US intensified its efforts. Grossman contacted high-ranking European diplomats. Greece was the point of focus in this process. Clinton made a phone call to the Greek PM Simitis.[193] Greek newspapers wrote that Simitis was inclined to say "yes" to Turkey's candidacy but that he would give his decision at the last minute since this would be the most difficult decision in his political career. The newspapers added that some of his preconditions would be satisfied by Germany and the US to help him make up his mind.[194]

In early November 1999, US Congressman Amo Houghton wrote a 'Dear Colleague' letter to Martti Ahtisaari, President of Finland, the country that held the presidency of the COEU. This letter was signed by 26 of Houghton's fellow congressmen from both parties. The letter stated that

> no progress was recorded in Turkey's membership while the EU expedited the membership procedures of Central European countries which had been under the communist rule until very recently. [. . .] Approval of its EU candidacy would pave the way to economic, political and social reforms. On the other hand, if it is rejected for the second time, Turkey will have to consider other alternatives which might bear unpleasant results also for the U.S., the letter explained.[195]

2.3.5 Last-Minute Preparations

A few days before the Council, Eric S. Edelman, the USAMB to Finland,[196] Marc Grossman, the ASSTSECSTATE for European Affairs, Nicholas Burns, the USAMB to Greece, Mark R. Parris, the USAMB to Turkey, and James F. Jeffrey, the DCM to Turkey, initiated a campaign for Turkey.[197]

In the meantime, the UN Secretary-General Kofi Annan started the Cyprus talks in New York. A Turkish diplomat foresaw that these talks and the Helsinki Council meeting would affect each other. He said if Turkey's candidacy was not declared at Helsinki, the Cyprus talks would be unlikely to bear fruit.[198]

On 9 December, one day before the European Council, Simitis came to Helsinki. He had a meeting with Paavo Lipponen, PM of Finland that held the Presidency of the Council, and Javier Solana, High Representative for the CFSP. He told them that if he was to approve Turkey's candidacy, he would not compromise on three of his demands:

1   Turkey's recognition of the ICJ's jurisdiction in the issue of the continental shelf in the Aegean (if the negotiations to be commenced with Turkey on this issue could not be concluded by 2003, the problem would be taken to the ICJ);
2   Accession of Cyprus to the EU under the governance of the present Greek Cypriot government who would also represent the Turkish Cypriots; and
3   Drawing up of a roadmap for Turkey's EU accession that would be separate from those of the other candidates.[199]

The first draft of the Presidency Conclusions that had been in preparation since October was finalized by incorporating the wishes of Simitis into the text. This draft reached Ankara in the morning of 9 December. Turks got disappointed with the text. Cem declared that they were not optimistic about the Helsinki Council and that Turkey would refuse the candidate status if this status was to be predicated on unacceptable conditions. His declaration alarmed the embassies of the EU MSs in Ankara; they started sending despatches marked 'urgent' to their capitals. In this strained atmosphere, Clinton wrote a letter addressed to Ecevit and Simitis. He requested from Simitis not to raise any difficulties and from Ecevit not to miss this opportunity.[200]

2.3.6 *Turks' Sensitivities Are Addressed*

In the morning session of the European Council on 10 December, a second draft of the Presidency Conclusions was completed. The only alteration made to the first draft was a change from '2003' to '2004' in the point pertaining to the ICJ. This text was immediately faxed to Ankara around 12:00. Then, there ensued a heated exchange of telephone calls between Helsinki and Ankara. Turks were unhappy with the imposition of the ICJ jurisdiction upon them and with the existence of a deadline for an ICJ settlement. For them, under these conditions, Cyprus's membership was not acceptable.[201] Concerning Simitis's third precondition, they doubted that the EU would extend the financial aid it had promised to Turkey.[202]

In line with Turkey's concerns, a few small modifications were made on the text. With the addition of a comma, the passage about the 2004 deadline was changed to mean that the deadline would be for the review of the European Council, not for the settlement of the disputes through the ICJ.[203] As for Cyprus, although the relevant section did state that the island was going to become an EU member regardless to whether a settlement is reached or not (which meant a possibility of exclusion of the TRNC) and although it was stipulated that Turkey's accession process would be influenced by the developments in the Cyprus issue, Turkey was comforted by the inferences that this paragraph referred to 'Cyprus' not 'the Republic of Cyprus,' and that a solution for the Cyprus problem was not a precondition for Turkey's EU membership.[204] At 16.00 Lipponen sent a fax message to Ankara in which he gave assurances on these points. Ankara and Helsinki agreed that Lipponen's fax be put into the form of an official letter that would be brought to Ankara by Solana and Günter Verheugen, European Commissioner for Enlargement.[205]

2.3.7 *The Text Is Finalized*

The relevant sections of the final draft of the Conclusions appeared as follows:

> Para. 4. The European Council reaffirms the inclusive nature of the accession process, which now comprises 13 candidate States within a single framework. The candidate States are participating in the accession

process on an equal footing. They must share the values and objectives of the European Union as set out in the Treaties. In this respect the European Council stresses the principle of peaceful settlement of disputes in accordance with the United Nations Charter and urges candidate States to make every effort to resolve any outstanding border disputes and other related issues. Failing this they should within a reasonable time bring the dispute to the International Court of Justice. The European Council will review the situation relating to any outstanding disputes, in particular concerning the repercussions on the accession process and in order to promote their settlement through the International Court of Justice, at the latest by the end of 2004. [. . .]

[. . .]

Para. 9. (a) The European Council welcomes the launch of the talks aiming at a comprehensive settlement of the Cyprus problem on 3 December in New York and expresses its strong support for the UN Secretary-General's efforts to bring the process to a successful conclusion.

(b) The European Council underlines that a political settlement will facilitate the accession of Cyprus to the European Union. If no settlement has been reached by the completion of accession negotiations, the Council's decision on accession will be made without the above being a precondition. In this the Council will take account of all relevant factors.

[. . .]

Para. 12 The European Council welcomes recent positive developments in Turkey as noted in the Commission's progress report, as well as its intention to continue its reforms towards complying with the Copenhagen criteria. Turkey is a candidate State destined to join the Union on the basis of the same criteria as applied to the other candidate States. Building on the existing European strategy, Turkey, like other candidate States, will benefit from a pre-accession strategy to stimulate and support its reforms.[206]

Now, what was left was to get the Turks' 'consent' to this final version.

2.3.8 Convincing the Turks

Grossman's recollection of this episode is revealing in the sense that it contains a Freudian slip. Perhaps as an indication of that the Clinton administration preferred to bypass Ecevit whenever possible, he confuses PM Ecevit and President Demirel:

> When the decision was taken in Helsinki, I believe that Solana then had to fly to Ankara to try to convince Mr. Demirel that it was a good decision. While he was flying there, he called me and said "Could you have President call PM Demirel to say this is a good deal?" And I said "I will

try." I called Sandy Berger, and Sandy Berger said: "Of course." [. . .] And President Clinton called Mr. Demirel or Mr. Ecevit, and said: "Look, it is not perfect, no, it is not perfect, but this is good. And please, please, if you can, say 'yes.'" [207]

Ecevit received Clinton's call at around 17:00. Clinton was calling from Air Force One on his way to his home state Arkansas. He congratulated Ecevit and told him that this outcome should be considered as a victory. Ecevit replied that unless his aforementioned concerns were addressed, it would be difficult for him to approach to the process positively. Ecevit and Demirel received similar calls from Chirac and Schröder.[208]

At 23.55, Ecevit finally convened with Solana and Verheugen. They talked for half an hour, and Solana gave him Lipponen's letter.

2.3.9 The Grand Finale

At 00.30, Ecevit made a historical declaration heralding Turkey's candidacy. A few hours later, Clinton issued a statement congratulating Turks and appreciating the efforts of the European leaders, particularly stating the names of Simitis and Lipponen.[209]

In the following days, Clinton sent letters to Simitis and Ecevit. He thanked Simitis for his 'responsible' stance in Helsinki. He said "your country can look forward to playing a leadership role in the region for the achievement of stability, prosperity and peace."[210] He wrote to Ecevit that recognition of Turkey's candidate status "would have lasting benefits [. . .] for all EU members and the United States."[211] On 17 December, Clinton received Ahtisaari, Lipponen, and Prodi. He told them that his administration was very much pleased with the EU's decision to offer candidacy to Turkey and Turkey's acceptance of it; this decision would have a positive impact on the future of Turkey and Europe as well as on the problems in Cyprus and in the Aegean.[212]

2.3.10 Garnering the Credit

Citing diplomatic resources, Turkish state television TRT reported that Turkey would have said "no" if Solana had not come to Turkey.[213] The Clinton administration had a different version of the story. On 17 January 2000, Clinton was at a reception held in his honor by John Catsimatidis, a Greek-American businessman who was one of the biggest fundraisers of Clinton. There, Clinton reiterated that the Cyprus problem was one of the core issues of the US FP agenda. He declared that he had emphasized to Turks that Turkey's admission to the EU was conditional upon improving Turkish–Greek relations and the solution of the Cyprus problem. In reply to the complaints that the US was unresponsive to the demands of the Greeks and Greek Cypriots, he revealed a detail which, if true, may be the best evidence of the extent of the US interference into the EU affairs in the Clinton era: He said it was he and Tony Blair who prepared the part of draft text the Conclusions of the Helsinki Council, wherewith Turkey's candidacy was proclaimed. The text, he added, was in line with the predilections of the Greek President Clerides and they had gotten Greek PM Simitis's approval of it before the other leaders.[214] In that atmosphere Clinton may have had to overstate his influence on the Helsinki Council, but Grossman, too, was using a similar hyperbolic discourse in an interview conducted for this book:

> It was very exciting, very interesting and very exhausting, but our ambassador to Finland at that time Eric Edelman who then became ambassador to Turkey, and Madeline Albright and the President, and Sandy Berger, and myself . . . Everyday. . . I tried really hard to support that effort in Helsinki in '99. It was a very big thing for us, and we were delighted, delighted, delighted when the EU made the offer and PM Ecevit accepted the offer. We thought it was a huge breakthrough. Then at that point, since the US is not a member of the EU, we continued to encourage the two to sides to get going. And then when negotiations opened formally on the chapters, I think people in the US said: "Well, our work here is basically completed; this is now going to go forward."
> [. . .]
> With Turkey and with the EU. . . With very forward-thinking people in Britain, in France, at that time, in Germany and in the EU. . . Dr. Solana . . . [. . .] The US and Bill Clinton, in particular, worked really hard. Do not forget: Helsinki is December '99. Right? Clinton was in Turkey in November '99, and gave a great speech to the Turkish Parliament. So, we showed, I think, we were trying our best. We really worked very hard to say to the EU "Please, this is your opportunity. 'Helsinki '99': This is the place to breakthrough here."[215]

2.3.11 The Immediate Post-Helsinki Period

Once Turkey's candidacy was secured, Turks temporarily desisted from importuning the US for help against the EU, but the Clinton administration did not stop furthering Turkey's prospects. In July 2000, James Dobbins, ASSTSECSTATE for European Affairs, visited Turkey. 'Turkey–EU relations' was a topic on his agenda. He had talks with the GOT, business circles, and civilian society organizations. He left Turkey with the impression that at all levels of the Turkish society those who favored Turkey's EU membership were in majority.[216] When the newly elected Turkish President Sezer was in the US for the Millennium Summit of the UN on 6–8 September, he was among the eight leaders Clinton made a personal appointment with (160 leaders participated in the Summit). His demands from Clinton were better terms for Turkey's textile exports to the US, increase in the investments of US firms in Turkey, and 'energetic efforts' against the Armenian lobby in the US Congress, but nothing about the EU. Nevertheless, Clinton did not forget to emphasize Turkey's European journey and Sezer's mission in it.[217] Previously, Sezer was the chief justice of the Turkish Constitutional Court and known for his dedication to secularism. Clinton had high expectations from him in the HR and democratization reforms required by the EU.

European leaders remained silent for some time after the Helsinki Council. Then, some of them expressed their discontent with the US intervention in the Council. In April 2000, Giscard d'Estaing, former President of France, said that Turkey had no place in the European project and that it was with the US pressure that Turkey had been given candidate status.[218]

2.4 The Accession Partnership Document

On 8 November 2000, the European Commission made public the APD for Turkey. Turkey's EU membership would depend on the country's realization of the objectives set out in this document.

On 4 December, the GAER of the EU agreed on the document. The final word would be with the Nice European Council to be held on 7–9 December. At this point, Clinton made a last intervention for Turkey, which would be a memorable way of bidding farewell. He instructed the DOS to take a series of steps to make sure that the text of the APD would not be offending for Turks. The main target of this initiative was Greece. The US contacted Germany, France, the UK, Italy, and Spain, and requested them to take action at the 'very high level' to draw Greece's attention to the possible adverse outcomes that might arise if Turkey–EU relations were damaged. Albright conferred with the Greek FM Papandreou in Vienna. Athens described Washington's moves as 'draining.'[219]

The APD was published in the Official Journal (OJ) of the EU on 24 March 2001.[220] Although we have no clue as to how much the Clinton administration could affect the outcome, the intensity of their efforts was undeniable.

2.5 The New Security Architecture of Europe

The US took pains to keep Turkey in the emerging security architecture of Europe. With the Brussels (1994) and Berlin (1996) summits of NATO, a European Security and Defense Identity (ESDI) was created within the Alliance. In October 1999, Albright tried to convince her Dutch counterpart Jozias van Aartsen of inclusion of non-EU countries such as Turkey into the ESDI, while Clinton was striving to persuade Prodi, President of the European Commission, for Turkey's candidacy. Both Aartsen and Prodi expressed their positive opinion but emphasized that they were not in a position to give a binding commitment.[221]

On 4 December 1998, French President Chirac and British PM Blair made a declaration in St. Malo wherein they stated that "the Union must have the capacity for autonomous action, backed up by credible military forces, the means to decide to use them, and a readiness to do so, in order to respond to international crises."[222] As Turkey was not an EU member, this would mean Turkey's staying outside of this process. Four days later, at the Ministerial Meeting of NATO in Brussels in 1998, Albright formally declared her administration's support to the Europeans in this venture but cautioned them against 'the three Ds': duplication (of what was already being done effectively in NATO), decoupling (of the US from the European defense), and discrimination (against those NATO allies—such as Turkey—who were not EU members).[223]

At the Turkish–US High Level Defense Meeting in Washington on 27–28 April 2000, the US reiterated its desire for Turkey's involvement in the ESDI.[224]

Towards the end of Clinton's term, the US advocacy of Turkey's EU membership dwindled. His administration surrendered to the pressure from the European leaders. At the FMs Meeting of NATO in Florence on 24–25 May 2000, Albright remained silent about Turkey, while the Netherlands, anxious to keep the transatlantic dimension intact in the security architecture of Europe, defended Turkey's interests.[225] Almost a month before he left the White House, Clinton made a request from Turks for the next FMs Meeting to be held in Brussels on 14–15 December. He had been appealed by his European friends to take such a step. On 11 December, he sent a letter to Ecevit, addressing him "my dear brother." The letter, written in a friendly style, was asking Ecevit not to veto the plans related to the cooperation between NATO and the EU's nascent rapid reaction force (RRF) to be discussed at the meeting. Clinton wrote that "if Turkey vetoed the new plan, this would open a crack in the Alliance. He made remarks along the lines of 'you too would be adversely affected by that; it is inevitable that in the future you will take part in the European army.'"[226] He offered Turkey bilateral consultations with Washington whenever Ankara had concerns about NATO's cooperation with the EU. Upon receiving Clinton's letter, a crisis committee composed of high-ranking officials, including Ecevit himself, was established.[227] The Committee concluded that NATO could not give the EU assured access to alliance military planning and that this access should be offered on a case-by-case basis. They were apprehensive that the RRF could become involved in areas where Turkey had interests, such as Cyprus or the Balkans. In such a case, this force would use the bases and equipment in Turkey, without Turkey having a say. In his reply to Clinton's letter, Ecevit wrote that Turkey would like to take part in the activities within the ESDI in peacetime and be included in the decision-making mechanism of the operations where the EU would use NATO's capabilities.[228] Clinton made a phone call to Ecevit on 14 December, asking him to take a softer line.[229] Ecevit's answer was again negative; he was trying to keep this trump card and not to repeat the mistake Evren made in his talks with General Rogers in 1980.[230] At the request of the US, a new mechanism was proposed that set forth an intensive consultation mechanism to be resorted to in case a NATO member who was not an EU member felt its national interests threatened.[231] At the Brussels meeting, Albright had two tête-à-tête talks with her counterpart Cem with the hope of convincing him. These efforts proved in vain, and Cem blocked the NATO–EU deal.[232] The issue came to a standstill, and the GOT decided to wait for the Bush administration to proceed.

3 Collaborators of the US

In its efforts for Turkey's European bid, the US received considerable assistance from the UK, Israel and Finland. In the case of Israel, Clinton was hoping that a rapprochement between this country and Turkey would also contribute to peace in the Middle East.

3.1 The UK

In Clinton's term, the UK translated its latent support for Turkey to an active endeavor in cooperation with the US. British Shadow FS Robin Cook came to Brussels sometime between 20 October 1994[233] and 13 December 1995[234] to convince those MEPs who were from the British Labor Party to vote in favor of Turkey's CU decision.[235]

On 9 December 1997, Turkish PM Yılmaz visited his British counterpart Blair. Blair promised to throw his weight behind recognition of Turkey's candidate status at the Luxembourg Council.[236] When it became clear that the Conclusions of the Luxembourg Council would be upsetting for Turks, Parris, the USAMB to Turkey, had a talk with Cem on 14 December and tried to comfort him by saying that in the upcoming British Presidency of the Council, the US would use its influence over the British. At around the same time, David Logan, the British ambassador, visited PM Yılmaz and promised him that in their Presidency, they would work for Turkey.[237] Towards the end of 1997, the UK made it manifest that its policy regarding Turkey–EU relations would be parallel to that of the US: Turkey should not be excluded from the EU's enlargement process, and the solution of the problems between Greece and Turkey should be made possible via Turkey's EU membership.[238]

When the UK assumed the Presidency in January 1998, it started working as expected by the US and Turkey. In his address to the EP on 14 January, now as the FS, Cook said Turkey had to be included in the enlargement process.[239] In May, Clinton visited Europe for six days. He first came to the UK for the abovementioned G8 Summit. He and Blair were in agreement that Turkey had to become an EU member. Blair promised to double his efforts for Turkey.[240]

GOT announced that it would not attend the AC meeting scheduled for 25 May, unless first, the Greek veto over 400 million dollars in development aid from the EU to Turkey was lifted, and, second, Turkey was given assurance that no political conditions on closer ties with the EU would be imposed at that meeting. Cook pledged to try to persuade Greece to lift its veto[241] but could not keep his promise. The European press accused Britain of "not bringing any concrete and new proposals to Turkey and of not overcoming the unconstructive attitude of Greece."[242] The meeting was not held.

In June, the Department of Trade and Industry of the UK started a campaign to trade with Turkey.[243] At the Cardiff European Council on 15–16 June 1998, Blair could not convince Greece to include Turkey in the list of candidates and asked for Clinton's help. Clinton's phone call to the Greek PM Costas Simitis did not change the result.[244]

As noted above, Clinton convened with 16 leaders of the Greek lobby in the US on 5 December 1999 to explain them his 'solution package' about Cyprus that included Turkey's EU membership. At this meeting, he declared that Blair backed this solution wholeheartedly.[245]

If Clinton's words about his collaboration with Blair in the preparation of the Conclusions of the Helsinki European Council are true, Blair seems to have played into the hands of those who accused the UK as the Trojan horse of the US in Europe.

3.2 Israel

The seeds of the close relations between Turkey and Israel sown in the Bush era yielded their fruits in his successor's term. Sometime between 14 July 1992[246] and 27 July 1994,[247] Shimon Peres, FM of Israel, called Hikmet Çetin, his Turkish counterpart, and informed him about the phone calls he had made to European politicians for Turkey.[248]

> Israeli diplomats were very active in support of Turkey's bid to have its customs union agreement with the EU ratified by the European Parliament in December 1995. Drawing on his Socialist International contacts, Israeli Prime Minister Shimon Peres telephoned such leading European socialists as Spanish Prime Minister Felipe González German socialist leader Rudolf Scharping, and British socialist leader Tony Blair to lobby on Turkey's behalf. Prior to ratification vote [. . .] the socialists were widely viewed as holding the balance of power what many thought would be a close vote. Çiller publicly thanked Israel for its efforts and sent Peres a personal note of gratitude [249]

Initially, Peres's efforts were concealed from the public. However, this secret was revealed in a floor debate at the EP when an MEP complained about the lobbying efforts on Turkey's behalf and cited Peres's calls as an example.[250]

In November 1994, Çiller visited Israel. She was the first Turkish PM who came to Israel. That year, Turkey and Israel signed a number of agreements on such issues as nature conservation or security. In March 1996, this time President Demirel visited Israel. Again, this was the first visit of a Turkish

President to Israel. Between 1996 and 1998 other agreements were signed to establish a FTA between the two countries, to increase the bilateral investments, and to prevent double-taxation.[251] In 1998, Israeli–Turkish bilateral trade was the largest between any two countries in the Middle East.[252] This improvement was reflected in Israel's approach to Turkey–EU relations.

At a date between 6 March 1995[253] and 28 June 1996,[254] Shimon Peres, this time as the PM of Israel, called Emre Gönensay, the Turkish FM, and told him that Israel's campaign for Turkey was going at 'full steam.' Peres had instructed the Israeli embassies to work as if they were representing Turkey and to promote Turkey's EU bid.[255]

In January 1998, the two countries together with the US started joint naval exercises called the Reliant Mermaid to be repeated twice a year.[256]

During his visit to the US, the Anti-Defamation League bestowed its Distinguished Statesman Award upon PM Mesut Yılmaz on 18 December 1998. At the ceremony, Abraham H. Foxman, the League's National Director, expressed his disappointment with the EU's exclusion of Turkey possibly on religious grounds. Several members of the DOS were present at the meeting.[257]

USAMB Grossman confirms that Israel was not acting independently but was 'listed' by the US for the campaign:

> [W]e listed Israel as well to work on people in Europe. . . .] Shimon Peres, for example, made many, many, many telephone calls to leaders in Europe saying "Please, these guys gotta get out." The Israelis were very active on behalf of Turkey in Europe. Peres, in particular, calling leaders in Europe, saying "please, this is really important."[258]

The US also tried to reinforce the trade relations between Israel and Turkey. In his visit to Turkey, Clinton proposed to include Turkey in the Qualifying Industrial Zones (QIZs) system between the US and Israel.[259] In this project, goods produced in a QIZ would have direct access to the US market without tariff or quota restrictions and be subject to only certain conditions. Textile, clothing, and leather products, Turkey's major export items, would be excluded from the QIZs system. The factor behind this exclusion was the textile lobby in the US [260] that met around 80 percent of the domestic demand. Turkey was never incorporated in the system.

In 2000, Israel's relations with Turkey were "second only to the closeness of Israel-US ties."[261] However, towards the end of Clinton's term, these relations showed signs of deterioration. On 19 October 2000, Clinton wrote a last-minute letter to Dennis Hastert, the Speaker of the HOR and stopped a Resolution on the alleged Armenian genocide from being brought to the floor.[262] The following day, Albright called his Turkish counterpart Cem and requested a favor in return: On that day, the UN was about to vote a Resolution[263] condemning Israel for excessive use of force in the Palestinian Territory. Would Turkey vote against this Resolution or at least abstain from voting? Much to her chagrin, the Resolution was adopted,[264] and Turkey happened to vote in favor. Albright sent a resentful letter to Cem. The Jewish lobby who had struggled for Turkey against the Armenian Resolution was also disturbed.[265]

3.3 Finland

In the Clinton era, Finland, a relatively small member of the EU, proved to be of much assistance to the US in the latter's campaign for Turkey. That the December 1999 European Council was held under Presidency of Finland and that Ahtisaari was the Finnish President at that time were two lucky strikes for the Clinton administration. Ten years later, Ahtisaari would speak as follows:

> If I'm asked in Washington or New York what the Americans should do, sometimes the best advice I can give is don't say a thing because we know what your good position is and very often some of us in Europe react that when there is a statement made by the leadership in this country you easily hear why are they talking about Turkey's membership in the European Union because they are not members. It sounds a little bit like some people would think that you are trying to sell the neighbor's house. But I have always welcomed that because as I said in the beginning, the positive thing is that if there were a transatlantic project, I could always count on U.S. support for these negotiations, and we need that sort of positive support, quietly perhaps talking to some of our friends in Europe and trying to also encourage them in those negotiations that we can move with the process as we should because I hate to be a member of the European Union if we lose our credibility of treating Turkey in a different fashion than we should.[266]

4 Mentality of the Clinton Administration

Some names in the Clinton administration maintained the Bush administration's mentality regarding Turkey, which was rather based on geopolitical formulae defined over the US interests in the Middle East and the Central Asia. For instance, in March 1995, Holbrooke characterized Turkey as "the pre-eminent 'front-line state' surrounded by nasty and chaotic neighbors."[267] Nonetheless, taking into consideration the majority of the members of the administration, we can assume that the transition from the Bush administration to Clinton administration meant not only a rise in the level of support for Turkey but also a change in the nature of this support, which was manifest in the increasing significance attributed to Turkey's identity and to Turkish–Greek relations. The following two sections examine these points in detail:

4.1 Turkey's Identity

Like his predecessors, Clinton was aware of Turkey's geopolitical importance. When Turkish PM Mesut Yılmaz was in the US in December 1997, he had a talk with Clinton. Clinton pointed to the 'global village' map on the wall and said he looked at that map every morning and realized how important Turkey's location was.[268] In his speech at the Turkish Parliament in November 1999, he referred to geopolitics once again:

> Turkey's ability to bridge East and West is all the more important when another fact of Turkey's geography is considered. You are almost entirely surrounded by neighbors who are either actively hostile to democracy and peace or struggling against great obstacles to embrace democracy and peace.[269]

Yet, in the same speech, he made it clear that Turkey's importance was not limited to geopolitics:

> There are still those who see Europe in narrower terms. Their Europe might stop at this mountain range or that body of water or, worse, where people stopped to worship God in a different way. But there is a growing and encouraging consensus that knows Europe is an idea as much as a place, the idea that people can find strength in diversity of opinions, cultures, and faiths, as long as they are commonly committed to democracy and human rights; the idea that people can be united without being uniform, and that if the community we loosely refer to as the West is an idea, it has no fixed frontiers. It stretches as far as the frontiers of freedom can go.

Years later, he would say that he saw Turkey as a 'strategic fulcrum,' and call it the fifth or sixth most important country in the world; along with Egypt, Indonesia, and, to a lesser extent, Pakistan, Turkey was offering the US a chance to help Islamic societies with modern democracy.[270]

Clinton wanted to see Turkey as a part of Europe rather than of the Middle East or the Central Asia. His vision of Turkey had a historical depth compared to that of Bush. He is said to have a special interest in history in general and in Ottoman/Turkish history in particular. On 28 September 1999, at the state dinner held at the White House in honor of Turkish PM Ecevit, he and Ecevit spent most of their conversation on Ottoman Empire and modern Turkey. Before attending the OSCE's Istanbul Summit, a number of books on Turkey were ordered for Clinton to read. As an anonymous American diplomat pointed out, Clinton's interest in this subject was not a simple intellectual pursuit; he believed that as the Ottoman Empire had left its mark on the twentieth century, modern Turkey would leave its on the twenty-first.[271]

When Ecevit visited the US in 1999, Clinton told him that Turkey was a secular and democratic 'model' for Islamic countries and that from time to time he even quarreled with European leaders while trying to convince them Turkey's eligibility for the EU.[272]

Several key figures in his administration shared the same view. Albright's book *The Mighty and the Almighty* contains a long section dedicated to Turkey:

> Like most exclusive clubs, the EU selects its own members. Meddling by American secretaries of state is not welcome. While in office, I nevertheless did my best to nudge my European colleagues in the direction of accepting Turkey. My view, reflected in U.S. policy, was that a prosperous, pro-western Turkey was needed to ensure stability in a sensitive region.
> [. . .]
> Turkey is uniquely important because it is the only member of NATO included in the Organization of the Islamic Conference, representing the world's Muslim states; it is also one of the few Muslim countries to have diplomatic relations with Israel.[273]

She, then, presents four principles—mainly related to Turkey's identity—to be kept in mind in Turkey–EU negotiations:

> First, [. . .] [i]f Turkey continues its rapid progress toward European standards, it has a right to expect European leaders to endorse its membership. [. . .]
> Second, Turkey's European identity should not be questioned. [. . .]
> [. . .]
> Third, Turkey's religious identity should not be relevant to its application to join the EU. [. . .]
> [. . .]
> Finally, it is unconvincing to argue, as some do, that Turkey's membership would disrupt the cultural harmony of Europe.[274]

4.2 Turkish–Greek Relations

As the Greek daily *Imerisia* wrote, Clinton was determined to make the Greek–Turkish matrimony possible.[275] However, remaining between Greeks and Turks was being between a rock and a hard place for him.

Clinton thought that Turkey's EU membership and improvement of Greek–Turkish relations would be mutually conducive. Before his visit to Turkey, he shared this idea with his audience at Georgetown University on 8 November 1999:

> The future can be shaped for the better if Turkey can become fully a part of Europe, as a stable, democratic, secular, Islamic nation.

> This, too, can happen if there is progress in overcoming differences with Greece, especially over Cyprus, if Turkey continues to strengthen respect for human rights, and if there is a real vision on the part of our European allies.[276]

A month later, when he visited Turkey, in his address to the Turkish Parliament, 'Greek–Turkish relations' was one of the topics he covered.[277] He used this theme even in the speech he delivered on the occasion of his reception of the International Charlemagne Prize in Aachen, Germany on 2 June 2000:

> I applaud the EU's decision to treat Turkey as a real candidate for membership. I hope both Turkey and the EU will take the next steps. It will be good for Turkey, good for Southeast Europe; good for more rapid reconciliation between Greece and Turkey and the resolution of Cyprus, and good for the entire world, which is still too divided over religious differences.[278]

The chess game between Turks and Greeks was in a stalemate where both parties had been stuck for years in such problems as Cyprus or the continental shelf in the Aegean. A corollary to this prolonged antagonism was the delay in Turkey's integration with Europe. To Holbrooke, Cyprus seemed to be the key piece to break the stalemate. He moved this piece 'towards Europe' and left Turks two options: either cooperate for a solution, or watch the island become an EU member without the Turkish Cypriots. The resentment Turks felt from this imposition made it difficult for them to appreciate

1. that it was thanks to this move that the Greek veto against Turkey's CU and candidacy could be lifted;
2. that, had Turks not insisted on the recognition of the TRNC as a party in the accession process of Cyprus, which was a hope for the impossible given the status of the TRNC in international law and the sensitivity of the Greeks in the issue, Cypriot Turks would not have been excluded;
3. that although the Cyprus move was risky, for Clinton the island was not a simple pawn to be sacrificed. He was unhappy with accession of Cyprus to the EU without the Turkish Cypriots. Towards the end of his term, he was still considering the Cyprus issue unresolved and was determined to work on it after his presidency until the issue was solved to everyone's satisfaction;
4. that Clinton's ultimate aim in his FP regarding this region, his checkmate on the Eurasian chessboard, would be Turkey's EU membership; and
5. that the accession of a divided Cyprus to the EU was undesirable not only for Turkey but also for Italy, Germany, France, and Belgium.[279] With the Cyprus move, Clinton was taking the risk of disturbing his European friends.

Most of these points can be identified in Clinton's unperturbed reply to the provocative pro-Greek question of a journalist:

Q: Mr. President, despite your personal involvement for a Greek-Turkish rapprochement over the Aegean and Cyprus, Ankara has become more aggressive against the territorial integrity of Greece and the Republic of Cyprus in the last days. May we have your comments?
THE PRESIDENT: [. . .] I can say that one of the relatively small number of real disappointments I have after eight years of working in the foreign policy field is that I have not made more progress in helping to resolve the Cyprus issue—because I have always felt that Turkey should be integrated into Europe, I have always felt that Turkey and Greece should be natural allies because they're allies in NATO [. . .].
[. . .]
There is actually some change we can make a little progress before I can leave office. If we don't, it's something I will keep an interest in and would be willing to keep working for even after I'm gone from here.[280]

5 Conclusion

The Clinton era was the *Belle Époque* in Turkey–US relations. The US backing for Turkey's EU prospects in this era was unprecedented and would not ever be equaled. This backing was strong enough to overshadow all the problems between the two countries. Clinton's patronage was much more than a lip-service. He mobilized all his horses and men from the Israeli government to American businessmen, from George H.W. Bush to Jiang Zemin (NRA7). He—together with Blair—went as far as making a few brushstrokes on the Conclusions of the Helsinki European Council (NRA2). It would not be an overstatement to say that in the Clinton era Turkey conducted its relations with the EU under US auspices.

Clinton promoted Turkey's interests not only in the EU but also in the rest of the world very strategically and tactfully. Whereas Turks had questioned the sincerity of Bush's commitment to Turkey's European aspirations, Clinton's genuineness was palpable for them and for the third parties. The atmosphere of friendship and trust that prevailed in Turkey–EU relations in this era did not fit in the pessimistic picture of world politics depicted by neorealists. True, at times the Clinton administration was soi-disant. For instance, although a considerable number of EU MSs were already advocating a CU with Turkey, Holbrooke made a declaration that he had mobilized all the US embassies in Europe to make Turkey's CU possible. Nonetheless, such small instances were far from affecting the reliability of the Clinton administration for Turks. In irrelevant contexts Clinton would reiterate his dedication to Turkey. The following quotation from his remarks at the

Legislative Convention of the American Federation of State, County, and Municipal Employees is an example of this:

> The second is the problem of Greece and Turkey. Why should that matter to you, unless you're Greek or Turk? Because Turkey has been a moderate Muslim state, a buffer between the West and radical, revolutionary—and I think, perverted—theories of Islam that are bubbling up in the Middle East, which is right next door.[281]

In his address to a group of Turkish businessmen, Clinton said he would not stop working for Turkey's EU membership till the end of his life.[282]

His courtesy to Turkey was unreserved. This attitude was, again, in contradiction with the assumption of neorealism pertaining to preference of states for relative gains (NRA5). Despite having been let down by Turks a few times in such cases as Turkey's vetoing the NATO–EU deal or the UN voting on Israel, Clinton did not reduce his support, or say "Turkey needs to reciprocate" as Carter once did. Nor did he make it conditional on some concessions as Ford did in the Cyprus issue. One may think that the 'Cyprus in return for the CU' and the 'helicopters in return for HR' trade-offs were exceptions to this. They were not:

In the case of the Cyprus/CU deal, although Turks felt it like a zero-sum game (NRA5)—and at the end, they lost the Cyprus leg of the game—Holbrooke's initial formula was intended to introduce a positive-sum game to Turkey, Greece and Cyprus, the EU and the US all. We should also keep in mind that after the completion of the CU, he continued to use Cyprus to convince Greeks for Turkey's EU membership: As mentioned previously, at the December 1998 meeting Clinton and Sandy Berger once again brought the issue to the attention of the leaders of the Greek lobby. Thus, although it looks like Turks 'lost Cyprus to Greece' in this period, a closer examination reveals that the Clinton administration did its best for Turkey to buy the most at this price. Turks could afford the CU and, if the remaining credit had been enough, they could have purchased the full-membership too.

In the helicopters/HR deal, 'support for Turkey's EU bid' was not subject to bargaining. With this deal, the US was trying to strengthen Turkey's hand against the US Congress and the EU—and, understandably, make some profit.

Clinton's campaign for Turkey was not simply a reward given to a loyal ally or a contribution to the solution of the problems between Turkey and Greece. He regarded Turkey's EU membership as a historical step towards reconciliation between the East and the West and between Christianity and Islam. Some sources alleged that it was Clinton's negligence that led to the 11 September tragedies,[283] but at least the zeal he and his team showed for Turkey's integration to Europe should be counted to his credit.

A few times Turks raised the threat that they were ready to severe their relations with the EU, which made the US step up its efforts. For Clinton, anchoring Turkey to the West by establishing closer ties, such as a Turkey–US CU was not an option. When Turks made eyes at the US in the aftermath of the Luxembourg Council, the Clinton administration tried to soothe them and convinced them to continue with their affair with the EU.

The EU members were initially attentive to the US demands for Turkey, but, then, they became unwelcoming. They requested Turkey to stop asking the US to mediate on its behalf.[284] After a point, Europeans became so inured to Clinton's adherence to Turkey that they did not mind asking his help in convincing Turkey in such cases as Solana's call to Grossman to secure Turkey's approval of the Conclusions of the Helsinki Council, or the European leaders' appeal to Clinton that made him send a letter to Ecevit before the FMs Meeting in December 2000.

To supplement Turkey's EU-membership project, the US proposed a number of initiatives including the common market project between Greece and Turkey, the SECI project in the Balkans or the FTA project between Israel and Turkey. These projects could not come to fruition.

Although Clinton was critical of some of Turkey's failures in such areas as HR, he kept Turkey–EU relations immune from those criticisms and caused some eyebrows to rise in the US Congress. The close US–Turkish relationship was annoying for the Greek lobby. As it was revealed in Clinton's visit to Athens in 1999, he lost the sympathy of Greek people. He also put a heavy pressure on the Europeans so as to impair the US–EU relations.

In the case of Turkey's CU and candidacy, it is difficult to know the role the US played in the change of mind of such MSs as Greece and Germany. It is also difficult to eliminate the effects of other factors such as Papandreou's becoming FM in Greece;

> [the] change in the attitude of human rights groups and even Kurdish nationalist groups—which opposed Turkish candidacy in 1997 but this time strongly favored it—apparently convinced that EU candidacy offered the best hope for Turkish reform; the goodwill many Europeans—particularly those on the left who now dominate EU governments—feel toward Turkish prime minister Bulent Ecevit, [. . .]; the Ecevit government's anti-torture reforms; earthquake-related sympathy for Turkey throughout Europe; [or] Turkey's ongoing anger over the 1997 decision, which demonstrated to many Europeans that the EU may indeed be pushing a strategically significant Turkey away from the West.[285]

Nevertheless, the influence of the Clinton administration is difficult to deny.

It is not difficult to guess that by the end of the 1990s, the Clinton administration had accepted the reality that it was not possible for Turkey to become an EU member in the foreseeable future. In 2002, after leaving his position as the DOS Spokesperson James Rubin—who had worked very closely with Albright—would say "I am sure that I will see Turkey joining the EU in my lifetime. However, do not forget that I am very young."[286] Nevertheless, not to demoralize the Turks, the Clinton administration did not share this conviction with them. Instead, they helped Turks regain their self-confidence. After having been shunned by 'the European half' of the West for decades, Turks were comforted by the warm embrace of 'the American half.' Turkey felt itself a member of the Western family and, therefore, eligible for the EU. As Cem pointed out, Clinton reminded Turks of their position, culture, and history.[287] Moreover, Clinton and his team should be appreciated for having strived to convince the GOT to implement the reforms necessary for EU accession. Once these reforms were implemented as much as possible, the US tried to sell them in Europe.

In the Clinton era, the economic dimension of Turkey–US relations remained weak as usual; the share of the US in Turkey's foreign trade was only 8.2 percent.[288] In his visit to the US in 1997, Turkish PM Yılmaz took several lucrative proposals with him such as Turkey's purchase of military equipment from the US and construction of nuclear power plants and pipelines by US firms. These projects were not realized.[289] Whereas the Turkey–EC CU envisaged entry of Turkish textile products into the European market without tariffs or quota restrictions, Clinton administration found it difficult to liberalize its own textile imports from Turkey. The increase in the quota from 1 to 1.1 billion dollars[290] was rather symbolic, and the exclusion of the textile, clothing, and leather products from the QIZ project, which may be attributed to the might of the textile lobby in the US, was disturbing for Turks. In Clinton's term, Turkey found itself in a strange triangular trade regime with the US and EU: After joining the EU's CU, Turkey started applying the EU's CCT to the imports from third countries. In the case of the textile products, the rate of CCT duties applicable to the goods originating from the US was 0–8 percent, whereas the US was applying a much higher rate (20–30) to textile imports from Turkey.[291] Nevertheless, Turks were satisfied with the financial aid they were receiving from the US. In 1999, Turkish President said Turkey was the best friend of the US. He supported his argument with the example of the 25 projects in the energy sector in Turkey financed by the US.[292]

In its relations with Turkey, the Clinton administration preferred cut-through driving. Although the President held a largely ceremonial role in Turkish politics, Clinton's team preferred to be in contact with President Demirel and circumvented PM Ecevit as much as possible. Ecevit was not as pro-American and pro-European as the Clinton administration would have liked him to be and was seriously ill.[293] Similarly, Holbrooke opted for cutting through the age-old Gordian knot of the Cyprus problem.

In this era, Israel, the UK, and Finland acted in concert with the US. For Clinton, Israel's involvement would also contribute to the dialogue between Muslims and Jews.

Consequentially, the Clinton era can be seen as a period when the US support for Turkey's EU membership increased to an unparalleled level and changed its character. The meaning of Turkey–EU relations that the previous administrations had constructed within neorealist paradigm against the background of Cold War gained a new frame of reference: the emerging East–West (or Islam/Christianity) divide viewed through the lens of idealism.

Notes

1 "Çankaya Presidential Campus." Available at www.tccb.gov.tr/pages/presidency/campuses/, accessed 19 September 2011; and Yılmaz Ergüvenç, "Çankaya Köşkleri." Available at www.kenthaber.com/Haber/Genel/Kose/yilmaz-erguvenc/2007, accessed 18 September 2011.
2 "Ağır misafir," *Zaman*, 15 November 1999; and "CIA ajanları Çankaya Köşkü'ndeydi," *Milliyet*, 14 January 2008.
3 "Remarks at a state dinner hosted by President Demirel in Ankara," *Weekly Compilation of Presidential Documents*, Washington: USGPO, Vol. 35, No. 46, 22 November 1999, pp. 2388–9.
4 "CIA ajanları Çankaya Köşkü'ndeydi," *Milliyet*, 14 January 2008.
5 Sedat Ergin, "Son yemekte ortaya çıkan gerçek," *Hürriyet*, 29 April 2000. For a different account of this event, see "Poised for a new president," *The Economist*, 4 May 2000, p. 54. The irony of fate had it that Sezer himself became the President in 2000.
6 Meral Tamer, "Depremzedenin oyu Clinton'a," *Milliyet*, 18 November 1999.
7 Mark R. Parris, "U.S.-Turkish Relations: How Firm a Foundation?" Speech given to the Economics Club in Memphis, TN. Available at http:/www.brookings.edu/research/speeches/2008/05/08-turkey-parris, accessed 25 June 2012.
8 "Halk ABD'yi değil Bush'u sevmiyor," *Yeni Şafak*, 13 March 2005.
9 Serpil Çevikcan, "Clinton'ın mektubu Ankara'yı karıştırdı," *Milliyet*, 5 February 1998; Sedat Sertoğlu, "Bir mektup," *Sabah*, 17 June 1998; and "Clinton mektubu," *Milliyet*, 17 June 1998.
10 "Türk gibi," *Sabah*, 16 November 1999. In the Turkish state system, the Presidency is largely a ceremonial office.
11 "Remarks to the Turkish Grand National Assembly in Ankara," *Weekly Compilation of Presidential Documents*, Washington: USGPO, Vol. 35, No. 46, 22 November 1999, pp. 2382.
12 Muharrem Sarıkaya, "Konuşmadan herkes istediğini aldı," *Hürriyet*, 16 November 1999.
13 "Bu sözler tarihe geçecek," *Sabah*, 16 November 1999; and "Türk gibi," *Sabah*, 16 November 1999.
14 Mark R. Parris, "U.S.-Turkish Relations: How Firm a Foundation?" Speech given to the Economics Club in Memphis, TN. Available at www.brookings.edu/research/speeches/2008/05/08-turkey-parris, accessed 25 June 2012.
15 Sami Kohen, "ABD, Avrupa'dan farklı düşünüyor," *Milliyet*, 17 December 1994.
16 Sami Kohen, "Clinton (ve ABD) neden AB'ye girmemizi istiyor?" *Milliyet*, 11 July 2002.
17 Kemal Kirişci and Gareth M. Winrow, *The Kurdish Question and Turkey: An Example of Trans-State Ethnic Conflict*, New York, NY: Routledge, 1997, p. 175. See also Yasemin Çongar, "Silahlara gözaltı," *Milliyet*, 26 May 1995.
18 Altan Öymen, "Denizliğe karşı," *Milliyet*, 28 August 1994.
19 Kemal Kirişci, "U.S.-Turkish relations: New uncertainties in a renewed partnership," in Barry M. Rubin and Kemal Kirişci (eds.), *Turkey in World Politics: An Emerging Multiregional Power*, Boulder, CO: Lynne Rienner Publishers, 2001, 129–50, p. 129.

20 Yasemin Çongar, "Clinton'dan reform desteği," *Milliyet*, 29 September 1999.
21 See, for example, Uğur Mumcu, "Taşeron," *Cumhuriyet*, 23 December 1992.
22 George Harris, "Turkish-American relations since the Truman Doctrine," in Mustafa Aydın and Çağrı Erhan (eds.), *Turkish-American Relations: Past, Present and Future*, New York, NY: Routledge, 2004, 66–88, p. 81.
23 Emin Çölaşan, "'Rose of Istanbul' ajan mı?" *Hürriyet*, 13 July 1997.
24 Kemal Kirişçi, "U.S.-Turkish relations: New uncertainties in a renewed partnership," in Barry M. Rubin and Kemal Kirişçi (eds.), *Turkey in World Politics: An Emerging Multiregional Power*, Boulder, CO: Lynne Rienner Publishers, 2001, 129–50, p. 129.
25 Nur Batur, "Avrupa, Türkiye'siz olmaz," *Milliyet*, 19 November 1992.
26 With some exceptions, the EC had abolished the import duties on Turkish industrial goods in 1971. As stated above, the Additional Protocol to the Ankara Agreement envisaged the gradual reduction in Turkey's customs tariffs applicable to the goods originating from the EC. This process would start with the entry into force of the Protocol in 1973 and be completed in 22 years. Turkey failed to honor its commitment to gradually reduce its customs duties; it made the last reduction in 1976 and froze its obligations in 1978. The EC suspended its relations with Turkey in 1982. The relations were revived in 1987, when Turkey made its application for full-membership. Turkey resumed the tariff reductions in 1988. Technical details of the CU to be established were determined in 1992.
27 In technical terms, Turkey's CU would be established not with the EU but with the EC.
28 Örsan Kunter Öymen, "Almanya ve Belçika'dan çatlak sesler," *Milliyet*, 11 March 1993.
29 "Yunanistan'a kardeş geldi," *Milliyet*, 15 February 1995.
30 "Türkiye-AT teknik işbirliği canlanıyor," *Milliyet*, 9 January 1992.
31 See page 40 endnote 39.
32 Ahmet Sever, "Türkiye-AT ilişkilerinde önemli gelişme," *Milliyet*, 11 November 1992.
33 "Türk-Yunan ortak pazarı," *Milliyet*, 9 May 1994.
34 Interview with Murat Karayalçın, Istanbul, 18 October 2012.
35 Taki Berberakis, "Atina ağız değiştirdi," *Milliyet*, 19 February 1995.
36 Zülfikar Doğan, "Gümrük Birliği'nde ilk raund yarın," *Milliyet*, 27 November 1994.
37 Ahmet Sever, "Gümrük Birliği'ne Yunan vetosu," *Milliyet*, 29 November 1994; and Ahmet Sever, "Yunanistan'ın istekleri bitmiyor," *Milliyet*, 30 November 1994.
38 Taki Berberakis, "Papandreu'ya 'Gümrük Birliği' baskısı," *Milliyet*, 1 December 1994.
39 Mehmet Aktan, "Zirveden yumuşak uyarı," *Milliyet*, 10 December 1994.
40 Mehmet Aktan and Ahmet Sever, "Gümrük Birliği tehlikede mi?" *Milliyet*, 11 December 1994.
41 Taki Berberakis, "ABD'den Atina'ya baskı," *Milliyet*, 16 December 1994.
42 Interview with James Howard Holmes, Washington, 6 May 2010.
43 Interview with Emre Gönensay, Istanbul, 8 November 2012. See also Birol Yeşilada, *EU-Turkey Relations in the 21st Century*, New York, NY: Routledge, 2013, p. 12; and Mehmet Ali Birand, *31 Temmuz 1959'dan 17 Aralık 2004'e Türkiye'nin Büyük Avrupa Kavgası*, Doğan Kitapçılık, 2005, p. 366.
44 Interview with Şükrü Sina Gürel, Istanbul, 9 November 2012.
45 Barçın Yinanç, "Clinton'dan mektup var," *Milliyet*, 2 March 1995.
46 Ahmet Sever, "Ankara'ya: Engel olma," *Milliyet*, 1 April 1998.
47 Interview with Murat Karayalçın, Istanbul, 18 October 2012; and Emil Edip Öymen, "Boru hatları da görüşülecek," *Cumhuriyet*, 2 February 1995. Karayalçın's critics maintained that with these moves recommended by some Turkish diplomats, he was just trying to save his face. See, for example, Bülent Akarcalı, "Kıbrıs'ı sattık mı?" *Vatan*, 2 August 2005.
48 Ömer Şahin and Ahmet Bıyık, "Yılmaz'ın 'Kıbrıs'ta taviz verdiniz' sözü Çiller'i kızdırdı," *Zaman*, 22 June 2002.
49 Interview with Nihat Akyol, Istanbul, 6 February 2013.

50 Birol Yeşilada, *EU-Turkey Relations in the 21st Century*, New York, NY: Routledge, 2013, p. 12.
51 Yasemin Çongar, "Washington niye devrede?" *Milliyet*, 18 February 1995.
52 Barçın Yinanç, "Yunanistan'a ABD uyarısı," *Milliyet*, 18 February 1995.
53 Örsan Kunter Öymen, "Kıbrıs'ta kim karlı," *Milliyet*, 9 February 1995; and Nilgün Cerrahoğlu, "Önce Türkiye, sonra Kıbrıs," *Milliyet*, 5 March 1995.
54 "Decision No 1/95 of the EC/Turkey Association Council of 22 December 1995 on implementing the final phase of the Customs Union" (96/142/EC). The Decision was published in the *OJ of the EU* after it was approved by the EP on 13 December.
55 "Briefing No. 1: Cyprus and the Enlargement of the European Union," *European Parliament*. Available at www.europarl.europa.eu/enlargement/briefings/pdf/1a1_en.pdf, accessed 12 April 2011.
56 "Statement by Murat Karayalçın, Foreign Minister of Turkey, on Greek Cypriot Application for EU-Membership on 6 March 1995 during the EU-Turkey Association Council in Brussels." Available at www.cypnet.co.uk/ncyprus/history/cyproblem/articles/bolum31.html, accessed 3 October 2012.
57 Soli Özel, "We have confidence in Turkish democracy," *Private View*, Istanbul: TÜSİAD, Vol. 2, 1996, 18–25, p. 25.
58 Interview with Marc Grossman, Washington, 11 May 2010.
59 New York, NY: The Modern Library, 1999, p. 61.
60 "ABD ile Avrupa'dan farklı bakış," *Milliyet*, 23 June 1995.
61 Interview with Thomas Miller, Washington, 15 April 2010. Miller referred to this deal in an interview published by the Greek daily *Kathimerini* in 2004. Source: "Türkler Gümrük Birliği'ne, Rumlar AB'ye," *NTVMSNBC*. Available at http://arsiv.ntvmsnbc.com/news/263466.asp, accessed 20 May 2011.
62 "Greece blasts 'cynical' treatment at Cannes summit," *Athens News Agency*, 29 June 1995. Available at www.hri.org/news/greek/ana/1995/95-06-29.ana.html, accessed 29 September 2011. See also Panayotis Tsakonas, "From 'perverse' to 'promising' institutionalism? NATO, EU, and the Greek-Turkish conflict," in Dimitris Bourantonis and Kostas Ifantis (eds.) *Multilateralism and Security Institutions in an Era of Globalization*, New York, NY: Routledge, 2008, 223–51, p. 248.
63 For example, Şükrü Elekdağ, "Yalan dolanla siyaset," *Milliyet*, 12 February 1995; Erol Manisalı, "Kıbrıslı Rumlara hükümranlık tanındı," *Milliyet*, 9 March 1995; or Mümtaz Soysal, "Tren," *Hürriyet*, 3 April 1998.
64 Semih Günver, "Yine Kıbrıs," *Milliyet*, 20 March 1995.
65 Uğur Akıncı, "Gurel: EU's wrong impressions not binding on Turkey," *TDN*, 9 June 1997.
66 Örsan Kunter Öymen, "ABD'den rahatlatıcı sözler," *Milliyet*, 22 February 1995; and Nilgün Cerrahoğlu, "ABD elçileri Türkiye için devrede," *Milliyet*, 24 February 1995.
67 Ahmet Sever, "Atina AB'yi bezdirdi," *Milliyet*, 2 November 1994.
68 Yalçın Doğan, "Atina'da veto hazırlığı," *Milliyet*, 24 November 1994.
69 Interview with Hikmet Çetin, Istanbul, 23 September 2011.
70 "Türkiye'ye krediler sürdürülmeli," *Milliyet*, 30 July 1995.
71 Interview with Marc Grossman, Washington, 11 May 2010.
72 Ed Whitfield, "Admit Turkey to the European Union," Speech in the HOR, *Congressional Record*, Vol. 141, No. 40, 3 March 1995, Washington: USGPO, pp. H2642–3.
73 Amo Houghton, "European Union should approve a customs union with Turkey," Speech in the HOR, *Congressional Record*, Vol. 141, No. 186, 20 November 1995, Washington: USGPO, p. E2227.
74 Derya Sazak, "Batı'dan bakınca," *Milliyet*, 26 May 1995; and Yasemin Çongar, "Türkiye GB'ye girmeli," *Milliyet*, 16 June 1995.
75 Taha Akyol, "Avrupa Parlamentosu," *Milliyet*, 7 April 1995.
76 Yasemin Çongar, "Türkiye GB'ye girmeli," *Milliyet*, 16 June 1995.

77 Barçın Yinanç, "Clinton Çiller'e mektup yolladı," *Milliyet*, 1 June 1995.
78 Yasemin Çongar, "Türkiye GB'ye girmeli," *Milliyet*, 16 June 1995.
79 Yasemin Çongar, "ABD'den büyük destek," *Milliyet*, 4 June 1995.
80 "ABD ile Avrupa'dan farklı bakış," *Milliyet*, 23 June 1995.
81 Interview with Marc Grossman, Washington, 11 May 2010.
82 Şeref Oğuz, "Erteleme felaket olur," *Milliyet*, 2 June 1995.
83 "Avrupa hareket bekliyor," *Milliyet*, 6 June 1995.
84 Yasemin Çongar, "ABD'den büyük destek," *Milliyet*, 4 June 1995.
85 Ahmet Sever, "GB için olumlu hava," *Milliyet*, 10 November 1995.
86 Ahmet Sever, "Clinton: Türkiye ile GB ya olacak, ya olacak!" *Milliyet*, 4 December 1995.
87 The period in which Gönensay was the FM.
88 Interview with Emre Gönensay, Istanbul, 8 November 2012.
89 William Hale, *Turkey, the US and Iraq*, London: The London Middle East Institute, 2007, p. 73.
90 "Erbakan'ın D8'i ümitsiz vaka," *Milliyet*, 15 June 1997.
91 Yasemin Çongar, "Clinton'a Türkiye önerileri," *Milliyet*, 16 March 1997.
92 Örsan Kunter Öymen, "Roma'da 'soğuk duş,'" *Milliyet*, 29 January 1997; and Şükrü Elekdağ, "Türkiye rest çekiyor," *Milliyet*, 10 February 1997.
93 The Copenhagen Criteria were defined at the Copenhagen Council (21–22 June 1993) of the EU: "Membership requires that the candidate country has achieved stability of institutions guaranteeing democracy, the rule of law, human rights and respect for and protection of minorities, the existence of a functioning market economy as well as the capacity to cope with competitive pressure and market forces within the Union. Membership presupposes the candidate's ability to take on the obligations of membership including adherence to the aims of political, economic and monetary union." (Source: European Council, *Presidency Conclusions*, Copenhagen European Council, 21–22 December 1997, Relations with the Countries of Central and Eastern Europe, para. iii.)
94 "The week in human rights: January 27 to February 2, 1997," *Derechos*. Available at www.derechos.org/human-rights/briefs/20297.html, accessed 7 July 2012; and Yasemin Çongar, "Avrupa'ya ABD köprüsü," *Milliyet*, 3 February 1997.
95 Yasemin Çongar, "Albright'in gündemi Türkiye," *Milliyet*, 16 February 1997.
96 Yasemin Çongar, "Hristiyanlık kıstas olamaz," *Milliyet*, 9 March 1997.
97 The Council was composed of the Chief of Staff, force commanders, certain members of the cabinet, and the President of the Republic. Civilian members of the Council were in minority.
98 A center-right European party group in the EP, dominated by European Christian Democratic Parties.
99 Chris Nuttall and Ian Traynor, "Kohl tries to cool row with Ankara," *The Guardian*, 7 March 1997; and Ahmet Sever, "Medeniyet bahanesi," *Milliyet*, 6 March 1997.
100 Kohl was not the 'President' of the EU. The President of the COEU was Wim Kok from the Netherlands, and Kok was not a Christian Democrat but from the Labor Party. This journalist may have meant Jacques Delors, President of the European Commission between 1985 and 1995, who was the victim of the same misunderstanding. (For Delors see: Ahmet Sever, "Fehmi Koru'ya zorunlu yanıt," *Milliyet*, 17 June 1997.)
101 Uğur Akıncı, "US hope shaken on Turkey's EU chances," *Hürriyet Daily News (HDN)*, 3 October 1997.
102 Barçın Yinanç, "ABD'den Türkiye'ye destek çağrısı," *Milliyet*, 10 March 1997; Yasemin Çongar, "ABD, Türkiye için seferber," *Milliyet*, 13 March 1997; and Yalçın Doğan, "Amerika seferber, Avrupa sinirli," *Milliyet*, 13 March 1997.
103 DOS Daily Press Briefing #60, 22 April 1997. Available at www.hri.org/news/usa/std/1997/97-04-22.std.html, accessed 23 June 2011.

104 Yasemin Çongar "'Gözümüz üstünüzde,'" *Milliyet*, 25 April 1997.
105 Yasemin Çongar, "Transatlantik, Türkiye ve Talbott," *Milliyet*, 12 May 1997.
106 James Warren, "Germany's Kohl remains Europe's most impressive figure," *Chicago Tribune*, 8 June 1997.
107 Yasemin Çongar, "Clinton: Ankara'yı destekleyin," *Milliyet*, 6 June 1997.
108 Ahmet Sever, "AB'de durum belirsiz," *Milliyet*, 20 June 1997.
109 Richard Burt, "Are we losing Turkey," *WSJ*, 21 June 1997.
110 "Kinkel: 'AB'ye alamayız," *Milliyet*, 29 June 1997.
111 European Commission, Agenda 2000: For a Stronger and Wider Union, *Bulletin of the EU*, Supplement 5/97, 15 July 1997.
112 David Hannay, *Cyprus: The Search for a Solution*, London: I.B. Tauris, 2005, p. 76.
113 Altan Öymen, "Refah'tan sonra AB," *Milliyet*, 22 July 1997.
114 Barçın Yinanç, "AB: Sorun çözülmeden tam üyelik olmaz," *Milliyet*, 21 July 1997.
115 "Byzantine diplomacy," *The Economist*, Vol. 344, 24 July 1997, p. 144.
116 "Kinkel: Rumlar'ın üyeliği zor," *Milliyet*, 30 July 1997.
117 Akay Cemal, "Bütünleşmenin temeli atıldı," *Milliyet*, 7 August 1997. The text of the agreement in Turkish is available at http://mevzuat.kamunet.net/mmd/uluslararasi_htm/09–1998.html, accessed 25 November 2012.
118 Yasemin Çongar, "AB bütünleşmeden rahatsız," *Milliyet*, 8 August 1997.
119 See page 114 and Yasemin Çongar, "ABD'nin Kıbrıs terennümü," *Milliyet*, 25 August 1997.
120 "Turkey favors free trade with US," *Pharos Tribune*, 17 August 1997; Sedat Ergin, "ABD ile bahar havası," *Hürriyet*, 17 August 1997; Yasemin Çongar, "ABD ile serbest ticaret," *Milliyet*, 18 August 1997; Sami Kohen, "Cem'in AB atağı," *Milliyet*, 19 August 1997; Yasemin Çongar, "AB ile serbest ticaret zor," *Milliyet*, 19 August 1997; and Üzeyir Garih, "U.S. wants strong Turkey," *TDN*, 19 August 1997.
121 Şükrü Elekdağ, "AB ateşle oynuyor," *Milliyet*, 1 September 1997.
122 Yasemin Çongar "Avrupa Birliği tavizini vermeyiz," *Milliyet*, 29 October 1997.
123 Barçın Yinanç, "KKTC'nin tam üyelik atağı," *Milliyet*, 10 November 1997.
124 David Hannay was the UK's special representative to Cyprus from 1996 to 2003 and one of the architects of the Annan Plan. He believed in a "painstakingly detailed approach" to the Cyprus problem. When Holbrooke was appointed as Presidential Special Envoy for Cyprus in June 1997, he had discussions with Hannay. After listening to Hannay's comprehensive 'briefings' on the issue, Holbrooke said: "[t]here must be some way of cutting through all this, of getting the key players to take the big decisions and to focus on the politics of the problem, not its technicalities." (Source: David Hannay, *Cyprus: The Search for a Solution*, London: I.B. Tauris, 2005, p. 76.)
125 Yalçın Doğan, "Brüksel randevusu," *Milliyet*, 12 November 1997.
126 Selin Çağlayan, "Holbrooke: Entegrasyondan vazgeçin," *Hürriyet*, 13 November 1997; and Barçın Yinanç, "ABD, Türkiye için ağırlık koyacak," *Milliyet*, 14 November 1997.
127 Ahmet Sever, "AB'ye 'karışma' mesajı," *Milliyet*, 28 November 1997.
128 Mine G. Saulnier, "Gündem yine Ankara'ydı," *Milliyet*, 6 December 1997.
129 Zülfikar Doğan, "Ekonomik alan önerisi," *Milliyet*, 12 December 1997.
130 Vera M. Budway and Erhard Busek, "From Dayton to Brussels: Ten years of moving from stabilization to integration," in Erhard Busek (ed.), *10 Years Southeast European Cooperative Initiative: From Dayton to Brussels*, New York, NY: Springer, 2006, 1–24, p. 2.
131 Paul J.J. Welfens, *Stabilizing and Integrating the Balkans: Economic Analysis of the Stability Pact, EU Reforms and International Organizations*, New York, NY: Springer, 2001, p. 75.
132 Işıl Cemali, "Güneydoğu Avrupa İşbirliği Girişimi (SECI)," TMFA. Available at www.mfa.gov.tr/guneydogu-avrupa-isbirligi-girisimi-_seci_.tr.mfa, accessed 3 November 2011.

133 European Council, *Presidency Conclusions*, Luxembourg European Council, 12–13, December 1997, A European Strategy for Turkey, para. 31.
134 Para. 33.
135 Para. 35.
136 Murat Yetkin, *Avrupa Birliği Bekleme Odasında Türkiye*, Istanbul: İmge Kitabevi, 2002, p. 13.
137 The Luxembourg Council decided to convene a European Conference to bring together the MSs and those European states aspiring to become EU member. The first meeting of the Conference would be in London in March 1998.
138 Sedat Ergin, "AB'ye 6 ay süre," *Hürriyet*, 18 December 1997; Derya Sazak, "AB Zirvesi ve Yılmaz," *Milliyet*, 18 December 1997; and Stephen Kinzer, "Turkey, rejected, will freeze ties to European Union," *NYT*, 15 December 1997.
139 Fikret Bila, "Yeni bir dünya," *Milliyet*, 13 December 1997.
140 "ABD ile ilişkiler daha gelişecek," *Milliyet*, 13 December 1997. This agreement on the avoidance of the double taxation had been signed on 28 March 1996. The agreement became effective on 1 January 1998.
141 Yasemin Çongar, "ABD'den sakin olun çağrısı," *Milliyet*, 16 December 1997.
142 Barçın Yinanç, "Broek: Başımız dertte," *Milliyet*, 18 December 1997. Author's translation.
143 "Chirac ve Clinton Türkiye'yi konuştu," *Hürriyet*, 24 December 1997.
144 "AB'ye süre restinde yumuşama," *Milliyet*, 21 December 1997; Sedat Ergin "Clinton'un Yılmaz'a AB sorusu: 'Buradan nereye gidiyoruz?'" *Hürriyet*, 21 December 1997; and Derya Sazak, "Clinton'ın küresi," *Milliyet*, 21 December 1997.
145 Zalmay Khalilzad, "Why the West needs Turkey," *WSJ*, 22 December 1997.
146 Derya Sazak, "Kıbrıs, AB, Türkiye," *Milliyet*, 19 December 1997.
147 John Tirman, "Improving Turkey's 'bad neighbourhood': Pressing Ankara for rights and democracy," *World Policy Journal*, Vol. 15, No. 1, Spring 1998, 60–7, p. 65. For a different version of the story, see Yalçın Doğan, "Amerika'da dersimiz demokrasi," *Milliyet*, 20 December 1997.
148 "Helikopter sorunu," *Milliyet*, 20 December 1997; and Yalçın Doğan, "Amerika'da dersimiz demokrasi," *Milliyet*, 20 December 1997.
149 Henri J. Barkey, "The United States, Turkey, and human rights policy," in Debra Liang-Fenton (ed.) *Implementing U.S. Human Rights Policy: Agendas, Policies, and Practices*, Washington, D.C.: United States Institute of Peace, 2004, 363–400, p. 376.
150 "Turkish Prime Minister confirms 49-plane order," 19 December 1997. Available at http://boeing.mediaroom.com/1997-12-19-Turkish-Prime-Minister-Confirms-49-Plane-Order, accessed 2 March 2014.
151 "AB'de kim yalan söylüyor," *Hürriyet*, 12 March 1998.
152 "Körfezin unutturdukları," *Milliyet*, 10 February 1998.
153 Taki Berberakis, "ABD'den ikili baskı," *Milliyet*, 22 March 1998.
154 Barçın Yinanç, "AB masasına oturun," *Milliyet*, 23 April 1998.
155 Akay Cemal, "Holbrooke'tan buruk veda," *Milliyet*, 5 May 1998.
156 "Albright'ın Türkiye çabası," *Milliyet*, 2 May 1998.
157 Münir Bağnaçık, "Kohl'e Clinton sürprizi," *Milliyet*, 14 May 1998; and "Clinton'dan Türkiye lobisi," *Hürriyet*, 11 May 1998.
158 Münir Bağnaçık and Mehmet Aktan, "Kohl, Clinton'a kızgın," *Milliyet*, 15 May 1998.
159 Yasemin Çongar, "Clinton'ın Türkiye kulisi," *Milliyet*, 18 May 1998.
160 "Schröder: Türkiye AB'ye girmeli," *Milliyet*, 5 August 1998.
161 Yasemin Çongar, "Schröder: Türkiye için çalışacağım," *Milliyet*, 7 August 1998.
162 Taki Berberakis, "Hedefim Türkiye'nin üyeliği," *Milliyet*, 6 December 1998.
163 "Programda AB yok," *Milliyet*, 13 January 1999.
164 Şahin Alpay, "Bizim için Türkiye adaydır," *Milliyet*, 3 February 1999.
165 "Türkiye'yi dışlamayalım," *Hürriyet*, 7 September 1998. Austria was opposed to Turkey's EU membership but did not prefer Turkey's complete exclusion. See also "Klima, Türkiye'nin adaylığı kabul edilemez," *Hürriyet*, 28 May 1998.

166 "Schroeder 'decisively' backs Turkey's EU bid," *TDN*, 12 April 1999.
167 İlter Türkmen, "Vuslat bir başka bahara," *Hürriyet*, 10 June 1999.
168 Hasan Cemal, "Washington'dan Ankara'ya mesajlar," *Milliyet*, 10 June 1999.
169 "Cohen ile kritik diyalog," *Milliyet*, 16 July 1999.
170 Philip T. Reeker, "U.S. Department of State Daily Press Briefing #115," 1 September 1999. Available at http://secretary.state.gov/www/briefings/9909/990901db.html, accessed 16 May 2012.
171 Chris Morris, "US promises aid to Turkey," *BBC News*, 5 September 1999. Available at http://news.bbc.co.uk/2/hi/europe/439254.stm, accessed 14 November 2011.
172 Zafer Arapkirli, "Helsinki'de son tango," *Milliyet*, 3 September 1999.
173 Doğan Heper, "Üç hayati konunun kesiştiği nokta," *Milliyet*, 12 September 1999.
174 Yasemin Çongar, "ABD'de 'kritik' iki hafta," *Milliyet*, 19 September 1999.
175 Fikret Bila, "Ufuk turu," *Milliyet*, 29 September 1999.
176 Şükrü Elekdağ, "Ecevit'in ABD gezisi: Ne kar ne zarar," *Milliyet*, 11 October 1999; and Güngör Uras, "'Şen' gidenler 'yaslı' dönecek," *Milliyet*, 1 October 1999.
177 "Üç destek bir fren," *Hürriyet*, 29 September 1999; and Aslı Aydıntaşbaş and Deniz Zeyrek, "Beyaz Saray'da mutlu son," *Radikal*, 29 September 1999. The quota was increased from 1 billion dollars to 1.1 billion dollars.
178 Yasemin Çongar, "İslam dünyası için modelsiniz," *Milliyet*, 30 September 1999.
179 "Ecevit ABD'den memnun döndü," *Radikal*, 3 October 1999.
180 Taki Berberakis, "Atina yön değiştiriyor," *Milliyet*, 1 October 1999.
181 "Ecevit tekelleri davet etti," *Evrensel*, 1 October 1999.
182 "Albright'tan iki müjde, iki destek," *Milliyet*, 6 September 1999.
183 European Commission, "1999 Regular Report from the Commission on Turkey's Progress towards Accession," 13 October 1999.
184 Anatolian Agency, "ABD, AB raporunu memnuniyetle karşıladığını bildirdi." Available at www.belgenet.com/arsiv/ab/ab_komisyon99_02.html, accessed 10 December 2011.
185 William J. Clinton: "Remarks to the American Embassy Community in Ankara, Turkey." Available at www.presidency.ucsb.edu/ws/?pid=56932, accessed 5 October 2011.
186 *Public Papers of the Presidents of the United States (PPPUS), William J. Clinton*, 1999, Book 2: July 1 to December 31, 1999, Washington: USGPO, p. 2103.
187 "Remarks by the President and President Demirel of Turkey in joint press availability." Available at http://clinton3.nara.gov/WH/New/Europe-9911/remarks/1999–11–15c.html, accessed 3 June 2011.
188 Yasemin Çongar, "Yunanistan'a jest istedi," *Milliyet*, 17 November 1999. Author's translation. The Halki school had been closed by Turkish authorities in 1971.
189 Aris Abatzis, "Ecevit denies that Clinton called for Turkish goodwill gesture towards Athens." Available at www.greekembassy.org/Embassy/content/en/Article.aspx?office=1&folder=285&article=4439, accessed 19 November 2011.
190 "AB'nin Türkiye büyükelçisi gibi," *Milliyet*, 17 November 1999.
191 Helena Smith, "Thousands vent anger at Clinton's Greek visit Athens," *The Guardian*, 20 November 1999.
192 Murat Yetkin, *Avrupa Birliği Bekleme Odasında Türkiye*, Istanbul: İmge Kitabevi, 2002, pp. 27–8; Yasemin Çongar, "Clinton ziyaretinden Helsinki zirvesine," *Milliyet*, 22 November 1999.
193 Yasemin Çongar, "ABD sürekli bastırıyor," *Milliyet*, 10 December 1999.
194 Taki Berberakis, "Atina'da ibre 'evet'te," *Milliyet*, 9 December 1999.
195 "27 Members of U.S. House of Representatives write letter to Finnish President Ahtisaari and ask Turkey's EU candidacy be approved," *Hellenic Resources Network*, 2 December 1999. Available at www.hri.org/news/turkey/anadolu/1999/99–12–02.anadolu.html, accessed 30 June 2012; Amo Houghton, "Supporting membership for Turkey in the European Union," Remarks in the US HOR, *Congressional Record, V. 146, Pt. 6, May 10, 2000 to May 23, 2000*, Washington: USGPO, 2000, pp. 8573–4; and "ABD basınında Clinton," *Hürriyet*, 16 November 1999.

196 After Finland, Edelman would work as the Principal Deputy Assistant to the Vice President for National Security Affairs and, then, be appointed as the USAMB to Turkey in 2003.
197 Murat Yetkin, "Sizden beklentimiz AB yolunda başarılı sonuç," *Radikal*, 18 May 2005.
198 Yasemin Çongar, "Kıbrıs, Helsinki'ye endeksli," *Milliyet*, 4 December 1999.
199 Barçın Yinanç and Güven Özalp, "Son dakika manevraları," *Milliyet*, 10 December 1999.
200 Murat Yetkin, *Avrupa Birliği Bekleme Odasında Türkiye*, Istanbul: İmge Kitabevi, 2002, pp. 28–9; Barçın Yinanç and Güven Özalp, "Son dakika manevraları," *Milliyet*, 10 December 1999; and Sami Kohen, "AB, Yunan vetosu kadar Türk reddini önlemeye çalışıyor," *Milliyet*, 10 December 1999.
201 "Kriz yaratan kararlar," *Milliyet*, 11 December 1999; and Güven Özalp, Barçın Yinanç, and Serpil Çevikcan, "Solana operasyonu," *Milliyet*, 11 December 1999.
202 Muharrem Sarıkaya, "Metin Ecevit'in daktilosundan çıktı," *Hürriyet*, 12 December 1999; and "AB'nin iki kişilik daveti nasıl üçe çıktı?" *Hürriyet*, 12 January 2000.
203 Barçın Yinanç, "Her şeyi değiştiren virgül," *Milliyet*, 12 December 1999.
204 Cf. Alan Makovsky, "US policy towards Turkey: Progress and problems," in Morton Abramowitz (ed.), *Turkey's Transformation and American Policy*, New York, NY: The Century Foundation Press, 2000, 219–66, pp. 264–5.
205 Demokratik Sol Parti, *Ecevit, Kıbrıs ve Helsinki Gerçeği*, Ankara: Pozitif Matbaacılık, 2004, pp. 26–8; and Güven Özalp, Barçın Yinanç, and Serpil Çevikcan, "Solana operasyonu," *Milliyet*, 11 December 1999; "İşte güvence mektubu," *Milliyet*, 12 December 1999.
206 European Council, *Presidency Conclusions*, Helsinki European Council, 10–11 December 1999.
207 Interview with Marc Grossman, Washington, 11 May 2010.
208 Murat Yetkin, *Avrupa Birliği Bekleme Odasında Türkiye*, Istanbul: İmge Kitabevi, 2002, p. 33; and Fikret Bila, "Ecevit nasıl ikna oldu," *Milliyet*, 11 December 1999.
209 William J. Clinton, "Statement on Turkey's European Union candidacy," *PPPUS, William J. Clinton*, 1999, Book 2: July 1 to December 31, 1999, Washington: USGPO, 2001, pp. 2279–80.
210 Athens News Agency, "Clinton congratulates Simitis." Available at www.hri.org/news/greek/apeen/1999/99-12-13.apeen.html, accessed 28 November 2011.
211 "The week in perspective," *TDN*, 19 December 1999.
212 Yasemin Çongar, "Clinton'un Helsinki sevinci," *Milliyet*, 19 December 1999.
213 "Helsinki-Gipfel: Türkei nimmt EU-Offerte an," *Spiegel Online*. Available at www.spiegel.de/politik/ausland/0,1518,56096,00.html, accessed 25 November 2011.
214 "Clinton: Helsinki metnini ben yazdım," *Hürriyet*, 17 January 2000.
215 Interview with Marc Grossman, Washington, 11 May 2010.
216 Murat Yetkin, "Amerika Türkiye'yi AB'de istiyor," *Sabah*, 6 July 2000.
217 Yasemin Çongar and Barçın Yinanç, "Avrupa Birliği size bağlı," *Milliyet*, 8 September 2000.
218 Güven Özalp, "Türkiye'nin Avrupa'da yeri yok," *Milliyet*, 16 April 2000.
219 Taki Berberakis, "Clinton Türkiye için bastırdı," *Milliyet*, 5 December 2000.
220 Decision 2001/235/EC (OJ L 85, 24. 3. 2001, p. 13).
221 Yasemin Çongar, "ABD'den çifte destek, *Milliyet*, 30 October 1999.
222 Christopher Hill and Karen Elizabeth Smith, *European Foreign Policy: Key Documents*, London: Routledge, 2000, p. 243.
223 Stanley R. Sloan, *NATO, the European Union, and the Atlantic Community, The Transatlantic Bargain Challenged*, Lanham, MD: Rowman and Littlefield, 2005, p. 191.
224 "US reiterates support for Turkey's involvement in ESDI," *TDN*, 2 May 2000.
225 Güven Özalp, "Karargahta yerimiz yok," *Milliyet*, 25 May 2000.
226 "Clinton'dan Ecevit'e mektup," *Milliyet*, 12 December 2000.
227 Murat Yetkin, "Türkiye, NATO-AB sınavında," *Sabah*, 14 December 2000.

228 Sibel Yeşilmen, "İşte Clinton'a cevap," *Sabah*, 14 December 2000.
229 "Ödün yok," *Milliyet*, 16 December 2000.
230 Murat Yetkin, "Clinton 10 bin metrede Ecevit'i iknaya çalışıyor," *Sabah*, 16 December 2000.
231 Barçın Yinanç, "Veto silahı hazır," *Milliyet*, 5 December 2000.
232 "Turkey blocks NATO-EU deal," *BBC News*. Available at http://news.bbc.co.uk/2/hi/europe/1072840.stm, 15 December 2000, accessed 1 December 2011; Sami Kohen, "Zorla güvenlik olmaz," *Milliyet*, 16 December 2000; Güven Özalp, "Türkiye direniyor," *Milliyet*, 15 December 2000; and "Ankara geçit vermedi," *Milliyet*, 16 December 2000; and Murat Yetkin, "Avrupa güvenliği konusunda istediğimizi aldık mı?" *Sabah*, 17 December 2000.
233 The date he became the Shadow FS.
234 The date the EP approved the CU decision.
235 Interview with David Robert Bowe, Istanbul, 11 October 2012.
236 "Blair: Türkiye meşru aday," *Hürriyet*, 10 December 1997.
237 Barçın Yinanç and Gülsen Solaker, "Blair'den 'sakin olun' mesajı geldi," *Milliyet*, 15 December 1997.
238 Ferai Tınç, "İngiltere'nin formülü," *Hürriyet*, 3 November 1997.
239 "Türkiye'yi genişleme sürecine çekmeliyiz," *Hürriyet*, 15 January 1998.
240 Zafer Arapkirli, "Clinton ve Blair yanıtladı," *Milliyet*, 19 May 1998; and "Clinton ve Blair'den Ankara'ya destek," *Hürriyet*, 19 May 1998.
241 "EU-Turkey Association Council," *Antenna: News in English*, 21 May 1998. Available at www.hri.org/news/greek/ant1en/1998/98-05-21.ant1en.html, accessed 5 January 2012; and "AB toplantısı olmayacak," *Hürriyet*, 24 May 1998.
242 "EU Council of Ministers' meeting starts," *Antenna: News in English*, 25 May 1998. Available at www.hri.org/news/turkey/anadolu/1998/98-05-25.anadolu.html, accessed 5 January 2012.
243 "İngilizler'in Türkiye kampanyası," *Hürriyet*, 25 June 1998.
244 Heinz Kramer, *A Changing Turkey: The Challenge to Europe and the United States*, Washington DC: Brookings Institution, 2001, p. 198, Zafer Arapkirli, "Lüksemburg delinmedi," *Milliyet*, 17 June 1998; and "AB yeni sayfa istıyor," *Milliyet*, 19 June 1998.
245 Taki Berberakis, "Hedefim Türkiye'nin üyeliği," *Milliyet*, 6 December 1998.
246 Peres's appointment as the Israeli FM.
247 The end of Karayalçın's term of office.
248 Interview with Hikmet Çetin, Istanbul, 23 September 2011.
249 Alan Makovsky, "Israeli-Turkish relations: A Turkish 'periphery strategy?'" Henri Barkey (ed.), *Reluctant Neighbor: Turkey's Role in the Middle East*, Washington, D.C.: US Institute of Peace, 1997, 147–70, p. 154. See also Amikam Nachmani, "A triangular relationship: Turkish-Israeli co-operation and its implications for Greece," *Cahiers d'Etudes sur la Méditerranée Orientale et le monde Turco-Iranien*, Vol. 28, 1970, 149–62, pp. 155–6.
250 Alan Makovsky, "Israeli-Turkish relations: A Turkish 'periphery strategy?'" Henri Barkey (ed.), *Reluctant Neighbor: Turkey's Role in the Middle East*, Washington, D.C.: US Institute of Peace, 1997, 147–70, p. 239.
251 WINEP, "Timeline of Turkish-Israeli relations, 1949–2006." Available at www.washingtoninstitute.org/documents/44edf1a5d337f.pdf, accessed 14 November 2011.
252 Amikam Nachmani, "The remarkable Turkish-Israeli tie," *The Middle East Quarterly*, June 1998, 19–29, p. 24.
253 Signing of the CU decision.
254 Gönensay's term in the office.
255 Interview with Emre Gönensay, Istanbul, 8 November 2012.
256 Orhan Babaoğlu, "Reliant Mermaid naval exercise: Increasing the peacetime role of navies," *Policy Watch* #943, WINEP, 18 January 2005. Available at www.washingtoninstitute.org/policy-analysis/view/reliant-mermaid-naval-exercise-increasing-the-peacetime-role-of-navies, accessed 21 November 2012.

257 Sema Emiroğlu, "Türkiye'ye moral," *Milliyet*, 19 December 1997; and "ADL presents Prime Minister of Turkey with Distinguished Statesman Award." Available at www.adl.org/presrele/Mise_00/3082-00.asp, accessed 25 October 2011.
258 Interview with Marc Grossman, Washington, 11 May 2010.
259 Barçın Yinanç, "Stratejik işbirliği dönemi," *Milliyet*, 15 November 1999.
260 MÜSİAD, "MÜSİAD Ürdün iş gezisi raporu 2002." Available at www.musiad.org.tr/detayDikRapor.aspx?id=5, accessed 12 November 2011.
261 Efraim Inbar, *The Israeli-Turkish Entente*, London: King's College London Mediterranean Program, 2001, p. 25
262 Turan Yavuz, *Çuvallayan İttifak*, Ankara: Destek Yayınları, 2006, p. 107. For the text of the letter, see Office of the Federal Register, National Archives and Records Service, General Services Administration, *Weekly Compilation of Presidential Documents*, Vol. 36, No. 42, 2000, p. 2517.
263 Resolution ES-10/7.
264 *Yearbook of the United Nations: 2000*, UN Publications, 2003, p. 421.
265 Yasemin Çongar, "ABD'den ağır sitem," *Milliyet*, 27 October 2000; and "Yahudi lobisi rahatsız," *Milliyet*, 29 October 2000.
266 Martti Ahtisaari, Remarks at the Brookings Institution, 23 September 2009, unedited transcript available at www.brookings.edu/~/media/events/2009/9/23%20turkey%20europe/20090923_turkey.pdf, accessed 18 June 2012.
267 Morton Abramowitz, "The complexities of American policymaking on Turkey," *Insight Turkey*, Vol. 2, No. 4, 2000, 3–35, p. 9.
268 Derya Sazak, "Clinton'ın küresi," *Milliyet*, 21 December 1997.
269 "Remarks to the Turkish Grand National Assembly in Ankara," *Weekly Compilation of Presidential Documents*, Washington: USGPO, Vol. 35, No. 46, 22 November 1999, pp. 2382.
270 Taylor Branch, *The Clinton Tapes: Wrestling History with the President*, New York, NY: Simon & Schuster, 2009, p. 139.
271 Sami Kohen, "Clinton'ın Türk tarihi merakı," *Milliyet*, 10 November 1999; and Yasemin Çongar, "Clinton halka inecek," *Milliyet*, 12 November 1999.
272 "Ecevit ABD'den memnun döndü," *Radikal*, 3 October 1999.
273 Madeleine Albright, *The Mighty and the Almighty*, New York, NY: HarperCollins, 2006, pp. 243–5.
274 p. 247.
275 "Türk-Yunan ortak pazarı," *Milliyet*, 9 May 1994.
276 "Bill Clinton's Remarks at Georgetown University," *William J. Clinton*, Washington: USGPO, 1998, pp. 2011–12.
277 "Remarks to the Turkish Grand National Assembly in Ankara," *Weekly Compilation of Presidential Documents*, Washington: USGPO, Vol. 35, No. 46, 22 November 1999, pp. 2383.
278 Philip E. Auerswald, Christian Duttweiler, and John Garofano, *Clinton's Foreign Policy: A Documentary Record*, New York, NY: Kluwer Law International, 2003, p. 116.
279 Fikret Bila, "Kıbrıs aleyhte, Lahey lehte," *Milliyet*, 1 December 1999.
280 "Remarks by the President on fiscal year 2001 budget," 27 October 2000, The White House, Office of the Press Secretary. Available at http://clinton4.nara.gov/WH/EOP/OP/html/Fri_Oct_27_144556_2000.html, accessed 30 November 2011.
281 "Remarks at the Legislative Convention of the American Federation of State, County, and Municipal Employees—March 23, 1999," *William Clinton: Book 2*, USGPO, 2001, p. 430.
282 Sami Kohen, "Clinton (ve ABD) neden AB'ye girmemizi istiyor?" *Milliyet*, 11 July 2002.
283 See, for example, Gerald Posner, *Why America Slept: The Failure to Prevent the 9/11*, New York, NY: Random House, 2003.

284 Barçın Yinanç, "Yunanistan'a ABD uyarısı," *Milliyet*, 18 February 1995.
285 Alan Makovsky, "Turkey: Europe-bound," *Policywatch*, No. 429, 15 December 1999. Available at www.washingtoninstitute.org/templateC05.php?CID=1307, accessed 13 February 2008.
286 Gila Benmayor, "Türkiye için en iyi lobi Irak operasyonu olur," *Hürriyet*, 2 May 2002. Author's translation.
287 Volga K. Çağlayangil and Sezin Öney, "AB ile aşka geleceğiz," *Milliyet*, 7 December 1999.
288 As of November 1999. (Source: TÜSİAD-USCC, *US-Turkish Economic Relations in a New Era*, Washington, 14 March 2012, p. 4.)
289 Yalçın Doğan, "ABD'ye cömert gezi," *Milliyet*, 18 December 1997.
290 See page 157 endnote 177.
291 Oya Karakaş, "Türkiye ile ABD arasında olası bir serbest ticaret anlaşmasının, Dünya Ticaret Örgütü ve Avrupa Birliği çerçevesindeki yükümlülüklerimiz açısından incelenmesi," *Uluslararası Ekonomik Sorunlar Dergisi*, No. 7, November 2002. Available at www.mfa.gov.tr/turkiye-ile-abd-arasinda-olasi-bir-serbest-ticaret-anlasmasinin_-dunya-ticaret-orgutu-ve-avrupa-birligi-cercevesindeki-yukumluluklerimiz-acisindan-incelenmesi.tr.mfa, accessed 6 February 2012. See also Muharrem Sarıkaya, "ABD, Ecevit'e 'serbest ihracat' jesti yapacak," *Hürriyet*, 28 December 2001.
292 Yasemin Çongar and Sinan Gökçen, "ABD'nin en iyi dostuyuz," *Milliyet*, 29 April 1999.
293 Ecevit had been afflicted by Parkinson's disease since 1997. He also developed myasthenia gravis, a neuromuscular disorder, in the early 2000s. (Source: Sedat Ergin, "Başbakan Ecevit ne hastası?" *Hürriyet*, 24 May 2002.)

10 The (George W.) Bush Administration (2001–2009)

An Underestimated Effort

Those who believed George W. Bush followed in his father's footsteps were not surprised to see him under the Baccarat chandelier in Dolmabahçe Palace at a state dinner on 28 June 2004. This time the chandelier was casting its light over 40 guests, the heads of state and of government from NATO member and partner countries, and their wives. Istanbul was the venue of a two-day NATO Summit, and the dinner was an event held on that occasion.

The circular dinner table under the chandelier was embellished with traditional Ottoman flower patterns. The tableware had been crafted by a prominent Turkish company ten days before the event. The plates for the main course, the glasses, and the napkins had a stylized Ottoman carnation pattern on them. The dessert plates were decorated with an Ottoman tulip pattern. The same tulip pattern had been drawn with syrup on the dessert on each plate. From above, the table was looking like an intricate arabesque.

When the guests entered into the hall, an expression of amazement flashed across their faces. This expression remained intact while 40 waiters each serving a guest brought the dishes one-by-one. British PM Blair, NATO's Secretary-General De Hoop Scheffer, and First Lady Bush . . . all kept asking complimentary questions about the menu, but the most laudatory reaction came from the French President Chirac. He had the chef de cuisine and the under-chefs summoned. Then in his French accent, he called out to Bush: "Come here, George. This wonderful meal has been prepared by these gentlemen."[1] Just as this little play Chirac put on was to compliment the chefs, it was also to break the ice between himself and Bush. Earlier that day, he had scolded Bush by saying: "He not only went too far, but he has gone into a domain which is not his own. He has nothing to say on this subject. It is as if I were to tell the United States how it should conduct its relations with Mexico." Chirac was known for his sharp tongue anyway, but even during the bitter disputes of the previous year over his opposition to war in Iraq, he had never hurled personal abuse at Bush.[2]

What had annoyed Chirac were the remarks Bush made on the previous day at the residence of the Turkish PM Recep Tayyip Erdoğan:

> I would remind the people of this good country that I believe you ought to be given a date by the E.U. for your eventual acceptance into the E.U. I also look forward to working with you on matters regarding the neighborhood, Iraq and elsewhere. I appreciate so very much the example your country has set on how to be a Muslim country and at the same time, a country which embraces democracy and rule of law and freedom.[3]

With these remarks Bush could not please anyone. Turkish President Ahmet Necdet Sezer reminded Bush that although more than 99 percent of the Turkish population was Muslim, Turkey was not an Islamic but a secular state.[4]

The 'Mexican theme' was Bush's leitmotif heard whenever he attempted to patronize Turkey against Europeans; Chirac's fortissimo rendition of this theme to an international audience at the NATO Summit was not the first time. Verheugen had improvised on the theme in an interview when he was in Ankara on 14–15 February 2002.[5] And it was heard as dinner music at the Copenhagen European Council on 12–13 December 2002:

> Anders Fogh Rasmussen, Denmark's prime minister, told Mr Bush caustically that Washington had failed to grasp the meaning of EU membership, which involves sharing a law-making parliament, a currency and a supreme court in a close-knit union.
>
> He asked: "If you are so keen on us letting the Turks into the EU, why don't you let Mexico into the United States?" Mr Bush deflected the rebuke by laughing [. . .].[6]

1 Changing US Policy

The Bush administration's endeavor for Turkey's EU bid was weaker and more parochial compared to that of the Clinton administration. His Turkey policy was less elaborate than that of Clinton; it was more like a shopping list: support Turkey's EU membership, request cooperation in Iraq, emphasize the compatibility between Turkey's blend of Islam with the values of the West . . . While, in the Clinton era, the cultural element in Turkey's importance had been accentuated at the expense of the geopolitical element (rather than for where it was, Turkey was valuable for what it was), with Bush, the significance of Turkey's geopolitical value—especially the fact that Turkey borders Iraq—increased. Bush resurrected his father's understanding of Turkey–EU relations. Once again, the US advocacy of Turkey's EU membership was—not expressly made conditional on but—connected to Turkey's cooperation with the US in the Iraq issue.

The 11 September attacks brought about a sharp turn in the FP of the US. In his memoir, *Decision Points*, Bush described this change as follows:

> After 9/11, I developed a strategy to protect the country that came to be known as the Bush Doctrine: First, make no distinction between the terrorists and the nations that harbour them—and hold both to account. Second, take the fight to the enemy overseas before they can attack us again here at home. Third, confront threats before they fully materialize. And fourth, advance liberty and hope as an alternative to the enemy's ideology of repression and fear.[7]

Now, the US was pursuing a more assertive and impetuous FP, which posed new risks. In particular, a crisis was brewing in Iraq due to the US war on terrorism, the noncompliance of Iraq with the resolutions of the Security Council of the UN on weapons of mass destruction, and the aspirations of the US to consolidate its control over the region.

Turkey–US relations got their fair share in this process. In an article he wrote in 2008, Mark R. Parris, the USAMB to Turkey from 1997 to 2000, maintained that the 2001–2008 period had been "the most problematic six years in U.S.-Turkish relations since the Cyprus crises of the seventies" and that the burden of responsibility lied with Washington. In his opinion, the following were the four major "sins of commission and omission" of the US:[8]

1   Exploitative myopia: The Bush administration paid attention to Ankara when it needed something, and in most cases this was done in a hurry. In most cases, it was Turkey's geopolitical value that the US wanted to exploit. This approach was manifest in Bush's words about the Iraq War:

> By March 2003, the battle plan was ready. [. . .] The one remaining uncertainty was the role of Turkey. For months, we had been pressing the Turks to give us access to their territory so that we could send fifteen thousand troops from the Fourth Infantry Division to enter Iraq from the north. We promised to provide economic and military aid, help Turkey access key programs from the International Monetary Fund, and *maintain our strong support for Turkey's admission to the European Union.*[9]

And when the Bush administration did refer to Turkey's identity, it was mostly for practical reasons. For instance, this administration sought Turkish soldiers for peacekeeping duty in Iraq in mid-2003.[10] This was partly because, within the NATO-led security mission International Security Assistance Force (ISAF), Turkish troops were the only ones who could mix with the local population.[11]

2   Insensitivity to Turkish interests: In the first years of the 2000s, Turks lost their belief in the effectiveness of the US ventures in their region

and were cautious towards US involvement in such issues as Black Sea security, strategic energy transport, and the 2008 Georgia crisis[12] or such projects as the Broader Middle East and North Africa (BMENA) initiative.[13] Thus, they developed a different set of priorities based, among other things, on establishing closer relations with Russia.

3 Inaction against the PKK: On 1 June 2004, PKK ended the cease-fire it had announced unilaterally on 1 September 1999.[14] Civilian and military casualties mounted rapidly thereafter. Turks believed that the inaction of the US towards PKK was deliberate. Turkey deployed 100.000 troops on its border with Iraq and declared that it would deal with the issue single-handedly.

4 Weak leadership on energy security: The AKP that came to power in the 2002 election in Turkey attributed particular importance to the Baku-Tbilisi-Ceyhan pipeline that had been on the country's agenda for more than a decade. While Russia was present at the highest levels in the project, representation of the US did not go beyond the Deputy ASSTSECSTATE level. The pipeline was formally opened on 13 July 2006.[15]

Parris added that polls conducted in Turkey since 2003 had consistently placed the US in first place among nations viewed as threatening Turkey's security, and prophesized as follows: "The next U.S. President will get a bounce in terms of Turkish public opinion just by not being George W. Bush."[16]

A few issues stood out against this background: the assistance extended by the IMF and the World Bank to the Turkish economy in the early 2000s, Bush's resistance against the activities of the Armenian lobby, and, most importantly, the US endeavor for Turkey's EU membership.

2 US Involvement in Turkey–EU Relations

US involvement in Turkey–EU relations in the first years of the Bush era was inconspicuous. When Turkish PM Ecevit was in the US between 14 and 18 January 2002, 'Turkey–EU relations' was not among the items of priority on his agenda.[17] Before the visit, Ecevit had signaled that strengthening Turkey's economy was crucial for him. He was hoping to secure an increase in trade quotas for Turkish exports to the US.[18] In his talks with Bush, references to Turkey–EU relations were casual. Bush reiterated the importance he attributed to Turkey's EU membership and delivered a one-liner: "Europeans do not like me much. They would probably like to see you rather than me among them."[19] A columnist, who drew up a balance-sheet of Ecevit's visit, mentioned 'Washington's support for Turkey's EU membership' only as the ninth item on the list of the outcomes of the visit.[20]

In these early years, the Bush administration was rather concerned with making sure that Turkey would not turn away from the EU,[21] because the coalition government formed in 1999 was showing two signs in that direction:

1. There was a disagreement between PM Ecevit and Deputy PM Bahçeli, the chairman of the Nationalist Movement Party, over the reforms necessary for Turkey to satisfy the Copenhagen political criteria. Bahçeli was against the abolition of capital punishment and the changing of the Articles 159 (on insulting the state) and 312 (on hate speech) of the Turkish Criminal Code. He threatened that if the rift in the GOT deepened, a restructuration would be necessary in the cabinet.[22]
2. When PM Ecevit's health started deteriorating in the spring of 2002, one of the fears of Washington was that Turkey would turn away from Europe after him since the possible winner of a general election would be the AKP whose dedication to the EU was unclear then.[23]

Americans were of the opinion that the GOT would not last long. In this hazy period, DOS Spokesperson Lynn Cassell said Turkey's EU membership was as crucial to US strategic interests as it was to those of Turkey.[24]

Between February and August 2002, the Ecevit government was able to endorse the first three harmonization packages, which included, among other reforms, amending the abovementioned two articles of the Criminal Code and abolishing the death penalty. Some US diplomats remarked that they were pleasantly surprised at this achievement and took it as a token of the pro-European preferences of the Turkish Parliament. They added that via diplomatic channels the US was continuing to recommend the Europeans that they should keep the door open for Turkey.[25] Marc Grossman (now the Under SECSTATE) met with Günter Verheugen in Brussels on 18 July and told him that Turkey's EU membership would be in the benefit of both the EU and US.[26]

The editorial of the 27 August 2002 issue of the *Washington Times* (*WT*) warned the Bush administration against the rise of the "the Islamic-style Justice and Development Party [(AKP)]" that was leading in polls. It claimed that "[w]hile secular, progressive parties would accelerate the momentum for Turkey's entry into the European Union, a triumph of the Islamic-leaning party could dampen Europe's already tepid enthusiasm for the country's membership." The concluding paragraph of the editorial was as follows:

> While the Bush administration is juggling many foreign-policy priorities right now, it must put Turkey's EU membership near the top. Mr. Bush should lean on his European friends, particularly British Prime Minister Tony Blair, to set a date for formal talks on Turkey's membership. While the union can't be expected to usher Turkey in until it meets the set criteria, it should demonstrate it does, ultimately, want Turkey the join the club.[27]

Although with less dedication—and perhaps skill—than his predecessor, Bush would try to keep the 'Turkey–EU relations' ball as high as possible in his FP juggling from the second half of 2002 onwards.

2.1 Getting a Date for the Opening of the Negotiations

The highlight of the Bush administration's involvement in Turkey–EU relations was its role in the process of Turkey's getting a date for the opening of the accession negotiations. This process involved three stages. In the first stage, the EU was convinced in principle. In the next stage, the EU gave a date—not to open the negotiations but to assess Turkey's eligibility therefor. In the final stage, Turkey was given a date. Let us examine these stages in detail.

2.1.1 The EU Agrees to Give a Date for the Opening of the Negotiations

In 2002, Turks and Americans were actively campaigning to get a date for the opening of Turkey's negotiations with the EU. Towards the end of May, the US diplomats in European capitals started promoting the idea that Turkey's stability was of key importance for the stability of the Balkans and the Middle East; if the EU failed to give a date to Turkey chaos would follow. The diplomats presented this view as the personal opinion of President Bush. Germany, France, the UK, and Italy were in the focus of this campaign, and special importance was attributed to Spain who held the Presidency of the Council, and to Denmark, the next country to hold the Presidency. US diplomats made individual appointments with the MEPs. German parliamentarians who constituted the majority in the EP declared that they were suffocated by the US pressure.[28]

It was around this time that Turkish private sector started lobbying in the US for Turkey's membership. Turkish Industrialists' and Businessmen's Association (TÜSİAD), the largest representative organization of the Turkish private sector, had opened up an office in Washington in November 1998. According to Abdullah Akyüz who established this office, 'working towards increasing the US support for Turkey's EU bid' was among the initial goals set for the office.[29] In May 2002, TÜSİAD organized a conference in Istanbul about Turkey–US relations. In his speech, Tuncay Özilhan, the chairman of the Association, expressed his expectation that the US would help Turkey secure a date at the Copenhagen Council.[30] In October, TÜSİAD representatives came to the US to lobby for a number of issues including the 'date' issue. They met with some key policy-makers such as Daniel Fried, Marc Grossman, and Richard Perle, and were informed about the intense efforts of the Bush administration on Turkey's behalf.[31]

When the Bush administration was planning the Iraq War, securing Turkey's cooperation emerged as a key determinant. Paul Wolfowitz (Deputy

Secretary of Defense—DEPSECDEF), Marc Grossman (DEPSECSTATE), and Joseph Ralston (US European Commander and SACEUR) came to Turkey on 16 July 2002.[32] Wolfowitz conferred with Turkish PM Ecevit. In particular, he was inquiring about the possibilities of launching attacks into Iraq from the bases on Turkish territory. Ecevit told him that Turkey wished that there would be no military intervention. Yet, he added, if there happened to be an intervention, Turkey would like to be informed thereof. He said Turkey would evaluate this issue in the context of its strategic partnership with the US. Wolfowitz took this as a positive answer. Turks presented a list of demands in exchange for their cooperation. A strong backing of Turkey's EU membership by the US was among them.[33]

Although at a lower key than that of the Clinton administration, the Bush administration, too, attributed importance to Turkey's domestic reforms in order to meet the Copenhagen criteria. When the Turkish Parliament adopted the third harmonization package on 3 August, an anonymous high-level US official praised Turkey's efforts and heralded that the US would maintain the level of support given in the Clinton period.[34]

On 30 August, the Bush administration publicly declared that it was in favor of Turkey's getting a date from the EU. Uğur Ziyal, Under Secretary of the TMFA, who was in Washington in those days, was informed about this policy.[35]

In the first week of October, at a Senior Level Group (SLG)[36] meeting in Washington, American officials led by Grossman requested from their European counterparts that Turkey be given a date. Meanwhile, Thomas Weston, the DOS special coordinator for Cyprus, was lobbying for Turkey in Brussels.[37]

The US support for Turkey had become conspicuous again. On 9 October, in his daily press briefing, DOS Spokesperson Richard Boucher was asked a question on this issue:

QUESTION: Diplomats in Washington and in capitals are saying that they are [. . .] under intense pressure by the United States to grant Turkey membership. Are you making such a push for other candidates?

MR. BOUCHER: I think we have made clear our view that expansion is a good thing and that we support it. [. . .] We've also made our views clear, I think, consistently that we think that better relations between the European Union and Turkey are important to us. [. . .] So the answer is yes, we've advocated both the general and some of the specifics.[38]

2.1.1.1 THE WEXLER-WHITFIELD-LANTOS RESOLUTION

On 16 October 2002, three members of the US Congress, Robert Wexler, Ed Whitfield, and Tom Lantos[39] submitted a resolution to the Congress.

The resolution emphasized the importance of Turkey's EU membership. Its 'resolved clause' was as follows:

> Now, therefore, be it
> Resolved, That it is the sense of the House of Representatives that—
>
> (1) the United States should continue to support the efforts of the Republic of Turkey to join the European Union; and
> (2) the European Union should recognize Turkey's comprehensive political and economic reforms and set a date for the initiation of accession negotiations at the meeting of the European Council in Copenhagen to be held on December 12–13, 2002.[40]

The resolution was referred to the CIR but 'died' there. Being one of the few instances of the involvement of the Congress in Turkey–EU relations, this resolution was of peculiar importance.

2.1.1.2 TARGETING GERMANS

The estrangement between Germany and the US prompted by Chancellor Schröder's re-election campaign, in which he assailed Bush's policies on Iraq, was being fueled by the pressure that was now directed at the German government after the German MEPs. In October 2002, the Bush administration gave a list to the German government. The list contained three demands to improve the US–German relations:

1. support for the Iraq operation at the Prague Summit of NATO to be held in November 2002;
2. support for the establishment of the RRF; and
3. support for Turkey's admission to the EU.[41]

As the December European Council approached, the US expanded the scope of its efforts. W. Robert Pearson, the USAMB to Turkey, announced that the US was expecting the EU to give a date to Turkey. He emphasized that he was saying this as a representative of President Bush.[42] A high-ranking US official declared that the US was doing its best at highest conceivable levels for Turkey to be given a date.[43] On 29 October, the seventy-ninth anniversary of the Turkish Republic, Bush sent his congratulations to Turkish President Sezer. In his message, he included a sentence assuring Turks of the US adherence to Turkey's European aspirations.[44]

In his visit to Washington in October, Germany's FM Joschka Fischer was unwelcome:

> [E]ven as Secretary of State Colin L. Powell met with the German foreign minister, Joschka Fischer—in a session delayed after several

American rebuffs to German entreaties for a meeting—the administration dealt the Germans another snub: a refusal to invite Mr. Fischer to the White House.[45]

Fischer's response in this 'antiphon' was once again the Mexican theme. He

> compared the likelihood of Turkey's admission into the EU with Mexico and Central America's admission into the United States. [. . .] [He] suggested that, while friends do many things for each other, getting married to a third party because a friend requests it is not one of them.[46]

Fischer repeated his witty complaint to a Greek official: "The US is trying to convince us to marry Turkey. This is like saying 'this female friend of mine is a good girl; do not miss this opportunity.'"[47]

It is difficult to assess the actual effect of these efforts of the US, but the Conclusions of the Brussels Council on 24–25 October 2002 made it clear that the Council was not negative anymore to the idea of the opening of Turkey's accession negotiations. The details for the next step would be determined at the Copenhagen Council in December.[48]

2.1.2 The EU Consents to Give a Date to Assess Turkey's Eligibility

The 47 days between the Brussels and Copenhagen Councils were critical for Turkey and the US. Both countries were trying hard to make sure that Turkey would be given a date in Copenhagen.

2.1.2.1 COMING TO POWER OF THE AKP

Some important parameters of Turkey–US relations would be altered by the general election to be held in Turkey on 3 November 2002 and by the planned launch of the Iraq War.

It was likely that AKP would win the election. The majority opinion was that Islam was a definitive element in the identity of the party; it was predicted that under the AKP government Turkey would turn away from the West.[49] Two months before the election, Wolfowitz said they did not know AKP well, but Turkey's destination in the long run was clear and evident. He remarked that those who attempted to impose the radical and strict religious practices of the Middle Ages were condemned to fail in Turkey and added that the 11 September attacks had once again emphasized Turkey's importance as a role model.[50]

In September, when Greek FM George Papandreou was in the US for a UN General Assembly meeting, SECSTATE Powell, ASSTSECSTATE Grossman, and some other high-ranking officials told him that they attributed great importance to the Progress Report the European Commission would publish on 9 October; this report would have a substantial impact on the results of the election, and Turkey's efforts to join the EU should be fostered.[51]

In the election, AKP garnered 34.2 percent of the vote and won 363 seats of the 550 seats in the Parliament, while the Republican People's Party (CHP), the main opposition party, received 19.4 percent. Since the AKP leader Erdoğan had been banned from politics,[52] Abdullah Gül from the same party became the PM while Erdoğan continued to lead the party unofficially.

Contrary to expectations, the AKP government soon made Turkey's EU membership a priority. Erdoğan declared that this membership would be one of the greatest steps in the modernization process of the country.[53] On 13 November 2002, he started a series of visits to European capitals. These were comforting signs for the Bush administration.

On 3 December 2002, Wolfowitz and Grossman came to Ankara. This was a 'reconnaissance flight' to make sure that the new government had no intention to alter Turkey's FP parameters and to see how the land lied for the demands the US might place on Turkey in case of an operation against Iraq. Before arriving in Ankara, Wolfowitz had spent a few hours for a stopover in London, advocating Turkey's European bid. Almost half of his speech at the International Institute for Strategic Studies (IISS) was devoted to the importance of Turkey's EU membership.[54] In Ankara, he expressed his support for AKP and for Turkey's EU membership and repeated that Turkey was a role model for Islamic countries (especially for Iraq in the post-Saddam period).[55] His discourse was indicative of that he

1. was convinced of Erdoğan's dedication to Turkey's EU cause;
2. was persuaded that Turkey would collaborate with the US in the planned operation in Iraq; and
3. was coupling this potential collaboration on Iraq with Turkey's EU ambitions:

[H]ere is a new Prime Minister with [. . .] a huge agenda of big issues and he's barely been in office and what he projects is somebody who is very very strongly supportive of Turkey going toward Europe, pressing very hard to gain a date for Turkey in Copenhagen. And he also, I think, understands fundamentally what we're trying to get at in terms of presenting Saddam Hussein with a unified world that will allow us to have some chance of achieving a disarmament of Iraq by peaceful means. [. . .] So I would say that the early signs of this government are very positive for Turkey and for Turkey's relations with the west—not only with Europe but ourselves.[56]

Wolfowitz demanded to base 80,000—according to the Turks, or less, according to the Americans—US troops in Turkey to open up a northern front in case of an operation against Iraq.[57] He extended a formal invitation from Bush to Erdoğan for an official visit to Washington.⁵⁸ This was to put some pressure on Erdoğan and to secure his assistance in the Iraq operation.

A few days later, Richard N. Haass, Director of the Policy Planning Office of the DOS spoke as follows:

> Europe needs to integrate Turkey and needs to give them an accession date. This is a major opportunity to bring Turkey into Europe. It would not simply be an error, but to paraphrase Bismarck, a blunder, if this opportunity were lost.⁵⁹

On 6 December 2002, DOS Spokesperson Richard Boucher declared that if the EU set a date for Turkey at the Copenhagen Council, this would encourage the political reforms in Turkey and contribute to the solution of the Cyprus problem.⁶⁰

2.1.2.2 ERDOĞAN'S VISIT TO THE US

On 10 December 2002, two days before the Copenhagen Council, Erdoğan was in the US for slightly longer than 24 hours as the AKP's chairman. His visit was filled with a series of intense negotiations. He was first briefed on Iraq by Wolfowitz for two hours. Thereafter, he was received by Bush in the White House. Also present at the meeting were Wolfowitz, Powell, Condoleezza Rice (NSA), and W. Robert Pearson (the USAMB to Turkey).⁶¹ As Erdoğan was not the PM yet then, the meeting was held in the Roosevelt Room.⁶² This small windowless room, which measures not more than 25 feet by 35 feet,⁶³ was filled with tension as the stakes were high for both sides.

From the Turks, the Bush administration had two demands:

1. That Turkey cooperate with the US in the Iraq crisis: Bush refrained from being specific about their demands from Turkey.⁶⁴ Later on, Turks learned that the Bush administration was requesting the use of six airbases and two seaports in Turkey. Besides, 60,000 US troops would be deployed in the country;⁶⁵ and
2. That Turkey put pressure on Turkish Cypriots for a solution on the island: Turks were asked to make a framework agreement within the scope of the Annan Plan's revised version in 2003.⁶⁶

Turks, too, had two demands:

1. That the US compensate Turkey's possible financial losses in case of a war in Iraq: The UN sanctions on Iraq had cost Turks between 40 and 80 billion USD.⁶⁷ They had raised a similar demand to Wolfowitz in his visit in December (the figure Turks had in mind was 20–25 billion dollars then);⁶⁸ and

2   That the US use its influence on the EU to give Turkey a date (if possible, a date earlier than 1 July 2005): According to the information leaked to the press, on 4 December 2002 German Chancellor Schröder and the French President Chirac had agreed on that the European Commission would be asked to prepare a report by the mid-2004 on the democratization process in Turkey. If this report found Turkey's progress satisfactory, the negotiations would start on 1 July 2005.[69] The year 2005 was not preferable for the Turks, because they were hoping to start negotiating with the EU while the Union still had 15 Members; it would be more difficult to take a decision on Turkey's accession—which would be subject to unanimity—in an EU with more than 20 Members after the upcoming enlargement in 2004.[70] Later on, this deadline clarified as 30 April 2004.[71]

Erdoğan was so preoccupied with securing US help against Europeans that he let the cat out of the bag early. In the exchange of remarks prior to the meeting, his first words were as follows:

> I thank you very much. We're very happy to be in the United States, who is our ally and friend, and also another source of happiness for us that Mr. President spare the time to meet with us.
>
> Undoubtedly, we see our bid to European Union membership as the most important modernization project of our country since the establishment of the republic. And this will serve as a great jump-start for democracy, enhancement of democracy.[72]

Reporters were hoping to catch a few valuable bits of information before the doors of the Roosevelt Room were closed for the meeting. They were focused on Bush's solicitation of cooperation from Europeans for Turkey. Although Bush did not allow them to ask questions, a reporter managed to pose one: He was wondering whether they could "expect some call for European Union." Bush did not ignore the question. "I made a lot of phone calls already" he said. "My administration is working hard on Turkey's behalf."[73]

At the meeting, Erdoğan did not make any commitment to meet the Americans' demands. Bush promised him financial backing and further support against Europeans;[74] he said that in the coming 48 hours, he would call the European leaders on Turkey's behalf once again.[75]

In his statement after the meeting, Erdoğan declared that most of the meeting was taken up by Turkey–EU relations.[76]

Bush kept his promise. He called Anders Fogh Rasmussen, President of the COEU and, as mentioned above, was made to listen to the Mexican theme on the phone. Powell announced that he was in continuous contact with his European counterparts.[77] He had written a letter to each of them for Turkey.[78] Certain names from the European Commission were contacted by the members of the Bush administration.[79]

As stated in the Introduction section, another option brought to the table by Erdoğan at the meeting was Turkey's admission to NAFTA. Some representatives of Turkish private sector opined that Erdoğan's proposal was nothing more than trying to show to the EU that Turkey had alternatives.[80]

2.1.2.3 REPERCUSSIONS OF BUSH'S EFFORTS

The reaction of the EU members to Bush's efforts for Turkey before the Copenhagen Council was in harmony with their views on Bush's Iraq policy. Those who approved this policy, namely the UK, Italy, Belgium, Portugal, Greece, and Spain concurred with the US in the issue of Turkey–EU relations.[81] In the case of the other EU members, Bush's intervention elicited a flurry of negative reactions.

> "It's certainly not up to the president of the United States to interfere in something so important and which mainly concerns Europeans," the French industry minister, Nicole Fontaine, told a radio interviewer.[82]

Swedish Premier Göran Persson remarked that although Bush had a right to declare his views, they would make their own decisions.[83]

François Bayrou, leader of the Union for French Democracy, a French centrist party, spoke as follows:

> Let us be honest! Actually, behind the candidature of Turkey for Europe stands the United States. For a long time, American diplomacy has considered the European Union as a simple regional alliance of the member countries of NATO. They view Europe eventually as the 'NATO club' on the Eastern side of the Atlantic. [. . .] The Americans are charmed to have a European puzzle inside of which they push their pawn.[84]

Members of the EU institutions, too, were irritated:

> Pat Cox, the president of the European Parliament, said: "Sometimes our friends in Washington are heavier handed than the situation might require, and this might have been one of those situations."
>
> And Pascal Lamy, a French EU commissioner, argued: "It's a classic US diplomacy to want to put Turkey in Europe. The further the boundaries of Europe extend, the better US interests are served."[85]

Günter Verheugen, European Commissioner for enlargement, described the situation as follows: "The veiled pressure and threats that came from within Turkey but also from the outside [. . .] caused a kind of overkill. [. . .] It was just a fraction too much, the fraction that triggered a negative reaction in Europe."[86]

2.1.2.4 THE CONCLUSIONS OF THE EUROPEAN COUNCIL

The relevant part of the Paragraph 19 of the Presidency Conclusions of the Copenhagen European Council appeared as follows:

> If the European Council in December 2004, on the basis of a report and a recommendation from the Commission, decides that Turkey fulfils the Copenhagen political criteria, the European Union will open accession negotiations with Turkey without delay.[87]

The Union was not giving a definite date for the opening of the negotiations. It was uncertain that the European Council in December 2004 would specify a date either. Some columnists claimed that under Turkey's conditions even this was an achievement and that most of the credit for this achievement should be given to the US.[88] However, in fact, these efforts of the US were rather counter-productive or at least ineffective. As indicated above, on 4 December 2002 Schröder and Chirac had agreed on that the European Commission would be asked to prepare a report by the mid-2004 on the democratization process in Turkey. If this report found Turkey's progress in this regard satisfactory, the negotiations would start on 1 July 2005. Paragraph 19 was almost a copy of the Schröder-Chirac agreement, with the exception that the '1 July 2005' date had been replaced with "without delay," which was a less concrete statement. Thus, the ten days between the signing of the agreement and the announcement of the Presidency Conclusions brought a deterioration rather than an improvement to the terms of the start of Turkey's negotiations. It is true that Turks' expectation of 2003 as the start of the negotiations was unrealistic, and the EU's decision in Copenhagen could have been much worse, but the actual contribution of the US efforts remains doubtful.

2.1.3 The EU Gives Turkey a Date

The year 2003 started with a new target for Turks and Americans: securing at the December 2004 European Council a date for the opening of Turkey's negotiations. This was already a difficult period for everyone, and with the coming of the Iraq and Cyprus issues to the table, the situation would get further complicated.

2.1.3.1 THE IRAQ CRISIS

The demand of the Bush administration to use Turkey as a passage in their planned offensive against Iraq was on Turkey's agenda since Wolfowitz's visit in July 2002. Turks were slow and reluctant in responding to this demand due to the following reasons:

1. They were apprehensive of being involved in a war against their next-door neighbor;

2   Domestic politics were undergoing a transition in Turkey: Running for the Parliament had become possible for Erdoğan.[89] In this period, the GOT was not ready to shoulder the responsibility of such a critical decision; and
3   Turkey was trying to get as much as possible from the US in return for being used a springboard to Iraq.

Turkey's procrastination was too much for the US for whom timing was important in opening up a northern front against Iraq. In a tense process—where, according to Calder, a textbook example of 'bazaar politics' was at work[90]—the US was striving to convince Turkey.

In this bargaining, whilst Turkey demanded such remunerations as a high 'toll for passage' or favorable terms for its textile exports, the US offered an attractive financial package. US support for Turkey's EU membership was not a part of this important deal; this support had already become a constant in the formula of Turkey–US relations. Moreover, once the verdict of the Conclusions of the Copenhagen Council was published with its goods and bads, the EU dimension had been shelved for the time being. Finally, the deal was forged and a memorandum of understanding was signed in February 2003. According to the memorandum, Turkish armed forces would have the total control of the management of the US forces on the soil and in the territorial waters of Turkey. Turkish soldiers would enter Iraq together with US soldiers, but they would not be involved in combat unless it was against PKK. After the signing of the memorandum, a US official jokingly said to the Turks: "You brought us to our knees."[91]

On the basis of this memorandum, the AKP government introduced a bill into Parliament on 26 February to allow the deployment of US troops, aircraft, and helicopters in Turkey for a period of six months. To the consternation of the Americans, the Turkish Parliament rejected the bill on 1 March 2003. Among the reasons of this rejection were the following:[92]

1   Some Turkish MPs thought that the scale of the proposed deployment was beyond the requirements of the planned operation in Iraq and that the US request to utilize some sea ports on Turkey's Black Sea coast was dubious. In their opinion, the US army would settle in Turkey for an indefinite time;
2   Religious and moral concerns about the probable civilian casualties in Iraq were voiced by MPs from both the government and the opposition; and
3   Germany and especially France warned the Turkish MPs not to approve the bill. The message coming from France was to the effect that if the bill was to be approved, Turks would have to forget about EU membership for a generation.

Turkey had left the US in the lurch.

> As a consequence of Turkey's failure to allow a real second front in the north of Iraq, Mosul and Kirkuk, not to mention Saddam Hussein's birthplace of Tikrit and much of the Sunni Triangle, remained unconquered [. . .]. This hiatus, of course, gave militants more opportunity to organize and stockpile for the savage guerrilla war that was ultimately to ensue than they otherwise would have enjoyed.[93]

It was only on 20 March, hours after the Iraq War commenced and six days after Erdoğan became the PM that the Turkish parliament allowed overflight rights to the US. This would enable the US air force to carry out airborne attacks of small scale. In return, the US allowed Turks to launch a land operation against PKK bases in Northern Iraq.[94] On 2 April, with a further agreement between Powell and Turkish FM Gül, Turkey allowed the use of its hospitals for the American soldiers wounded in Iraq and consented to the supply of logistics to the US troops via Turkish soil.[95]

Turkey–US relations continued to sour, and on 4 July 2003 another crisis occurred: US forces captured a group of Turkish soldiers operating in northern Iraq, put hoods on their heads and interrogated them. The soldiers were accused of planning an attack on the interim governor of Kirkuk. In retaliation, Turkey closed Habur border gate, the only crossing point for aid and goods between Turkey and Iraq. It also threatened to close Turkish airspace to US military flights, stop the use of the southern Incirlik air base and send more troops into northern Iraq. The Turkish soldiers were released 60 hours later following a 30-minute telephone conversation between Turkish PM Erdoğan and US Vice President Dick Cheney. An official from the TMFA described the detention of the soldiers as the worst incident in Turkey–US relations in 50 years. Turkish newspapers used such headlines as "Ugly American," and wrote that the soldiers had been treated as shabbily as al-Qaeda detainees.[96] A Turkish journalist, who wrote a book on the incident, claimed that the order for the arrest had come from Wolfowitz as retaliation to the uncooperative attitude of the Turks.[97] Wolfowitz denied this claim.[98]

The effect of the Iraq crisis on Turkey–EU relations was equivocal:

1. On the positive side, the crisis reaffirmed Turkey's military and geopolitical value. Even the US, a superpower, was seeking Turkey's cooperation when necessary. Turkey's admission to the EU would increase the relative weight of the EU in international politics.
2. As another positive point, Turkey's initial resistance to the US demands showed Europeans that it would be unfair to treat Turkey as a potential Trojan horse in the EU. However, this impression soon changed when Turkey started cooperating with the US on 20 March. Each step Turkey took with the US in Iraq fueled the dislike of those EU members,

especially France and Germany, who were against the Iraq policy of the US. As explained above, this could be one of the reasons behind their refusal to give Turkey an earlier and more concrete date at the Copenhagen Council.
3   On the negative side, the crisis increased the uneasiness of some EU members with the possibility of Turkey's accession. France and Germany were even less willing now to admit to the Union a Turkey that had a long border with crisis-prone countries of the Middle East and that seemed to be inclined to meddle in those crises.[99]
4   The biggest uncertainty was whether the US would retaliate against Turkey's intransigence by reducing or even ending its efforts for the latter's European prospects.

2.1.3.2 A MOMENT'S HESITATION

In the spring of 2003, Turks contemplated putting some distance between the US and themselves, and drawing closer to Europe[100] on the following grounds:

1   They were expecting to be punished by the US. Probably, the Bush administration would not be so willing to put its weight behind Turkey's accession.
2   The US efforts for Turkey had started to become deleterious for Turkey's interests. An interview with Verheugen published in April 2003 contained a clear expression of this situation:

> Mr Verheugen says US pressure has been "counter-productive" to the Turkish cause and insists it is better for the EU to conduct negotiations with Ankara in a low-key atmosphere.
>   With tensions between the US and some European countries still high after the Iraq war, Mr Verheugen urged Washington to stay out of what are likely to be difficult talks with Turkey.
>   [. . .]
>   [Verheugen] says Washington's push to bring Turkey into the EU at the earliest opportunity annoyed many Europeans at last December's Copenhagen summit, when Ankara's membership bid was discussed.[101]

3   There were some encouraging signals from the EU, which meant that Turkey's need for the US help was lesser. Michael Christides, the Ambassador of Greece—the country that held the Presidency of the Council—to Turkey said the Iraq War had increased Turkey's importance for the EU, and Turkey's attitude in the war had proven once again that Turkey was a European country.[102] At the AC meeting between Turkey and the EU on 15 April 2003, Verheugen stated that if Turkey

fulfilled the Copenhagen political criteria and if the Cyprus problem was solved, Turkey could become an EU member in 2011–2012.[103] Furthermore, the draft text[104] of the Treaty Establishing a Constitution for Europe that was presented to the Thessaloniki European Council to be held on 19–20 June 2003 did not contain a reference to Christianity. Such a reference, advocated by several circles including the Vatican,[105] would have alienated Turkey.

Yet, it did not take Turkey long to notice that the signals coming from Europe were nothing more than to console Turkey while ten candidate countries were signing their treaties of accession[106] in Athens on 16 April 2003. The EU was not only reluctant to assist Turkey to recover the country's likely financial losses due to the Iraq war but was also against the entry of the Turkish forces into northern Iraq. Turkey's pressing demands for financial assistance notwithstanding, the European Commission's pre-accession package remained limited to 1 billion euros.[107] "If Turkish troops cross the border, it would be a serious act which would contradict a whole series of undertakings by the Turkish government" President of the European Commission Prodi declared. Belgian FM Louis Michel spoke as follows: "Very strong pressure must be put on Turkey to let it know that taking such action will be a determining factor in refusing its entry to Europe."[108] In September 2003, Giscard d'Estaing, President of the Convention on the Future of Europe, claimed that efforts to make Turkey an EU member would never come to fruition and that Turkey–EU relations should be inspired by US–Mexico relations.[109]

Turks realized that despite the troubles between the two countries, they still needed the US support.

2.1.3.3 NO INTERRUPTION IN THE US SUPPORT

On 6 May 2003, two Turkish journalists interviewed Wolfowitz in Washington. He was still resentful to Turkey. He said

> I suppose I could say we are not the ones who said get out of Incirlik. It was the moment when one might have expected an ally to say, okay, all of the restrictions are off, you use Incirlik for anything you need to. Instead we were told Operation Northern Watch is finished so leave. We don't want to be in places where we are not wanted and we don't want to be in places where we may be wanted but are no longer needed.[110]

Even in that mood and state of mind Wolfowitz was supportive of Turkey's EU membership. The 'coda' of the interview was as follows: "Mr. Secretary, I should say [. . .] thank you very much for joining us. I want one reply, yes or no. This administration is going to back Turkey for EU membership or is it out of [incomplete]?" Wolfowitz's answer was "Yes."

At the EU–US Summit in Washington on 25 June 2003, Bush came together with Prodi and Simitis, Greek PM and President of the COEU. To his two guests Bush emphasized the importance of encouraging Turkey's reforms.[111]

The Brussels European Council to be held in December 2004—where Turkey was hoping to get a date—was on the horizon. In this critical period, a decrease in the US engagement would not be in Turkey's benefit. For Europeans, the Brussels Council would be a kind of a 'return game' of the Helsinki Council. In November 2003, Jacques Simonet, the SECSTATE for European Affairs of Belgium, remarked as follows:

> When we really opened the door to Turkey in 1999, this was done for very wrong reasons, under pressure from Americans who certainly did not pursue an objective of consolidating the process of European construction. [. . .] It's good to give a political signal, but those who want join the Union must meet certain political and economic standards—this will be verified in December 2004.[112]

2.1.3.4 THE YEAR 2004

The US approach to Turkey–EU relations underwent two transformations in 2004:

1   In the first half of the year, the Cyprus issue overshadowed Turkey–EU relations, because 24 April 2004, the date of the referenda[113] to be held in the Turkish and Greek parts of the island, was approaching. In Erdoğan's visit to the US between 26 and 31 January 2004[114] 'Turkey–EU relations' was not an important item of in his talks with Bush, which was unusual taking into consideration the upcoming Brussels Council. In their remarks following their discussions at the White House on 28 January, Bush and Erdoğan addressed several issues of common concern including Cyprus but not Turkey–EU relations.[115] The opinion of the Bush administration was that the solution of the Cyprus problem would strengthen Turkey's hand in its negotiations with the EU. Turks were dissatisfied with Álvaro de Soto as the intermediator and inquired about the possibilities of having a US intermediator appointed. Erdoğan's visit could not render this possible, but it was agreed that Colin Powell would step in on the Cyprus issue.[116]

Nevertheless, backing Turkey's European vocation was not put aside completely. In the context of the Greater Middle East Initiative,[117] which the US had started promoting in the late 2003, Turkey maintained a special place. In a bill prepared by senators Chuck Hagel and Joe Lieberman to authorize programs to assist the countries involved in this initiative, Turkey was the only country for which a paragraph was devoted. This paragraph contained a special reference to the need to facilitate Turkey's accession to the EU.[118] This bill was introduced on 8 April 2004 but was not enacted.

2 In the second half of 2004, Bush's involvement in Turkey–EU relations first took a pompous tone but soon became inconspicuous. When he came to Ireland to attend the EU–US Summit to be held on 26 June, he was welcomed by Prodi and Bertie Ahern who was the Irish PM and the President of the COEU. In their press availability, shortly after the introductory sentences of his speech, Bush brought up the topic of Turkey's EU membership with a *lapsus linguae*:

> Tomorrow I will travel to Turkey for the NATO summit—actually, today I will travel to Turkey. (Laughter.) Tomorrow is the NATO summit. Turkey is a proud nation that successfully blends a European identity with the Islamic traditions. As Turkey meets the E.U. standards for membership, the European Union should begin talks that will lead to full membership for the Republic of Turkey.[119]

As we have seen above, at the NATO Summit, his words about Turkey–EU relations attracted fierce criticism from European leaders. This repulse did not deter the Bush administration but only make it change its strategy. In October, an anonymous US diplomat declared that the US support for Turkey's EU bid was continuing; the US was taking steps in this direction at every level, albeit more tactfully this time. According to him, Rice and Powell were involved in this campaign, and the administration was getting the intended results thanks to its initiatives made without causing any annoyance.[120]

The new modus operandi of the US was in line with the recommendations of the Atlantic Council. A policy paper published by the Council in August 2004 contained a multidimensional analysis of the upcoming Brussels Council and recommended the Bush administration not to "campaign openly in [. . .] countries such as Germany or France where public efforts are likely to be counterproductive."[121]

The presidential election to be held in the US on 2 November further constrained the US campaign. On 12 November, one month before the Brussels Council, Rockwell Anthony Schnabel, the USAMB to the EU, stated that an optimistic atmosphere was prevailing both in the EU and in Turkey and that Turkey would get a date at the Brussels Council.[122] On 13 December, three days before the Brussels Council, Eric S. Edelman, the USAMB to Turkey, assured Erdoğan about the determination of the Bush administration.[123] Edelman was cooperating with the British ambassador Peter Westmacott.

2.1.3.5 THE BRUSSELS EUROPEAN COUNCIL

The Brussels Council came without the usual tumult orchestrated by the Americans. At the Council, on 16–17 December 2004, a heavy pressure was put on the Turkish delegation led by Erdoğan to sign—or at least initial—an additional protocol to extend the Ankara Agreement to new MSs. For Turks, this would mean recognition of the Greek Cypriots as the sole representative of the island before the start of Turkey's negotiations. Tony Blair—together with Silvio Berlusconi, PM of Italy—were the only two figures who tried to sympathize with the Turks. The Bush administration was closely following process but was not intervening. During the Council meeting, the Turkish delegation received a phone call from Laura Kennedy, US Deputy ASST-SECSTATE for EUR. She was saying that a crisis desk had been established in Washington and that they were ready to step in if the delegation needed any help. Finally, the Turks agreed to initial the protocol (as an indication of their intention to sign it), with the reservation that their initialing would not mean recognition of the Greek Cypriot administration.[124]

Paragraphs 19 and 22 of the Conclusions of the Council appreciated Turkey's declaration of intent to sign the protocol and heralded that Turkey's accession negotiations would open on 3 October 2005.

On 17 December, White House Press Secretary Scott McClellan declared that the US welcomed the EU's decision.[125] Four days later, Bush himself called Erdoğan and congratulated him on the EU's decision.[126]

2.1.3.6 THE WIKILEAKS PHENOMENON

On 28 November 2010, Wikileaks, which described itself as a not-for-profit media organization operating online,[127] began releasing purportedly secret information including some documents presented as classified cables that had been sent to the DOS by its consulates, embassies, and diplomatic missions around the world. The authenticity of these documents was questionable. Nevertheless, their impact on politicians and public was evident. Some of the 251,287 documents released had references to Turkey–EU relations. Two of these were cables that had allegedly been created in December 2004, the first being an account of the Brussels Council and the second an evaluation of the performance of the AKP government and of Erdoğan by the USAMB Edelman.

2.1.3.6.1 The Wikileaks Account of the European Council Of the Wikileaks documents, one, in particular, dated 23 December 2004, looked like the script of a farce. Entitled "Turkey Accession/EU: The Mysterious Case of the Missing Declaration," this document was alleged to have been prepared by the US Embassy in The Hague. It was presented as two insiders' recounting of the behind-the-scenes dimension of the December 2004 Brussels European Council. According to the document, during the last hours of the Council, while French President Chirac gently coerced Cypriot President Papadopoulos to settle for a mere initialing of the protocol by the Turks, the British PM prevented his Turkish counterpart Erdoğan from abandoning the meeting. The document claimed that the GOT's declaration of intent to sign the protocol, mentioned in Paragraph 19 of the Presidency Conclusions, had no official evidence. It was Pieter de Gooijer, Director of the European Integration department of the Dutch Foreign Ministry—one of the two insiders—who tore from his notebook the page on which the final version of the Paragraph was written and managed to have it signed by the Turks. Commissioner Olli Rehn signed it on behalf of the European Commission and the Dutch State Secretary Arzo Nicolai for the Netherlands as the MS that held the Presidency of the Council. De Gooijer then made the page 'disappear,' perhaps as a 'remuneration' to—or a part of a collusion with—Erdoğan.[128]

On 3 March 2005, EU officials declared that they hoped that signing of the protocol would happen soon "to prevent any slippage."[129]

Turkey's procrastination in signing the protocol prompted the Greek lobby in the US Congress to initiate a resolution "Urging the Republic of Turkey to comply with all European Union standards and criteria prior to its accession to the European Union."[130] Submitted by Robert Menendez and a group of co-sponsors on 28 July 2005, this resolution was inviting Turkey, *inter alia*, to extend its CU to 'all' the EU members and to end its 'invasion' of Cyprus. The Resolution died in the CIR. On 29 July, Turkey finally signed the Protocol through an exchange of letters with the Presidency of the COEU and with the European Commission. In its letter, Turkey noted that its signature did not betoken recognition of the Greek Cypriot administration.[131]

The significance of the abovementioned Wikileaks document stems from the purported process of leakage of information to the US about Turkey as much as the leaked information itself. If this cable is accurate, we can surmise that the US Mission to the EU (USEU) was trying to make the most of every opportunity to be informed about Turkey–EU relations and report this information to the DOS duly. According to the document, de Gooijer related his story to the DCM and the Political Officer of USEU at a reception hosted by the DCM on 20 December. The second insider was "a Council staffer who was note-taking for the final session" of the meeting. This staffer shared his experiences with the Political Officer. This particular cable was also an evidence of the willingness of the Dutch government to cooperate with the US for Turkey.

2.1.3.6.2 Edelman Evaluates the Aftermath of the European Council A cable, asserted to have been created on 30 December 2004 and written by Edelman, the USAMB to Turkey, contained an evaluation of the first two years of the AKP and of Erdoğan in power. The text was critical of the GOT and pessimistic about Turkey's EU prospects. It claimed that some "core institutions of the Turkish state"—probably referring to the army—and "nationalists on right and left" were accusing the Erdoğan government of having sold out "Turkey's national interests (Cyprus) and Turkish traditions." According to the cable, not much had been done to prepare the bureaucracy and the public opinion for the changes necessary for EU membership. Lack of confidence at Turkey's ability to join the EU was prevalent in AKP, and there was a widespread doubt that the EU would be around in attractive form in ten years. There had been a noticeable tension between Erdoğan and FM Gül during the Brussels Council in particular and in Turkey–EU relations in general. It was a Turkish journalist who had informed Edelman of the rift between Erdoğan and Gül. The same journalist had told Edelman that when the negotiations were stuck on 17 December, Erdoğan advisors got phone calls from Russian President Vladimir Putin's advisors who recommended them to walk out. Within AKP there was a discord over the meaning of Turkey's EU membership: For some, Turkey's role was "to take back Andalusia and avenge the defeat at the siege of Vienna in 1683" and for some others Turkey's accession process was an opportunity "to marginalize the Turkish military and what remains of the arid 'secularism' of Kemalism." While Euro-aversion prevailed in the cabinet, the ministries of the AKP government were incompetent to advance the country's harmonization process with the EU, because these ministries were hiring "on the basis of 'one of us,' i.e., from the Sunni brotherhood and lodge milieu that ha[d] been serving as the pool for AKP's civil service hiring."[132]

In short, the cable was describing Erdoğan and his cabinet as unqualified and unwilling to conduct relations with the EU; the advisors of this government were receiving recommendations from Russia.

If this cable was indeed sent to the DOS, it must have increased the Bush administration's determination to further Turkey's EU bid, because the Turkey depicted in Edelman's cable was one that was more likely to drift away from the West.

2.2 Countdown to the Opening of the Negotiations

In accordance with the Paragraph 22 of the Conclusions of the Brussels Council, the European Commission was required to submit to the COEU a proposal for a framework for negotiations with Turkey. Then, the Council would try to agree on that framework with a view to opening the negotiations on 3 October 2005.

This process did not run smoothly. A few MSs were claiming that Turkey should be given a 'privileged partnership' status instead of full-membership. Although 'privileged partnership' was never defined formally and clearly, it surely referred to a serious downgrading in the status to be accorded to Turkey. This concept, often associated with Wolfgang Schäuble, a German politician from the Christian Democratic Union (CDU), had been around since 2002.[133] Privileged partnership remained mere rhetoric until Angela Merkel, the Chairperson of the CDU, actively promoted it in 2004 and 2005 hoping to mold the public opinion, to muster up support from some fellow European politicians, and to convince Turks for this option before 3 October 2005.[134] The Austrian government and the French presidential candidate

Nicolas Sarkozy were also advocating this status for Turkey. On several occasions, the GOT vehemently denied this option.[135]

In this process, the Bush administration tried to make sure that Turkey–EU relations would not lose the full-membership perspective and the negotiations would be opened on 3 October 2005. They were maintaining their restrained approach. Especially in this period when they were trying to mend their relations with Germans. The September 2005 general election to be held in Germany would be an opportunity for the US, because it was probable that Chancellor Schröder who was opposed to the US-led war in Iraq would lose the election to Merkel who promised a more pro-American policy. For Turks, on the other hand, this was an unwelcome possibility. While Schröder was in agreement with Bush that Turkey should join the EU, as noted above, Merkel was advocating the privileged partnership option.[136]

2.2.1. Enter Rice

In the first months of 2005, Erdoğan and Merkel were trying to improve their relations with Bush, while Bush was having a difficult job of restoring Germany's friendship without sacrificing Turkey's EU prospects. For Bush, one sensible move in this predicament would be to put a fresh face to the forefront of the administration's support for Turkey, whereas he himself stayed aside. This face would be Rice's.

Rice became the SECSTATE on 26 January 2005. In her first foreign travel, she visited Ankara after London, Berlin, and Warsaw.[137] 'Turkey–EU relations' was not a primary topic she discussed with Turkish officials.[138] Nevertheless, on several occasions, she assured Turks that despite the resentment of her administration due to the Turkey's stance in the Iraq crisis, the US interest in Turkey's EU ambitions was intact. In response to a question she said the following:

> Well, it was certainly a disappointing decision given our long alliance and the need to transport American forces, and I think we made no secret of that. I think whatever the relationship was to what happened subsequently is really speculative but we are moving on in our relationship. If we were not moving on, it would not be the case that the United States has been so strongly supportive of Turkish European Union or the support for the Turkish economic reforms and its IMF program.[139]

A few months later, in a public speech she delivered in San Francisco, she emphasized the importance of Turkey's EU membership to prevent a clash of civilizations between Muslim Turkey and multi-religious but Christian Europe.[140] In June, in her meeting with three European leaders Rice stated that Turkey should be a vital part of an enlarging Europe.[141]

2.2.2. The BMENA Alternative

On 8 June 2005, Bush welcomed Erdoğan to the White House. Despite the fact that prior to the meeting, Scott McClellan, the White House Press Secretary, had declared that this meeting would "provide the opportunity to invigorate U.S.-Turkish cooperation with respect to Turkey's European Union aspirations,"[142] neither of the leaders spoke publicly on Turkey's candidacy. In this low-key approach of the Bush administration, some alternative opinions from within the administration became more audible. For example, Zoellick, now Rice's deputy, spoke as follows:

> It's important for Turkey reform orientation to look beyond the European Union to a global context. [. . .] It's important that our bilateral ties not be too constrained by the effort at EU accession. [. . .] The European Union is clearly important to Turkey's future, but so are the countries of the broader Middle East.[143]

This was not a good idea for Turks. For them, Turkey's possible position in the BMENA initiative could never be lumped together with the country's European vocation. In his visit to the US in January 2004 and at the G8 Summit in June 2004, Erdoğan had expressed his interest in the initiative; in his opinion, Turkey's involvement in this initiative would prevent the country's isolation from the processes that would shape the region.[144] Beyond that, Turks would not like to be categorized as Middle Easterners. Thus, their commitment to the initiative remained limited.[145]

2.3 The EU Decides to Open the Negotiations

In June 2005, Schäuble came to Washington to represent Merkel.

> Originally, Schäuble was scheduled to meet solely with US national security adviser Stephen Hadley. But, in a sign that Washington is interested in improving US-German relations should the Conservatives sweep September's election as many predict, Schäuble got the red carpet treatment—an unscheduled 45-minute meeting with President George W. Bush and Secretary of State Condoleezza Rice.
> [. . .]
> There was a difference of opinion on Turkey's prospective membership in the EU, however, as Schäuble made clear that Merkel's party remains opposed to full membership, preferring instead to pursue a 'privileged partnership'—something that is 'not quite the position of Washington.' [146]

On 16 September, the *Financial Times* (*FT*) published an article by Grossman who had retired from the DOS the same year. Grossman wrote that

Americans should hope that Blair would keep the EU focused on Turkey. He was recommending that the Bush administration be prepared to sign a free-trade agreement with Turkey if the 3 October meeting of the COEU gave Turkey the red light.[147]

As the meeting of the Council approached, the Americans speeded up their efforts. Nicholas Burns, Under SECSTATE for Political Affairs, and Daniel Fried, ASSTSECSTATE for EUR, started communicating with Europeans, while Ambassador Edelman intensified his communication with his British counterpart Westmacott.[148]

On 29 September, Turkish FM Gül called Rice. He revealed her his concerns over a possible imposition of 'privileged partnership' and his unhappiness with a certain paragraph in the draft decision of the Council. If finalized, this paragraph would enforce Turkey to lift its veto to the membership of Cyprus to NATO.[149] Rice immediately got down to the job. She summoned the EU ambassadors in Washington and reaffirmed her administration's commitment to Turkey.

Rice remained in touch with the British FS Jack Straw before and during the Council meeting. Luckily, the UK was holding the Presidency of the Council in this term. Austria was the main obstacle to the opening of the negotiations. Ursula Plassnik, the Austrian FM, was insisting on the privileged membership option, and 80 percent of Austrians as well as the main political parties of the country were opposed to Turkey's membership. In the night before the meeting, Straw had taken pains to convince Plassnik whereas Blair telephoned Wolfgang Schüssel, the Austrian Chancellor. Meanwhile, Rice called Erdoğan and comforted him that Turkey could conclude any agreement it was pleased with the EU, having the peace of mind that that agreement would not bind Turkey in NATO, "because" she said "we do not think that this will be the case."[150]

The outcome of the meeting of the COEU on 3 October 2005 was pleasing for Turks: The Council approved the opening of the accession negotiations.

After the Council meeting, Gül thanked Rice and requested her to convey his gratitude to Bush, Hadley, and (Nicholas) Burns.[151] Three months later, Erdoğan hosted a dinner for the EU ambassadors in Istanbul. In his remarks at the dinner, he specifically thanked Blair and Straw in their absence. He then turned to Westmacott, thanked him too and said: "That last night must have been a very exhausting one for you."[152]

2.3.1 A Weird Combination

While the Bush administration was trying to secure a positive outcome from the meeting of the COEU, a strange development took place at the US Congress. On 29 June 2005, two bills were introduced that were sponsored[153] and co-sponsored[154] by Congressman Adam Schiff, known for his efforts in addressing Armenian-American issues. Although these two bills aimed at upholding the interests of Armenians and Armenia, they had references to Turkey–EU relations as well.

The first bill, sponsored by Schiff, was aimed at commemorating the alleged Armenian Genocide and urging Turkey not only to acknowledge the claimed role of its predecessor state, the Ottoman Empire, in the issue but also to reach a 'just resolution' with the Armenian people. Interestingly, the bill was offering support to Turkey's European bid. However, this support was conditional on Turkey's

1 acknowledgment of the 'culpability' of the Ottoman Empire;
2 rapprochement with the Republic of Armenia and the Armenian people, and
3 fulfillment of the accession criteria determined by the EU.

The bill was introduced and referred in the HOR.

The goal of the second bill co-sponsored by Schiff was to end the Turkish 'blockade' of Armenia. The bill was drawing attention to that "[Turkey had] been repeatedly urged by the European Union to open the last closed border of Europe," and claiming that the EU's security and economic interests necessitated Turkey's lifting its blockade of Armenia. The bill was introduced in the HOR. Schiff would introduce this bill once again on 15 May 2008.[155]

Although the two bills in question did not have a concrete effect on the official policy of the Bush administration regarding Turkey–EU relations, they were important in two senses:

1 These were the first bills that had reference to Turkey–EU relations, submitted 14 years after Solarz's resolution, which could be interpreted as a sign of the insignificance of the issue for the Congress; and
2 They were evidence of the complex nature of Turkey–EU relations and the multitude of the stakeholders including Armenians.

2.3.2. Negotiations Start

The efforts of the Bush administration for Turkey did not stop after securing the opening of Turkey's accession negotiations. On 18 October 2005, Bush met with José Manuel Barroso, President of the European Commission, at the White House to discuss the transatlantic agenda.[156] 'Turkey–EU relations' was a topic they talked about.[157] At the oath-taking ceremony of Ross Wilson, newly appointed USAMB to Turkey, on 30 November,[158] Rice noted that US backing for Turkey would continue and emphasized the importance of maintaining the EU membership prospect of Turkey as a secular and democratic country the majority of whose population is Muslim.[159]

Wilson met regularly with EU ambassadors for the same cause. He spoke to the whole group of EU ambassadors twice in formal meetings and also worked with smaller groups of ambassadors. Like his predecessor Edelman, he cooperated closely with Westmacott.[160]

In January 2006, Fried said Turkey's EU membership "would be a good thing for Europe, a good thing for the Middle East." Such a move would show that "the European Union [was] not a Christian club. It would be a club of European countries linked by values and aspirations."[161]

On 27 April 2006, Rice arrived in Ankara. She and Turkish FM Abdullah Gül agreed to prepare a statement of the strategic vision for US–Turkish relations.[162] This statement was made public on 5 July in Gül's visit to the US.[163] Since the early 1990s, the two countries had attempted to define their relations by using special terms. In Camp David on 22–23 March 1991, Özal invited George H.W. Bush to upgrade the relations between the two countries to a new model based on strategic cooperation and consultation. Özal called this new model 'strategic partnership.' The two leaders agreed on this idea in principle and remained in close consultation during the Gulf War.[164] In her visit to the US in October 1993, Turkish PM Çiller introduced another model that she called 'enhanced partnership.' This new model would include cooperation, consultation, and coordination in several fields including trade, agriculture, or health. Clinton was positive towards this proposal. Working groups were established to take concrete steps.[165] However, neither Özal's 'strategic partnership,' nor Çiller's 'enhanced partnership' was put into written form, nor did they contain a specific reference to Turkey–EU relations. The strategic vision document declared by Rice and Gül, was offering again a 'strategic partnership' but was now

1 secured in writing; and
2 contained a specific reference to Turkey–EU relations: "The United States strongly supports Turkey's accession to the European Union and the accession process now underway."[166]

This statement was a concrete evidence of the opening of a new page in Turkey–US relations and a symbolic contract that would 'obligate' the US to promote Turkey's European prospects.

On 12 June 2006, Turks eagerly started their accession negotiations with the EU. The negotiation framework specified 35 chapters.

Erdoğan made a phone call to Bush on 8 September. Besides such issues as Iran, Syria, or Iraq, the two talked about Turkey–EU relations. Bush assured Erdoğan of the US efforts for Turkey.[167] In his visit to the US between 30 September and 2 October 2006, Erdoğan's summary of his talk with Bush included the following:

> We have [. . .] discussed Turkey's progress and reforms with regards to the European Union—the Copenhagen political criteria, as well as Maastricht criteria, and the recent work that is ongoing with the screening process at the EU for Turkey's accession.[168]

2.4 Negotiations Come to a Grinding Halt

Turks' happiness lasted only a few months. On 29 November 2006, the European Commission recommended suspension of talks on eight of the 35 chapters on the ground of Turkey's refusal to open its trade to vessels from Cyprus.[169] Congressman Frank Pallone delivered a speech against Turkey in the HOR on 7 December 2006. He recommended that the EU FMs approve the recommendation of the European Commission. He called Turkey to end its 'occupation' of the northern Cyprus.[170] On 11 December, EU FMs agreed to follow the Commission recommendation and decided to suspend talks on eight chapters and not to close the other chapters until Turkey changed its policy.[171] The US found it prudent to stand aside again. To a question inquiring the US position in this regard, ASSTSECSTATE for European and Eurasian Affairs Daniel Fried responded as follows:

> I'm not going to comment on the specifics. For one thing, these discussions are still in motion, and there are many things I could say, many things the United States could say that would not help the process, so I will let caution be my watchword in describing this.[172]

'Turkey' had become a 'constant' in the French formulation of anti-Americanism. In an interview published by *Le Monde* on 9 September 2006, when asked whether the Europe he was defending was subservient to America, French presidential candidate Nicolas Sarkozy replied furiously:

> Under no circumstances and in no way! .... How can you ask such a thing? Who wanted Turkey in Europe?: President Bush ... And you ask me if I am aligned with the Americans! It is you who were aligned with the Americans, you, *Le Monde*, calling me a populist because I was opposed to the entry of Turkey into the EU. This is a major issue where I opposed head-on—because I am attached to a political Europe—to a US strategy.[173]

There was now a considerable gap between Turks' expectations and what the US could do under these conditions. At a roundtable at the Washington Foreign Press Centre on 9 January 2007, Clayland Boyden Gray, the USAMB to the EU, received a detailed and demanding question from a Turkish journalist. Gray's answer was distant—in literal sense—and measured:

> QUESTION: Would you talk about the Turkey-EU negotiation process? It seems that Cyprus is the main obstacle now. And Turkey—the EU expects Turkey to combine its obligations which is opening its ports to the Cyprus Government. And Turkey expects the EU to ease the embargo of Northern Cyprus before opening its ports. What can the U.S. Government do to help this process go any further and how do you see the latest development?

AMBASSADOR GRAY: Well, step back. I mean, there really is not much the U.S. can do actively to resolve this issue. This is really a European problem and I think the position of the U.S. is—the President expressed this recently—we would very much hope that Turkey would gain admission but we're not taking an active role in lobbying the member states or taking any other actions to deal with this.[174]

The UK, too, had to cut down its activities that, under the present conditions, were being prejudicial to the interests of not only Turkey but also of the UK itself; especially the French were irritated.[175] Following the 11 December meeting, "the train is still on the tracks" said the British FS Margaret Beckett,[176] but her declaration did not change the fact that she had consented to the suspension of the negotiations on eight chapters, which was decided unanimously.

In those days, the only voice heard in Turkey's favor was that of Wexler who was taking heart from the fact that the speech he delivered in the Rayburn House Office Building situated on the Capitol Hill on 15 March 2007 was inaudible from Europe. His speech, addressed to the Subcommittee on Europe of the COFA of the HOR, included the following:

> While I respect my European colleagues and their concerns about possible membership, Turkey's eventual full inclusion in the EU so clearly benefits Europe's long-term interests, as well as those of the United States. I urge the EU and its members not to close the door on Turkey and create the conditions that will promote further political and economic reform in Turkey.[177]

Sarkozy's taking over the Presidency on 16 May 2007 was another adverse event for Turks. At first, Sarkozy said he did not want to be involved in a fight on Turkey to avoid complicating talks on the proposed Reform Treaty at the Brussels Council to be held between 22–23 June, but he could not wait so long. Around 12 June, Merkel (Germany was holding the Presidency of the Council then) declared that she hoped to open three more chapters in Turkey's negotiations. These were Statistics, Financial Control, and Economic and Monetary Policy. France warned that it had particular problems with the third of these chapters and was reserving its position on all the three chapters.[178] On 25 June, Sarkozy blocked the third chapter.[179] In the second half of 2008, France held the Presidency of the Council. On 27 August, Sarkozy said he would veto the five chapters that he considered directly relevant to Turkey's accession. Together with the eight chapters previously suspended by the Council, the total number of the blocked chapters rose to 12 (one chapter was common in the two lists).[180]

Bush refrained from confronting Sarkozy. Turkey would have to wait for the next American president for US patronage against France.

2.4.1 Rising Anti-Americanism and Anti-Europeanism in Turkey

Towards the end of Bush's term, the dissatisfaction of the Turkish public with the policies of the US and of the EU reached a record high.

While the AKP government and the Bush administration quickly bound up the wounds of the 2003 crisis at the official level, anti-Americanism continued to brew in Turkish public opinion. In Turkey, works of fiction that depicted the two countries at armed conflict became best-sellers and box-office hits. *Metal Storm*, a novel published in Turkish in December 2004, told the story of a war between the Bush administration and the Erdoğan government. In the novel, while the US army was invading Turkey, Turkey was making allies with China, Russia, and Germany. A nuclear bomb was being detonated in Washington. A Turkish movie, *Valley of the Wolves: Iraq*, released in February 2006, depicted a Turkish special forces unit that infiltrated into Iraq to hunt down the US commander who had ordered the aforementioned capture of the Turkish soldiers in July 2003. Especially the sections of the movie that showed American forces raiding a wedding, killing innocent civilians, and torturing prisoners had a cathartic effect on the Turkish viewers. A survey conducted by an American research center and released in June revealed that the image of the US was the worst in Turkey among the 47 countries covered by the survey; 83 percent of the Turks entertained negative sentiments towards the US.[181]

Likewise, the EU's reluctance towards Turkey's membership in general and the suspension of eight chapters in Turkey's negotiation process in particular decreased Turks' enthusiasm for EU membership and their trust in the Europeans. While in the spring of 2004, 71 percent of the Turks had been in favor of EU membership, in the autumn of 2008, this rate dropped to 42 percent. The rate of those who trusted in the EU dropped from 51 percent to 27 percent between the autumn of 2004 and the autumn of 2008.[182]

In February 2007, Seyfi Taşhan, a commentator known for his belief in the necessity of anchoring Turkey to the West wrote as follows: "Some of the actions and measures taken by both Europe and the United States smack of an undeclared Cold War by the West towards Turkey."[183]

If translated into political action this popular indignation could inflame Turkey's relations with the West. Even worse, the elixir—his touting of Turkey—Bush kept near at hand and applied onto Turkey against such inflammations was causing an allergic reaction in Europeans now. It was again Rice who, like a dexterous nurse, came to his rescue. Reminiscent of Clinton, Rice never missed an opportunity to argue for Turkey. Even in her remarks upon her reception of the Eric M. Warburg Prize in Germany on 31 May 2007, she said Turkey's inclusion in the EU would strengthen Europe.[184] At the American–Turkish Council, she preferred to emphasize the importance of Turkey's domestic reforms.[185] In their remarks she and her cadre were careful in choosing their words not to offend Turks or give the impression of intervening in the domestic affairs of Turkey: when Turkey's constitutional court was considering arguments for closing down AKP and banning its leadership from politics for threatening the secular nature of the Turkish state, "we don't take sides" remarked the head of the DOS's European Bureau.[186]

Once or twice, Bush attempted to use his elixir timidly while there was no European around. When Turkish President Abdullah Gül visited him at the White House on 8 January 2008, he said "I view Turkey as a bridge between Europe and the Islamic world, a constructive bridge." He described Turkey as a "great strategic partner and 'a fantastic example' of democracy co-existing with Islam and added 'I strongly believe that Europe will benefit with Turkey as a member.'"[187] His words soon backfired. Elmar Brok, a German politician and the EP's enlargement rapporteur,

> criticized Bush's government of asking the EU to bear the consequences of full freedom of movement to all Turkish citizens while the U.S. is building high security fences to stop Mexican immigrants along the Rio Grande.[188]

A few days after Bush's declaration, Turkey, Germany, and France agreed to hold a tripartite summit in March. According to Turks who have always been inclined to see Europe at the disposal of the US, Bush's efforts were one of the factors that convinced France and Germany to participate this summit.[189] However, it soon became evident that the real intention of the French and Germans was to impose Turks a status less than full-membership. The summit was cancelled due to Turks' refusal to participate.[190]

There was one case, though, where Bush at least intended—but could not find "a lot of time"—to clarify the US position to Europeans for the n-th time: One of the early paragraphs of the speech he delivered after the EU–US Summit in Slovenia on 10 June 2008 was as follows:

> And, by the way, one subject we didn't spend a lot of time on that I'd like to clarify the U.S. position on is, we strongly believe Turkey ought to be a member of the EU, and we appreciate Turkey's record of democratic and free market reforms, and working to realize its EU aspirations.[191]

This was a final hit-and-run for Bush who would leave the office almost six months later.

2.4.2 "They Won't Admit Us to the EU"

Turks' pessimism about the country's EU prospects continued to grow in the summer of 2008. On 11 June, a major pro-opposition Turkish daily *Cumhuriyet* claimed that Turkish FM Ali Babacan, who was on a state visit in Washington, had complained to his counterpart Rice about Europeans: "We know that Turkey will not be accepted to the EU. Nevertheless, we solicit you to put pressure on the French so that this negative atmosphere could be dissipated and the reaction of the Turkish public mitigated."[192] On the same day, TMFA denied the claim.[193] Although an unreliable source, the minutes of the Babacan–Rice meeting published by Wikileaks[194] do not contain any such complaint by Babacan either. True or not, *Cumhuriyet*'s story was a reflection of the cynical *mise-en-scène* of Turkey–EU relations in 2008.

2.5 Other Related Issues

In the W. Bush era, Turkey–EU relations were affected by the following issues: the Cyprus question, the status of the Turkish army in domestic politics and in the new European security structure, Turkey's financial problems, the trade dimension of Turkey–US relations, and the terrorism problem in Turkey. These issues are examined below:

2.5.1 The Cyprus Question

The Clinton administration's initial ideal of maintaining simultaneity between the accession processes of Cyprus and of Turkey to the EU had long collapsed before coming into power of the Bush administration. While the accession negotiations of Cyprus had been going on since 1998, those of Turkey would have to wait until 2005 to start. Even so, the Bush administration continued to support the accession of both Cyprus and Turkey and to observe the link between the two processes. Wolfowitz would describe the revised understanding of this link as follows:

> Although the two issues in principle are separate, both Turkish and European leaders acknowledge that Turkey's EU application and the long-standing Cyprus problem are linked at the practical level. The plan put forward last month by the UN Secretary General provides the basis for a just and lasting solution.[195]

As a more feasible project than Turkey's accession, accession of Cyprus had gained priority. Now, the support extended to Turkey was rather to secure its consent to the EU membership of Cyprus than to make Turkey's own membership possible. Greeks were aware of this. The Greek newspaper *Ethnos*, wrote that economic aid, support in its relations with the EU, and a place in the decision-making mechanism of the ESDI would be promised to convince Turkey to assume a more cooperative stance in the Cyprus issue.[196] In March 2001, Grossman, Under SECSTATE for Political Affairs, revealed that a prospect for accession to the EU would be an important reward to convince Turkey and the TRNC to come back to the negotiation table;[197] once the Cyprus issue was solved, this would improve Turkey's chances of joining the EU.[198]

2.5.1.1 TOWARDS THE COPENHAGEN EUROPEAN COUNCIL

Until the mid-2002, in accordance with Turkey's preferences, the US refrained from influencing the Cyprus negotiations. When it became clear that the deadlock in the negotiations would have a negative effect on Turkey's EU prospects and on the future of the island itself, the US changed its strategy.[199] Bush requested some concrete steps from Turkey in Erdoğan's abovementioned visit in December 2002. What Bush was expecting from Turks was to convince Denktaş to assume a more cooperative stance. One month before Erdoğan's visit to the US, on 11 November 2002, Álvaro de Soto, Special Adviser to the UN Secretary-General Kofi Annan, had presented the two sides of the issue a comprehensive plan (Annan Plan I) for the resolution of the problems. Taking the feedback of the parties into consideration, a revised version of the plan (Annan Plan II) was prepared and again presented to the parties on 10 December, two days before the Copenhagen Council. Annan was hoping that the new version of the plan would help the parties reach an agreement before the Council. Erdoğan was under an intense pressure from de Soto,[200] from Solana,[201] and from Denmark that held the Presidency of the Council.[202] He reflected this pressure onto Denktaş. Denktaş resisted the pressure, and the relations between the TRNC and Turkey deteriorated to an unprecedented degree.[203]

Initially, Turks were in agreement with the Americans and Europeans that the Cyprus issue and Turkey–EU relations could be dealt with together[204] because with this strategy Turkey would be able to use the Cyprus card in exchange for a date for the opening of the accession negotiations. Upon encountering Denktaş's tenacity, Erdoğan changed his discourse and started to defend the idea that the two issues should be considered separately. He said the EU should take the first step and give Turkey a date—then the solution of the Cyprus problem would follow.[205] Around 9 December, Erdoğan sent a letter to Rasmussen, PM of Denmark and the President of the COEU. Erdoğan committed himself that if Turkey was given a date in Copenhagen, he would convince the Turkish Cypriots for a solution.[206] Turkish Cypriots were expected to sign the plan before the Conclusions of the Council. During the Council meeting, in a distressing and theatrical process de Soto kept the text of the plan on a table until 17.30 on 14 December, waiting in vain to have it signed by the parties.[207]

As stated above, the Copenhagen Council confirmed the successful completion of the accession negotiations of Cyprus and set 28 February 2003 as the deadline for the parties of the Cyprus issue to reach an agreement so that the whole process could be completed before Cyprus's signing of its accession treaty on 16 April 2003.[208]

2.5.1.2 THE REFERENDA

After the Copenhagen European Council, the US continued to be involved in the Cyprus issue. In 2003, Weston made several visits to Turkey and

Greece.²⁰⁹ His main aim was to end the division of Cyprus before the admission of the island to the EU in May 2004.²¹⁰ He said solution of the Cyprus issue would facilitate Turkey's accession to the EU.²¹¹

The third and fourth versions of the Annan Plan were rejected by the parties, and the 28 February deadline was missed. Finally, the fifth version of the plan satisfied both of the parties. Simultaneous referenda were held in the Greek and Turkish parts of Cyprus on 24 April 2004 on the reunification of the island on the basis of the Annan Plan. Whereas a majority of the Turkish Cypriots (65 percent) voted for the plan, Greek Cypriots (75 percent) voted against it. Thus, the plan could not be implemented. On 1 May, the Greek part of Cyprus representing the whole of the island acceded to the EU. The following quotation is indicative of the Americans' frustration with the Greeks:

> "We do think that there was a lot of manipulation by the Greek Cypriot leaders in the run-up to the election; that the outcome was regrettable but not surprising given those actions," said the State Department spokesman, Richard A. Boucher.
> [. . .]
> The United States sought to improve the chances of its ally Turkey to enter the European Union through a 'yes' vote and lobbied Cypriots hard to accept the United Nations-proposed peace plan.²¹²

In 2010, Marc Grossman expressed their disappointment as follows:

> the Annan Plan came; there was the vote; and amazingly enough, it was the Turkish Cypriots who voted 'yes' and the Greek Cypriots who voted 'no.' One should not speak ill of the dead, but I sometimes think that what if Mr. Clerides had still been the President of Cyprus, or others who had been the President of Cyprus before? . . . That deal²¹³. . . That might have happened. The Greek Cypriots and the Turkish Cypriots might have voted 'yes'; that was our hope, that was our goal. Then, a unified, bizonal, federated Cyprus would have gotten into the EU. It was obviously a great disappointment when that did not work out. The beginning of that policy gets into people's minds during the time that Holbrooke is Assistant Secretary.²¹⁴

On the whole, the US involvement in the Cyprus issue did not bring about the intended consequences on Turkey–EU relations. The solution conceived by the Clinton and Bush administrations was to make the accessions of Cyprus and Turkey to the EU possible along two separate but mutually contributing tracks, whilst, in reality, the membership of Cyprus to the EU did not prove to be conducive to Turkey's accession for two reasons:

1   In the short term, new problems arose between Turkey and the EU. Turkey refused to open its ports and airports to Cyprus, whereas, mainly

due to the veto of Cyprus, eight chapters were suspended in Turkey's accession negotiations.
2   In the long term, the accession of Cyprus meant likelihood of one more veto on Turkey's prospective accession decision to the EU which would be subject to unanimity.

The accession of Cyprus left a number of issues unsolved and at least one of the parties to the Cyprus dispute dissatisfied: First,

> [t]he 1959 Zurich and London Agreements that established Cyprus as an independent country stipulated that this country could not join international organizations or pacts of alliance of which both Turkey and Greece were not members [. . .]. Second, the 1960 Treaty of Guarantee contains the provision that Cyprus cannot participate in whole or in part, in any political or economic union with any state whatsoever. Third, the EU never consulted with the Turkish Cypriots over Greek Cypriots' application for membership.[215]

2.5.2 Security Issues

For the Bush administration, the concept of security was relevant to Turkey–EU relations on two grounds:

1   In the Bush era, Turkey's domestic politics entered into a process of demilitarization. To continue with the harmonization of Turkish laws with the EU's acquis, the Turkish Parliament passed the seventh harmonization package, which, among other amendments, aimed at limiting the role of the military. The *FT* called this harmonization package a 'quiet revolution.'[216] For the Americans, this process warranted more efforts for Turkey's EU membership for two reasons:

    a   As the military dimension was the strongest leg of Turkey–US relations, the decline of the influence of the army in Turkish politics also meant a decrease in the 'area of the surface of contact' between the two countries, and a weaker organic link between Turkey and the West.
    b   Constraining the military's room for maneuver in favor of the civilian element in the domestic politics of Turkey would improve the country's prospects for EU membership. However, this process could also be a sign of Islamization of Turkish politics. Traditionally, Turkish army had seen itself as the 'guarantor' of the secular character of the Republic, and it was a possibility that with these steps the AKP government was getting closer to the establishment of a more Islamic regime in the country. Turkey's EU membership would prevent this possibility.

2   After the Clinton administration, Turks maintained their concern over being left outside of the new security architecture of Europe. For them, "EU decisions with regard to Turkey's place in emerging European defense initiatives [had] become a key test of whether Brussels [was] serious about Turkey's new candidacy."[217]

2.5.2.1 THANKS TO SADDAM

The first comments of the Bush administration were in line with the Turkish position regarding European security. At the first NAC/PSC (Political and Security Committee) meeting between NATO and the EU on 5–6 February 2001, Donald Rumsfeld, the US SECSTATE, declared that the emerging security structure of Europe should be open to all the NATO members. A high-ranking Turkish official interpreted these words to mean that the US was now lending an ear to Turkey's demand; in his opinion, Europeans had been shocked by Cem's blocking of the NATO–EU deal in December 2000.[218] However, on 8 February 2001, Powell invited Turkish FM Cem to find 'a middle way,' while telling him that the US took Turkey's concerns seriously. According to European diplomats, Powell had told them that the impression that the US was against the formation of a European army was wrong; this, they said, would correct the Turks' misconception. Indeed, Cem stepped back and said that they did not intend to block the functioning of NATO.[219] In the spring of 2001, the US continued to put pressure on Turkey in this direction[220] while Turkey continued to drag its feet.[221]

The US became more tolerant towards Turkey's concerns in the summer of 2001, since Turkey's help was needed against Saddam. In his visit to Turkey in June 2001, Rumsfeld declared that he understood Turkey's apprehension about the ESDP issue and added that the restructuration of the security architecture of Europe should reserve a right of refusal for NATO.[222]

At the NATO Headquarters Summit on 13 June 2001, Turkish PM Ecevit was prepared to face some pressure to change Turkey's position. To his surprise, Bush and Blair told him that they were behind Turkey in every way. Yet, they added, they expected a solution from Turkey in the ESDP issue.[223] In Ecevit's visit to the US between 14 and 18 January 2002, Bush promised to side with Turkey in the ESDP disagreement.[224]

2.5.2.2 THE ANKARA DOCUMENT

Bush and Blair continued to work together to convince Turkey to take a softer line in the ESDP issue. British and American diplomats had a series of informal negotiations with Ecevit[225] who also received a formal letter from Blair. Remembering the mistake Evren had made by being contented with a verbal guarantee given by Rogers, Turks were trying to secure the promises of their counterparts in a written agreement.[226] On 26 November 2001, the US, UK, and Turkey privately formulated a text—known as the Ankara Document—that assured Turks that the ESDP would not be used against non-EU NATO members (i.e., Turkey). The agreement guaranteed that Turkey would be closely consulted in the case of an intervention by the EU's RRF in any contingency that might occur in Turkey's geographic vicinity or that could affect Turkish security interests.[227] In early December, certain details of the agreement were leaked to the press. Greek FM Papandreou called his American and British counterparts Powell and Straw and asked the meaning of the news circulating in the media. Unsatisfied with the answers they received, the Greek government declared that they would not be bound by such an agreement.[228] Meanwhile, the GOT gave its consent to the agreement, which meant a determination to lift its veto. At around the same time, Greek and Turkish Cypriot communities restarted their talks that had remained dormant for almost a year. This was surprising given the fact that only a few weeks earlier Ecevit had threatened to annex Northern Cyprus if the Cyprus Republic was to be admitted to the EU without an agreement between the Greek and Turkish communities. According to Missiroli, the simultaneity between Turks' change of mind in the ESDP and Cyprus issues was a sign of a coupling between these two issues.[229]

The Americans and Turks were naively confident that the rest of the process would run smoothly.[230] At the Laeken Council on 14–15 December 2001, Greece rejected the Ankara Document and forestalled its implementation.[231] Nevertheless, Turks were not disappointed with the Conclusions of the Council. Cem stated that they had tried their best in the ESDP issue and that for the first time their negotiating position was included in an official document of the EU.[232] PM Ecevit said that in the negotiations that took nearly two-and-a-half years, Turkey did its utmost and that now the problem was between Greece and the EU.[233]

In the following months, Americans focused on Greeks. In February 2002, Weston and Lynn Pascoe, Deputy ASSTSECSTATE for EUR, had talks with Papandreou in Athens.[234] Together with Hannay, the UK's special representative to Cyprus, Weston visited Ankara.[235] In June, US officials declared their approval of the Ankara Document.[236]

In the rest of the process, Turkey secured some concrete gains:

1   The Ankara Document was approved at the Brussels Council held on 24–25 October 2002.[237] The Conclusions of the Council assured Turkey that under no circumstances, would the ESDP be used against an ally,[238] and that in the case of an EU-led operation using NATO assets and capabilities, non-EU European allies would, if they wished, participate in the operation and be involved in its planning and preparation in accordance with the procedures laid down within NATO.[239]

2   The following sentence was included in the Conclusions of the Copenhagen Council convened on 12–13 December 2002:

> If the European Council in December 2004, on the basis of a report and a recommendation from the Commission, decides that Turkey fulfils the Copenhagen political criteria, the European Union will open accession negotiations with Turkey without delay.[240]

3   A discrimination was made in favor of Turkey. Cyprus and Malta, whose treaty of accession to the EU had been signed on 16 April 2003, were banned from all EU–NATO consultations with a NAC decision taken on 13 December 2003.[241]

In return, Turkey lifted its veto, paving the way for the so-called Berlin Plus agreement. The conclusion of the agreement, announced on 16 December 2002, enabled the EU to engage in limited crisis management in its neighborhood by using NATO assets and capabilities.[242]

Most of the negotiations on the cooperation between the EU and NATO occurred behind closed doors, and the texts of the Ankara Document and Berlin Plus agreement were never made public. The Annex II of the Presidency Conclusions is believed to be a verbatim reproduction of the Ankara Document.[243]

2.5.3 Turkey's Economic Problems

In the first two years of the Bush era, Turkey experienced a severe economic crisis under the coalition government led by Ecevit. The crisis reached its peak on 21 February 2001, Turkey's Black Wednesday, the day when banks withdrew billions of dollars from the Central Bank in hours, repo interest rates peaked at close to 7.500 percent, and the Istanbul Stock Exchange's main ISE-100 index plunged by 18.1 percent.[244] Turkey's candidate status had just been approved, and these economic problems increased doubts about the country's ability to meet the economic criteria of EU membership.[245]

Between 1999 and 2002, Turkey received a series of rescue packages from the IMF, the total of which amounted up to 35 billion dollars. Pearson, the USAMB to Turkey, declared that the US had been instrumental in the payment of these packages. He revealed that 17 billion dollars of this aid was sustained by American taxpayers.[246] A commentary published in the *NYT*, evaluating the latest of these packages, included the following sentence: "The rescue package for Turkey comes only a few weeks after the I.M.F. cut off aid to Argentina, which shares Turkey's chronic economic difficulties but not its strategic importance."[247] According to Pearson, the economic aid the US extended to Turkey was not primarily intended to support Ecevit, his government, or the IMF but to enable Turkey to continue with its reforms on its way to EU membership.[248]

In several places, the EU's 2003 Regular Report on Turkey appreciated the contribution of the IMF to Turkey's economy.[249]

2.5.4 The Trade Dimension of Turkey–US Relations

During the Bush presidency, Turks were dissatisfied with their trade relations with Americans as usual—with one difference: Now the EU had become an important factor in these relations. Turkey had been a part of the CU of the EU since 1 January 1996. The functioning of this CU put Turkey in a disadvantageous position in its trade with the US. The rates of the CCT applicable to many of the goods originating from the US were low, and Turkey's imports from the US were subject to these rates. On the other hand, the US was applying higher rates to its imports from Turkey. Especially in the case of textile and clothing sector, this unfair situation was more pronounced.

In the Clinton era, Turks had accepted this situation as it was and did not voice any complaints; for them, this was a small price for Clinton's favor towards Turkey, but when Bush took office, this issue came to the fore. In the lead-up to the Iraq War, when asked about what the possible demands of Turkey could be in return for its assistance to the US against Iraq, Perle and some Turkish businessmen recommended asking for favorable trade terms.[250] In September 2001, four major unions and associations representing Turkish textile and clothing industrialists established a working-group to redress this imbalance. Among the tasks of this group was to choose a lobbying firm in the US. This firm would work for the recognition of the same status to Turkish textile exports to the US as that was enjoyed by those originating from the EU,[251] for lifting of the quotas, and for the establishment of a QIZ in Turkey as a springboard for, inter alia, textile exports to the US in favorable terms.[252] The firm selected was Patton Boggs. These efforts did not bring about any concrete change.[253] The might of the American industrialists and the interests of Jordan and Israel in the case of QIZs were the impeding factors for Turkey. Unable to obtain their objective in Washington, the Turkish textile lobby hammered out an interesting deal to be put into effect in Istanbul: They brought together in the city the representatives of the textile and clothing sectors from 36 countries including Turkey. On 3 March 2004, these representatives signed a text known as the Istanbul Declaration.[254] Among other details, this declaration was inviting the representatives to lobby their governments to make sure that the WTO would continue to allow quota protection through 2007. This was a gesture from Turks to protect the domestic textile market of the US against Chinese exporters. In return, the Americans were supposed to forgo their objection to inclusion of textile and clothing sectors in QIZs and ease their pressure on their government so that textile imports from Turkey could have access to the US on more favorable terms. However, the Americans remained reserved towards both issues.[255]

Turks considered the option of negotiating a free-trade agreement with the Americans. Before Ecevit's aforementioned visit to the US in January 2002, this option was discussed in Turkey. It was concluded that first, such an agreement would be incompatible with Turkey's CU with the EC, and second, although customs tariffs Turkey applied to US exports were not high, reduction of these tariffs to zero would be compelling for Turkish industrialists.[256] Ecevit decided to demand a PTA from the US.[257] Bush told Ecevit that he was sympathetic to the idea and set up a commission chaired by Alan Larson, Under SECSTATE for Economic, Business and Agricultural Affairs, to work to this aim.[258] In the end, a PTA could not be concluded either. Instead, Turkey was kept on the list of the beneficiaries of the GSP of the US reauthorized in 2002[259] until 31 December 2006, and in 2006[260] until 31 December 2008.

2.5.5 The Terrorism Problem in Turkey

As noted above, PKK's terrorist activities had been a serious problem for Turkey since the late 1970s. Following the 11 September attacks, the COEU adopted a Common Position on the application of specific measures to combat terrorism.[261] This document included a list of persons, groups, and entities involved in terrorist acts. This was—colloquially referred to as—the EU's first 'terror list.' Turkey requested the names of PKK and the Revolutionary People's Liberation Party–Front (DHKP-C) be included in this list. Germany, Belgium, and the Netherlands were not amenable to the idea, whereas the US and the UK were on Turkey's side.[262] Behind closed doors, the Bush administration strived to convince the Europeans to extend the list.[263] In the Council Decision of 2 April 2004,[264] PKK and DHKP-C were included in the list.

3 Collaborators of the US

The UK, Israel, and the Netherlands were the main companions of the Bush administration in its campaign for Turkey.

3.1 The UK

Compared to the Clinton administration, the Bush administration had a limited room for maneuver in Europe to work for Turkey. Thus, the need for the UK as an 'insider' was greater. The UK did not disappoint the US in this sense.

Around March 2001, the US and the UK were trying to put on the final scene of Holbrooke's plan. The steps to be taken were to complete the accession negotiations of Cyprus in June 2001, to bring the full-membership of the island onto the agenda of the Union in the Presidency of Denmark in the second half of 2002, and to put pressure on Turkey when Greece took over the Presidency in the first half of 2003 (with this pressure, Turks would be expected to assume a more cooperative attitude in the Cyprus issue). The three British diplomats to be starring in the key roles in this scene were David Hannay, Brian Cowe, and Michael Leigh.[265] As explained above, this scene did not have a happy ending for Turks.

On several occasions, the British government comforted the Turks. It is worth remembering the assurance Blair—and Bush—gave to Ecevit at the NATO Summit in June 2001 by telling him that they were behind Turkey in every way. On 20 November 2002, Erdoğan met with Blair in London. Blair promised him 'full-support,' and told him that he would talk to Schröder for Turkey.[266]

The UK also encouraged Turkey's domestic reforms. In July 2002, the Turkish Parliament was considering to hold an early election in November. The UK feared that the political instability that would ensue in this process could drive Turkey away from the EU. British Ambassador Westmacott expressed his hope that Turkey would not slow down its reforms on the way to the EU membership.[267]

It was together with the help of the UK that the US negotiated the Ankara Document with Turkey in November 2001, and it was the UK who brought the Document to the negotiating table at the Brussels Council in October 2002.[268]

Towards the critical Copenhagen Council of December 2002, the presence of the UK in the game became more pronounced.[269] In the speech he delivered one day before his visit to Turkey, Wolfowitz gave examples of how Turkey's unique secular approach to Islam was appreciated by the US and the UK alike. He said: "My boss, Secretary Donald Rumsfeld, has observed that 'everything [is] easier' when British forces are with you."[270]

Jack Straw, the SECSTATE for Foreign and Commonwealth Affairs of the UK, came to Turkey on 3 December 2002, the same day Wolfowitz and Grossman came. He declared his country's support for Turkey's getting a date at the Copenhagen European Council:[271]

> Prime Minister Tony Blair of Britain had joined the United States in pushing for Turkey's candidacy. Blair had said he believed that allowing Turkey to join the EU would send "an important signal to the Islamic world," according to his official spokesman, Tom Kelly. "We think a firm date is necessary, and we want that as soon as possible," Kelly said before the decision was made [at the Copenhagen Council].[272]

Before the Copenhagen Council, Blair made a last-minute call to Chirac for Turkey on 13 December.[273] When Blair arrived at Copenhagen, he called the Council to set a concrete date for Turkey. In his opinion, the year 2005 would be too late "to send a signal to the wider Islamic world that we want to engage with them." He went to a pre-Council meeting with Erdoğan. His discourse was in conformity with that of Bush. He told his Cabinet that the Copenhagen Council "could transform relationships with Turkey." "We cannot afford to pass up the chance of placing Turkey on the path to modernisation" he added.[274] After the Council, Blair was the person Turkish PM Gül called and complained about Chirac.[275]

Blair would not conceal that Turkey's being an ally of the US was a factor contributing to his position. In the speech he delivered at the Lord Mayor's Banquet on 10 November 2003, he said the following:

> Europe is already the largest economic market and political alliance in the world. It will become bigger and the symbolism of Turkey, a Moslem nation and American ally, joining the EU could not be more epochal.[276]

From December 2004 onwards, while the US stepped back, Britain assumed an even more active role. The abovementioned efforts of Blair, Straw, and Westmacott before and at the 3 October 2005 meeting of the COEU are an example of this situation. Westmacott was close to Erdoğan with whom he could converse in Turkish. Whenever Erdoğan had a problem with the EU, he would turn to the people around him and ask: "Where is Peter?" After completing his tenure in Turkey, Westmacott was appointed as the Ambassador to France where he continued to promote Turkey's interests in the EU.[277] In October 2012, Turkish President Gül awarded Straw the Order of the Republic.[278]

In the Bush era, similar to the case in the US politics, support for Turkey's EU bid was an issue above the party politics in the UK: not only the Labor government but also the Conservatives were actively promoting Turkey. On 28 October 2008, Conservative Friends of Turkey (CFT), a group associated with the British Conservative Party, was officially launched. At the cocktail reception organized on this occasion, William Hague, the Shadow FS, referred to Turkey–EU relations: "The Conservative Party is energetically in favor of Turkey's accession to the European Union."[279]

3.2 Israel

In coordination with Jewish organizations in other countries, the Jewish lobby in the US tried to make sure that the high level of backing they provided to Turkey in the Clinton era was maintained in the Bush era. On 13 April 2001, Bruce M. Ramer, President of the American Jewish Committee (AJC), and its Acting Executive Director Shulamith Bahat wrote a letter to Bush. He emphasized the importance of extending economic assistance to Turkey and working for the country's EU membership:

> As you prepare for your discussions with Turkish officials in the coming days, we wish you to know of our appreciation for the U.S.-Turkey partnership—and the ongoing and vital relationship between Turkey and Israel—as well as our support for the Turkish Government's efforts

to stabilize its economy, and our endorsement of that nation's aspiration to become a full member of the European Union.[280]

Four days after the adoption of the Conclusions of the Brussels Council of December 2004, which included a decision to start the accession negotiations with Turkey, David A. Harris, the Executive Director of the ACJ, published an open letter with started with the following paragraph:

> The European Union's invitation to Turkey last week to open negotiations for membership is truly momentous. No, this isn't hyperbole. If anything, it's an understatement.[281]

The same letter had a reference to Israel too:

> And, in Israel, the EU's announcement will also be welcomed. Israel has publicly declared its support for Turkey's accession. Even though, like Washington, Jerusalem runs the risk of slippage in its thriving bilateral ties with Ankara should Turkey's foreign policy become "Europeanized," it believes the overall benefits for Turkey and the eastern Mediterranean make the risk well worth taking.

Turkish Parliament's adoption of the 3 August 2002 harmonization package to meet the Copenhagen criteria was applauded by the Jewish lobby in Washington. Tom Lantos, the most senior member of the Jewish lobby in the US HOR, praised Turkey's reforms and invited the EU to give Turkey the earliest date at the Copenhagen Council to be held in December 2002.[282]

Turkish–Israeli relations started deteriorating in 2006. Turkey sent troops to Lebanon as part of the international peace-keeping force after Israel's military campaign against Hezbollah. In the same year, Turkey became the first NATO country to host the Hamas leader Khaled Mashaal.[283] This deterioration found its reflection in Israel's policy towards Turkey–EU relations. From 2006 onwards, no Israeli initiative was taken for Turkey's EU bid.

3.3 The Netherlands

In the Bush era, the opinion of the Dutch citizens on Turkey's EU membership was positive in general; in the average of the January 2001 and April 2008 period, 42 percent of them were in favor of Turkey's EU membership. This rate was above the EU average (30 percent) and was slightly lower than the highest rate that belonged to Spain (42 percent).[284] Dutch politicians in government and opposition alike were positive towards Turkey's membership. They preferred a 'strict but fair' approach to Turkey and believed that Turkey's EU membership would be a positive message to the Islamic world.[285]

Even if we disregard the Wikileaks account of the December 2004 Brussels Council, the fact that the Council was convened under Dutch Presidency remains meaningful. News reports from the period recount the impressive efforts of the Dutch PM Jan Peter Balkenende for Turkey on the eve of the Council. On 7 December, he embarked on a European tour to talk to Greek, Greek Cypriot, German, French, Hungarian, Danish, and British leaders for Turkey (with the other leaders, he would talk on the phone). His tour included a meeting with Erdoğan in Brussels.[286]

Here, the critical question is whether this courtesy to Turkey contained any element of cooperation with the Americans for Turkey's EU membership. There was a conducive atmosphere for such cooperation:

1   Soon after the 11 September 2001 attacks, the Netherlands became another country threatened by Islamist terrorism. On 6 May 2002, Pim Fortuyn, a Dutch politician and professor known for his anti-immigrant and anti-Muslim views, was murdered by a left-wing activist who confessed that he shot Fortuyn to defend Dutch Muslims from persecution.[287] Then, on 2 November 2004, Theo van Gogh, a Dutch film director and producer, was also murdered. A documentary van Gogh co-produced had been regarded by his murderer as an insult to Islam.[288] Many Dutch politicians were of the idea that Turkey's EU membership would be a wise move in view of this alarming state of affairs. In 2006, Jan Jacob van Dijk from the Christian Democratic Appeal (CDA), a Dutch political party that participated in all but two governments since 1977, expressed this rationality as follows: "among all the reasons we have for our support of Turkey, the most important one is that we believe Turkey's EU accession will disprove Huntington's idea of a 'clash of civilisations.'"[289] In an interview, Balkenende commented on the historical importance of Turkey's EU membership by referring to the 11 September attacks.[290]

2   The US, the Netherlands and Turkey were in close cooperation within NATO. On the eve of the Iraq War, on 10 February 2003, Turkey invoked Article 4 of the North Atlantic Treaty in the event of a potential threat to its territory or population as a consequence of the crisis. France, Germany, and Belgium cast a veto on this request. Following a contentious process, it was "decided that NATO military authorities should provide military advice on the feasibility, implications and timelines of three possible defensive measures to assist Turkey."[291]

> The Dutch would play an important role in this process. Three Patriot fire units were loaned from Germans via the Netherlands, picking up Dutch crews in order to keep Schröder's campaign pledge of abstention from the war. Three-hundred seventy troops were sent to man the missile systems. The Dutch mission continued until 16 April.[292]

In appearance, the cooperation of the Dutch government with the Bush administration for Turkey's EU membership was ambivalent. In his visit to the US in March 2004, Balkenende admitted that he did not rule out Washington's support for Turkey.[293] However, when Bush spoke in favor of Turkey in Ireland in June 2004, the same Balkenende declared that Bush's views would not have any effect on Turkey–EU relations.[294] Apparently, the extent of the cooperation between two countries for Turkey reflected in the media was only the tip of the iceberg. Among the Wikileaks documents, besides the abovementioned cable from 23 December 2004 about de Gooijer's prestidigitation, there are some other cables that altogether depict a different Netherlands than that was reflected in the media:

According to a cable from 1 December 2004, after resolving an internal dispute whether to keep secret the draft Conclusions of approaching Brussels Council, the government of the Netherlands "concluded that a last-minute attempt by Heads of State to deal with previously unseen texts could precipitate a disaster worse than the negative reactions an early release might provoke." On 29 November they circulated the draft and spent four hours reviewing the draft in detail with Turks. Both the Turks and the Dutch were in contact with the Americans in this process. The next day, Gooijer told the US DCM that engineering a 'yes' at the Brussels Council was the essential act of the Dutch Presidency.[295]

A second cable dated 6 December 2004 is indicative of the zeal of the Balkenende government. This zeal was so strong as to risk the relations of the Netherlands with the other EU members:

> Rob Swartbol (PM Balkenende's diplomatic advisor) (STRICTLY PROTECT) told Ambassador Sobel[296] late December 6 he was alarmed about efforts by France, Austria and Denmark to promote a third way/ privileged partnership alternative for Turkey. He said that the Dutch were working to get Germany and the UK together to counterbalance them. Balkenende may travel to the UK to meet PM Blair on Friday. He will meet Erdogan in Brussels on Thursday night and plans to see Schroeder and Chirac next week in capitals.
>
> In a separate conversation with the DCM, Pieter de Gooijer [. . .] (STRICTLY PROTECT) said he believed the Turkey accession talks are still on track for a positive result December 17 although they need careful steering by the Dutch to keep them there. The Dutch had reassured the Turks that there was nothing to rumors of Dutch willingness to support movement toward a third way. The Dutch will keep holding the line on accession talks leading to full membership, de Gooijer promised.
>
> [. . .]
>
> De Gooijer shared the redrafted Council Conclusions that will be circulated to member states for the December 8 COREPER meeting (full text faxed to EUR/ERA). De Gooijer said he and the Dutch had

been accused by the French and others of deliberately leaking the previous version to create favorable momentum for Turkey.[297]

The first paragraph of a third cable from 22 August 2005 underscores the importance of the Netherlands for the US with reference to the Iraq crisis:

> With the EU divided and its direction uncertain, the Dutch serve as a vital transatlantic anchor in Europe. As one of the original six EU members, the Dutch ally with the British to counter Franco-German efforts to steer Europe off a transatlantic course.[298]

The following paragraph of the same cable explains Balkenende's ambivalent position:

> We are fortunate to have in the Balkenende government an outward-looking partner for whom working with the U.S. and the U.K. comes naturally. Balkenende and FM Bot[299] take pride in building bridges between the U.S. and Europe. Nowhere was this more evident than during the Dutch presidency of the EU. On two issues of great importance to the U.S.—the China Arms Embargo and accession talks for Turkey—the Dutch moved, with our active urging, from following an EU 'consensus' set by others to redefining the issue on their, and our, terms. In both cases, Bot and Balkenende overcame initial skepticism and concluded that Dutch and U.S. interests coincided [. . .] Despite Balkenende's personal skepticism about bringing Turkey into the EU, he and Bot (a former Ambassador to Turkey) worked hard to ensure that Turkey got its date to start accession talks with the EU during the Dutch presidency, and want to see the agreement they helped negotiate successfully implemented. We will want the Dutch to continue to draw on the relationships they developed during the presidency to coax both sides to move in the right direction as October 3[300] approaches.

4 Mentality of the (George W.) Bush Administration

In the first years of his term, the reason behind Bush's efforts for Turkey's EU bid was the same as that of his father: securing Turkey's cooperation against Iraq. His focus was on Turkey's geopolitical value of which Turks, too, were aware: In June 2002, Turkish FM Cem said that Turkey was making the best of its [geo]strategic advantage.[301]

In the late 2003 and on the eve of the December 2004 European Council, several sources from the W. Bush administration declared that, within the ideational and institutional framework of the transatlantic relations, Turkey–EU relations were not in conflict with but complementary to Turkey–US relations. A Turkey that had adopted the EU norms and solved the Cyprus problem would be a better strategic partner for the US. Turkey's exclusion by the EU would stall Turkey's domestic reforms and provoke nationalist reactions. Turkey's EU membership would also be the best response to the 'clash of civilizations' thesis.[302] This rationale was widely accepted after the 11 September attacks.[303]

While Clinton had seen Turkey's value at a global scale, Bush focused on Turkey's possible regional role in the stability of the Balkans and the Middle East. The May 2002 'promotion campaign' the Bush administration launched in Europe for Turkey was based on this theme. Turkey's inclusion in the BMENA project was another step in this direction. By publicly expressing his backing for Turkey, Bush was also trying to reverse the tide of anti-American sentiments in the Turkish public.

Bush maintained the Cyprus strategy initiated by Clinton, with a twist: Bush's strategy was based on using the EU to convince the GOT and the Cypriot Turks to assume a more cooperative position and to facilitate the EU–NATO cooperation. The accession processes of Cyprus and of Turkey would be mutually conducive and should run *pari passu* as much as possible. However, with the accession of Cyprus, Turkey's relations with Greece and Cyprus worsened, Turkey's EU prospects dimmed, and the connection between the two accession processes got lost.

5 Conclusion

Turkey–US relations underwent serious problems in the Bush era. Both sides felt betrayed and questioned each other's reliability. Turkish public opinion turned negative against the US. Nevertheless, while Turkey continued soliciting help from the US against the Europeans, the US did not cease upholding Turkey's EU dreams.

Although one may expect the issues surrounding a war to be better explained by using neorealism, the US policy towards Turkey's EU bid before, during, and after the Iraq war in the Bush era defied some key neorealist assumptions. For instance, contrary to the assumption of the neorealists, in this period the Bush administration did not calculate its gains in relative terms (NRA5) and never used its 'support against the EU' as a 'carrot.' It was the GOT who included that support in the list of demands given to Wolfowitz in July 2002, or who asked for that support in the negotiations at the White House in December 2002 as a quid pro quo for Turkey's involvement in the Iraq war. As far as the available information suggests, the administration never threatened the Turks with the 'stick' of decreasing its support either.[304] Not even in the February 2003 negotiations wherein the US anxiously sought Turkey's assistance for the approaching Iraq war . . . It was again the Turks who demanded increased support for their EU bid in exchange for their backing of US policies in Iraq. In the Cyprus issue, the US could have decreased its support and forced Turkey to assume a more cooperative position, but it did not. On the contrary, in some cases, the Bush administration increased its support unconditionally either when Turkey asked for it or on its own accord. The ESDP issue was an example of this. By following this strategy, the Bush administration sometimes risked its relations with the German and French governments.

In this sense, the approach of the Bush administration towards Turkey–EU relations was not much different from that of the Clinton administration. Nevertheless, we should keep in mind that Bush did not harbor Clintonesque dreams about the historical significance of Turkey's EU membership, and his campaign for Turkey was more modest compared to that of Clinton. Besides the personal differences between the two presidents, the following factors may have been behind this decline:

1 After all, a spectacular undertaking would be too much for Turkey who had disappointed the US in the Iraq issue;
2 Due to the conjuncture, the Bush administration had to attribute more importance to maintenance of security and stability in Turkey's neighborhood than to cultural issues;
3 After the massive pressure the Clinton administration had put on Europeans, it would be prudent to maintain a low level of intervention not to annoy them further;
4 With such exceptions as Rice, Bush's diplomatic team was not so proficient and not so prone to devote time and effort to Turkey:

> Between the Iraqi invasion of Kuwait and the commencement of Operation Desert Storm, Secretary of State James Baker visited Turkey four times. Aside from a brief 2001 visit, Secretary of State Colin Powell did not travel to Turkey until a month after the National Assembly's vote. Powell's failure to visit Turkey in late 2002 and early 2003—while he found time to fly to Angola, Cape Verde, and Columbia—was indicative of the failure in American public diplomacy under Powell.
> [. . .]
> During pre-war negotiations, Ambassador W. Robert Pearson leaked derogatory comments about Turkey to the American and Turkish press. He had a tin-ear for Turkish politics. Despite private entreaties by Turkish officials, he ignored warnings that the presence of American diplomats in the Grand National Assembly on the day of the vote would spur a nationalist backlash against the American deployment. He also shirked his own responsibilities. He shocked American policymakers when, shortly before his departure, he remarked [. . .] that he had spent the day before the vote playing golf with [a] Turkish businessman;[305]

and

5 In the first two years of the Bush administration, the primary request of Turks from the US was economic assistance.

After the inactivity of the first two years, the supportive voice of the Bush administration for Turkey's European journey gradually became louder. Through a strenuous process, Turkey first got a date for the start of its negotiations, which could only be made possible through three challenging stages. Then, Turkey's negotiations started. In the second half of 2004, intensity of the US efforts reached its peak. However, the negative reaction of the Europeans soon made the Bush administration turn the volume down. From 2005 onwards

1 the activities of the US became less evident;
2 it was mostly through Rice's mouth that the Bush administration was speaking; and
3 the US focused on encouraging Turkey's democratization reforms.

In the processes where it had to remain silent, the Bush administration stood on alert and followed the events closely. Towards the end of the Bush era, the EU suspended its negotiations on eight of the 35 chapters. This was a deadlock in Turkey–EU relations.

After 2005, the Bush administration improved its strained relations with Turkey. This improvement culminated in the signing of the strategic partnership document in 2006. With this document, the relations between the two countries were bolstered and the US confirmed its backing for Turkey in writing.

With the ebbing of the US support for Turkey after the Clinton administration, neorealist variables resurfaced. Although the Turkish Parliament's initial resistance to the US requests seemed in line with the preferences of the Germans and the French (NRA2), the quick recovery of Turkey–US relations aroused the Europeans' dislike and increased their concern that Turkey could be a Trojan horse of the US in the EU (NRA8). Turkey's geopolitical position was another concern for the European leaders who did not like the idea of an EU that would be bordering Iraq in the case of Turkey's accession to the EU.

Domestic actors such textile lobby imposed constraints on the support the Bush administration to Turkey (DF). For Turkey, Bush took some risks in domestic politics, such as financing half of the IMF aid packages extended to Turkey from the US budget.

In accordance with the role it envisaged for Turkey, the Bush administration tried to complement Turkey's European openings with a Middle Eastern dimension by including Turkey in the BMENA project. Turks showed an interest in the project but argued against being identified as a Middle Eastern country. Another alternative that emerged in this period was the 'privileged partnership' idea. Turks and the Bush administration fervently objected to this idea.

The Bush administration indirectly influenced Turkey–EU relations in four other contexts:

The Cyprus issue was the first of them. The Bush administration maintained the connection between the negotiations of Cyprus and Turkey, established by the Clinton administration: The two countries would accede to the EU simultaneously. When the accession of Cyprus to the EU became certain, the Bush administration started using the EU to convince the Turks to assume a more cooperative position in the Cyprus issue.

Security was another context. In this context, the US tried to convince Turkey to lift its veto on the EU's accession to NATO assets and capabilities. The Bush administration played a role in comforting Turkey with the formulation of some guarantees and with the inclusion of the possibility of opening Turkey's accession negotiations in the Conclusions of the 2002 Brussels Council.

Third, the US extended financial aid to Turkey via the IMF. The improvement brought by this aid to Turkish economy was appreciated by the EU. The trade dimension of Turkey–US relations was still weak, and Turkey's disadvantaged position in the trilateral Turkey–EU–US trade did not change.

Finally, in the field of combatting terrorism, with help of the Bush administration, PKK and DHKP-C were added to the EU's list of terrorist organizations.

As Bush had to scale down his efforts for Turkey in 2004, his need for the UK as a collaborator increased. The Blair government—together with Berlusconi—did not disappoint the Americans and Turks. Israel—in connection with the Jewish lobby in the US—too, assisted the US. If Wikileaks documents are to be believed, the collaboration of the Netherlands with the US for Turkey was very intense.

Notes

1 Elif Berköz, "NATO liderlerini onlar doyurdu," *Milliyet*, 4 July 2004. Author's translation.
2 "Chirac tells Bush to keep his nose out," *The Telegraph*, 29 June 2004; Ian Black, Michael White and Giles Tremlett, "Angry Chirac puts Bush in his place," *The Guardian*, 29 June 2004; and Joshua Chaffin, "EU anger as Bush calls for Turkish membership," *FT*, 30 June 2004.
3 *PPPUS, George W. Bush*, 2004, Book 1: January 1 to June 30, 2004, Washington: USGPO, 2007, p. 1142.
4 Fikret Bila, "Sezer'den Bush'a: "Türkiye İslam devleti değil," *Milliyet*, 28 June 2004.
5 Sedat Ergin, "ABD, AB'yi ikna edebilir mi?" *Hürriyet*, 13 December 2002.
6 Ambrose Evans-Pritchard, "Europe dismisses Bush plea to let Turkey join earlier," *The Telegraph*, 14 December 2002.
7 George W. Bush, *Decision Points*, New York, NY: Crown Publishers, pp. 396–7.
8 "Common values and common interests? The Bush legacy in US-Turkish relations," *Insight Turkey*, Vol. 10, No. 4, 2008, 5–14, pp. 6–9. Parris's examples have been reinforced with further references.
9 George W. Bush, *Decision Points*, New York, NY: Crown Publishers, p. 250. Emphasis added. This may be seen as an evidence of the element of conditionality in the Bush administration's support, but as we will see, eventually it was the Turks who made their cooperation conditional to increased support from the US.

10 Rajan Menon and Henri Barkey, "Stationing Turks in Iraq could endanger region," *LAT*, 9 October 2003.
11 Murat Erdin, "Barışın nöbetçileri," *Hürriyet*, 30 May 2002.
12 A crisis broke out between Russia and Georgia in 2008 when both countries accused each other of military build-up near the separatist regions Abkhazia and South Ossetia.
13 BMENA initiative is a group of projects introduced by the US in 2004 to enable cooperation between the G8 and European nations on the one hand and the countries located in the BMENA region on the other. Its aim is to strengthen freedom, democracy, and prosperity in the region.
14 Mohammed Ahmed, Michael Gunter, *The Evolution of Kurdish Nationalism*, Costa Mesa, CA: Mazda Publishers, 2007, p. 94.
15 "Timeline of the Baku-Tbilisi-Ceyhan pipeline," *TDN*, 13 July 2006.
16 "Common values and common interests? The Bush legacy in US-Turkish relations," *Insight Turkey*, Vol. 10, No. 4, 2008, 5–14, pp. 7 and 13.
17 "Ecevit'ten 3 somut istek," *Milliyet*, 16 January 2002.
18 Murat Yetkin, "Ecevit: 'ABD'de önceliğimiz ekonomi,'" *Radikal*, 23 December 2001.
19 Sedat Ergin, "Bush: Saddam is a bad guy," *Hürriyet*, 18 January 2002. Author's translation.
20 Fikret Bila, "Gezinin bilançosu," *Milliyet*, 18 January 2002.
21 Perle, now the Chairman of the Defense Policy Board Advisory Committee, was an exception in this regard. In March 2002, he said he did not believe that the EU would accept Turkey in the near future. His alternative was conclusion of an agreement between Turkey and the US, which would be similar to NAFTA. This agreement would not contradict with Turkey's EU membership perspective. (Sources: Yasemin Çongar, "'AB zor, NAFTA gibi anlaşma yapalım,'" *Milliyet*, 19 March 2002; Yasemin Çongar, "Washington'dan görünen," *Milliyet*, 15 July 2002; and Yılmaz Polat, *CIA Pençesinde Açılım*, Ankara: Ulus Dağı Yayınları, 2010, p. 118.)
22 "Devlet Bahçeli: 'Anlaşmazlıklar artarsa hükümetin şekli değişir,'" *Zaman*, 24 February 2002.
23 Yasemin Çongar, "Ecevit sonrasına ABD'den bakışlar," *Milliyet*, 3 June 2002. When Erdoğan, the leader of the AKP, visited the US in January 2002, he was received coldly. Because, AKP was seen as a mild Islamist party by the US, and had voted against sending troops to Afghanistan. (Source: Hasan Cemal, "ABD'de Tayyip ile ilgili soru işaretleri," *Milliyet*, 17 September 2002.)
24 Yasemin Çongar, "Washington'dan görünen," *Milliyet*, 15 July 2002.
25 Yasemin Çongar, "AB'den Baykal'a, Özkök'ten Irak'a," *Milliyet*, 5 August 2002.
26 Murat Yetkin, "AB reformları ve bazı riskler," *Radikal*, 19 July 2002.
27 "In Turkey, it's the EU stupid," *WT*, 27 August 2002.
28 Zeynel Lüle, "ABD'den AB'ye baskı," *Hürriyet*, 31 May 2002.
29 Interview with Abdullah Akyüz, Washington, 25 May 2010.
30 "Özilhan: AB için ABD'ye güveniyoruz," *Hürriyet*, 15 May 2002.
31 "TÜSİAD ABD temaslarını tamamladı," *Hürriyet*, 10 October 2002; and "TÜSİAD: AB, Türkiye'ye kondüsyonlu tarih verebilir," *Hürriyet*, 10 October 2002.
32 Deniz Zeyrek, "Ev ödevlerimiz var," *Radikal*, 18 July 2002.
33 Sedat Ergin, "İşte kritik pazarlığın dökümü," *Hürriyet*, 19 July 2002; Murat Yetkin, "ABD ile Irak-Kıbrıs pazarlığı," *Radikal*, 21 July 2002; Murat Yetkin, *Tezkere: Irak Krizinin Gerçek Öyküsü*, Istanbul: Remzi Kitabevi, 2004, pp. 51 and 63–6; and Kent E. Calder, *Embattled Garrisons: Comparative Base Politics and American Globalism*, Princeton, NJ: Princeton University Press, 2007, p. 143.
34 Kasım Cindemir, "ABD: Bravo Ankara," *Hürriyet*, 5 August 2002.
35 "ABD: Avrupa, Türkiye'ye müzakere tarihi versin," *Hürriyet*, 31 August 2002; and "Ziyal in Washington," *TDN*, 28 August 2002.

36 Senior officials from the European Commission, the EU Presidency, the Council Secretariat, and the DOS meet four to six times a year to oversee the work in the Transatlantic Agenda. (Source: European Commission, *The European Union and the United States: Global Partners, Global Responsibilities*, Brussels: Publications Office of the EU, 2004, p.3.)
37 Yasemin Çongar, "ABD: Türkiye'ye haksızlık yapıldı," *Milliyet*, 10 October 2002.
38 "Daily Press Briefing for October 9 —Transcript." Available at http://usinfo.org/wf-archive/2002/021009/epf302.htm, accessed 3 February 2009.
39 Wexler and Whitfield were two of the three co-founders of the Congressional Caucus on Turkey and Turkish Americans, and Lantos was the Chairman of the CIR of the HOR.
40 107th Congress, H. Con Res. 594.
41 "Eine 'Liste' Washingtons für Berlin Forderungen zur Verbesserung der Beziehungen / Irak, Schnelle Eingreiftruppe, Türkei," *Frankfurter Allgemeine Zeitung*, 23 October 2002.
42 "Pearson: AB Türkiye'ye bir an önce tarih versin," *Hürriyet*, 25 October 2002.
43 Kasım Cindemir, "Bush da Türkiye'nin AB üyeliği için uğraşıyor," *Hürriyet*, 30 October 2002.
44 "Bush'tan AB için yanınızdayız mesajı," *Hürriyet*, 31 October 2002.
45 Steven R. Weisman, "Germany and U.S. tentatively ease chill in relationship," *NYT*, 31 October 2002.
46 "Germany: No Turkey in the EU," *WT*, 1 November 2002.
47 Nur Batur, "ABD bizi kız arkadaşıyla zorla evlendirmek istiyor," *Hürriyet*, 21 November 2002. Author's translation.
48 European Council, *Presidency Conclusions*, Brussels European Council, 24–25 October 2002, para. 6.
49 "AKP explains charter changes, slams foreign descriptions," *HDN*, 28 March 2010.
50 Kasım Cindemir, "Şahin'in makamından Türkiye'ye mesajlar," *Hürriyet*, 1 September 2002.
51 Yorgo Kırbaki, "ABD, tarih için bastırıyor," *Milliyet*, 17 September 2002.
52 See endnotes 25 and 821.
53 "Erdoğan: Şahinlik sonuç vermez," *Hürriyet*, 21 November 2002.
54 "Building Coalitions of Common Values," key address delivered by Paul Wolfowitz on 2 December 2002, US Deputy Defense Secretary, *IISS*. Available at www.iiss.org/recent-key-addresses/wolfowitz-address/, accessed 10 March 2012; Richard Norton-Taylor, "US hawk wants Turkey in EU," *The Guardian*, 3 December 2002; and Vernon Loeb and Bradley Graham, "Turkey has conditions for support of war," *WP*, 4 December 2002.
55 "Wolfowitz: AB Türkiye'siz olmaz," *Hürriyet*, 4 December 2002.
56 "Deputy Secretary Wolfowitz media availability in Ankara, Turkey," *US Department of Defense (DOD)*. Available at www.defense.gov/transcripts/transcript.aspx?transcriptid=2824, accessed 10 March 2012.
57 Michael R. Gordon, "Turkey's reluctance on use of bases worries U.S.," *NYT*, 9 January 2003.
58 "Wolfowitz Airport Departure Stakeout, Ankara," *US DOD*. Available at www.defense.gov/transcripts/transcript.aspx?transcriptid=2920, accessed 7 March 2013.
59 "Turkey renews pressure to win firm date for EU entry talks," *FT*, 4 December 2002.
60 "ABD: Türkiye'ye kesin tarih verilmeli," *Amerika'nın Sesi*, 6 December 2002. Available at www.amerikaninsesi.com/content/a-17-a-2002-12-06-7-1-87876012/800595.html, accessed 4 November 2010.
61 Turan Yılmaz and Kasım Cindemir, "Liderliğinizden etkilendik," *Hürriyet*, 11 December 2002.
62 Heads of state or government are hosted in the Oval Office.

63 "Roosevelt Room." Available at www.whitehousemuseum.org/west-wing/roosevelt-room.htm, accessed 15 March 2014.
64 "ABD'ye kısmi destek," *Hürriyet*, 11 December 2002.
65 Sedat Ergin, "Zor karar," *Hürriyet*, 13 December 2002.
66 "Bush: Sizinle omuz omuzayız," *Milliyet*, 11 December 2002. For more information, see the "2.5.1 The Cyprus Question" title.
67 Mark Parris, "Turkey and regime change in Iraq," *Policywatch*, No. 644, 2 August 2002. Available at www.washingtoninstitute.org/policy-analysis/view/turkey-and-regime-change-in-iraq, accessed 28 September 2014.
68 Fikret Bila, "Türkiye'nin ABD'ye koşulları," *Milliyet*, 4 December 2002; and Barkın Şık and Utku Çakırözer, "Saddam'a karşı 'caydırıcı işbirliği,'" *Milliyet*, 4 December 2002.
69 "Müzakere tarihi 1 Temmuz 2005," *Hürriyet*, 5 December 2002.
70. Deniz Zeyrek, ""Köşk: AB iyi ama 2005 olmaz," *Radikal*, 11 December 2002; and Ünsal Turan, "2005 olmaz," *Hürriyet*, 12 December 2002.
71 Art. 2 of the Treaty of Accession of the ten candidate states signed on 16 April 2003 stipulated that the Treaty would enter into force on 1 May 2004, provided that by 30 April 2004 all current MSs and at least one candidate country had submitted the ratification documents to the government of Italy, the MS who held the Presidency then. (Source: *OJ of the EU*, L 236, 23 September 2003.)
72 "Remarks prior to discussions with chairman Recep Tayyip Erdoğan of Turkey's AK Party and exchange with reporters," *PPPUS, George W. Bush*, 2004, Book 1: January 1 to June 30, 2004, Washington: USGPO, 2007, p. 2180–1.
73 Ibid., p. 2181.
74 "ABD'ye kısmi destek," *Hürriyet*, 11 December 2002.
75 "Erdoğan: Bush AB liderlerini bir kere daha arayacak," *Hürriyet*, 10 December 2002.
76 Turan Yılmaz and Kasım Cindemir, "Liderliğinizden etkilendik," *Hürriyet*, 11 December 2002.
77 Mehmet Ali Birand, "Bush olmasa bu sonuç çıkmazdı," *Hürriyet*, 21 December 2002; "ABD'den son dakika baskısı," *Hürriyet*, 12 December 2002; and John Vinocur, "Support for Turkey spurs officials' anger: French accuse U.S. of meddling," *NYT*, 13 December 2002.
78 Mehmet Ali Birand, "Bush olmasa bu sonuç çıkmazdı," *Hürriyet*, 21 December 2002.
79 Interview with Volkan Vural, Istanbul, 6 September 2011. Vural was the Secretary-General for EU Affairs in Turkey between 2000 and 2003.
80 Doğan Uluç, "Bizi NAFTA'ya alın Mr. Bush," *Hürriyet*, 12 December 2002.
81 Zeynel Lüle, "Grazie, Signor Primo Ministro," *Hürriyet*, 13 December 2002.
82 Keith B. Richburg, "EU rejects Turkey's bid for early talks: Some leaders upset by Bush's lobbying," *WP*, 13 December 2002.
83 "Kasımpaşa-Teksas usulü ters mi tepti?" *Hürriyet*, 14 December 2002.
84 Beyza Ç. Tekin, *Representations and Othering in Discourse: The Construction of Turkey in the EU Context*, Amsterdam: John Benjamins Publishing Company, 2010, p. 149.
85 Stephen Castle, "Turkey furious at leaders' 'prejudice' on early entry," *The Independent*, 14 December 2002.
86 Philip Robins, "Confusion at home, confusion abroad: Turkey between Copenhagen and Iraq," International Affairs, Vol. 79, No. 3, 2003, 547–66, p. 556.
87 European Council, *Presidency Conclusions*, Copenhagen European Council, 12–13 December 2002.
88 For example, see Mehmet Ali Birand, "Bush olmasa bu sonuç çıkmazdı," *Hürriyet*, 21 December 2002.
89 In December 2002, the Supreme Election Board canceled the election results from Siirt, a small city, due to voting irregularities. A new election was scheduled for the city for 9 February 2003. Erdoğan was listed as a candidate for this election, which he eventually won. Gül handed the post over to him in March 2003.

90 Kent E. Calder, *Embattled Garrisons: Comparative Base Politics and American Globalism*, Princeton, NJ: Princeton University Press, 2007, pp. 143–6.
91 Fikret Bila, "PKK'yı bitirecek imzalar atılmıştı," *Milliyet*, 22 September 2003 (includes the text of the memorandum in Turkish); Fikret Bila, "Özel amacı aşan faaliyetler yasak," *Milliyet*, 24 September 2003.
92 Faruk Mercan and Ufuk Şanlı, "4 Temmuz'un üç generali neden emekliye sevkedildi?" *Aksiyon*, 2 July 2007; and Ümit Enginsoy, "Fransa, Türkiye'nin ABD'ye desteğini engelledi," *NTVMSNBC*. Available at http://arsiv.ntvmsnbc.com/news/212226.asp, accessed 5 May 2012.
93 Kent E. Calder, *Embattled Garrisons: Comparative Base Politics and American Globalism*, Princeton, NJ: Princeton University Press, 2007, p. 145.
94 Barkın Şık et al., "Havayı verdik, karayı aldık," *Milliyet*, 22 March 2003; "Irak'a girdik," *Milliyet*, 22 March 2003.
95 Fikret Bila, "2003 yılındaki Abdullah Gül-Colin Powell gizli anlaşmasını açıklıyoruz," *Milliyet*, 12 September 2013.
96 Michael Howard and Suzanne Goldenberg, "US arrest of soldiers infuriates Turkey," *The Guardian*, 8 July 2003; and "Turkish fury at US Iraq 'arrests,'" *BBC News*, 5 July 2003. Available at http://news.bbc.co.uk/2/hi/middle_east/3048090.stm, accessed 27 March 2012; "US frees Turkish troops," *Al Jazeera*. Available at www.aljazeera.com/archive/2003/07/200841013184338965.html, accessed 28 March 2012; and "Turkey expects U.S. to free troops," *CNN*. Available at http://articles.cnn.com/2003-07-06/world/turkey.us_1_turkish-soldiers-turkish-special-forces-kurdish-governor?_s=PM:WORLD, accessed 27 March 2012.
97 Turan Yavuz, *Çuvallayan İttifak*, Ankara: Destek Yayınları, 2006, pp. 205–6.
98 Derya Sazak, "Kitaptaki 'çuval emrine' Paul Wolfowitz'ten itiraz," *Milliyet*, 1 April 2006.
99 Derya Sazak, "Üç cephede savaş," *Milliyet*, 5 December 2002.
100 Fikret Bila, "Gül'in sitemi," *Milliyet*, 5 April 2003.
101 George Parker and Judy Dempsey, "US warned to keep out of Turkey's EU talks," *FT*, 22 April 2003. See also Oktay Ekşi, "Kırmızı çizgiler," *Hürriyet*, 4 December 2004.
102 "Savaş, Türkiye'nin önemini arttırdı," *Milliyet*, 2 April 2003.
103 "Nihayet Avrupa Ankara'ya tarih verdi," *Milliyet*, 25 April 2003.
104 The European Convention, *Draft Treaty Establishing a Constitution for Europe*, CONV 850/03 of 19 July 2003.
105 "Vatican doubt over Turkey EU bid," *BBC News*, 26 May 2003. Available at http://news.bbc.co.uk/2/hi/europe/2937464.stm, accessed 3 January 2012.
106 *OJ of the EU*, L 236, 23 September 2003.
107 Judy Dempsey and Hugh Williamson, "Turkey in struggle to deal with Iraq crisis," *FT*, 25 March 2003; and Güven Özalp, "Avrupa 'niyetlendi,'" *Milliyet*, 22 March 2003.
108 "Turkey's EU hopes threatened by Iraq war," *Agence France-Presse*. Available at www.lebanon.com/news/local/2003/3/24.htm, accessed 29 March 2012.
109 Güven Özalp, "Giscard: 'Türkiye, AB'yi hazmedemez,'" *Milliyet*, 4 September 2003.
110 "Deputy Secretary of Defense Wolfowitz interview with CNNTurk," 6 May 2003, *US DOD*. Available at www.defense.gov/transcripts/transcript.aspx?transcriptid=2572, accessed 1 March 2012.
111 Yasemin Çongar, "Bush'tan Ankara'ya AB desteği," *Milliyet*, 27 June 2003.
112 Sabine Verhest, "Belge mais 'pas dindon de la farce,'" *La Libre Belgique*, 2 November 2003. Author's translation.
113 See the section 2.5.1.2.
114 This visit was an important step to mend the frayed relations between the two countries. In the text delivered to the Turks, the Americans used the term 'strategic partnership' to define the relationship between the two countries. (Source: Yasemin Çongar, "Erdoğan'ın ABD ziyareti ve Kıbrıs," *Milliyet*, 2 February 2004.)

115 "Remarks following discussions with Prime Minister Recep Tayyip Erdogan of Turkey," *PPPUS, George W. Bush*, 2004, Book 1: January 1 to June 30, 2004, Washington: USGPO, 2007, p. 150.
116 Fikret Bila, "Arabulucu," *Milliyet*, 28 January 2004; Fikret Bila, "Yansımalar," *Milliyet*, 30 January 2004; and Yasemin Çongar, "Erdoğan'ın ABD ziyareti ve Kıbrıs," *Milliyet*, 2 February 2004.
117 This initiative was aiming to promote liberal democracy, market economy, and educational reforms in a group of countries located in the Middle East, North Africa, and in Central Asia. Later, it was transformed into the BMENA initiative explained in endnote 745.
118 U.S. House. 108th Congress, 2d Session, "S. 2305, A Bill to authorize programs that support economic and political development in the Greater Middle East and Central Asia and support for three new multilateral institutions, and for other purposes," 8 April 2004, para. 8.
119 "The President's News Conference with European Union leaders in Shannon, Ireland, 26 June 2004," *PPPUS, George W. Bush*, 2004, Book 1: January 1 to June 30, 2004, Washington: USGPO, 2007, 1135–41, p. 1136.
120 "ABD'den Türkiye'ye lobi desteği," *Hürriyet*, 6 October 2004.
121 Morton Abramowitz et al., "Turkey on the threshold: Europe's decision and U.S. interests," Policy Paper 8, Washington: Atlantic Council of the United States, 2004, p. vii.
122 Ardıç Aytalar, "17 Aralık'ta tarih alacaksınız," *Hürriyet*, 13 November 2004.
123 Turan Yavuz, *Çuvallayan İttifak*, Ankara: Destek Yayınları, 2006, p. 240.
124 Bülent Aydemir and Evren Mesci, "Tarihi rest," *Sabah*, 18 December 2004.
125 "Press Briefing by Scott McClellan, December 17, 2004," *The American Presidency Project*. Available at www.presidency.ucsb.edu/ws/?pid=66113, accessed 3 February 2012.
126 "Press Briefing by Scott McClellan, December 21, 2004," *The American Presidency Project*. Available at www.presidency.ucsb.edu/ws/?pid=66114, accessed 3 February 2012.
127 "What is Wikileaks," *Wikileaks*. Available at www.wikileaks.org/About.html; and "Secret US embassy cables," *Wikileaks*. Available at www.wikileaks.org/cablegate. html#, both accessed 28 May 2012.
128 "Turkey Accession/EU: The Mysterious Case of the Missing Declaration," *Wikileaks*, 23 December 2004. Available at http://wikileaks.org/cable/ 2004/12/04THEHAGUE3333.html#, accessed 27 May 2012.
129 "EU/Turkey: Initialling of 'Ankara Agreement' sought as Rehn visits," *Europolitics*, 3 March 2005. Available at www.europolitics.info/eu-turkey-initialling-of-ankara-agreement-sought-as-rehn-visits-artr176909-44.html, accessed 1 June 2012.
130 109th Congress, H. Res. 411. With some minor changes, this resolution was once again introduced on 29 September 2006 (109th Congress, H. Con. Res. 493).
131 "Türkiye-AB ilişkileri," *TMFA*. Available at www.mfa.gov.tr/turkiye-ab-iliskileri. tr.mfa, accessed 28 May 2012.
132 "Erdogan and AK Party after two years in power," *Wikileaks*, 30 December 2004. Available at http://wikileaks.org/cable/2004/12/04ANKARA7211.html#, accessed 26 May 2012.
133 Cemal Karakaş, "Abgestuft integrieren statt privilegiert ausgrenzen. Zum mühsamen Beginn der EU-Beitrittsverhandlungen mit der Türkei," *Zeitschrift für Türkeistudien*, Vol. 1–2, 2005, 79–104, p. 97.
134 For example, in her visit in Istanbul on 15–17 February 2004, Merkel tried to convince Turks on the 'merits' of the privileged partnership status. (Source: "Almanya Hıristiyan Demokrat Birlik Partisi (CDU) Genel Başkanı Merkel'in konuşma metni," Konrad-Adenauer-Stiftung Turkey Office. Available at www.konrad.org. tr/index.php?id=574, accessed 8 April 2012. See also Fadi Hakura, "Partnership is

no privilege: The alternative to EU membership is no Turkish delight," Chatham House Briefing Paper 05/02, September 2005.)
135 Lionel Barber, "Erdogan points finger at Merkel and Sarkozy," *FT*, 17 September 2005.
136 "Schroeder in U.S. for Bush talks," *CNN World*. Available at http://articles.cnn.com/2005-06-27/world/schroeder.us_1_merkel-s-christian-democrats-bush-and-schroeder-german-chancellor-gerhard-schroeder?_s=PM:WORLD, accessed 8 April 2012.
137 "Travels of Secretary of State Condoleezza Rice," *US DOS*. Available at http://history.state.gov/departmenthistory/travels/secretary/rice-condoleezza, accessed 17 June 2012.
138 "Rice Ankara'ya geldi," *Hürriyet*, 5 February 2005.
139 Condoleezza Rice, "Interview with Metehan Demir of Turkey's Kanal-D TV," *US DOS*, 6 February 2005. Available at http://2001-2009.state.gov/secretary/rm/2005/41856.htm, accessed 17 June 2012. An almost identical question was asked and received an almost identical reply in another interview on the same day: "Interview with Banu Guven of Turkey's NTV," *US DOS*, 6 February 2005. Available at http://2001-2009.state.gov/secretary/rm/2005/41855.htm, accessed 17 June 2012.
140 "Amid EU jitters, Bush to assure Erdogan over Western ties," *HDN*, 7 June 2005.
141 Brian Knowlton, "Bush praises Turkish democracy," *NYT*, 9 June 2005.
142 Zeynep Gürcanlı, "Erdogan to Visit US 3 times in 4 Months," *The Journal of Turkish Weekly*, 6 June 2005. Available at www.turkishweekly.net/news/12042, accessed 7 April 2012.
143 Brian Knowlton, "Bush praises Turkish democracy," *NYT*, 9 June 2005.
144 Yakup Beriş and Aslı Gürkan, "Broader Middle East initiative: Perceptions from Turkey," *Turkey in Focus*, TÜSİAD Washington Office, No. 7, July 2004.
145 Soner Çağaptay, "Where goes the U.S.-Turkish relationship?" *Middle East Quarterly*, Fall 2004, 43–52, p. 43.
146 "Merkel's envoy lauds meeting with Bush," *Deutsche Welle*. Available at www.dw.de/dw/article/0,,1662225_page_0,00.html, accessed 7 April 2012.
147 Marc Grossman, "US should be ready to fill the void on Turkey," *FT*, 16 September 2005.
148 Interview with Ross Wilson, Washington, 25 May 2010.
149 Değer Akal, "ABD devrede," *ABHaber*. Available at www.abhaber.com/haber.php?id=7580, accessed 10 May 2012.
150 Anthony Browne, "Turkey left out in cold as Austria digs in heels over EU entry talks," *The Times*, 3 October 2005; Zeynel Lüle and Uğur Ergan, "Ankara'nın resti, Condi'nin müdahalesi," *Hürriyet*, 5 October 2005; "Avusturya'yı iknaya İngiliz desteği," *Hürriyet*, 2 October 2005; and Birol Yeşilada, *EU-Turkey Relations in the 21st Century*, New York, NY: Routledge, 2013, p. 19.
151 "Rice'a şükran sunuldu," *Radikal*, 6 October 2005.
152 "Erdoğan AB elçileriyle buluştu," *Hürriyet*, 20 January 2006. Author's translation.
153 109th Congress, H. Con. Res. 195.
154 109th Congress, H.R. 3103.
155 110th Congress, H.R. 6079.
156 Delegation of the European Commission to the USA, "Barroso & Bush meet at White House," *Euinsight*, October 2005, p. 1.
157 "Bush ile Barroso Türkiye'nin AB sürecini görüştü," *Hürriyet*, 18 October 2005.
158 "List of Chiefs of Mission as of December 20, 2006," *US DOS*. Available at www.state.gov/documents/organization/78328.pdf, accessed 10 April 2012.
159 "ABD'nin yeni Ankara büyükelçisi yemin etti," *Hürriyet*, 1 December 2005.
160 Interview with Ross Wilson, Washington, 25 May 2010.
161 US Embassy in Ankara, "Bush, Turkish Prime Minister Erdogan to meet in October," 12 September 2006. Available at http://turkey.usembassy.gov/news_09122006.html, accessed 3 April 2012.

162 "ABD ile yeni stratejik ortak vizyon belgesi oluşturulacak," *Hürriyet*, 25 April 2006.
163 US Embassy in Ankara, "Remarks with Deputy Prime Minister Abdullah Gul after their meeting," 5 July 2006. Available at http://turkey.usembassy.gov/news_07042006.html, accessed 23 April 2012.
164 Cüneyt Ülsever, "Camp David'de başladı 1 Mart 2003'te bitti," *Hürriyet*, 13 June 2005.
165 Sami Kohen, "Yeni ortaklık anlayışı," *Milliyet*, 19 October 1993.
166 US Embassy in Ankara, "Shared vision and structured dialogue to advance the Turkish-American strategic partnership," 5 July 2006. Available at http://turkey.usembassy.gov/statement_070508.html, accessed 5 May 2010.
167 "Bush assures Turkey of US support for its EU bid," *TDN*, 12 September 2006.
168 "Remarks following discussions with Prime Minister Recep Tayyip Erdogan of Turkey-2 October 2006," *George W. Bush: July 1 to December 31, 2003*, Vol. 2, USGPO, 2006, 1742–3, p. 1743.
169 "Commission wants partial suspension of talks with Turkey," *EurActiv*. Available at www.euractiv.com/enlargement/commission-wants-partial-suspension-talks-turkey/article-160112, accessed 20 April 2012.
170 Frank Pallone, "Turkey must open ports to Cyprus; European Union must not allow defiance to continue," Speech in the HOR, *Congressional Record*, Vol. 152, No. 18, 7 December 2006, Washington: USGPO, pp. 22900–1.
171 Council of the EU, "Press Release," GAER, 2770th meeting, Brussels, 11 December 2006.
172 Daniel Fried, Press Roundtable, Washington, 12 December 2006. Available at http://statelists.state.gov/scripts/wa.exe?A2=ind0612c&L=dossdo&P=184, accessed 2 February 2008.
173 Patrick Jarreau et al., "Nicolas Sarkozy: 'J'aime l'énergie et la fluidité de l'Amérique,'" *Le Monde*, 9 September 2006. Author's translation.
174 "Ambassador Gray discusses priority U.S.-E.U. economic issues after Bush, Barroso, Merkel meetings," *USEU*, 9 January 2007, available http://useu.usmission.gov/gray/jan0907_gray_fpc.html, accessed 24 April 2012.
175 "Ingiltere'nin AB desteği, Fransa'da Türkıye karşıtlığını artırdı," *Hürriyet*, 20 September 2006.
176 Mark Mardell, "Turkey's EU membership bid stalls," *BBC News*, 11 December 2006. Available at http://news.bbc.co.uk/2/hi/europe/6170749.stm, accessed 23 April 2012.
177 U.S.-Turkish Relations and the challenges ahead: Hearing before the Subcommittee on Europe of the Committee on Foreign Affairs of the House of Representatives, No. 110–30, 110th Congress, 15 March 2007.
178 George Parker et al., "France in threat to Turkey's EU hopes," *FT*, 12 June 2007.
179 Dan Bilefsky, "Turkish entry into Europe slowed by Sarkozy move," *NYT*, 25 June 2007. The blockage decision was formalized the following day.
180 Ali İhsan Aydın, "Askıya alınan müzakere fasıllarını 12'ye çıkardı," *Zaman*, 29 August 2007.
181 Pew Research Center, *Rising Environmental Concern in 47-Nation Survey: Global Unease with Major World Powers*, Washington, 27 June 2007, p. 3. Available at www.pewglobal.org/files/pdf/256.pdf, accessed 25 April 2012.
182 Armağan Emre Çakır, "Introduction," in Armağan Emre Çakır (ed.), *Fifty Years of EU-Turkey Relations: A Sisyphean Story*, New York: Routledge, 2011, pp. 1–9, 5.
183 Seyfi Taşhan, "Is it a 'Cold War' for Turkey?" *Foreign Policy Institute*, 27 February 2007. Available at www.foreignpolicy.org.tr/documents/270207_b.html, accessed 12 July 2012.
184 Condoleezza Rice, "Remarks upon reception of the Eric M. Warburg Prize." Available at www.atlantik-bruecke.org/service/dokumente/rice-remarks-upon-award-reception.pdf, accessed 10 April 2012.

185 US Embassy in Ankara, "Remarks by Secretary of State Condoleezza Rice at the American-Turkish Council luncheon, "Washington, 15 April 2008. Available at http://turkey.usembassy.gov/statement_041408.html, accessed 25 April 2012.
186 Mark A. Parris, "Turkey's courts should respect the will of the people," *WSJ*, 17 May 2008. The head of the Bureau was Daniel Fried then.
187 David Stout, "Bush calls Turkey a 'great strategic partner' after talks with Gul," *NYT*, 8 January 2008.
188 Cansu Çamlıbel, "Bush told not to get involved in Turkey's EU bid," *HDN*, 11 January 2008.
189 Uğur Ergan, "Türkiye için üçlü zirve," *Hürriyet*, 12 January 2008.
190 "No summit to discuss Turkish accession," *HDN*, 8 March 2008.
191 "President Bush participates in joint press availability with Slovenian Prime Minister Janša and European Commission President Barroso." Available at http://georgewbush-whitehouse.archives.gov/news/releases/2008/06/20080610-10.html, accessed 26 April 2012.
192 "'Bizi almayacaklar,'" *Cumhuriyet*, 11 June 2008. Author's translation.
193 "Dışişleri'nden Cumhuriyet'e yalanlama," *Zaman*, 11 June 2008.
194 "Secretary Rice's Meeting with Turkish FM," *Wikileaks*, 8 June 2008. Available at http://wikileaks.org/cable/2008/06/08STATE65812.html, accessed 27 May 2012.
195 "Building Coalitions of Common Values," Address by Paul Wolfowitz on 2 December 2002, *IISS*. Available at www.iiss.org/recent-key-addresses/wolfowitz-address/, accessed 10 March 2012.
196 Yorgo Kırbaki, "Batı'dan Rum rüşveti," *Milliyet*, 10 May 2001.
197 "Grossman'dan Kıbrıs desteği," *Milliyet*, 22 March 2001.
198 Yasemin Çongar, "Kıbrıs müzakereleri ve ABD," *Milliyet*, 16 February 2004.
199 Murat Yetkin, "Moralinizi bozmayın, AB umudu bitmedi," *Radikal*, 9 June 2002.
200 "De Soto'nun ikinci adresi Türk Dışişleri," *Milliyet*, 3 December 2002.
201 "Solana'dan AKP'ye 'Kıbrıs'ı çöz' baskısı," *Milliyet*, 15 November 2002.
202 Abdullah Karakuş and Utku Çakırözer, "Bu fırsatı kaçırmayın," *Milliyet*, 3 December 2002.
203 Birol Yeşilada, *EU-Turkey Relations in the 21st Century*, New York, NY: Routledge, 2013, p. 16; "Denktaş'ı ikna etmeye gitti," *Milliyet*, 24 November 2002; and Utku Çakırözer, "Masadan kaçanın tezi de yoktur," *Milliyet*, 27 November 2002.
204 Abdullah Karakuş, "Erdoğan: Başımızı kumdan çıkaralım," *Milliyet*, 21 November 2002.
205 Utku Çakırözer, "Kıbrıs başka, AB başka," *Milliyet*, 26 November 2002.
206 İrfan Kurtulmuş, "Tarih verin, Kıbrıs'ı çözelim," *Milliyet*, 10 December 2002.
207 Fikret Bila, "Kıbrıs ve Irak," *Milliyet*, 14 December 2002.
208 Para. 10.
209 Mustafa Sağıroğlu, "ABD baskıyı arttırıyor," *Radikal*, 15 January 2003; "ABD Kıbrıs Koordinatörü Weston Ankara'da," *Hürriyet*, 6 March 2003; "Weston: Çözüm için kritik tarih 1 Mayıs 2004," *Hürriyet*, 19 December 2003; and Tom Ellis, "Weston says US wants restart of Cyprus talks as soon as possible." Available at www.greekembassy.org/embassy/content/en/Article.aspx?office=3&folder=92&article=11997, accessed 22 March 2012.
210 See page 215 endnote 71.
211 "Weston: Kıbrıs'ta farklı sayfa açılacak," *Hürriyet*, 15 April 2003.
212 "U.S. accuses Greek Cypriot leaders of derailing unification vote," *NYT*, 27 April 2004.
213 Refers to Holbrooke's deal.
214 Interview with Marc Grossman, Washington, 11 May 2010.
215 Birol Yeşilada, *EU-Turkey Relations in the 21st Century*, New York, NY: Routledge, 2013, p. 12.

216 "A quiet revolution: Less power for Turkey's army is a triumph for the EU," *FT*, 31 July 2003.
217 Ian Lesser, "Turkey and the United States: Anatomy of a strategic relationship," in Lenore G. Martin and Dimitris Keridis (eds.), *The Future of Turkish Foreign Policy*, Cambridge, MA: MIT Press, 2004, 83–99, p. 91.
218 Güven Özalp, "ABD'den tam destek," *Milliyet*, 7 February 2001.
219 Yasemin Çongar, "Ankara'yı ters köşeye yatırdı," *Milliyet*, 1 March 2001.
220 Judy Dempsey and Alexander Nicoll, "EU and NATO to hold talks on military planning," *FT*, 24 April 2001.
221 Murat Yetkin, "Ankara, Avrupa'nın oyununu bozuyor," *Radikal*, 6 June 2001; and "NATO toplantısından sonuç yok," *Hürriyet*, 29 May 2001.
222 Uğur Ergan, "ABD'ye Irak mesajları," *Hürriyet*, 5 June 2001.
223 Güven Özalp, "Arkanızdayız," *Milliyet*, 14 June 2001.
224 Sedat Ergin, "Bush: Saddam is a bad guy," *Hürriyet*, 18 January 2002.
225 Murat Yetkin, "Avrupa Birleşik Devletleri Türkiye'siz olur mu?" *Radikal*, 28 November 2001, "Avrupa ile aramızdaki sırat köprüsü," *Radikal*, 1 December 2001, and "Top Ankara'dan çıktı," *Radikal*, 3 December 2001.
226 Murat Yetkin, "Zor karar ve 'asker sözü' baskısı," *Radikal*, 2 December 2001.
227 Martin Reichard, *The EU-NATO Relationship: A Legal and Political Perspective*, Aldershot: Ashgate Publishing, 2006, pp. 155–6.
228 Murat Yetkin, "Atina Kıbrıs pazarlığına mı başladı?" *Radikal*, 4 December 2001.
229 Antonio Missiroli, "EU-NATO cooperation in crisis management: No Turkish delight for ESDP," *Security Dialogue*, 2002, 9–26, p. 20.
230 Judy Dempsey and Leyla Boulton, "Turkey lifts objections to EU force," *FT*, 4 December 2001; Murat Yetkin, "Powell'den teşekkür, Pearson'dan iftar," *Radikal*, 5 December 2001, and "Ankara'da iyimser bekleyiş," *Radikal*, 7 December 2001. See also Çınar Özen, "ESDP-NATO relations: Considerations on the future of European security architecture," *Turkish Yearbook of International Relations*, 2002, 231–55, p. 249.
231 F. Stephen Larrabee and Ian Lesser, *Turkish Foreign Policy in an Age of Uncertainty*, Santa Monica, CA: Rand Corporation, 2003, p. 66; and "Greece makes pressure on changing ESDP," *TDN*, 29 June 2002.
232 Murat Yetkin, "Avrupa Birliği, Kıbrıs ve ABD," *Radikal*, 16 December 2001.
233 Murat Yetkin, "Ecevit: ABD'de önceliğimiz ekonomi," *Radikal*, 23 December 2001.
234 Murat Yetkin, "Avrupa'nın kabusu Kıbrıs," *Radikal*, 2 March 2002.
235 Murat Yetkin, "Moralinizi bozmayın, AB umudu daha bitmedi," *Radikal*, 9 June 2002.
236 "US stands for Ankara agreement on ESDP," *TDN*, 3 July 2002.
237 European Council, *Presidency Conclusions*, Brussels European Council, 24–25 October 2002, Annex II.
238 Para. 2.
239 Para. 11.
240 European Council, *Presidency Conclusions*, Copenhagen European Council, 12–13 December 2002, para. 19.
241 Frank Stadelmaier, *On the Emergence of ESDP and EU-NATO Cooperation*, Munich: GRIN Verlag, 2009, p. 62.
242 EU-NATO Declaration on ESDP, 16 December 2002, NATO Press Release (2002) 142 and 42 ILM 242 (2003).
243 Martin Reichard, *The EU-NATO Relationship: A Legal and Political Perspective*, Aldershot: Ashgate Publishing, 2006, p.156 ff and p. 274.
244 Hürrem Şatıroğlu, "Faiz, tarihi rekora uçtu: Yüzde 7500," *Hürriyet*, 22 February 2001; and "Turkey marks 10th anniversary of 2001 crisis," *HDN*, 20 February 2011.
245 Alan Makovsky, "Step up U.S. involvement in Turkish economic crisis," *PolicyWatch*, No. 521, WINEP, 1 March 2001. Available at www.washingtoninstitute.org/templateC05.php?CID=1399, accessed 6 February 2012.

246 "ABD'linin ödediği verginin 17 milyar doları size aktı," *Hürriyet*, 6 March 2002.
247 Joseph Kahn, "I.M.F. offers Turkey $16 billion in loan aid," *NYT*, 5 February 2002.
248 Ferai Tınç, "Türkiye'ye dış desteğin anlamı," *Hürriyet*, 25 February 2001.
249 The European Commission, "2003 Regular Report on Turkey's progress towards accession." Available at www.avrupa.info.tr/Files/File/Docs/2003.pdf, accessed 2 February 2012. See, for example, p. 48 or 94.
250 Yasemin Çongar, "Cheney'nin dönüşü," *Milliyet*, 25 March 2002.
251 See the Conclusion section of the previous chapter.
252 "İhraç pazarında etkinlik için geniş işbirliği: Hedef, Türkiye-ABD Serbest Ticaret Anlaşması," *Tekstil İşveren*, No. 261, September 2001.
253 Interview with M. Haluk Özelçi, Permanent Representative of the Turkish Textile and Clothing Exporters' Association, Istanbul, 10 February 2012.
254 M. Ulric Killion, "The new millennium: APEC and emerging China," in Lawrence Z. Pelzer (ed.), *New Developments in Macroeconomics Research*, 1–45, p. 42ff. The text of the Declaration is available at www.ncto.org/quota/Idec.pdf, accessed 4 January 2012.
255 Şevket Sürek, "Nitelikli sanayi bölgeleri hikayesi ve Obama," *Referans*, 9 April 2009.
256 Vahap Munyar, "ABD ile 'tercihli' mi 'serbest' ticaret mi?" *Hürriyet*, 16 January 2002.
257 Sedat Ergin, "Ecevit ABD'den ne alabilir?" *Hürriyet*, 14 January 2002; Ertuğ Yaşar, "Başbakan ABD'de," *Akşam*, 16 January 2002; and Ertuğ Yaşar, "Tercihli ticaret anlaşması," *Akşam*, 18 January 2002.
258 Mehmet Ali Birand, "Nakit para yok, ancak Türkiye kazançlı," *Hürriyet*, 18 January 2002.
259 Section 4101 of the Trade Act of 2002, Pub. L. 107–210.
260 Section 8002 of the Tax Relief and Health Care Act of 2006, Pub. L. 109–432.
261 "Council Common Position of 27 December 2001 on the application of specific measures to combat terrorism," *OJ of the EU*, No L 344, 28 December 2001, pp. 93–6.
262 "Sesimizi ABD duydu," *Milliyet*, 2 January 2002.
263 Mehmet Ali Birand, "Hollanda ve Belçika hala direniyor," *Posta*, 17 April 2002.
264 "Council Decision of 2 April 2004 implementing Article 2(3) of Regulation (EC) No 2580/2001 on specific restrictive measures directed against certain persons and entities with a view to combating terrorism and repealing Decision 2003/902/EC," *OJ of the EU*, No L 99, 3 April 2004, pp. 28–9.
265 Murat Yetkin, "Denktaş'tan mektup var: 'Kıbrıs'ta AB komplosu," *Radikal*, 2 April 2001.
266 Abdullah Karakuş, "Erdoğan: Başımızı kumdan çıkaralım," *Milliyet*, 21 November 2002.
267 Murat Yetkin, "AB reformları ve bazı riskler," *Radikal*, 19 July 2002.
268 Miguel Medina-Abellan, "Turkey, the European Security and Defence Policy, and accession negotiations," SInAN Working Paper, No. 1, Middle East Technical University, Ankara, 24 April 2009. Available at http://sinan.ces.metu.edu.tr/dosya/miguelwp1.pdf, accessed 3 December 2011.
269 Caroline Daniel, "Bush and Powell press EU to take Turkey as member," *FT*, 28 November 2002.
270 "Building Coalitions of Common Values," Key Address by Paul Wolfowitz on 2 December 2002, US Deputy Defense Secretary, *IISS*. Available at www.iiss.org/recent-key-addresses/wolfowitz-address/, accessed 10 March 2012.
271 "Straw'dan tarih desteği," *Milliyet*, 4 December 2002.
272 Keith B. Richburg, "EU rejects Turkey's bid for early talks: Some leaders upset by Bush's lobbying," *WP*, 13 December 2002.
273 Stephen Castle, "Turkey furious at leaders' 'prejudice' on early entry," *The Independent*, 14 December 2002.

274 Philip Webster and Rory Watson, "Rebuff for Britain as EU delays Turkey entry talks," *The Times*, 13 December 2002.
275 Philip Webster and Rory Watson, "Bush angers Europe as Ankara is rebuffed," *The Times*, 14 December 2002.
276 "PM's speech at the Lord Mayor's Banquet, November 10, 2003." Available at www.acronym.org.uk/docs/0311/doc08.htm, accessed 5 March 2012.
277 Interview with İlter Türkmen, Istanbul, 13 June 2008; and Mehmet Ali Birand, "Türkiye bir dostunu daha kaybediyor," *Hürriyet*, 7 October 2006.
278 "Former UK Foreign Secretary awarded Order of the Republic," *TZ*, 12 October 2012.
279 Press Release, *Conservative Friends of Turkey*, 30 October 2008. Available at www.cfot.org.uk/resources/CFT_official_launch-28Oct08.pdf, accessed 16 June 2012.
280 "Israelis say they are shocked by the news," *HDN*, 10 May 2001. See also "Musevi lobisinden Türkiye'ye destek," *Hürriyet*, 17 April 2001.
281 David A. Harris, "Letter from Turkey." Available at www.ajc.org/site/apps/nlnet/content2.aspx?c=ijITI2PHKoG&b=838459&ct=1084461, accessed 14 January 2012.
282 "Belçika basını: Türkiye er geç AB üyesi olacak," *Hürriyet*, 6 August 2002, and "Musevi lobisi: Sıra AB'de," *Hürriyet*, 7 August 2002.
283 Robert Tait, "Erdogan risks mediator role," *The Guardian*, 31 January 2009.
284 Figures generated on the *Eurobarometer* website. The direct link to the results is http://ec.europa.eu/public_opinion/cf/showchart_column.cfm?keyID=261&nationID=5,&startdate=2001.01&enddate=2008.04, accessed 6 June 2015.
285 European Stability Initiative, *Beyond Enlargement Fatigue? Part I The Dutch debate on Turkish Accession*, 24 April 2006, p. ii.
286 "Balkenende, Avrupa'da Türkiye turuna çıkıyor," *Milliyet*, 6 December 2004.
287 Ambrose Evans-Pritchard and Joan Clements, "Fortuyn killed 'to protect Muslims,'" *The Telegraph*, 28 March 2003.
288 Jason Burke, "The murder that shattered Holland's liberal dream," *The Guardian*, 7 November 2004.
289 European Stability Initiative, *Beyond Enlargement Fatigue? Part I The Dutch debate on Turkish Accession*, 24 April 2006, p. 6. Available at www.esiweb.org/pdf/esi_document_id_74.pdf, accessed 14 February 2011.
290 "Hollanda: Türkiye'nin üyeliği AB'nin yararına olacaktır," *Milliyet*, 11 September 2004.
291 "NATO and the 2003 campaign against Iraq," NATO, 25 July 2012. Available at www.nato.int/cps/en/natolive/topics_51977.htm, accessed 10 January 2013.
292 Elizabeth Pond, "The dynamics of the feud over Iraq," in David M. Andrews (ed.), *The Atlantic Alliance under Stress: U.S.-European Relations after Iraq*, Cambridge University Press, 2005, 30–55, p. 38ff.; and Netherlands Ministry of Defence, "Dutch participation in display deterrence." Available at www.defensie.nl/english/nimh/history/international_operations/mission_overview/48168763/operation_display_deterrence_turkey/dutchcontribution/, accessed 1 June 2012.
293 Orhan Alpdündar, "Hollanda, Türkiye'nin üyeliğine sıcak," *NTVMSNBC*, 18 March 2004. Available at http://arsiv.ntvmsnbc.com/news/262101.asp, accessed 30 May 2012.
294 Yusuf Bakırcı, "Hollanda Başbakanı: AB'nin Türkiye kararında Bush etkili olamaz!," *Milliyet*, 28 June 2004.
295 "EU/Turkey: Dutch comment on decision draft," *Wikileaks*, 1 December 2004. Available at http://wikileaks.org/cable/2004/12/04THEHAGUE3140.html#, accessed 7 June 2012.
296 Clifford Sobel, USAMB to the Netherlands.
297 "EU/Turkey: Dutch issue rev 2 draft text," 6 December 2004, *Wikileaks*. Available at http://wikileaks.org/cable/2004/12/04THEHAGUE3178.html#, accessed 7 June 2012.

298 "Ambassador's parting thoughts on taking the Dutch to the next level," *Wikileaks*, 22 August 2005. Available at http://wikileaks.org/cable/2005/08/05THE HAGUE2309.html#, accessed 3 June 2012.
299 FM Ben Bot.
300 Refers to the abovementioned 3 October 2005 meeting of the COEU where a decision for opening of Turkey's accession negotiations was expected to be taken.
301 Murat Yetkin, "Kıbrıs gerilimi artıyor," *Radikal*, 26 June 2002.
302 Yasemin Çongar, "ABD, AB'nin alternatifi değil," *Milliyet*, 24 December 2003; Yasemin Çongar, "Genişleyen AB, ABD ve biz (1)," *Milliyet*, 3 May 2004; and Yasemin Çongar, "Genişleyen AB, ABD ve biz (2)," *Milliyet*, 10 May 2004.
303 See, for example, David L. Phillips, "Turkey's dreams of accession," *Foreign Affairs*, Vol. 83, No. 5, 2004, 86–97, p. 87.
304 See also Ömer Taşpınar, "The US and Turkey's quest for EU membership," in Joseph Joseph (ed.), *Turkey and the European Union: Internal Dynamics and External Challenges*, Palgrave Macmillan, 191–210, p. 199.
305 Michael Rubin, "A Comedy of Errors: American-Turkish Diplomacy and the Iraq War," *Turkish Policy. Quarterly*, Spring 2005, 69–80, pp. 72–3.

11 The First Obama Administration (2009–2013)
Decline

The summer of 2009 was distressing for French President Sarkozy. Since 1 July, he had had to live and breathe Turkey. One day there was an open-air activity, entitled '*Café Turc*' and held in the Tuileries Gardens, during which Turkish coffee and dishes were served, another day the Eiffel Tower was illuminated with the colors of the Turkish flag . . . These activities, totaling approximately 600, were organized in the framework of the 'Turkish Season in France' project. Conceived in 2006, this project was the brainchild of the former Turkish President Ahmet Necdet Sezer and the former French President Jacques Chirac. Chirac's replacement by Sarkozy and the problems developing between the two countries in the following years had reduced the length and scale of the Season. French authorities were hosting the events half-heartedly while from time to time Turks were considering cancelling the project due to the unwelcoming attitude of the French. The official visit of the Turkish President Abdullah Gül to Paris was supposed to be the 'culminating point' of the Season.[1]

Gül was in France between 6 and 9 October 2009. Sarkozy's treatment of Gül was contemptuous. When Gül arrived in Paris, there was no minister from Sarkozy's cabinet present at the airport—let alone Sarkozy himself—to receive him.[2] He would have to wait for a few days to see Sarkozy. At the dinner hosted by the French Institute of International Relations in Gül's honor on 7 October, no French minister was present, again. On 8 October, Gül was able to see PM François Fillon, President of the Senate Gérard Larcher, and some officials responsible for economic policies.[3]

It was on 9 October that Gül could meet Sarkozy. That day, Sarkozy and Gül were to inaugurate an exhibition entitled 'From Byzantium to Istanbul: One Port for Two Continents' and held at the Grand Palais. Sarkozy was late to the inauguration. He chewed gum during the event and took pains to look nonchalant while the guide of the exhibition was introducing him the artifacts. Whereas Gül wrote a whole page in the visitors' book, Sarkozy first rapped his pen on the book with a nervous attitude, waited for a few seconds and only signed the book.[4] After the exhibition, Sarkozy and Gül parted, to come together again at the Élysée Palace for a working lunch.

The lunch, where a few ministers from both sides were also present, lasted an hour. The two leaders decided not to talk on 'the sensitive issues.'[5] Although holding a press briefing is customary after such events, no briefing was held after this one. Gül left the Palace without making any statement. Journalists were not allowed to follow the lunch and had to settle the account of the event with an advisor from the Palace. The advisor remarked: "Between friendly countries, we can talk frankly." French daily *Le Monde* covered the event with the title "Minimum Service at the Élysée Palace for Turkish President."[6]

1 Little Room for Maneuver

Besides his general averseness to Turkey, Sarkozy's attitude was a kind of reaction to the Obama administration. Four months earlier, on 6 June he had had an unpleasant experience because of Turkey. On the occasion of the sixty-fifth anniversary of the D-Day landings, Sarkozy welcomed Obama in Caen. At their press conference, Obama had a disagreement with Sarkozy. "I've said publicly that I think Turkish membership in the EU would be important" Obama told the reporters after their talk and continued as follows:

> I think that Europe and France have a role to play just as the United States does, to send a signal to Muslims around the world that we welcome and want their participation in a world community that is peaceful, that is prosperous, that is developing in favor of all people.

Sarkozy stood his ground. He stated that

> France would continue to oppose Turkey's membership in the EU, although he said he agreed with Obama that close ties with Turkey should be maintained. "It's very important for Europe to have borders. For me Europe is a force of stability in the world and I cannot allow that force for stabilization to be destroyed," he said.[7]

This was neither Obama's first declaration of support for Turkey, nor the first opposition from Sarkozy. In his first visit to Europe in April, Obama had come to the Czech Republic, then holding the Presidency of the Council. At the luncheon with the leaders of the 27 EU MSs, Obama said

> The United States and Europe must approach Muslims as our friends, neighbors and partners in fighting injustice, intolerance and violence, forging a relationship based on mutual respect and mutual interests. [. . .] Moving forward toward Turkish membership in the EU would be an important signal of your (EU) commitment to this agenda and ensure that we continue to anchor Turkey firmly in Europe.[8]

Here, Sarkozy did not answer Obama directly but told France's TF1 television that he had always been opposed to Turkey's entry to the EU. He was uncompromising:

> I have always been opposed to this entry [. . .] I still am and I think I can say that the immense majority of member states shares the position of France. [. . .] Turkey is a very great country, an ally of Europe, an ally of the United States. It will stay a privileged partner. My position hasn't changed and it won't change.[9]

A majority of MSs shared France's position. For example, when asked to comment on Obama's remarks, German Chancellor Merkel said that "the form of any future connection between the EU and Turkey was still not clear." Silvio Berlusconi, PM of Italy, however, said he backed Obama's support for Turkey.[10]

In the terms of office of the previous three presidents, there were a series of hurdles Turkey had to jump over such as the establishment of the CU or the opening of the accession negotiations. The referees in this run were the MSs. What the US had to do to help Turkey was to influence the decision of these referees. True, this was easier said than done, but Obama's job was even more difficult, because, now, Turkey was stuck in the mud pool of the race track. To accede to the EU, Turkey had to complete its negotiations in all of the 35 chapters. This was a gargantuan task for Turkey—and for the US—since

1   In the case of some of the chapters such as Agriculture and Rural Development or Environment, Turkey would need a serious overhaul of its relevant legislation, institutions, management capacity, and administrative system. This would also necessitate substantial social and technological changes. There was not much the US could do in this process.
2   The substance of the negotiations would be conducted in an intergovernmental conference with the participation of all the MSs and Turkey, where decisions would require unanimity. The COEU, acting by unanimity on a proposal by the Commission, would lay down benchmarks for the provisional closure and, where appropriate, for the opening of each chapter.[11] Turks were happy that these procedures were intergovernmental in nature, since the US could influence the MSs before the intergovernmental conferences or before the relevant meetings of the Council, just as it had done so before. Nevertheless, in reality the job of the US was more difficult now due to the following causes:

   a   The existence of 35 chapters with their different characteristics meant a multiplicity of targets for the US. The meaning and importance of each chapter was different for individual MSs. For example, for France, the Agriculture and Rural Development Chapter was critical.

b   Opening and closing of the chapters would require consideration of the technical benchmarks to be proposed, in some cases, by the Commission; there would be less room for political influence.
c   Once all the chapters were 'closed,' a treaty of accession would be prepared by the Commission and the Council, and submitted to the EP's approval. It would be difficult for the US to influence the EP whose 754 members do not necessarily come from the parties that run the government in their respective countries.

On the Cyprus front, things were not going well. Following the GAER Council meeting on 7–8 December 2009, Markos Kyprianou, FM of Cyprus, declared that "Cyprus intended to set conditions for the opening of six future chapters to secure Turkey's compliance with the 2005 agreement."[12]

As if all these constraints were not enough, the Treaty of Lisbon entered into force on 1 December 2009. The Treaty introduced a mutual defense clause:

> If a Member State is the victim of armed aggression on its territory, the other Member States shall have towards it an obligation of aid and assistance by all the means in their power, in accordance with Article 51 of the United Nations Charter.[13]

In the light of this clause, Turkey's possible conflicts with Iraq, Iran, Syria, or Israel would make Europeans think twice about this country's EU membership.[14]

Turkey's hopes were dim, and Obama had little leeway to succor Turkey.

2 US Involvement in Turkey–EU Relations

The Obama administration witnessed some significant changes in the key parameters of Turkish FP. Behind these changes was Ahmet Davutoğlu, a political scientist. In shaping the FP of the Erdoğan government, Davutoğlu had already been influential as a chief advisor before Obama assumed the office. When Davutoğlu became the FM on 1 May 2009, that is less than four months after Obama's inauguration, he found an opportunity to put his ideas into practice. Davutoğlu's aim was to transform Turkey into a global as well as a regional player. This strategy was in line with US interests. Such moves as Turkey's active involvement in ISAF in Afghanistan since 2002,[15] its efforts to contribute to the solution of the conflicts between Georgia and Russia in 2008,[16] or Bosnia and Serbia[17] increased Turkey's importance as an ally for the US. The Obama administration curiously watched Turkey's moves as the Erdoğan government started pursuing an active FP in the Balkans or the Middle East and established close relations with far away countries such as Brazil.

Nevertheless, some other details in Turkey's new FP orientation, including Erdoğan's red-carpet treatment to Sudanese President Omar al-Bashir who visited Ankara twice in 2008, or his clash with Israel's Shimon Peres in January 2009[18] raised doubts since Erdoğan and Davutoğlu were known for their Islamic background. In December 2009, Kürşat Tüzmen, Deputy Chairman of AKP, summarized Turkey's developing trade relations with its southern, eastern, and northern neighbors and said that

> [t]rade with Iran [had] increased tenfold in the last seven years, reaching $10 billion. He pointed out that Turkey's trade with Syria and Iraq, which was less than half a billion dollars, [had] increased to around $5 billion and that Turkey [had] become an important trade partner with Iran as well as with Russia, with which it [had] a trade volume of $50 billion.[19]

On 17 May 2010, Turkey, Iran, and Brazil signed a deal whereby Iran agreed to ship a certain amount low-enriched uranium to Turkey in exchange for nuclear fuel rods for a medical research reactor. The deal was intended to alleviate the crisis over Iran's nuclear aspirations and to obviate further sanctions against this country.[20]

Was Turkey's FP shifting away from the transatlantic axis? Although it was difficult to answer this question, there was one thing certain: in the broadening focus of the Turkish FP, the EU's relative weight was lower now: "Turkish frustration with a series of setbacks for its bid to join the European Union [had] triggered a search for a foreign policy that reflect[ed] its historical interests in the Middle East, Caucasus and Islamic world."[21] On 15 February 2009, Obama called Turkish President Gül and PM Erdoğan and praised Turkey's leadership in its region. Afghanistan, the Caucasus and the Middle East were the primary focus of their talks although they also "touched upon" the EU.[22]

On 7 March, US SECSTATE Hillary Clinton visited Ankara. She met with President Gül, PM Erdoğan, and FM Babacan. The following quotation from Babacan's remarks following his meeting with Clinton is an evidence of how unimportant 'Turkey–EU relations' was in their talk:

> We have [. . .] spoken about the Middle East, Israel-Palestine, Israel-Syria, Israel-Lebanon, Iraq, Afghanistan, Pakistan, developments in those countries—we've discussed those; the Balkans, the Caucasus; Cyprus was also on our agenda; *Turkish-EU relations was another topic we spoke about*; energy, from especially a regional perspective was another area of cooperation we discussed. And our good-excellent cooperation in the fight against terrorism.[23]

Clinton's reference to the issue was also habitual: "I reiterate the Obama administration's support for Turkey's membership in the European Union.

The United States believes it will strengthen Turkey, Europe, and our transatlantic partnership." In a detailed interview conducted with her, there was no reference to Turkey–EU relations.[24]

On 21 March, in his speech at Princeton University, Davutoğlu tried to put at ease the minds of those who were apprehensive of the FP choices of the Erdoğan government. "Our approach and principles are almost the same, very similar [to those of the US] on issues such as the Middle East, Caucasus, the Balkans and energy security. [. . .] By all means, the axis of our foreign policy is toward NATO, the EU and the transatlantic process."[25]

2.1 The Curious Tale of Two Chapters

In his first trip to Europe, Obama attended the NATO Summit in Strasbourg and Kehl, and the EU–US Summit in Prague. The aforementioned disagreement between Obama and Sarkozy in Prague was reliably covered by the media, whilst the coverage of a similar disagreement that occurred at the NATO Summit on 3–4 April 2009 in newspapers was imprecise and dubious: At the Summit, a heated discussion took place about the candidacy of the Danish PM Anders Fogh Rasmussen for the Secretary-General of the Alliance. Whereas the US, Germany, and other major NATO members had already shown their predilection for Rasmussen, Turkey was opposed to him. Turkey's position[26] was based on Rasmussen's

1. tolerance to the activities of PKK in Denmark;
2. indifference to the sensitivity of Muslims in the 'cartoon crisis';[27] and
3. opposition to Turkey's entry to the EU.

Finally, with a deal brokered by Obama who spoke with Gül face-to-face at the Summit and with Erdoğan on the phone,[28] Turkey was convinced to withdraw its opposition. Newspapers were in agreement up until this point. As for what Turkey got in return, however, they disagreed. Some newspapers reported that Turkey was promised senior military command posts and the post of the Alliance's deputy secretary general.[29] Some added 'membership in the European Defense Agency' to the deal.[30] According to some others, Rasmussen "would publicly address the concerns of the Muslim world about his response on the cartoons, possibly as soon as [the] Monday [of the respective week]"[31] or take some measures against the Denmark-based Kurdish broadcaster Roj TV.[32] The most important claim for our purposes here was that Turkey had been promised opening of two of the eight chapters frozen in December 2006.[33] None of these chapters were unfrozen in the following days. French daily *Le Monde* claimed that these rumors had been spread by Ankara,[34] and a Turkish columnist opined that by spreading these rumors the AKP's 'spin doctors' were trying to conceal the government's defeat in the Rasmussen issue.[35] European Commissioner for Enlargement Olli Rehn denied that there was a correlation between Rasmussen's appointment and Turkey's accession negotiations.[36]

2.2 Obama in Turkey

Only a month after Hillary Clinton's visit, this time President Obama came to Turkey on 6 April for two days to attend an annual forum of the Alliance of Civilizations. He had included Turkey in his first European trip, which was a privilege for Turks.[37] The EU was not among the priority issues on his agenda. In his remarks to the Turkish Parliament, he shortly repeated his conviction that Turkey belonged to Europe and underscored the importance of Turkey's—own—reforms.[38] Nevertheless, a strong reaction to his words came from the Christian Social Union of Bavaria (CSU), one of the three members of the coalition government in Germany. Bernd Posselt, foreign affairs spokesperson of the CSU in the EP said that this was "interference in the internal affairs of Europe" and continued: "The EU is not Obama's plaything. [. . .] Then Obama should just admit Turkey as a 51st state of the US." Another CSU member, Markus Ferber, spoke as follows: "[I]n NATO the US has something to say, there is no question about that. However, about the membership of its own club, the EU takes its decisions on its own." CSU's Vice Secretary-General Dorothee Bär's reaction was similar. "We do not need tutoring from abroad" she said. Manfred Weber, a member of the CSU executive board, joined the chorus with a familiar tune: "In the case of the US too, it would be difficult to imagine the admission of Mexico as a new state." The CDU, another member of the coalition, was also critical of Obama's comments albeit at a lower level, whereas the SPD, the third member of the coalition, was close to Obama's position. SPD was against the imposition of the 'privileged partnership' option to Turkey.[39]

In Erdoğan's visit to the US on 7 December 2009, 'the EU' was not referred to in the remarks by Obama and Erdoğan after their meeting.[40]

2.3 Wikileaks Strikes Again

Four Wikileaks cables, allegedly created in the late 2009 and early 2010 had notable references to Turkey–EU relations.

The first of these cables was dated 16 September 2009. It was about the meetings of Philip Gordon, ASSTSECSTATE for EUR, with French policy-makers in Paris in the same month. In one of these meetings, Gordon had a conversation on Turkey with Jean-David Levitte, a diplomatic advisor to President Sarkozy, and a former French ambassador to the US:

> Levitte informed [. . .] Gordon that there had been no change in the French position advocating a "privileged partnership" between the European Union and Turkey [. . .]. However, he emphasized that France was not preventing accession negotiations from progressing on all the EU chapters that do not pre-suppose membership. There remain plenty of chapters of the acquis to open, so if progress is not being made, the

fault lies with Turkish intransigence on Cyprus. Unfortunately, Ankara is not completing the required necessary reforms and progress has stalled. Levitte anticipated a negative report this fall on Turkey's failure to fulfill the Ankara Protocol.[41] [. . .] Gordon said that Turkey was caught in a vicious cycle and it is not completing necessary reforms because the Turks do not believe that their EU candidacy will be allowed to progress, and at the same time, their negotiations are not progressing because they aren't completing the required reforms.[42]

The second cable, dated 27 November 2009, provided a summary of the conversation between Secretary Clinton and Guido Westerwelle, Vice-Chancellor of Germany and Chairman of the Free Democratic Party, had in Berlin on 9 November. When Clinton asked him why Germany feared having Turkey in the EU

> Westerwelle said [. . .] [that] [i]f Germany had to decide now on Turkish access to the EU, the decision would be a clear no. [. . .] However, Westerwelle pointed out that his Free Democratic Party (FDP) had made clear to the Chancellor's Christian Democratic Union (CDU) that a decision on Turkey was not required this year, but rather in five or six years. Therefore, the FDP believed that it was important to keep the door open until that time, so that Turkey had good reason to work for better structures. Otherwise, he explained, if Germany slammed the door shut now, this would affect the entire internal situation in Turkey. He suggested the day might come when the EU would actually invite Turkey in, but Turkey would decline. Westerwelle continued noting that Turkey at present faced West, but it could change to face East. This was important, he said, for both NATO and the EU.[43]

The third cable was from 4 February 2010. It was reporting a meeting between Secretary Clinton and Catherine Ashton, High Representative of the EU for Foreign Affairs and Security Policy on 21 January.

> The Secretary said Turkey was giving up hope on EU membership, and this represented a missed opportunity. Ashton replied that Turkey should be in the EU, but it was not working towards it. The EU's official position remains that Turkey is a membership applicant. Assistant Secretary Gordon said EU membership was the only leverage to sway Ankara on key regional issues, and urged Ashton to speak publicly about Turkey's EU path.[44]

The fourth cable, also dated 4 February 2010, was about the third US–France Strategic Dialogue meeting on 20 January, where Under SECSTATE Bill Burns and Under Secretary of Defense for Policy (USD[P]) Michele

Flournoy hosted their French counterparts Jacques Audibert and Michel Miraillet.

> USD(P) asked whether the EU was closer to identifying a way that it could signal to Turkey that the door was open to a closer relationship, such as observer status in the European Defense Agency. Audibert noted that President Sarkozy had been particularly upset with the Turkish position on Rasmussen at Strasbourg and that Sarkozy's objection to Turkish membership in the EU was one of five pillars on his political campaign that the public still remembered. Further, when France tried to move forward with closer NATO-EU ties during its 2008 EU presidency, Turkey rejected every plan that was put on the table. For these reasons, it would be difficult for France to see any opening on EU membership for Turkey in the near future. All French interlocutors agreed that a 'more arrogant' Turkey could present a problem during NATO Strategic Concept discussions this year. In response, Flournoy, Vershbow[45] and Gordon reiterated that by closing the door on the Turks, the EU was creating a vicious circle that fueled Turkish obstructionism at NATO.[46]

The following two inferences can be drawn from the four cables above assuming that these cables are authentic:

1. The US advocacy for Turkey continued behind closed doors; it was not just a 'dog and pony show' staged to please Turkey. Clinton, Gordon, Vershbow, and Flournoy tried to convince the Europeans to offer better prospects and more optimistic signals to Turks.
2. According to Americans, even if Turkey's EU membership was not possible in the short term, keeping this dream alive for Turks was necessary to secure their cooperation in regional issues and in NATO and to ensure the continuity of their domestic reforms. Certain European figures such as Westerwelle were in agreement with the Americans on this issue.

2.4 Turkey Recalls Its Ambassador

On 4 March 2010, COFA of the US HOR passed a non-binding measure, calling on the administration to ensure that US policy formally referred to the 1915–1923 events as genocide. Previously, the attempts of the Armenian lobby to obtain recognition from various levels of the Congress had been thwarted by the previous administrations that lent an ear to Turkey's sensitivity. This time, Turks felt betrayed by the Obama administration. Şükrü Elekdağ, a former Turkish ambassador to the US and a deputy from the main opposition party CHP, said "the U.S. administration has left Turkey alone." Turkey recalled its ambassador Namık Tan minutes after the decision.

Tan returned to Washington a month later following a one-hour telephone conversation between Secretary Clinton and Davutoğlu.[47]

2.5 The Summer of 2010

Owing to the diplomatic 'investments' made since the coming into power of AKP in 2003, Turkey started to pursue a more active FP from the mid-2010 onwards, which was not in line with US preferences. Davutoğlu summarized Turkey's new FP openings based on "active involvement in all international organizations and on all issues of global and international importance" as follows:

> Turkey became a non-permanent member of the U.N. Security Council and is chairing three critical commissions concerning Afghanistan, North Korea, and the fight against terror. Turkey undertook the chairmanship-in-office of the South-East European Cooperation Process, a forum for dialogue among Balkan states and their immediate neighbors, for 2009 and 2010. Turkey is also a member of G20, maintains observer status in the African Union, has a strategic dialogue mechanism with the Gulf Cooperation Council, and actively participates in the Arab League. Turkey has also launched new diplomatic initiatives by opening 15 new embassies in Africa and two in Latin America, and is a signatory to the Kyoto Protocol. These developments show a new perspective of Turkey, one that is based on vision, soft power, a universal language, and implementation of consistent foreign policies in different parts of the world.[48]

The summer of 2010 started with two critical events. The first of these events was the Gaza flotilla raid and the second one was the adoption of a UN resolution on measures against Iran.

2.5.1 The Gaza Flotilla Raid

The deterioration that started in Turkish-Israeli relations in the mid-2000s continued in the Obama era. Following the Davos crisis between Erdoğan and Peres, Turkey banned Israel from an international air force drill, whereas Israel denied Davutoğlu's request to visit the Gaza Strip from Israeli territory.[49] The nadir of the relations between the two countries occurred when a flotilla carrying humanitarian aid and HR activists of mainly Turkish nationality and heading to Gaza was stormed by Israeli commandos on 31 May 2010. Nine people were killed and several others injured in the incident.[50]

The title of a *NYT* article from 8 June that summarized this new orientation of Turkey's FP was appropriate: "Turkey Goes from Pliable Ally to Thorn for U.S."[51]

The response of the Obama administration to the incident was cautiously pro-Turkish. On 1 June, Robert Gibbs, the Press Secretary of the White House, was answering the questions from members of the press:

Q: [. . .] On the Mideast, does President Obama condemn Israel's raid of the aid ship headed to Gaza?

MR. GIBBS: [. . .] [L]et me simply restate what the international community and the United States supported early this morning at the U.N. Security Council through a presidential statement. The Security Council deeply regrets the loss of life and injuries resulting from the use of force during the Israeli military operation in international waters against the convoy sailing to Gaza. [. . .]

Q: So that would seem to cover President Obama's personal feeling, while some of the allies are looking for a stronger statement from him directly.

MR. GIBBS: Again, this is supported not just by the United States but by the international community.[52]

2.5.2 The UN Resolution

As stated above, in mid-May, Turkey, Iran, and Brazil signed a deal that, they hoped, would demonstrate the cooperative attitude and peaceful intentions of Iran in its nuclear program. To this deal

> Washington's response was ambivalent. A statement said the potential transfer of Iran's enriched uranium abroad would be 'a positive step', while adding that the fabrication of 20% enriched uranium was 'a direct violation of UN security council resolutions." The White House also pointed out that the agreement was vague on Iran's future talks with major powers on its nuclear programme.[53]

Turkey and Brazil did not stop there. Being two of the ten non-permanent members of the UN Security Council, on 9 June they voted against a UN resolution[54] that aimed to impose further sanctions on Iran. The resolution was adopted anyway. An analysis published in the *WP* commented that "[t]he 'no' votes cast by Turkey and Brazil might embolden Tehran to keep standing firm."[55]

The Obama administration had difficulty crafting a stable and consistent policy for this unexpected pattern of behavior of the Erdoğan government. Secretaries of State and Defense seemed relatively tolerant towards Turkey. "We disagreed with their vote. [. . .] But I can understand from a diplomatic perspective why they might be able to make a convincing case for how they voted today"[56] remarked SECSTATE Clinton, while SECDEF Robert Gates said "I'll be honest, I was disappointed in Turkey's vote on the Iranian sanctions. [. . .] Allies don't always agree on things, but we move forward from here."[57]

Philip Gordon, ASSTSECSTATE for EUR, known as a diplomat who attributed importance to keeping Turkey–US relations free from strain,[58] indicated that the US expected Turkey to prove that it remained fully committed to NATO, the EU and the US, else would risk losing America's support *on certain issues*.[59]

Obama's personal reaction behind closed doors was grim initially. Then, he came to terms with the stance of the Erdoğan government:

> Obama and Erdogan had a showdown later that month [June 2010] at the G-20 summit in Toronto. Obama protested, "You knew how important this was to me, and you didn't come with me," recalls a senior administration official. Erdogan responded equally bluntly. Over several hours, they moved into "a long discussion about evolving trends in the world and what it means to be allies." Turks agree that a real partnership was born at that meeting.[60]

2.5.3 Implications for Turkey–EU Relations

Surprisingly, the effect of these two issues on Turkey–EU relations was likely to be positive for three reasons.

1. For the Obama administration, the flotilla incident was a conclusive evidence of that the focus of Turkish FP had shifted from the West to the East. The administration accused the Europeans for this. With reference to the incident, Gates said the following:

   > I personally think that if there is anything to the notion that Turkey is, if you will, moving eastward, it is, in my view, in no small part because it was pushed, and pushed by some in Europe refusing to give Turkey the kind of organic link to the West that Turkey sought.[61]

Obama himself remarked that he

saw reluctance to let Turkey in as a factor behind changes seen in its traditionally West-facing foreign policy.
Obama said he thought the unwillingness in Europe was not the only factor in the shift observed in Turkey. [. . .]
"But it is inevitably destined to play a role in how the Turkish people see Europe," Obama said. "If they do not feel themselves part of the European family, it is natural that they should end up looking elsewhere for alliances and affiliations."[62]

This view of the Obama administration garnered some approval in the US media. Thomas Friedman from the *NYT* wrote "The EU's rejection of Turkey, a hugely bad move, has been a key factor prompting Turkey to move closer to Iran and the Arab world."⁶³ In Europe, certain columnists found this view unsettling.⁶⁴

2   Just as it had been the case in 2003, Turkey was taking steps contrary to US preferences. The 'Turkey as a Trojan horse in the EU' argument was less tenable now.
3   As a stronger and more assertive player in international politics, Turkey's contribution to the EU's FP dimension could be higher than before.

Nonetheless, the words of two members of the HOR were challenging for Turks. Mike Pence, a member of COFA and "a self-described proponent of Turkey" told the Turkish ambassador the following: "[W]ith regard to Capitol Hill, with regard to the Congress of the United States, there will be a cost if Turkey stays on its present heading of growing closer to Iran and more antagonistic to the state of Israel." It is not clear whether 'toning down the support for Turkey's European cause' was included in the calculation of this cost, but it is clear that in another invoice, drawn up by Representative Shelley Berkley, the chair of the US delegation to the Transatlantic Legislators' Dialogue, this item was at the top.

> "They will not come into my office, they will not be welcome in my office until I see a change of policy. Because I think the current trajectory the Turkish government is on is not only dangerous for Israel, it's dangerous for the United States of America," Berkley told reporters.
> [She] said, "[Turkey doesn't] deserve [EU] recognition until they start behaving more like the European nations and a whole less like Iran."
> Berkley added that she would "speak actively against" Turkey's bid to become a part of the European Union.⁶⁵

2.5.4 "A Smarter American Policy"

On 20 July 2010, the *Los Angeles Times* (*LAT*) published a commentary by Henri Barkey. Entitled "Don't Blame Europe for Turkey's Moves away from the West" this commentary was a criticism of the aforementioned remarks by Gates and Obama blaming the Europeans. In Barkey's opinion, Turkey had two fundamental problems that would remain the main impediments to progress for EU membership. These problems were the Kurdish question and poor record of rule of law promotion. Barkey was recommending a change in the discourse of the Obama administration:

> Both of these impediments will take years, if not decades, to deal with. Therefore, to blame Europe for Turkey's difficulties is unfair and unnecessarily alienates the Europeans. It made sense for the U.S. to push the Europeans on Turkey in the 1990s when Europe was pushing Turkey

away. Now, however, a process has been put in place for Turkey to pursue EU membership. The current U.S. rhetoric and silence on domestic issues relieve Turkish leaders from the burden of reform and from being honest with their public about the travails ahead for EU membership. It does not do Turkey any favors; on the contrary, it solidifies the distance between Turkey and the EU.

A smarter American policy would focus on pushing the Turks to reform. [. . .] The U.S. must align itself with Turkish and European advocates of change and help transform Turkey into a more tolerant and democratic society.[66]

In the autumn of 2010, other points of disagreement arose between Turkey and the US. In September

> Turkey's trade minister said [. . .] that the American-led campaign to ban all banking transactions with Iran was a mistake. Turkish officials said it was up to Turkey's banks and companies to decide whether to go along with tougher unilateral sanctions decreed by the United States and the European Union.
>
> "If the demand is for Turkey not to have any trade, any economic relations with Iran," Mr. Gul[67] said, "it would be unfair to Turkey." He claimed that some American and European companies continued to do business with Iran under new names, circumventing the sanctions.[68]

Turkey also showed reluctance to endorse NATO-wide missile defense plans that included construction of a radar base in Turkish territory.[69]

Contrary to the views of some columnists who thought that the US would be less enthusiastic to promote Turkey's EU bid during those days,[70] the support of the Obama administration remained immune to—or even fueled by—these problems. On 14 October, Hillary Clinton and Catherine Ashton were interviewed for the BBC. Clinton emphasized Turkey's increasing weight, underscored the importance of Turkey–US relations, and expressed her belief that Ashton was as much committed to Turkey's EU prospects as herself was. Ashton was walking on eggshells:

> HIGH REPRESENTATIVE ASHTON: Well, as Hillary says, Turkey's position for me is a very important one. [. . .]
> In terms of what then for the member states need to do is to move forward. I mean, Turkey is a candidate country. [. . .] And I work on that basis and so do they. It's a long-term and challenging route to get to EU membership in any event.[71]

In another interview, published in *La Repubblica* on 19 November 2010, this time President Obama reiterated his dedication to Turkey's European bid and—as reminded by Barkey—stressed the importance of Turkey's domestic reforms:

> We urge Turkey to continue the reforms necessary for its accession which is an open-ended process. We believe that a Turkey that is able to meet the criteria for accession to the European Union would make a contribution to the EU itself.[72]

SECSTATE Clinton followed a similar track. In July 2011, she said "Washington was counting on [Turkey] to live up to the standards of its founder, Mustafa Kemal Ataturk." She added that "the recent arrests of dozens of journalists and curbs placed on religious freedom were 'inconsistent' with Turkey's economic and political progress."[73]

The Obama administration's policy towards Turkey–EU relations was 'smarter' now.

2.6 The Arab Spring or Being In-between

A series of popular uprisings broke out against oppressive regimes in a number of Arab countries from December 2010 onwards. In this process known as the 'Arab Spring,' the protesters were demanding improvement in such areas as democracy, HR, education, and economy. In a matter of months, Egypt, Tunisia, and Libya overthrew their monarchies. Turkey strongly encouraged this process. In September 2011, Erdoğan visited these three countries and was warmly welcomed by politicians and public alike. In implicit terms, he was trying to promote Turkey as a model for the countries involved in the Arab Spring. The *FT* compared his popularity to that of the Shia regime of Iran, another player who aspired to be influential in these countries:

> There are those who argue he is the non-Arab leader Arabs have most admired since Saladin—a Kurd from Mesopotamia—recaptured Jerusalem from the Crusaders in 1187.
>
> [. . .]
>
> According to this year's Arab Attitudes, the authoritative annual survey [. . .], Mr Erdogan's ratings are so high he could be forgiven for believing (as his enemies whisper) he could recreate a neo-Ottoman sultanate. Turkey's policies are a hit from Morocco (80 per cent approval) to Saudi Arabia (98 per cent); Iran's are not, with 14 and 6 per cent respectively.
>
> Even in Lebanon, stronghold of Hizbollah, Tehran's Shia Islamist proxy, 93 per cent have a favourable view of Turkey and 87 per cent like Mr Erdogan.[74]

The article also referred to the popularity of the Americans in these countries: "President Barack Obama and the US score well below Iran everywhere except Saudi Arabia."

The results of a similar survey were made public by an Italian news agency:

> Turkey beat EU as a 'supporter' of the Arab Spring countries. [. . .] The investigation was carried out between December 2011 and February 2012 in the 43 Member States of the Union for the Mediterranean. [. . .] On a 01–10 scale, Turkey ranks first among countries supporting the Arab Spring countries, with an average score of 5.9 in replies.
>
> The European Union ranks second on the same list (5.4), then come the Arab League (4.4), the Gulf Cooperation Council (3.7), Saudi Arabia (3), China (2.9), Russia (2.8) and Iran (2.2.).[75]

Turkey's involvement in this process demonstrated once again that Turkey was 'in-between':

1. Turkey was in-between amid the West and the East politically. With the sympathy it received from the Arab world, Turkey proved to be a more valuable ally for the US and a more valuable candidate for the EU. Secretary Clinton was happy with this new potential already bearing its fruits:

   > Turkey has a unique opportunity in this time of great historic change, with the so-called Arab Awakening, to demonstrate the power of an inclusive democracy and responsible regional leadership. For example, we have worked closely with Turkey on supporting the central institutions of Iraq and helping to integrate Iraq economically into a larger region. Turkey has been vocal in its condemnation of President Asad's brutal campaign of violence against its own people, and Syrian opposition groups have met and organized in Turkey. And Turkey has opened its arms and hearts to more than 7,000 Syrians who have found refuge across the border.[76]

2. However, Turkey was also in-between in terms of the democracy and HR standards of the West and the East. While Turkey was trying to improve its own record of democracy and HR taking the EU as a reference, it was aspiring to be a role-model for the Arab states. *The Economist* called Turkey 'a flawed example,'[77] and the 'Turkey' chapter of the *World Report 2012* of the Human Rights Watch started with the following paragraph:

   > As the [. . .] AKP government focused on promoting Turkey's regional interests in response to the pro-democracy Arab Spring movements, human rights suffered setbacks at home. The government has not prioritized human rights reforms since 2005, and freedom of expression and association have both been damaged by the ongoing prosecution and incarceration of journalists, writers, and hundreds of Kurdish political activists.[78]

2.7 The Contractor

The pro-active and venturous FP of the Erdoğan government captured everyone's imagination and raised the expectations to unreasonable levels. While Erdoğan was delivering a speech at the FMs' meeting at the Arab League's Cairo headquarters, demonstrators gathered outside the building to express their sympathy to him. The sign one of these demonstrators held up read "If Erdogan had been our leader, we would have liberated our Jerusalem."[79] This ordinary man was not the only one captivated by Erdoğan's confrontational style. The author of the leading article of *The Times* on 11 August 2011 was expecting bold steps from Erdoğan. While speculating Assad's atrocities against Syrian people, the article made a far-fetched surmise:

> Turkey has now given Damascus a two-week deadline to halt the killing machine. The alternative is not spelt out. But it is clear: a Turkish military incursion, to "protect Turkish interests."[80]

Although Assad did not yield to this threat, no military incursion followed, proving wrong—not Erdoğan—but *The Times*.

In this atmosphere, *The Middle East Newsline*, an online "defense news service by independent journalists"[81] published a spectacular claim on 1 March 2011: Erdoğan had made an offer to the US and EU. He would send the Turkish navy to overthrow the Gaddafi regime in Libya. If the operation was successful, the EU would accept Turkey as a full-member in return. While the Americans and the Saudis endorsed the plan, the website claimed, Europeans (especially Sarkozy) opposed it despite US pressure.[82] Turks had won numerous construction contracts in Libya in the past, but this one would have been the most unusual and profitable of all. The coverage of the rest of the process in the mainstream media, however, casts doubt on the claims of *The Middle East Newsline*. Based on a UN Security Council Resolution,[83] a multi-state military intervention was carried out between 19 March and 31 October 2011.[84] When the intervention started, Turkey called for an immediate Western cease-fire and drew attention to civilian deaths. After a while, when NATO got involved in the process, Turkey participated in the coalition on 8 June but did not take part in airstrikes and as a NATO member vetoed several proposals. This position put Turkey at odds with its Western allies.[85] Gates criticized Turkey, Spain, and the Netherlands as these three NATO members had chosen not to take part in the airstrikes.[86] According to *Der Spiegel*, Turkey's position was based on its concerns about its standing in the Muslim world.[87] For a Turkey who—even as a member of a coalition—was worried about a possible negative reaction from its fellow Muslim countries, it would be unimaginable to attack Libya single-handedly. Although the claim of *The Middle East Newsline* may not be true, it still shows the prevalent impression of Turkey who is ready to do anything to become an EU member. This impression would soon change.

2.8 The EU Loses Its Relative Importance for Turks

In the Obama era, Turks never abandoned the quest for EU membership. Nevertheless, as they improved their economy, constructed new FP avenues, and gained self-confidence, they grew lukewarm towards EU membership and tried to divest themselves of the image of a nation that is ready to sacrifice anything to attain it.

While the EU members were suffering a sovereign-debt crisis that emerged around late 2009, Erdoğan was priding himself on the success of his economic policies. In June 2012, he declared that Turkey's economy had grown at an annual average of 5.3 percent since 2002 (the fastest rate of any country in the OECD), GDP had more than tripled (as had its foreign reserves), and foreign investment had increased more than 16 times.[88]

In December 2011, Volkan Bozkır, Chairman of the Foreign Affairs Commission of the Turkish Parliament, remarked that he identified a paradigm change in Turkey–EU relations. He said that with its welfare level, Turkey did not need the EU for economic reasons anymore. Raising Turkey's laws to the level of the EU's was still an important target for Turkey, but even this could be achieved without becoming a member, he added. He claimed that Turkey was working on the chapters that had not been opened by the EU and that by the year 2013 the body of legislation covered by these chapters would have been harmonized with the corresponding sections of the EU law. In other words, Turkey would have unofficially 'closed' these chapters by 2013, although they had not been 'opened' officially in the first place yet, which would be ironic, Bozkır concluded.[89] Bozkır was a diplomat with considerable professional experience in Turkey–EU relations and had been the Secretary-General for EU Affairs in the 2009–2011 period.

On 21 September 2011, Erdoğan said they did not want to be the side that would sever the relations, unless the EU took a step in that direction.[90] A few months later, his economy minister Zafer Çağlayan would refer to the economic crisis in Europe contemptuously: "Those who called us 'sick' in the past are now 'sick' themselves. May God grant them recovery."[91]

2.9 The EU Is Taken Out of the Agenda of Turkey–US Relations

In Obama's first term, Erdoğan visited the US four times.[92] He also met with Obama at various international summits. 'Turkey–EU relations' was not among the primary topics discussed in their *tête-à-tête* talks.[93]

After 2010, the Obama administration did not take any concrete step for Turkey other than voice their support on a few occasions. They did not seem particularly interested in and competent at Turkey–EU relations. A few days after the EU released Turkey's Progress Report on 12 October 2011, DOS Spokesperson Victoria Nuland was asked her opinion about the Report. She said that she had not read it and habitually added that they wanted to see Turkey as an EU member.[94] In the framework of Obama's re-election campaign,

Vice President Joe Biden spoke to members of the Turkish-American community in April 2012.

> [He] stated, "Like the President (Obama), I criticize some of our European allies for not completely accepting Turkey into the economic union[95] and for not considering Turkey as a complete part of Europe."[96]

In the visits of Secretary Clinton (on 10–12 August 2012),[97] and Bill Burns—now DEPSECSTATE—(on 10 September 2012)[98] to Turkey, the Syrian civil war was in focus and 'Turkey–EU relations' was not an item on the agenda.

Obama was re-elected on 6 November 2012, and his first term in office ended on 20 January 2013 against this background.

3 Collaborators of the US

The strain between Turkey and Israel affected the attitude of the Jewish lobby in the US Congress towards Turkey. Turks' loss of support of this lobby was one of the reasons behind the result of the voting on the alleged Armenian genocide at the US HOR in March 2010. After James Jeffrey, the USAMB to Ankara, was named Ambassador to Iraq in July in 2010, the US could not appoint a new ambassador to Ankara for five months due to the opposition of this lobby.[99]

On 4 February 2011, Davutoğlu announced that Israel's diplomatic presence in Turkey was being reduced to second secretary level, which meant expulsion of the Israeli ambassador and senior level diplomats. He added that Turkey was suspending military agreements with Israel.[100] On 23 January 2012, *Jerusalem Post* underscored Turkey's close relations with Iran and Hamas and claimed that Turkey was supporting 'anti-Israel Islamic terrorists.'[101] Turkey also vetoed Israel's participation in the NATO Summit in Chicago on 20–21 May.[102]

In Obama's first term, Israel did not enter into any co-ordination with the US to back Turkey's EU bid, whereas some MEPs claimed that with an austere anti-Israel course, Turkey was not making any friends in Europe.[103] *Haaretz* quoted an anonymous senior European official who said "Erdogan wants to be part of the European Union, but now he can forget about it."[104] As noted above, Shelley Berkley, a member of the US HOR, declared that she would work against Turkey's accession to the EU.

A Turkish newspaper used the following quotation from Wikileaks documents: "Israelis [. . .] blamed the Europeans, and especially France, for this shift in Turkey's policy. They said that if Europe had more warmly embraced Turkey, then the Turks would not be taking steps to earn approval in the Arab and Muslim world at the expense of Israel."[105]

There was a change in the case of the Netherlands too. In the 9 June 2010 election, CDA lost half of its seats in the Parliament and dropped from first to fourth place. What was worse for Turks was that Geert Wilders's party,

Party for Freedom, came in third in the election. Wilders was known for his anti-Islamic and anti-Turkish discourse. Upon his request, the coalition protocol of the government included an article about modifying the association agreement Turkey had signed with the EEC in 1963.[106]

The UK and Italy, on the other hand, continued to work with the US for Turkey.

3.1 The UK

In Obama's first term, the UK remained a staunch defender of Turkey. When the Greek Cypriot representatives, at the 7–8 December 2009 meeting of the COEU, threatened to veto the opening of six chapters in Turkey's accession negotiations, British FS David Miliband walked out of the hall to protest the Cypriots.[107] At the same meeting, Miliband also quarreled with his French counterpart Bernard Kouchner for Turkey.[108]

In June 2010, at a meeting of the CFT, Liam Fox, Shadow SECSTATE for Defense, stated that Turkey's exclusion from the EU would lead the country to turn its face to Russia and the Middle East. He promised that when the Conservative Party came to power they would work for Turkey.[109]

William Hague, now the FS, was equally positive:

> We should [. . .] see the value of Turkey's future membership of the European Union in this light. Turkey is Europe's biggest emerging economy and a good example of a country developing a new role and new links for itself, partly on top of and partly outside of existing structures and alliances. It is highly active in the Western Balkans, the wider Middle East and Central Asia. We will make a particular diplomatic effort to work with Turkey, starting with a major visit by the Turkish Foreign Minister to Britain next week at my invitation.[110]

Hague's words provoked reaction from his own party as well as from the opposition. Roger Helmer, an MEP from the British Conservative Party, said "British voters won't stand for Turkish membership—nor will other EU states"[111] while the British National Party accused Hague of subjecting the FP of Britain to America's interests.[112]

On 26 July 2010, British PM David Cameron visited Turkey. His speech at the Union of Chambers and Commodity Exchanges of Turkey was comparable to Bill Clinton's speech at the Turkish Parliament. In magniloquent terms, he expressed his country's backing for Turkey's EU membership and established a parallel between de Gaulle's vetoing of the UK's accession to the EEC and Turkey's case.[113] Cameron convened a joint press conference with his counterpart Erdoğan, where Erdoğan voiced his gratitude to the UK:

> [A]s my dear friend David also said before, there is no party in the UK that opposes Turkey's accession to the EU. [. . .] That observation is very

important because in the seven and a half years that we have been in power here in Turkey we have always experienced great support from British governments.[114]

In return, Cameron emphasized Turkey's importance for the economy and security of Europe. On 6 August 2010, in their conversation on the phone, Cameron 'updated' Obama on his visit to Turkey.[115]

When the Dutch scaled down their campaign for Turkey, the British lobbied for Turkey in the Netherlands. On 9 March 2011, in his address to the Confederation of Netherlands Industry and Employers, David Lidington, British Minister of State for Europe, invited Dutch investors to Turkey and explained them the potential economic benefits of Turkey's EU membership.[116]

In 2011, Hague confirmed the connection between his policies towards Turkey and those of the US. He said Davutoğlu and Clinton were his two colleagues he made the most phone calls to.[117]

3.2. Italy

Italy's support for Turkey increased in the Obama era. As noted above, Berlusconi openly declared his concurrence with Obama in the latter's visit to Europe in April 2009. On 10 June 2010, *Frankfurter Allgemeine Zeitung* published an interview with Italy's FM Franco Frattini who said the EU's refusal to embrace Turkey had pushed Ankara 'eastwards.'[118] As indicated above, on 9 June *Reuters* had quoted the words the US SECDEF Gates that reflected the same understanding.[119] Probably, it had been Gates's words that inspired Frattini.

Whereas for the British, Turkey's potential contribution to the EU would be rather in terms of economy and security, for Italians, Turkey's identity, geopolitical value, and new FP options were important. In November 2009, Italian President Giorgio Napolitano drew attention to Turkey's "potential contribution to the moderate evolution of the Muslim world by acting as a bridge between Europe and Islam" and expressed his hope for Turkey's EU membership.[120] In May 2012, Mario Monti, PM of Italy, said Turkey's close relations with the Middle Eastern, African, and Arab countries would contribute much to the EU's influence in international politics.[121] He added that Italy's backing for Turkey was not a strategic choice of certain governments but a policy of Italy as a state. Therefore, he said, before his own government, the Berlusconi and Prodi governments had favored Turkey.[122]

Following the change of government in France, Italy found an opportunity to 'sell' Turkey to the new French cabinet. When the new French FM Laurent Fabius visited Rome in June 2012, his Italian counterpart Giulio Terzi elaborated on Turkey's importance for the EU and said that a concrete answer should be given to Turkey.[123]

4 Mentality of the Obama Administration

Turkey's perception by the Obama administration underwent a process of transformation that comprised two stages:

1. The first stage that lasted until the mid-2010 was marked by incertitude. It took some time for the Obama administration to develop a coherent policy—and a politically correct discourse—in dealing with the Islamically inclined AKP government. In her visit to Turkey in March 2009, Secretary Clinton was cautious not to emphasize Turkey's Islamic identity:

> QUESTION: [. . .] Now, how do you qualify Turkey today? I mean, previous administrations used the terminology "moderate Islam." Now, will you be using the same terminology? Is it—
> SECRETARY CLINTON: No. We're not going to characterize any country's religious affiliation. We're looking for an opportunity to strengthen and deepen our relationship with Turkey.
> Turkey is many things. Turkey has many aspects to it. [. . .] The fact that Turkey is a predominantly, but not exclusively Muslim nation, that there are varying levels of society that are moving forward together, we find all of that very exciting. So we want our relationship to be with the Turkish people.[124]

Only a month later, when Obama visited Turkey, he seemed much more comfortable with Turkey's Muslim identity. He said the following:

> I think where there's the most promise is in the idea that Turkey and the United States can build a model partnership in which a majority Christian and a majority Muslim nation, a Western nation and a nation that straddles two continents—that we can create a modern international community that is respectful, secure and prosperous.[125]

In the words of Jackson Diehl of the *WP*, "'Islamist-oriented' governments [including that of Turkey were] about to become the new normal in a region dominated for decades by secular autocrats and pro-American generals." Turkey's cooperation with the US in denying al-Qaeda a safe haven in Pakistan or Afghanistan, its neighborhood and acquaintance with Iran, and its potential contribution to the solution of Israel's problems with Syria and Palestine were important assets.[126]

In this first stage, the US support for Turkey's EU membership was a kind of safety precaution. The EU was seen as a center of gravity to keep Turkey in orbit in the Western planetary system. With this policy,

the US also hoped to regain the confidence and sympathy of the Turkish people.
2   From the mid-2010 onwards Turkey pursued an active and assertive FP that at times drew the disapproval of the US. Oddly, this new bearing of Turkey elevated Turkey's stature as an ally for the US. Stephen Kinzer wrote the following in 2010:

> [B]y showing its independence from Washington, Turkey has further strengthened its credibility in the Middle East. This credibility can be a strategic asset for the west, because Turkish diplomats can go places, talk to factions and make deals that Americans cannot. Yet the US has not been able to take advantage of it.[127]

Two other developments accompanied this process:
First, the EU lost its importance for Turkey in relative terms, because

    a   Turkey's accession process came to a deadlock;
    b   the EU was hit by an economic crisis; and
    c   Turks created FP alternatives to the EU.

Second, Europeans grew completely intolerant of US interventions. European diplomats interviewed for this book in Washington in 2010 unanimously indicated that they had closed their ears to the US advocacy for Turkey. "When our American colleagues start talking about Turkey-EU relations, we show signs of exasperation. Even in social events such as cocktails, we don't let them talk about Turkey. For the last few months Americans have gone cold turkey in this sense, and it is quite a weight off our mind" one of them said jokingly.

As a result, in this second stage, the Obama administration was rather concerned with keeping Turkey's interest in and hopes for Europe alive and ensuring the continuation of Turkey's domestic reforms.

5 Conclusion

In the Obama era, Turkey's FP went through some major changes. Turkey 'broke up' with Israel, established close relations with Iran, and aspired to play a role in the Arab Spring; it was not the predictable and tame ally it once had been. According to some observers, Turkey was drifting away from the West, and a similar process was observed in domestic politics in the country. In their opinion, AKP-based Islamists were utilizing the political reforms undertaken to facilitate the country's accession to the EU "as a means to achieving a hidden agenda of Islamization in Turkey." Nevertheless, it was again the EU that had a potential to "consolidate democratic laws and practices and stabilize state-religion relations in the country."[128] Notwithstanding this necessity, the actual support—if not the intention—of the Obama administration for Turkey's accession to the EU dwindled gradually. This had a number of reasons:

1. An erosion of the global hegemonic position of the US had been going on for almost a decade. The US influence over the EU was even lesser in Obama's first term compared to that of his predecessors. Several American officials interviewed for this book put forward arguments along the lines of "we are not so powerful anymore" to explain the decrease in the US support for Turkey.[129]
2. Turkey's improving economic indicators and increasing political influence boosted Turks' self-confidence. They felt less need for Americans.
3. 'Relations with the EU' was downgraded on Turkey's list of FP priorities because of
    a. the technical and political difficulties brought about by the chapters;
    b. Turks' perception of being unfairly treated; and
    c. the new openings on the FP agenda of the Erdoğan government.
4. Europeans became completely intolerant of US interventions.
5. It was impossible for the Europeans to give any more concessions to the Turks. For them, the 35 chapters they were negotiating with the Turks were the last 35 'bastions' defending the continent against a Turkish invasion; 'closing' of these chapters would 'open' the door to Turkey's accession.

The combination of the unwavering US backing for Turkey with Turkey's unusual FP moves stimulated the creativity of conspiracy theorists: Some claimed that the US convinced Turkey to lift its objection to the appointment of Rasmussen as the Secretary-General of NATO in return for opening of two chapters in the accession negotiations, whereas some others claimed that Turkey offered to topple down Gaddafi at a price of EU membership.

The Obama administration also worked for the prevention of replacement of Turkey's full-membership prospect with privileged partnership. If Wikileaks documents are any indication, the US advocacy of Turkey's interests against the Europeans continued *in camera*.

In the last two years of the first term of the Obama administration, the US support for Turkey's EU bid dwindled to an imperceptible level for the first time for decades, while Turks themselves started confidently saying that they could do without the EU.

Due to the problems between Turkey and Israel, the latter discontinued its efforts for Turkey's European aspirations. A governmental change resulted in a similar situation in the case of the Netherlands. The UK and Italy continued to collaborate with the US for Turkey.

Notes

1 "Years and Seasons of Turkey recently organized in other countries," *TMFA*. Available at www.mfa.gov.tr/years-and-seasons-of-turkey-recently-organized-in-other-countries.en.mfa, accessed 6 May 2012; "Sarkozy's stance clouds Turkey Season in France," *HDN*, 8 October 2009; and "Turkish Season in France to go on despite tension," *TZ*, 20 June 2009.
2 "Ankara'da Sarkozy'ye soğuk karşılamayla misilleme yapıldı," *EurActiv*. Available at www.euractiv.com.tr/yazici-sayfasi/article/ankarada-sarkozyye-soguk-karsilama-016022, accessed 10 May 2012.
3 Arnaud Leparmentier, "Service minimum à l'Elysée pour le président turc," *Le Monde*, 8 October 2009.
4 Aslı Aydıntaşbaş, "Gül'ü ağzında sakızla karşıladı," *Akşam*, 10 October 2009.
5 Read 'Turkey's accession to the EU.'
6 Arnaud Leparmentier, "Service minimum à l'Elysée pour le président turc," *Le Monde*, 8 October 2009; and "Sarkozy et Gül constatent leur désaccord, mais promettent de mieux coopérer," *Le Parisien*, 9 October 2009.
7 "Obama, Sarkozy clash over Turkey's EU bid, headscarf issue," *Sunday's Zaman*, 8 June 2009.
8 Kerstin Gemhlich and Mark John, "Paris, Berlin bristle as Obama backs Turkey for EU," *Reuters*, 5 April 2009. Available at www.reuters.com/article/2009/04/05/us-obama-europe-turkey-sb-idUSTRE53421U20090405, accessed 11 May 2012.
9 "Obama calls for nuclear-free world," *Al Jazeera*. Available at www.aljazeera.com/news/europe/2009/04/20094574117841403.html, 6 April 2009, accessed 15 March 2012.
10 Kerstin Gemhlich and Mark John, "Paris, Berlin bristle as Obama backs Turkey for EU," *Reuters*, 5 April 2009. Available at www.reuters.com/article/2009/04/05/us-obama-europe-turkey-sb-idUSTRE53421U20090405, accessed 11 May 2012.
11 European Council, *Presidency Conclusions*, Brussels European Council, 16–17 December 2004, para. 23.
12 "EU regrets Turkey's lack of progress on Cyprus," *EurActiv*. Available at www.euractiv.com/enlargement/eu-regrets-turkey-lack-progress-cyprus/article-188158, accessed 13 May 2012.
13 Article 42(7) of the Treaty on European Union.
14 Erwan Lagadec, *Transatlantic Relations in the 21st Century: Europe, America and the Rise of the Rest*, New York, NY: Routledge, 2012, p. 127.
15 "Turkey takes over ISAF Kabul command," *TZ*, 2 November 2009.
16 Alexander Jackson, "The limits of good intentions: The Caucasus as a test case for Turkish foreign policy," *Turkish Policy Quarterly*, March 2011, 81–92, pp. 85–6.
17 James Traub, "Turkey's rules," *NYT*, 20 January 2011; and "Davutoğlu meets with foreign ministers of Bosnia, Serbia," *TZ*, 12 October 2009.
18 On 29 January 2009, an angry exchange of words took place between Turkish PM Erdoğan and the Israeli President Shimon Peres at the World Economic Forum in Davos.
19 Ali Aslan Kılıç, "Turkey's independent foreign policy advantageous to US," *TZ*, 6 December 2009.
20 Julian Borger, "Iran-Turkey nuclear swap deal 'means new sanctions are unnecessary,'" *The Guardian*, 17 May 2010. For the text of the agreement, see Julian Borger, "Text of the Iran-Brazil-Turkey deal," *The Guardian*, 17 May 2010.
21 Damien McElroy, "Turkey's moves towards Iran concerning United States," *The Telegraph*, 7 December 2009.
22 "Obama Cumhurbaşkanı Gül'ü aradı," *Hürriyet*, 16 February 2009.
23 US Embassy in Ankara, "Remarks with Turkish Foreign Minister Ali Babacan," 7 March 2009. Available at http://turkey.usembassy.gov/statements_03072009.html, accessed 16 May 2012. Emphasis added.

24 US Embassy in Ankara, "Interview with Mehmet Ali Birand of Kanal D TV Hillary Rodham Clinton," 7 March 2009. Available at http://turkey.usembassy.gov/statement_030709.html, accessed 17 May 2012.
25 "Davutoğlu rules out shift from transatlantic axis," *TZ*, 23 March 2009; and Amberin Zaman, "Turkey and Obama: A golden age in Turkish-U.S. Ties," *On Turkey*, Washington: GMFUS, 20 March 2009.
26 Summarized from Sedat Laçiner, "Rasmussen, Turkey and the NATO," *The Journal of Turkish Weekly*. Available at www.turkishweekly.net/news/70547/rasmussen-turkey-and-the-nato.html, accessed 19 May 2012.
27 On 30 September 2005, Danish daily *Jyllands-Posten* published some cartoons of Muslims and their prophet Muhammad. These cartoons provoked a wave of protests by Muslims from around the world.
28 Matthias Gebauer, "Obama rettet Nato-Regierungen vor Gipfelblamage," *Spiegel Online*, 4 April 2009. Available at www.spiegel.de/politik/ausland/0,1518,617474,00.html, accessed 27 May 2012.
29 Bruno Waterfied, "Rasmussen 'to give Turkey senior posts in Nato,'" *The Telegraph*, 6 April 2009.
30 Toby Vogel, "Obama reiterates call for Turkey to join the EU," *European Voice*, 6 April 2009.
31 Steven Erlanger and Helene Cooper, "Europeans offer few new troops for Afghanistan," *NYT*, 4 April 2009.
32 Matthias Gebauer, "Obama rettet Nato-Regierungen vor Gipfelblamage," *Spiegel Online*, 4 April 2009. Available at www.spiegel.de/politik/ausland/0,1518,617474,00.html, accessed 27 May 2012. For Turks, Roj TV was a mouthpiece of the PKK.
33 Mark Champion and Farnaz Fassihi, "Obama urges EU to accept Turkey, but member nations remain cool," *WSJ*, 6 April 2009; Steven Erlanger and Helene Cooper, "Europeans offer few new troops for Afghanistan," *NYT*, 4 April 2009; and Nikos Konstandaras, "The EU's Turkey test," *Ekathimerini*, 6 April 2009. Available at www.ekathimerini.com/4dcgi/_w_articles_columns_100006_06/04/2009_106082, accessed 3 April 2010.
34 Jean-Pierre Stroobants, "La 'méthode' d'Ankara pour adhérer à l'UE crée le malaise à Bruxelles," *Le Monde*, 10 April 2009.
35 Kadri Gürsel, "Palavra, mübalağa ve azıcık hakikat," *Milliyet*, 11 April 2009.
36 Joachim Zepelin und Fidelius Schmid, "Nato bezahlt hohen Preis für Rasmussen," *FT Deutschland*, 5 April 2009. Available at www.ftd.de/politik/international/:poker-um-posten-nato-bezahlt-hohen-preis-fuer-rasmussen/497030.html, accessed 27 May 2012. Author's translation.
37 Clive Leviev-Sawyer, "Greek ire at Obama trip to Turkey," *The Sophia Echo*. Available at http://sofiaecho.com/2009/03/10/686987_greek-ire-at-obama-trip-to-turkey, accessed 9 May 2012.
38 "Remarks by President Obama to the Turkish Parliament," The White House, 6 April 2009. Available at www.whitehouse.gov/the_press_office/Remarks-By-President-Obama-To-The-Turkish-Parliament, accessed 14 May 2012.
39 Sebastian Fischer, "CSU entdeckt das Obama-Bashing," *Spiegel Online*, 6 April 2009. Available at www.spiegel.de/politik/deutschland/0,1518,617698,00.html, accessed 19 May 2012. Author's translation.
40 "Remarks by President Obama and Prime Minister Erdogan of Turkey after meeting," The White House, 7 December 2009. Available at www.whitehouse.gov/the-press-office/remarks-president-obama-and-prime-minister-erdogan-turkey-after-meeting, accessed 24 July 2012.
41 On 13 June 2005, the GAER Council of the EU approved the signing of an additional protocol to the association agreement with Turkey. This protocol, known as the Ankara Protocol, would extend the CU agreement to the 10 new MSs, including the Greek Cypriot administration.

42 "A/S Gordon's meetings with policy-makers in Paris: A tour d'horizon of Europe and Afghanistan," *Wikileaks*, 16 September, 2009. Available at http://wikileaks.org/cable/2009/09/09PARIS1254.html, accessed 31 May 2012.
43 "Secretary Clinton's November 9, 2009, meeting with German Foreign Minister Guido Westerwelle," *Wikileaks*, 27 November 2009, http://wikileaks.org/cable/2009/11/09PARTO112705.html, accessed 2 June 2012.
44 "Secretary Clinton's January 21, 2010 meeting with EU Hirep Ashton," *Wikileaks*, 4 February 2010. Available at http://wikileaks.org/cable/2010/02/10STATE11453.html, accessed 23 May 2012.
45 Alexander Vershbow, ASSTSECDEF for International Security Affairs.
46 "Readout of January 20 U.S.-France strategic dialogue," *Wikileaks*, 4 February 2010. Available at http://wikileaks.org/cable/2010/02/10STATE13750.html#, accessed 28 May 2012.
47 "Turkey condemns house panel endorsement of Armenian 'genocide' resolution," *HDN*, 3 April 2010; and "Ambassador Tan returns to US after 'genocide' row," *TZ*, 7 April 2010.
48 Ahmet Davutoğlu, "Turkey's zero-problems foreign policy," *Foreign Policy*, 20 May 2010, 1–6, p. 3.
49 Barak Ravid, "Israel hits back at Turkey over scuppered air force drill," *Haaretz*, 11 October 2009. Available at www.haaretz.com/news/israel-hits-back-at-turkey-over-scuppered-air-force-drill-1.6319, accessed 20 May 2012.
50 UN Human Rights Council, *Report of the International Fact-Finding Mission to Investigate Violations of International Law, Including International Humanitarian and Human Rights Law, Resulting from the Israeli Attacks on the Flotilla of Ships Carrying Humanitarian Assistance*, A/HRC/15/21, 22 September 2010, para. 21.
51 Sabrina Tavernise and Michael Slackman, *NYT*, 8 June 2010.
52 "Press briefing by Press Secretary Robert Gibbs, 6/1/10," *The White House*. Available at www.whitehouse.gov/the-press-office/press-briefing-press-secretary-robert-gibbs-6110, accessed 19 June 2012.
53 Julian Borger, "Cool response to Iran's nuclear fuel swap with Turkey," *The Guardian*, 18 May 2010.
54 UN Security Council, Security Council resolution 1929 (2010) [on measures against Iran in connection with its enrichment-related and reprocessing activities, including research and development], 9 June 2010, S/RES/1929 (2010). Available at www.unhcr.org/refworld/docid/4c1f2eb32.html, accessed 19 June 2012.
55 Glenn Kessler, "U.N. vote on Iran sanctions not a clear-cut win for Obama," *WP*, 9 June 2010.
56 Mark Landler, "Clinton says opponents of penalties can still aid diplomacy," *NYT*, 9 June 2010.
57 James Kanter, "Gates criticizes Turkey vote against sanctions," *NYT*, 11 June 2010.
58 "Assembly praises Senator Menendez for tough questioning of nominee Philip Gordon," Armenian Assembly of America, 26 March 2009. Available at www.aaainc.org/index.php?id=7&no_cache=1&newsID=183, accessed 22 August 2012.
59 Linda S. Heard, "West must commit to Turkey," *Gulf News*, 29 June 2010. Available at http://gulfnews.com/opinions/columnists/west-must-commit-to-turkey-1.647476, accessed 22 August 2012. Emphasis added.
60 David Ignatius, "U.S. and Turkey find a relationship that works," *WP*, 8 December 2011.
61 Adam Entous, "U.S. concerned at Turkey shift: Gates," *Reuters*, 9 June 2010. Available at www.reuters.com/article/2010/06/09/us-turkey-israel-usa-idUSTRE65811220100609, accessed 1 August 2014.
62 "EU pushes Turkey to look elsewhere, Obama says," *HDN*, 9 July 2010.
63 Thomas Friedman, "Letter from Istanbul," *NYT*, 15 June 2010.
64 See, for example, Charlemagne, "Turkey and the EU: America's unhelpful interventions on Turkey," *The Economist*, 10 June 2010. Available at www.economist.com/blogs/charlemagne/2010/06/turkey_and_eu, accessed 10 August 2012.

65 Molly K. Hooper, "Pence: 'There will be a cost' for Turkey drawing toward Iran," *The Hill*. Available at http://thehill.com/homenews/house/103571-lawmakers-there-will-be-a-cost-for-turkey-drawing-toward-iran, accessed 19 June 2012.
66 Henri Barkey, "Don't blame Europe for Turkey's moves away from the West," *LAT*, 20 July 2010.
67 Turkish President.
68 Mark Landler, "At the U.N., Turkey asserts itself in prominent ways," *NYT*, 22 September 2010.
69 Daniel Dombey et al., "US and Turkey clash looms over Nato," *FT*, 28 October 2010.
70 Mehmet Ali Birand, "ABD ile itişmenin faturası hazırlanıyor," *Hürriyet*, 26 November 2010.
71 Catherine Ashton "Interview with Shirin Wheeler of BBC," *US DOS*, 14 October 2010. Available at www.state.gov/secretary/rm/2010/10/149538.htm, accessed 21 June 2012.
72 Federico Rampini, "Obama: 'Serve un'America forte per la ripresa globale'," *La Repubblica*, 19 November 2010. Author's translation.
73 Matthew Lee, "Clinton chides NATO ally Turkey on rights curbs," *The Guardian*, 16 July 2011.
74 David Gardner, "Erdogan's brand benefits Arabs and the west," *FT*, 15 September 2011.
75 "EU beaten by Turkey at support to Arab spring," *ANSAmed*. Available at www.ansamed.info/ansamed/en/news/nations/lebanon/2012/06/13/EU-beaten-Turkey-support-Arab-spring-study_7029632.html, accessed 24 June 2012.
76 Hillary Clinton, "Remarks at the 2011 Annual Conference on U.S.-Turkey Relations," *US DOS*. Available at www.state.gov/secretary/rm/2011/10/176445.htm, accessed 20 June 2012.
77 "A flawed example," *The Economist*, 24 September 2011.
78 Available at www.hrw.org/world-report-2012/world-report-2012-turkey, accessed 21 June 2012.
79 Heba Saleh and Daniel Dombey, "Erdogan rallies Arab League against Israel," *FT*, 13 September 2011.
80 "Ankara at crossroads," *The Times*, 11 August 2011.
81 "About us," *Middle East Newsline*. Available at www.menewsline.com/1128-About-Us.aspx, 1 March 2011, accessed 22 June 2012.
82 "Turkey offers to invade Libya," *Middle East Newsline*, available at www.menewsline.com/article-22151-Turkey-Offers-To-Invade-Libya.aspx, accessed 22 June 2012.
83 UN Security Council, Security Council resolution 1973 (2011), 17 March 2011, S/RES/1973(2011). Available at: www.unhcr.org/refworld/docid/4d885fc42.html, accessed 23 June 2012.
84 "Nato chief Rasmussen 'proud' as Libya mission ends," *BBC News*. Available at www.bbc.co.uk/news/world-africa-15516795, accessed 23 June 2012.
85 Ian Traynor and Nicholas Watt, "Libya no-fly zone leadership squabbles continue within Nato," *The Guardian*, 23 March 2011, and "Libya: Nato to control no-fly zone after France gives way to Turkey," *The Guardian*, 25 March 2011.
86 David Cloud, "Shaky Libya campaign shows NATO's weaknesses, Gates says," *LAT*, 10 June 2011.
87 "Command conflict: Turkey blocks NATO mission in Libya," *Spiegel Online*, 21 March 2011. Available at www.spiegel.de/international/world/command-conflict-turkey-blocks-nato-mission-in-libya-a-752222.html, accessed 24 June 2012.
88 "PM Erdoğan: Obama's friend in Turkey," *TZ*, 8 June 2012.
89 Cansu Çamlıbel, "Beşar Esad uzun süre dayanabilir," *Hürriyet*, 4 December 2011.
90 Charlie Rose's interview with Recep Tayyip Erdogan, 21 September 2011. Available at www.charlierose.com/view/interview/11905, accessed 21 June 2012.
91 Dan Bilefsky, "For Turkey, lure of tie to Europe is fading," *NYT*, 4 December 2011.

92 "Visits by Foreign Leaders of Turkey," *US DOS*. Available at http://history.state.gov/departmenthistory/visits/turkey, accessed 23 June 2012.
93 US Embassy in Ankara, "Başkan Obama'nın Başbakan Erdoğan ile görüşmesi," 14 April 2010. Available at http://turkish.turkey.usembassy.gov/pr_041410.html, accessed 24 June 2012; "Başbakan Erdoğan'ın Obama görüşmesi sonrası açıklamaları," *Hürriyet*, 21 September 2011; or "Erdoğan, Obama discuss Syria, Iran at Seoul meeting," *TZ*, 25 March 2012.
94 "Türkiye'yi AB'de görmek istiyoruz." Available at www.trthaber.com/haber/dunya/turkiyeyi-abde-gormek-istiyoruz-12848.html, accessed 10 December 2012.
95 Probably refers to the European Union.
96 "Biden criticizes EU on Turkey," *Sabah English*, 28 April 2012. Available at http://english.sabah.com.tr/World/2012/04/28/biden-criticizes-eu-on-turkey, accessed 13 August 2012.
97 "Secretary Clinton: Travel to Turkey." Available at www.state.gov/secretary/trvl/2012/196350.htm, accessed 10 December 2012.
98 "Travel of Deputy Secretary Burns to Jordan, Iraq and Turkey." Available at www.state.gov/r/pa/prs/ps/2012/09/197557.htm, accessed 10 December 2012.
99 "Ricciardone: Dağ dağa kavuşmaz insan insana kavuşur," *Hürriyet*, 20 January 2011.
100 Herb Keinon, "Turks reduce Israel's diplomatic presence, expel envoys," *The Jerusalem Post*, 9 February 2011. Available at www.jpost.com/DiplomacyAndPolitics/Article.aspx?id=236437, accessed 28 May 2012.
101 Nitsana Darshan-Leitner, "Perry was right on Turkey and Islamic terror," *Jerusalem Post*, 23 January 2012.
102 NATO Secretary-General declared that Israel had not been invited to the Chicago Summit anyway. (Sources: Serkan Demirtaş, "Turkey blocks Israel from NATO summit," *HDN*, 23 April 2012; Muddassar Ahmed, "Turkey risks walking off the Nato tightrope," *The Telegraph*, 24 May 2012; and Yossi Lempkowicz, "Despite Turkish official statement, NATO Secretary General denies Israel not invited to Chicago summit because of Turkey's veto," *European Jewish Press*, 13 May 2012. Available at www.ejpress.org/article/news/france/57957, accessed 28 May 2012.)
103 Annett Meiritz, "'Erdogans Macho-Gehabe ist gefährlich,'" *Spiegel Online*. Available at www.spiegel.de/politik/ausland/kritik-an-ankaras-anti-israel-kurs-erdogans-macho-gehabe-ist-gefaehrlich-a-785994.html, accessed 28 May 2012.
104 Yoav Stern and Barak Ravid, "Israel: Erdogan's Davos behavior may ruin Turkey's EU chances," *Haaretz*, 1 January 2009. Available at www.haaretz.com/print-edition/news/israel-erdogan-s-davos-behavior-may-ruin-turkey-s-eu-chances-1.267033, accessed 13 April 2012.
105 "Wikileaks: Israel tells US it has 'bad feeling' about Turkey," *TZ*, 1 December 2010.
106 "Hollanda Türkiye'nin AB üyeliğine taş koymak istiyor," *CNN Türk*. Available at www.cnnturk.com/2010/dunya/10/11/hollanda.turkiyenin.ab.uyeligine.tas.koymak.istiyor/592612.0/index.html, accessed 10 June 2012.
107 Fulya Özerkan, "Turkey urged not to be provoked by 'unilateral' Greek Cypriot move," *HDN*, 17 December 2009.
108 "AB zirvesinde Türkiye kavgası," *Milliyet*, 9 December 2009.
109 "İngiltere'nin Türkiye umudu," *CNN Türk*, 24 June 2009. Available at www.cnnturk.com/2009/dunya/06/24/ingilterenin.turkiye.umudu/532192.0/index.html, accessed 15 June 2012.
110 "Britain's Foreign Policy in a Networked World," British FS William Hague's speech at the Foreign and Commonwealth Office, London, on 1 July 2010. Available at www.fco.gov.uk/en/news/latest-news/?view=Speech&id=22472881, accessed 16 June 2012.
111 "Cameron's Turkey remarks shake up British diplomacy," *TZ*, 30 July 2010.

112 British National Party "William Hague not vague about betraying Britain's interests." Available at www.bnp.org.uk/news/william-hague-not-vague-about-betraying-britain%E2%80%99s-interests, accessed 15 June 2012.
113 "A transcript of a speech given by Prime Minister David Cameron in Ankara, Turkey, on 27 July 2010," *Number 10: The Official Site of the British Prime Minister's Office*. Available at www.number10.gov.uk/news/pms-speech-in-turkey/, accessed 15 June 2012.
114 "A transcript of a joint press conference given by Prime Minister David Cameron and Turkish Prime Minister Recep Tayyip Erdogan in Ankara, Turkey, on 27 July 2010," *Number 10: The Official Site of the British Prime Minister's Office*. Available at www.number10.gov.uk/news/ress-conference-with-turkish-pm/, accessed 15 June 2012.
115 "Readout of the President's Call with British Prime Minister Cameron," The White House, 6 August 2010. Available at www.whitehouse.gov/the-press-office/2010/08/06/readout-presidents-call-with-british-prime-minister-cameron, accessed 15 June 2012.
116 David Lidington, "European Union enlargement: Tulips, trade and growth," Speech at the VNO–NCW in The Hague. Available at http://ukinnl.fco.gov.uk/en/news/?view=Speech&id=562922482, accessed 1 June 2012.
117 Andrew Rawnsley and Toby Helm, "William Hague: 'We have to build new alliances with the emerging powers,'" *The Guardian*, 1 October 2011.
118 "Die Spekulanten waren die besseren Schachspieler," *Frankfurter Allgemeine Zeitung*, 10 June 2010.
119 Gates's words were published in mainstream media on 10 June (see, for example, Marc Champion, "Gates says EU pushed Turkey away," *WSJ*, 10 June 2010).
120 "Italian President hints at Turkey's future EU role," *HDN*, 18 November 2009.
121 Yasemin Taşkın, "Türkiye bizim için bir hazine," *Sabah*, 8 May 2012. See also "Türkiye-İtalya Siyasi İlişkileri," *TMFA*. Available at www.mfa.gov.tr/turkiye-italya-siyasi-iliskileri-.tr.mfa, accessed 17 June 2012.
122 "AB'ye destekte dürüstüz," *Hürriyet*, 7 May 2012.
123 "İtalya ve Fransa Dışişleri Bakanları Türkiye-AB ilişkilerini ele aldı," *Zaman*, 5 June 2012.
124 US Embassy in Ankara, "Interview with Mehmet Ali Birand of Kanal D TV Hillary Rodham Clinton," 7 March 2009. Available at http://turkey.usembassy.gov/statement_030709.html, accessed 17 May 2012.
125 "Obama declares Turkey model partner of values," *TZ*, 7 April 2009.
126 Jackson Diehl, "Turkey's government is the new normal in the Middle East," *WP*, 23 January 2012. See also "Remarks by President Obama to the Turkish Parliament," The White House, 6 April 2009. Available at www.whitehouse.gov/the_press_office/Remarks-By-President-Obama-To-The-Turkish-Parliament, accessed 14 May 2012.
127 Stephen Kinzer, "Turkey and America should kiss and make up," *The Guardian*, 15 June 2010.
128 Birol Yeşilada, *EU-Turkey Relations in the 21st Century*, New York, NY: Routledge, 2013, p. 84 and 85.
129 See also Zbigniew Brzezinski, *The Waning of the American Dream*, New York, NY: Basic Books, 2012; Patrick J. Buchanan, *Suicide of a Superpower: Will America Survive to 2025?*, New York, NY: Thomas Dunne Books, 2011; Mark R. Lewin, *Ameritopia: The Unmaking of America*, New York, NY: Threshold Editions, 2012; Thomas Friedman and Michael Mandelbaum, *That Used To Be Us: How America Fell Behind in the World We Invented—and How We Can Come Back*, New York, NY: Thorndike Press, 2011. On various occasions, Noam Chomsky also spoke or wrote on the topic.

Conclusion

As denoted in the Introduction section, there seems to be a commonality among the works examining the US involvement in Turkey–EU relations: These works focus on the last two or three decades of the story, because they depart from the presumption that "[d]uring the Cold War the US had not shown any particular keenness on assisting Turkey's bid for accession to the then European Community."[1] The present volume, on the other hand, is premised on the idea that the whole of the story of the US involvement in Turkey–EU relations from the 1950s till the end of 2012 reveals a remarkable process in which we see a Turkey transforming from a pauper who begs for wheat from the US into an agha who aspires to be a regional power, an EU transforming from a keen groom who marries Turkey in haste to a sophisticated ladies'-man who repents at leisure, and a US transforming from an inexperienced salesclerk who tries to weigh Turkey's geopolitical value with cotton bolls or tobacco leaves to an assertive dealer who strives to market Turkey to Europeans. Thus, while acknowledging the fact that it was in the post-Cold War that the US started actively promoting Turkey's EU bid, our analysis here includes the Cold War era as well. Employing such a large timeframe allows us to develop the following two deductive hypotheses:

Hypothesis 1: *Turkey–US relations have always been a key variable in Turkey–EU relations.*

Perhaps with the exception of the Johnson and Carter eras, Turkey–EU relations have never been free from strong US influence. So much so that without the US interference, Turkey could not have made it to the point where it is now in its relations with the EU . . . In a state-centric game, with a number of hit-and-runs, the American *Realpolitik* tattooed the Turkish crescent on the skin of 'soft power' Europe. This being the case, Europeans should reassess the EU's competence as an international actor, whereas

Turks should reconsider their conviction that it is the Europeans who take Turkey–EU relations to an unfair ground where not right but might matters.

Nevertheless, while some seasoned Turkey-watchers seem to be subscribed to the fallacy that the US has favored Turkey's close relations with the EU always in full force, there were, in fact, salient differences between presidential eras in this regard:

In the Eisenhower era, the US was prudently supportive of closer relations between Turkey and the EEC; Turkey submitted its application for associate membership with the 'consent' of the US. With the Kennedy administration, on the basis of its commercial interests, the US turned against the Turkey–EEC association, but taking Turkey's geopolitical value into consideration, refrained from undermining Turkey–EEC relations. In the Johnson era, 'Turkey-EEC relations' was not a significant concern for the US. In its first four years, the Nixon administration remained against Turkey's association. It was only in 1973, that is ten years after the signing of the Ankara Agreement, that the US acknowledged the Turkey–EEC association. The Ford administration made its support conditional on Turkey's cooperation in the Cyprus issue and revealed that it was not against Turkey's full-membership to the EEC. However, the US support was weak in this period. In the Carter era, the EEC once again disappeared from the agenda of Turkey–US relations.

In the post-Cold War era, in the cases presented in the following non-exhaustive list, the hand of the US extended to Europeans across the table was a significant factor in Turkey–EU relations:

Towards the end of the Reagan era, the relative importance of Turkey–EEC relations on the US FP agenda increased. The US declared that it supported Turkey's EEC membership, although this support remained rather in rhetoric. With the H.W. Bush administration, the US got actively involved in the issue with some concrete results. The Clinton era was where the US efforts peaked. The US involvement began to fade with W. Bush, eventually sputtering out in the Obama era. The main instances where the US influenced Turkey-EU relations are as follows:

The Reagan Era

1 The US tried to convince the Europeans to assume a more tolerant stance towards the Turks after the 1980 coup (late 1981–early 1982). The effect of this effort on the Europeans was limited;
2 The US brokered a deal whereby Turkey lifted its veto on Greece's return to NATO's integrated military structure in exchange for a promise that Greece would not put any obstacles in front of Turkey in the EEC (September–October 1980). The US could not enforce the deal in its entirety; and
3 The US affirmed that it was in favor of Turkey's full-membership application but added that it would refrain from taking any initiative in this direction (February and then April 1987).

The George H.W. Bush Era

1 The US offered to interfere while Turkey was waiting for the European Commission's response to its full-membership application (August–December 1989), and promised support for a subsequent application (August 1990). Turks appreciated the first offer but refused it fearing that such an interference might irritate the Europeans. Turks never made use of the second offer since they did not submit a second application;
2 SECSTATE James Baker sent a letter to the FMs of the MSs of the EEC, explaining the potential benefits of Turkey's accession (July 1990); and
3 As a message to the EEC, the US and Turkey declared that they were planning to sign a free-trade agreement (September 1990).

The Clinton Era

In each of the five cases below, the US intervention was substantial and had a decisive impact on the result:

1 Establishment of the Turkey–EC CU (December 1995);
2 Recognition of Turkey's eligibility for membership at the Luxembourg Council (December 1997);
3 Approval of Turkey's candidate status at the Helsinki Council (December 1999);
4 Approval of the APD in favorable terms for Turkey at the Nice Council (December 2000); and
5 Inclusion of Turkey in the new security architecture of Europe (from December 1998 onwards).

The George W. Bush Era

The US was influential in the following six cases:

1 Preventing Turkey's exclusion from the new security architecture of Europe with the formulation of the Ankara Document (November 2001) and its approval at the Brussels Council (October 2002);
2 Maintaining the momentum of Turkey's domestic reform process (from 2002 onwards);
3 Setting favorable terms for Turkey's accession negotiations (2002–2004);
4 Inclusion of PKK and DHKP-C in the EU's 'terror list' (April 2004);
5 Turkey's getting a date for the opening of the accession negotiations (December 2004); and
6 Eliminating the 'privileged partnership' option for Turkey (from 2004 onwards).

The Obama Era

The US had some success in influencing the Europeans in the following three cases:

1. Denying the privileged partnership option (from 2009 onwards);
2. Convincing the Europeans not to close the door to Turks (from 2009 onwards); and
3. Encouraging Turkey's domestic reforms (from 2009 onwards).

On the other hand, in some periods, the efforts of the US for Turkey proved to be counterproductive; angered by the American interference, Europeans gave Turks less than they would have otherwise done. The Conclusions of the European Council of December 2002 was an example of this. In 2003 and 2004, on various occasions such as Verheugen's interview published in April 2003, Europeans stated that US effort undermined Turkey's chances.

Within individual presidential eras themselves, too, the US support was not constant. For example, in the H.W. Bush era the US went into action after a few years' inertia. In the W. Bush and Obama eras, the US support started with pomp, but then it had to be reduced due to the EU's reaction.[2]

This stocktaking of the US involvement in Turkey–EU relations brings us to our second hypothesis.

> **Hypothesis 2:** In the Cold War era, Turkey and the US missed a large window of opportunity where Turkey's EEC membership could have become reality with the help of the US.

The neorealist analysis of the US involvement in Turkey–EEC relations in the Cold War era reveals an anomaly: Syllogistic neorealist reasoning would assume that the US support for Turkey's EU bid in the Cold War era was stronger than in the post-Cold War era, because in the Cold War era, the US, as an alliance leader, had greater influence over Europeans; in the Cold War era, many would agree with Ecevit who, in 1978, said the West was not anything more than the US. With this dominance, the US was doing its best to tie firmly to the West a Turkey flirting with the Soviets. Turkey's EEC membership would improve Turco–Greek relations and bolster the southeastern flank of NATO. The EEC was more open to US influence since it had fewer members—who were willing to co-operate with the US—and its supranational core as well as the foreign and security policy dimension was in formation. Turkey's accession would have been easier technically since the Community acquis was easier to adopt, accession conditions were not formalized much, and the number of the MSs whose unanimous decision on this accession would be required was less. Turkey's geostrategic position and military capabilities had an appeal for Europeans.

However, in reality, US advocacy of Turkey integration into Europe was less conspicuous in the Cold War than in the post-Cold War era. Because of a number of factors, a stronger US influence would have been prejudicial to US interests and unnecessary in the Cold War era. Most of these factors are still within the purview of neorealism, whereas some others such as domestic determinants remain outside:

1. Turkey was not strong enough economically; Europeans would not have found Turkey's EEC membership in their benefit (NRA8).
2. In the early years of the Cold War era, for the US, the EEC was a fledgling organization and had little significance in strategic terms (NRA2); it was rather a source of financial aid for Turkey (NRA7).
3. From the US perspective, Turkey was not a European but a Near Eastern country, which remained an official policy until 1974.
4. Especially in the Eisenhower era, both Turkey and the US preferred IMF or OECD—two organizations that the US dominated—to the EEC as sources of financial aid to Turkey (NRA4).
5. In the Kennedy era, mainly due to the influence of the agriculture lobby, economic interests started to have a decisive impact on American FP (DF). In this era, Turkey started competing with the UK and the LDCs for US favor (NRA5).
6. In the Johnson era, the US avoidance of supporting Turkey's European orientation was due to three reasons:

    a. Economic interests of the US continued to prevail over its strategic interests (NRA4).
    b. Turkey was already benefiting from the favorable economic conditions of the preparatory stage of its association with the EEC (NRA7).
    c. As an alliance leader, the US was trying to 'discipline' Turkey, thereby solving this country's problems with Greece, and safeguarding the integrity of the Western bloc (NRA6 and 7).

7. In the Nixon era, the agriculture lobby was against Turkey's association (DF). The Nixon administration was able to reduce the influence of this lobby on the US FP but had to remain against Turkey's EEC membership.
8. In the Ford era, as an alliance leader, in accordance with the relative gains assumption (NRA5), the US decreased its support for Turkey, trying to elicit a cooperative attitude from Turkey in the Cyprus issue (NRA7).
9. For Carter, the EEC was not a significant international political actor; his policy towards Europe was based on relations with individual MSs (NRA2). Furthermore, since Turks froze their relations with the EEC, there was not much for the US to sell to Europeans.

After the end of bipolarity, some key elements in international politics described by neorealism survived into the early years of the post-Cold War era. As the US was able to assert itself as a hegemonic power in the Gulf War in a process where a group of EU MSs preferred to bandwagon with the US, the window of opportunity remained open for Turkey—and the US—till the end of the H. W. Bush administration, but when Clinton assumed the office, Europeans had become more self-confident and less tolerant to US advances on behalf of Turkey. They were trying to establish a CFSP. Turkey's window of opportunity was closing. A significant erosion was apparent in the relevance of neorealism to international politics.[3] The Clinton administration relocated the US FP to a new ground. Discussing the nature of this shift is beyond the scope and space constraints of this book. Nevertheless, the approach of this administration to Turkey–EU relations gives us an opportunity to have a short discussion here. Some authors contend that by supporting Turkey, the Clinton administration was working for US interests rather than ideals. One commentator wrote in 1998 as follows: "In fact, probably in no other internal EU issue has the U.S. been so actively involved and asserted a right, *on the basis of its own interests*, to speak out."[4] However, drawing on our presentation of the approach of the Clinton administration to Turkey–EU relations, it seems plausible to claim that this approach was developed on the basis of quasi-Wilsonian ideals—in particular, the democratic peace theory that holds that democracies rarely wage war on one another.[5] For this administration, a Turkey whose democratic standards have been 'ensured and certified' by the EU would constitute a prime role model for Islamic states. Democratization of Turkey would contribute much to the peaceful coexistence between Turkey and Greece.[6]

If the Clinton administration was able to extend that much support to Turkey even though

1   the US was not an undisputed alliance leader anymore, and
2   EU members had developed a CFSP and grown intolerant of US interventions,

we can infer that in the Cold War era, Turkey and the US missed a large window of opportunity where Turkey's EEC membership could have become reality with the help of the US.

From our account of the US influence on Turkey–EU relations, we can also derive the following findings:

Finding 1: *The main method the US followed in supporting Turkey was trying to 'convince' the European decision-makers through lobbying.*

American FP conduct has been marked by straightforwardness and a predilection for direct and high-level contacts and for shortcuts. In our context,

Holbrooke's dialogue with Hannay[7] where the former tried to circumvent the complexities of the Cyprus crisis may be an example of this style. It is not infrequent to see American politicians and diplomats making a distinction between the preferences of the 'governments' and 'people' of other countries, which is exemplified by Daniel Fried who, in his visit to Turkey in 2006, spoke as follows:

> Some [Europeans] look at Turkey and say: "Oh, my God! This is not Europe. They do not look like Europeans. They live in villages and wear hijab. How can Muslims be European?" *Of course, this is not the view of the governments but of the European people.*[8]

These two traits led the Americans to use all the diplomatic/political channels—preferably informal ones—available at all levels to influence the European decision-makers on Turkey's behalf.

In this endeavor that we call the 'hands-across-the-table approach,' the intensity of the efforts of the Americans sometimes became suffocating for the Europeans. In trying to influence the European decision-makers, Americans used the following channels:

1. The most creative initiative was taken by Albright who, in her visit to China in April 1998, requested help from Zemin to convince Germans;
2. When necessary, US presidents, secretaries, and ASSTSECSTATEs contacted their European counterparts. The dinner Clinton had with Kohl in June 1997 can be cited as an example. In the Clinton era, even an ex-President, H.W. Bush, made phone calls to Europeans;
3. Institutionalized transatlantic contacts where Turkey's NATO membership strengthened the Americans' hand were good opportunities. At the NATO summits (for example, the ones in June 2001, June 2004, and April 2009), the EU–US summits (such as the ones in June 1995, December 1995, June 2003, June 2004, and June 2008), and the SLG meetings (such as the one in October 2002) American participants were able to 'sell' Turkey to the Europeans sotto voce;
4. The US 'diplomatic forces' stationed in Europe also deserve credit. USEU was the main operational base of these forces.[9] To make Turkey's CU with the EC a reality, Eizenstat, the USAMB to the EU was rushing from pillar to post between Brussels, Strasbourg and Istanbul.

The US embassies in European capitals had acquired a considerable experience:

> There is a long track record of messages, instructions sent to our embassies in the EU capitals—and the EC capitals before the EU was established—to make points on behalf of the US government on Turkey's EU accession effort, both as part of the general messages

that we conveyed or at the time of specific EU meetings [. . .] if we thought we had some reasonable standing to do so.¹⁰

The co-ordination of the following names among themselves and with the DOS prior to the Helsinki Council of 1999 was an example of outstanding operational performance:

- Eric S. Edelman, the USAMB to Finland,
- Nicholas Burns, the USAMB to Greece,
- Mark R. Parris, the USAMB to Turkey,
- James F. Jeffrey, the DCM to Turkey, and
- Marc Grossman, the ASSTSECSTATE for European Affairs.

Even low-ranking European diplomats interviewed for this book stated that they had been approached by their American counterparts for Turkey;

5 The US also focused on the EP and the European Commission. The campaign of the Clinton administration on the EP is worth remembering. The efforts of Israel and the UK and Amo Houghton's invitation to the HOR to influence the EP were important contributions to Clinton's campaign.

Contacts of the US with the European Commission for Turkey were more established and less strained. In September 1959, Under SECSTATE Dillon contacted Marjolin, Vice President of the Commission, for the financial assistance to be extended to Turkey. In November, Secretary Herter conversed with the Commission President Hallstein and inquired about the association processes of Turkey and Greece. In December, Dillon had talks with some officials from the Commission, including Rey, Commissioner for External Relations. They informed Dillon about the preparation of the association agreements of Turkey and Greece. In March 1970, Rey had to defend against the US the preferential treatment Greece and Turkey were enjoying. Following the 1980 coup in Turkey, Secretary Haig got in touch with the Commission President Thorn to prevent a freezing of the credit the EEC was expected to extend to Turkey. The relations between the US and the Commission saw a marked improvement at the end of the 1980s. In 1989, H.W. Bush came together with the Commission President Delors five times, and the Commission's Delegation to Washington was upgraded to full diplomatic status. In June 1995, at the EU–US Summit in Washington, Clinton and Christopher talked to the Commission President Santer and emphasized the importance of the EP's approval of the CU decision. Meanwhile, Eizenstat was seeking talks with the chairpersons of the political groups in the EP. Prior to the Luxembourg Council of December 1997, Albright contacted, Commissioner Brittan and Commissioner van den Broek. In

October 1999, Clinton strived to persuade the Commission President Prodi for Turkey's candidacy. During the Helsinki Council of December 1999, Commissioner Verheugen was together with the members of the Clinton administration. After the Council, Clinton received Prodi and tried to convince him further. W. Bush got in touch with some officials from the Commission to have Turkey's negotiations started in 2003. Prior to the Brussels and Copenhagen Councils of 2002, American officials had talks with some members of the Commission; and

6   Although occasionally, the US also resorted to the help of its private sector. In the SECI project initiated in December 1996, the US private sector would play an important role. In November 1997, Holbrooke conferred with some American businessmen about the economic cooperation schemes applicable among Cyprus, Greece, and Turkey.

Finding 2: *The US assiduously invented alternative methods to accompany its lobbying efforts for Turkey.*

The first of these methods was to introduce or support some projects to substitute or facilitate Turkey's EU membership. Plans to establish a US–Turkish FTA or to sign a PTA came to the table several times. Clinton proposed a Greek–Turkish common market in April 1994. Turkey was included in SECI established in December 1996. Between 1996 and 1998, agreements were signed to establish a FTA between Turkey and Israel. With these projects, the Americans and Turks were also hoping to make the Europeans think that they would lose Turkey to the US, but except in such rare cases as the Kohl–Chirac meeting in December 1997, Europeans took no account of these moves.

Second, in at least five cases, the US attempted to devise deals:

1   the 'return of Greece to NATO/assurance given to Turkey' deal (September-October 1980);
2   the 'Cyprus/CU' deal (1995–96);
3   the 'helicopters/HR reforms' deal (December 1997);
4   the 'appointment of Rasmussen' deal (it is unclear what Turkey gained here) (March-April 2009); and
5   the 'ESDP/Ankara Document + reference to the December 2004 European Council + banning of Cyprus and Malta' deal (November 2001-October 2002).

It is remarkable that in none of these deals did the US risk its own direct interests. The first two of these deals were diplomatic lessons for the Turks and the Americans; they learned the importance of securing the promises of their counterpart in writing. Lipponen's letter of December 1999 and the Ankara Document of December 2004 came into being out of this concern.

Third, the US focused on Turkey's improvement of its own economy, democracy, and HR record. Americans sometimes encouraged Turks in this direction and sometimes put pressure on them; in the field of HR, the Clinton administration twisted their arm so hard as to cause a crisis in Turkey–US relations. The W. Bush administration welcomed Turkey's August 2002 harmonization package. The US encouragement of Turkey's democratic reforms became more perceptible with Rice's stepping into Turkey–US relations.

> **Finding 3:** The US dedication to Turkey's European vocation has been a bipartisan policy.

The diplomats, politicians, analysts, and academics interviewed for this book concurred that Turkey's EU membership had become an official, bipartisan policy of the US. As early as 1959, Bowles, a Democrat member of the HOR, was in agreement with the Republican Eisenhower administration in working for Turkey's associate membership in the EEC. In later years, Republicans such as Whitfeld and Houghton, endorsed Democrat Clinton's efforts for Turkey.

In supporting Turkey, the US was acting quite monolithically as foreseen by neorealists. Nevertheless, some differences of opinion emerged in the state machinery on the following grounds:

Ideological Ground

Except some extreme personal views that are rarely translated into political action,[11] the neo-conservative frame of mind is the only one marked with an established doubt about—but not an actual struggle against—Turkey's close relations with the EU:

> Many neo-conservatives [...] are much more concerned about Turkey's strategic role in the Middle East than its ties to Europe. They believe that Turkey should pay less attention to Europe and instead strengthen its ties to the U.S. and Israel. Many would actually not be unhappy if the EU refused to open accession negotiations with Ankara because they believe this would force Turkey to rely more heavily on the U.S. and Israel.[12]

Perle, for example, was of this opinion. In March 2002, he declared that he did not believe that Turkey would join the EU in the near future; a free-trade agreement between Turkey and the US would be a better alternative for Turks. In 2005, Perle explained his reasons as follows:

> Well, I think we [Americans] are more open to all cultures. I think Europe is in fact much more inward looking. And it's going to be quite a long time before Turkey achieves membership. I also think the heavy emphasis within Europe on the involvement of government in the daily lives of citizens and their economy is a less effective environment for economic growth and development. The prevailing attitudes in the US are more conducive to growth and development. There are deeply entrenched interests in Europe that are not terribly competitive and depend on government to protect them. And for a rising, young economy like Turkey's, that's not good.[13]

Some circles[14] in Turkey mistook Perle's words for the official position of the US and concluded that the US support was not genuine.

Federal Executive Departments

Occasionally, certain executive departments had a negative impact on the US backing for Turkey's European project. The protective attitude of the DOA in the 1960s and 1970s was an early example. The resistance of the NEA of the DOS to Turkey's transfer to EUR in 1974 was thwarted by Kissinger, and the EUR's opposition to favoring Turkey's EEC bid publicly in the early 1990s was overcome by Zoellick. With the Clinton administration, the DOS would turn into one of the engines of the US support for Turkey.

The Congress

"By and large the Congress is not much help to a president in matters of FP because of the lack of political profit in it"[15] wrote Nicholas deB. Katzenbach, the Under SECSTATE between 1966 and 1969. In particular, issues related to the EU have never been of much interest to the Congress, where a European Caucus was established as late as 2005.[16] Thus, the influence of the Congress on Turkey–EU relations has not been substantial. This being the case, we should appreciate the vision of Bowles, a Member of the HOR, who was able to develop a sound opinion in 1959 about the possible associate memberships of Turkey and Greece in the EEC.[17]

Turks were lucky to have by their side such Members of Congress as Stephen Solarz who "earned a reputation as a micromanager of foreign policy [. . .] who in a post-Watergate era put the HOR on a competitive footing with the Senate in foreign policy discussions" and is remembered as a Congressman "whose concerns went beyond traffic lights and beach erosion in his Brooklyn district to nuclear weapons [and] the Middle East."[18] He—together with Dan Burton—sponsored the first bill to argue for Turkey's European bid in April 1991. Robert Wexler, Ed Whitfield, and Tom Lantos submitted a similar bill in October 2002, and Chuck Hagel and Joe Lieberman did so in April 2004. None of these bills could win Congressional approval. The proposals of Phil Gramm (August 1997) and Mark Kirk (December 2003) to sign a Turkey–US free-trade agreement were nice gestures for Turks. In November 1995, Amo Houghton invited the members of the HOR to influence the EP for Turkey's CU decision, and in November 1999, he wrote a letter to the Finnish President Ahtisaari in favor of recognition of Turkey's candidate status at the Helsinki Council.

These individual efforts for Turkey were overshadowed by the opposition of some other Members of the Congress whose stance was

1   not specifically directed towards Turkey–EU relations but was a part of a general anti-Turkish attitude; and
2   was predicated rather on ethnic grounds than US interests.

Certain members of the Congress who were close to Greek, Armenian, and—later—Jewish diasporas tried to undermine Turkey–EU relations. Such names as Paul Sarbanes (of Greek origin), Adam Schiff (Jewish by origin but had a large Armenian community in his district), Frank Pallone (Roman Catholic but the co-chairman of the Armenian Caucus), Robert Menendez (a member of the Armenian Caucus), Shelley Berkley (of Greek-Jewish origin), Claiborne Pell (known for sympathizing with Greek Americans) worked against Turkey's European bid, sometimes by sponsoring a resolution, sometimes making negative statements to the press.

Interest Groups and Lobbies

The agriculture lobby (composed mainly of tobacco farmers and exporters) in the US cast its shadow on Turkey–EEC relations until the mid-1970s when the clamor of the strategic necessities of the transatlantic relations finally overwhelmed the voice of the American farmers.

The textile lobby, too, was a source of concern for Turkey. Among US presidents "Kennedy sought votes from textile states with industry-specific promises in 1960, and Nixon, bested in that encounter, emulated him eight years later."[19] This lobby worked for maintenance of a quota to imports from Turkey and was critical of the advantageous status of the Turkish textile products within the Turkey–EC CU. It opposed to the signing of a free-trade agreement between the US and Turkey in 1997 and the establishment of a QIZ between Turkey and Israel in 1999. Although Turkish textile industrialists resorted to the help of a US lobbying firm in 2001, not much improvement was seen in this regard.

From the mid-1970s onwards, the Greek lobby started campaigning against US efforts for the improvement of Turkey–EEC relations. Greeks were trying to gain leverage against Turks in the Cyprus issue. Their close relations with Carter provided a fertile ground for their campaign to germinate. In May 1978, Turkish PM Ecevit was complaining that "[t]here was too much inter-relationship between United States' internal and external policies."[20] Carter's successors, too, could not distance themselves from the Greek lobby. Clinton was not an exception among them. He tried hard to secure the cooperation of this lobby hoping to solve the Cyprus issue and make Turkey's EU membership possible. His courtesy towards the Turks drew the reaction of the Greeks. The Greek lobby was an important factor behind the Resolution submitted to the Congress in July 2005, calling Turkey, among other things, to extend the CU to Cyprus.

Just as Turks were absorbed with securing their EU membership, Armenians were preoccupied with having Turks acknowledge the claim of genocide. Surprisingly, the cases where the Armenian lobby tried to undermine Turkey's European prospects were few. The resolution proposed to the US Congress in July 2005 by Adam Schiff was a curious example in the sense that it was urging Turkey to acknowledge the 'genocide' while expressing support for Turkey's EU membership. The Armenian lobby was hoping that after becoming an EU member, Turkey would admit the 'genocide' and normalize its relations with Armenia.[21] Furthermore, with this membership, Armenia would also become next-door neighbor to the EU.

In the H.W. Bush era, due to their uneasiness with the activities of the Greek and Armenian lobbies, and thanks to their developing relations with Israel, Turks established close contacts with the Jewish lobby. The concrete benefits of this process for Turkey–EU relations came in the Clinton era. In the second half of the 1990s, the intensity of the activities of the Jewish lobby and Israel increased to an annoying level for Europeans. The Jewish lobby tried to maintain its support in the W. Bush era especially with the efforts of the AJC. With the emergence of the problems between Turkey and Israel in the Obama era, the Jewish lobby first 'switched' its support off and then—as it was evident in the statements of Mike Pence and Shelley Berkley—started working in the contrary direction.

It is difficult to say that the Turkish lobby in the US made a considerable contribution to Turkey–EU relations. According to the results of the 2010 census, 195,283 US citizens were of Turkish origin, compared to, say, 1,315,775 citizens of Greek origin.[22] The impact of this small Turkish population on US politics has been low. 'Turkey–EU relations' has not been an important item on the agenda of such entities as the Turkish-American Business Council[23] or the Assembly of Turkish American Associations.[24] Among the representative offices of the Turkish interest groups, TÜSİAD's is an exception for it has had 'improvement of Turkey–EU relations' on its list of priorities since its establishment in 1998.

The GOT has always conducted a vigorous lobbying campaign on Capitol Hill. As of 2009, Turkey was the fifth biggest spender on lobbying and public relations campaigns in the US (3,524,632 dollars) and had tallied the highest number of congressional contacts (2,268).[25] The contracts Turkey concluded with its lobbying firms contain numerous—and sometimes trivial—activities such as "preparing and distributing press releases and background documents on the Smyrna burning"[26] or "arranging meetings with members of Congress, staff assistants, and other U.S. Government officials to discuss issues related to the status of Turkish hostages in Iran."[27] 'Turkey–EU relations' exists only in one of these reports. For the 12-month period ending 31 December 1995, Abernathy/MacGregor Group, Inc.

> provided counsel and coordination of communications activities in Europe and the United States of other agencies performing advocacy functions on behalf of the Government of Turkey. The registrant's primary activity was to generate support for Turkey's admission to the European Customs Union.[28]

Of course, not all the activities of the lobbying firms are documented. For example, the submission of the Wexler–Whitfield–Lantos resolution to the Congress in October 2002 may have been orchestrated by the Livingston Group; Ackley states that Wexler and Whitfield are known to be among the network of contacts of this firm.[29]

Think Tanks

Certain think tanks in the US followed Turkey–EU relations closely and published detailed studies containing recommendations for the USG. For instance, in preparing its aforementioned policy paper before the critical 2004 European Council,

> [t]o explore the likely course of Turkish-EU-U.S. relations, and how best U.S. foreign policy might play a constructive role, the Atlantic Council sent a delegation of U.S. leaders and experts to Europe [. . .]. The delegation met with key government and private sector policy makers in Brussels, Berlin, Ankara, Istanbul and Athens for discussions about prospects for the December 2004 decision and its aftermath.[30]

Overall, these think tanks have been in favor of US support for Turkey's EU membership:

Publications by Brookings Institution has mostly advocated for closer relations between Turkey and the EU since the 1960s. The aforecited study from 1968 by Krause[31] cogently argued for Turkey's association with the EEC. In later years, numerous other studies published by Brookings, such as Kramer's study[32] mentioned previously, or Gordon and Taşpınar's book entitled *Winning Turkey: How America, Europe, and Turkey Can Revive a Fading Partnership*,[33] invited the USG to work for Turkey's cause. Brookings hosted a number of events[34] where the same theme was among the topics discussed.

Council on Foreign Relations, another influential think tank, has also favored closer Turkey–EU relations. In *Foreign Affairs*, a magazine published by the Council, there appeared several articles that underlined the benefits of Turkey's EU membership for the US; Philips's article[35] referred previously is one example of them. An analyst from the Council, Steven A. Cook, once wrote that "Turkey ha[d] veered from what was once a promising path of liberal democracy—and the European Union [could] pull it back."[36]

The research at the Washington Institute for Near East Policy (WINEP) which "has remained a staunch supporter of Israel"[37] "include[d] a special focus on Turkey and the rise of Islamic politics"[38] especially after the coming into power of the AKP government. This focus is most evident in the analyses written by Soner Çağaptay, the director of the Turkish Research Program of the Institute: Çağaptay's analyses have always been in favor of US support for Turkey's EU membership, although his reasons leading to this position were different before and after the coming into power of the AKP government. In the pre-AKP period, Çağaptay claimed that Turkey's accession to the EU was important since it would anchor a pivotal ally in the European continent and establish Turkey as a model for the larger Islamic world by binding this country to a family of democratic and secular nations.[39] In his opinion, the Turkey under the AKP government, on the other hand, was anti-Western in nature, and insincere in its professions for Turkey's EU membership. Thus, the US had to contribute to Turkey's EU accession, thereby guaranteeing Turkey's alignment with the West.[40]

German Marshall Fund of the United States (GMFUS), a fourth prominent think tank relevant to our purposes here, has a special Turkey program. The Fund has contributed much to the monitoring and evaluation of Turkey–EU relations in the US with the commentaries and analyses of its experts and with the help of its offices located in several major cities of the world. ASSTSEC of EUR Philip Gordon's reference to the Transatlantic Trends Surveys of the GMFUS in his dialogue with French policy-makers in September 2009 is an indicator of the importance of the work of the Fund.

Finding 4: *Turkey's geopolitical position has been an important factor in the support the US extended to Turkey's European aspirations.*

Thomas Miller expressed this importance of Turkey's geopolitical position as follows: "Turkey inhabits some of the most critical real estate in the world. [. . .] Suppose Turkey was located off the coast of Africa. Would we care? Probably not . . ."[41]

In the Cold War era, Turkey's geopolitical position was defined with reference to the division between the East and West and was an important asset for Turkey. After the Cold War, with the George H.W. Bush administration, Turkey's geopolitical position was redefined with reference to the Middle East. To Iraq in particular . . . This definition would remain the most parochial view of Turkey's location and was a bathos for Turkey in geopolitical terms. Yet, there was an increase in the intensity of the US advocacy for Turkey in this era thanks, primarily, to Özal's pro-US policies.

With Clinton, Turkey's geopolitical importance was elevated to an unprecedented level and complemented with a profound conception of Turkey's identity. In this understanding, Turkey's unique location and culture would make it a key piece in bridging the inter-civilizational fault line. Clinton continuously underlined Turkey's Europeanness.

In rhetoric, George W. Bush maintained Clinton's geopolitical view of Turkey, but for him Turkey's presence in the Balkans and especially in the Middle East was more important.

Finally, in the Obama era, with the distance developing between Turkey and the EU and due to the instability hanging over Syria, Iraq, and Iran, Turkey's geopolitical value came to be defined, rather, with reference to the Middle East once again.

> **Finding 5:** While the support of Europeans for Turkey's EU membership was proportional to Turkey's assets, that of Americans was to Turkey's problems.

The US policy-makers believed that Turkey's EU membership could be a panacea for most of the ailments of Turkey such as its unpromising economic indicators, its frequent advances to the Soviets, its problems with Greece, its intransigence in the Cyprus issue, the objections it raised to European defense initiatives, or the Islamic resurgence in its domestic politics.

The possibility of 'losing Turkey' was a perpetual concern for the US and a common theme in the media and in academic writings.[42] In the Eisenhower, Kennedy, Johnson, Ford, and Carter eras, Americans feared to lose Turkey to the Soviets. In the Clinton, W. Bush, and Obama eras, Turkey's Islamization became an alarming contingency. To prevent these two 'perils,' in most cases the Americans increased their support for the improvement of Turkey–EU relations.

The effect of Turkey's troubled HR record on the support the country received from the US has been negligible or positive. Turkey's fight with acts of terrorism, first by left- and right-wing organizations in the 1970s and then by the PKK from the late 1970s onwards gave rise to accusations of HR violations. Especially after the 1980 coup, Turkey–EU relations were negatively affected by these accusations, whereas the US was more tolerant towards Turkey. The Clinton administration's critical stance was an exception that was dictated by the Congress. This administration tried to make the sale of the combat helicopters to Turkey contingent on Turkey's HR reforms and encouraged Turks to implement these reforms. Albright, Talbott, and (Nicholas) Burns tried to convince the Europeans that the HR issue should not be a reason to refuse Turkey's EU membership. They claimed that the increase in HR violations in Turkey after 1997 was due to the country's casting aside by the Luxembourg Council. After the Clinton era, the HR issue did not occupy an important place in the US policy towards Turkey–EU relations.

Finding 6: *Since the Ford era, Cyprus problem has been an important factor in the US involvement in Turkey–EU relations.*

In the Ford era, the EEC started influencing the Cyprus issue and put pressure on Turks to make them assume a more cooperative attitude. Turks were unhappy with this pressure and asked for US intervention to alleviate it. The US was unwilling to intervene. Shortly after Turkey launched a military operation in Cyprus in July 1974, the US imposed an arms embargo on Turkey. Some individual MSs of the EEC made their unhappiness with the embargo known to the US in the Carter era. Carter lifted the embargo in September 1978.

In the H.W. Bush era, Cyprus emerged as an important factor again. The US attempted to give Turkey a guarantee that unless the Cyprus talks were concluded with an agreement, Cyprus would not become an EEC member. Meanwhile, the Greek lobby in the US Congress was promoting the idea that the Cyprus problem was an important obstacle in front of Turkey's EEC membership. This sensitivity of the Congress would continue in the Clinton and W. Bush eras. In May 1995, the Congress made 10 percent of the American military aid to Turkey conditional on Turkey's improvement of its policies on Cyprus and Kurdish issues.

The Cyprus policy of the Clinton administration was the most sophisticated and empathetic. This administration established a connection between the Cyprus issue and the CU Turkey was hoping to complete with the EC. It seems possible to claim that among the Americans, Europeans, Greeks, and Turks a deal was made whereby Greece would not object Turkey's CU whereas Turkey would assume a more cooperative attitude in the Cyprus issue allowing the establishment of a 'United Republic of

Cyprus' that would become an EU member. The first half of the plan worked fine and the CU was established, whereas the 'Cyprus' half of the plan miscarried; the 'no' vote of the Greek Cypriots to the Annan Plan in April 2004 meant accession of Cyprus to the EU as a divided island. The Cyprus problem remained unsettled. When the Agenda 2000 document of 1997 signaled that the EU was prepared to admit Cyprus as it was, Turkey and the TRNC signed an agreement that envisaged partial integration in economy and defense. Mainly due to US objections, this agreement was not implemented. Instead, the idea of establishing a Turkish–US FTA resurfaced and was, once again, discarded. A few times, Turkey attempted to undermine the accession process of Cyprus but was stopped by the US.

In the early days of the W. Bush administration, 'accession of Cyprus to the EU' became an important aim for the US. The Bush administration tried to convince Turkey to drop its objections to this accession. One major reason behind this effort was the belief that the possibility of the accession of Cyprus would compel the Turks into coming to the negotiation table and that the solution of the Cyprus problem would increase Turkey's own chances of EU membership. However, due to Turkey's refusal to extend its CU with the EC to Cyprus and the negative attitude of Greeks and Greek Cypriots towards Turkey's EU membership, Cyprus remained a problem in Turkey–EU relations.

> **Finding 7:** Conception of Turkey's Europeanness by the US underwent a transformation in the timespan covered here.

Until the early 1970s, for the US, Turkey was not fully European geographically, let alone culturally. The dropping of the objections of the US to Turkey's association agreement in October 1973, which was also an indirect recognition of Turkey's Europeanness, and the transfer of Turkey from NEA to EUR within the DOS in July 1974 were the early signs of recognition of Turkey's Europeanness by the US at least in geographical terms. This formal recognition did not entail an immediate and commensurate change in mentality. Even in the H.W. Bush era, Turkey's Middle Easternness would still outweigh its Europeanness. For Clinton, Turkey was certainly European; it was a bridge that belonged to Europe, connecting the East and the West. Among the recent US presidents, perhaps Obama was the one who happened to question Turkey's Europeanness in his mind most frequently since he encountered the pro-Islamic and anti-Israeli moves of the AKP government in various cases.

Finding 8: *Europeans were not categorically against US involvement in Turkey–EU relations.*

In the Eisenhower era, Europeans kept the Americans informed about their relations with the Turks and accepted Turkey's association application as, among other reasons, a gesture to the Americans. In the later decades, even when the US intervention became overwhelming, in a few cases such as the following ones this intervention still proved to be acceptable—or even preferable—for the Europeans:

1 A considerable progress was recorded in the Cyprus issue. Holbrooke's deal came close to bringing about an outcome that would have been satisfying for everyone. Had the Greek Cypriots voted in favor of the Annan Plan, the EU would have been credited with having solved the decades-old Cyprus problem. Although far from perfect, the actual result was still satisfying for the EU since the accession of Cyprus to the EU was made possible. The EU membership of Cyprus made Turkey's presence on the island more questionable and dimmed Turkey's European aspirations further, neither of which were bad news for the majority of Europeans;
2 With the assurance given by the US to Turkey, the return of Greece to the integrated military command of NATO became possible;
3 The US exerted substantial effort to convince Turkey to lift its veto on the formation of the ESDP. By following a kind but firm approach and inventing such 'tricks' as the Ankara Document, the US paved the way for the so-called Berlin Plus agreement; and
4 It was mainly thanks to the US that Turkey lifted its veto on the appointment of Rasmussen as the Secretary-General of NATO.

Finding 9: *The Greek and Armenian lobbies in the US were not totally bothered by the US involvement in Turkey–EU relations.*

As Ifantis noted, "[t]he policy implications [of the trilateral relations between the US, Turkey and Greece] for Greece are that the longer the relationship between Turkey and the EU remains overshadowed by uncertainties, the more the US remains 'the only and undisputed arbiter in an essentially balance-of-power game.'[43] The same was true for Armenians.

The US interventions gave the Greek and Armenian lobbies in the US some opportunities such as the following:

1. They were able to put further pressure on Turkey to attain their aims. For example, the resolution submitted by Adam Schiff in June 2005, invited the Congress to support Turkey's EU membership on the condition that Turks admit the culpability of the Ottoman Empire, and improve their relations with the Republic of Armenia and the Armenian people. Greeks, on their part, would probably acknowledge that without the US, the accession of Cyprus to the EU would be even more difficult; and
2. They had a chance to combine their efforts with those of the Greek and Armenian lobbies in the EU MSs. Especially the Greek lobbies in the US Congress and in the EP, which were coordinated by Greece, worked in harmony against Turkey.

Finding 10: *Since most of the US initiatives for Turkey took place in private, these initiatives seemed 'larger than life' to many and was sometimes exaggerated/misrepresented.*

The confidentiality of the US efforts for Turkey created a hazy atmosphere that was in everyone's benefit. Sometimes Americans used this environment to exaggerate their own efforts. For instance, in 1995, Holbrooke made a great display of having mobilized the US embassies in European capitals for Turkey's CU, although almost all the MSs were already sympathetic to the CU idea. Holbrooke would make phone calls from various European cities to Gürel, Turkish State Minister Responsible for Cyprus and EU Affairs, and tell him that while being in that particular city for a different reason, he had managed to say a few words to the Europeans about Turkey.[44]

Turks, too, took the advantage of this haziness. According to *Le Monde*, in April 2009, to bolster its domestic support, the AKP government spread the rumor that in return for lifting its veto on Rasmussen's appointment as the Secretary-General of NATO, Turkey had been promised opening of the two chapters frozen previously.

The most interesting claim in this context came from a third party, the online *Middle East Newsline* that, in March 2011, argued that Erdoğan had made an offer to Americans and Europeans: Turkish army would overthrow the Gaddafi regime and be admitted to the EU as a reward.

Finding 11: *Collaboration of the US with third countries increased the effect of the US interventions considerably.*

In furthering Turkey's interests in the EU, from the Reagan administration onwards, the US resorted to the help of certain EU and non-EU states. The UK was always among them. Especially after the Europeans grew intolerant of direct American interference, the assistance of the UK proved to be instrumental. This assistance was not only to please the US and Turkey but were also in harmony with the traditional British policy of working for an intergovernmental Europe.

In the early 1990s, Israel started cooperating with the US for Turkey's EU bid. Together with the Jewish lobbies in the US and in Europe, Israel was the right hand of the Clinton administration in supporting Turkey. In this period, Israel–Turkey relations were at their best. The efforts of Israel and the Jewish lobbies continued in the W. Bush era. Due to the problems between Israel and Turkey in the Obama era, Israel reversed its support.

In the Clinton era, the Netherlands emerged as another collaborator. The understanding of the majority of the Dutch political parties was that Turkey's EU membership would be an important precaution against a possible 'clash of civilizations.'

In the Obama era, Italy, who had intermittently collaborated with the US for Turkey, came to the forefront. The Italian position was based on the fear of losing Turkey to the Islamic world.

Finding 12: *'Financial aid to Turkey' has always been an important determinant in the approach of the US to Turkey–EU relations.*

Until the Reagan era, the US saw the international financial aid extended to Turkey as an alternative to the economic assistance Turkey could get from the EEC. From the Reagan era onwards, this aid was a part and parcel of the US 'support package' for Turkey's close relations with the EEC/EU.

Initially, the US preferred to keep financial aid schemes for Turkey under the control of international organizations such as the IMF where the influence of the US was considerable. This understanding was most perceptible in the Eisenhower and Carter eras. Later, the US changed this policy and argued for any economic assistance to Turkey as a means to advance this country's membership prospects.

Finding 13: *The intensity of the US efforts for Turkey's European aspirations decreased in the first Obama term in both intention and action.*

This decline was the result of the following developments:

1 Turkey–EU relations reached an impasse;
2 Turkey's growing economy and FP openings decreased its need for the EU and US;
3 The US influence over the EU gradually waned parallel to the decline of the US as a world power;
4 Europeans became allergic towards American initiatives on behalf of Turks; and
5 Turkey's relations with the US and Israel—a powerful collaborator of the US in supporting Turkey—were fraught with some serious problems.

Notes

1 Constantinos Koliopoulos, "The strategic implications of Turkey's EU membership," in Meltem Müftüler-Baç and Yannis Stivachtis (eds.), *Turkey-European Union Relations: Dilemmas, Opportunities, and Constraints*, Lanham, MD: Lexington Books, 2008, 93–111, p. 98.
2 Frances G. Burwell, a Vice President of the Atlantic Council, is of the same opinion. (Source: Interview with Burwell, Washington, 23 April 2010.)
3 For Waltz's counterarguments, see Kenneth Waltz, "Structural Realism after the Cold War," *International Security*, Vol. 25, No. 1, 2000, 5–41.
4 Alan Makovsky, "Turkey's faded European dream," in *Conference Report: The Parameters of Partnership: Germany, the U.S., and Turkey*, Washington: American Institute for Contemporary German Studies, 1998, p. 60. Emphasis added.
5 Bill Clinton, "Address before a joint session of the Congress on the State of the Union, January 25, 1994" in National Archives and Records Administration, Office of the Federal Register, *PPPUS, William J. Clinton, 1994, Book 1: January 1 to July 31, 1994*, Washington: USGPO, 1995, 126–35, p. 132.
6 See also Constantinos Koliopoulos, "The strategic implications of Turkey's EU membership," in Meltem Müftüler-Baç and Yannis Stivachtis (eds.), *Turkey-European Union Relations: Dilemmas, Opportunities, and Constraints*, Lanham, MD: Lexington Books, 2008, 93–111, p. 99.
7 See page 155 endnote 124.
8 "ABD: Türkiye'yi AB davet etti, varış noktası değiştirilmemeli," *Milliyet*, 5 May 2006. Author's translation. Emphasis added.
9 Interview with Volkan Vural, Istanbul, 6 September 2011.
10 Interview with Ross Wilson, Washington, 25 May 2010.
11 For example, journalist Steve Sailer maintains that Turkey's EU membership "would be bad for America, Turkey, and the Muslim world as a whole" and that, therefore the US should not push "this dangerous step." (Source: Steve Sailer, "Save Europe! Keep

Turkey out of the EU," *VDARE*, 19 September 2004. Available at www.vdare.com/articles/save-europe-keep-turkey-out-of-the-eu, accessed 17 August 2012.)

12 F. Stephen Larrabee, "American perspectives on Turkey and Turkish-EU relations," American Institute for Contemporary German Studies. Available at www.aicgs.org/c/larrabee_turkey.shtml, 30 September 2004, accessed 4 June 2006.

13 Nigar Göksel, "Pitfalls and opportunities for the US-Turkish Alliance: A TPQ exclusive interview with Richard Perle," *Turkish Policy Quarterly*, Vol. 4, No. 1, Spring 2005. Available at www.turkishpolicy.com/dosyalar/files/TPQ2005-1-perle.pdf, accessed 10 July 2012.

14 See, for example, Mehmet Ali Kışlalı, "Perle-Cheney ve TSK," *Radikal*, 21 March 2002. For a criticism, see Yasemin Çongar, "Genişleyen AB, ABD ve biz (1)," *Milliyet*, 3 May 2004.

15 Nicholas deB. Katzenbach, *Some of It Was Fun: Working with RFK and LBJ*, New York, NY: W.W. Norton & Company, 2008, p. 257.

16 "U.S. lawmakers introduce Congressional European Union Caucus," *USEU*. Available at www.useu.be/TransAtlantic/May0405CongressEUCaucus.html, accessed 6 January 2008.

17 Thanks to his erudition in the field of FP, Bowles became a FP adviser to Senator Kennedy in 1960 and Under SECSTATE in 1961.

18 Adam Bernstein, "Stephen Solarz dies: Former N.Y. Congressman was 70," *WP*, 29 November 2010; and Douglas Martin, "Stephen J. Solarz, former N.Y. Congressman, dies at 70," *NYT*, 29 November 2010.

19 Ian M. Destler, *American Trade Politics*, NYU Press, 1992, pp. 31–2.

20 Henry Stanhope, "Turkey may change relationship with NATO," *The Times*, 16 May 1978.

21 "Armenians against and for Turkey's European Union membership," *Armenpress*. Available at http://armenpress.am/eng/news/518696/.html, accessed 24 April 2014.

22 Statistical data retrieved from http://factfinder2.census.go (no direct link to the results is available), accessed 17 August 2012.

23 Interview with Brent Scowcroft, Washington, 14 May 2010.

24 Interview with Ross Wilson, Washington, 25 May 2010.

25 Anupama Narayanswamy and Luke Rosiak, "Adding it up: The top players in foreign agent lobbying," *ProPublica*, 18 August 2009. Available at www.propublica.org/article/adding-it-up-the-top-players-in-foreign-agent-lobbying-718, accessed 15 August 2012.

26 From the contract concluded with Fleishman-Hillard, Inc. in 1998. (Source: Report of the Attorney General to the Congress of the United States on the Administration of the Foreign Agents Registration Act of 1938, as amended, for the six months ending June 30, 1998, Washington: US Department of Justice, 1999, p. 315.)

27 From the contract concluded with the Livingston Group in 2005. Three Turkish nationals had been taken hostage in Iran in December 2005. (Source: Report of the Attorney General to the Congress of the United States on the Administration of the Foreign Agents Registration Act of 1938, as amended, for the six months ending June 30, 2005, Washington: US Department of Justice, 2006, p. 226.)

28 Report of the Attorney General to the Congress of the United States on the Administration of the Foreign Agents Registration Act of 1938, as amended, for the calendar year 1995, Vol. II, Washington: US Department of Justice, 1996, p. 705.

29 Kate Ackley, "Livingston Group's access opens doors for Turkey." Available at www.influence.biz/cgi-bin/display_news.pl?&id=20040927152840, accessed 30 August 2012.

30 Morton Abramowitz et al., "Turkey on the threshold: Europe's decision and U.S. interests," Policy Paper 8, Washington: Atlantic Council of the United States, 2004, p. v.

31 Lawrence B. Krause, *European Economic Integration and the United States*, Washington, D.C.: Brookings Institution, 1968, pp. 200–1.

32 Heinz Kramer, *A Changing Turkey: The Challenge to Europe and the United States*, Washington DC: Brookings Institution, 2001.
33 Washington DC: Brookings Institution, 2008.
34 Such as the panel discussion on 13 April 2009. Available at www.brookings.edu/events/2009/04/13-us-turkey, accessed 22 August 2014.
35 David L. Phillips, "Turkey's dreams of accession," *Foreign Affairs*, Vol. 83, No. 5, 2004, pp. 86–97.
36 Steven A. Cook, "How Europe can save Turkey," Council on Foreign Relations. Available at http://blogs.cfr.org/cook/2013/06/10/how-europe-can-save-turkey/, accessed 10 June 2014.
37 Mark Landler, "Trying to break logjam, scholar floats an idea for a Palestinian map," *NYT*, 22 January 2011.
38 "Our History," *WINEP*. Available at www.washingtoninstitute.org/about/mission-and-history, accessed 23 August 2014.
39 See for instance, "Turkey's quest to join the European Union: Implications for American policy," *Policy Watch*, No: 648, *WINEP*, 14 August 2002. Available at www.cagaptay.com/648/turkeys-quest-to-join-the-european-union, accessed 10 July 2014.
40 For example, "Turkey's Anti-European Rhetoric Challenges U.S. Policy," *Policy Watch*, No: 1775, *WINEP*, 11 March 2011. Available at www.washingtoninstitute.org/policy-analysis/view/turkeys-anti-european-rhetoric-challenges-u.s.-policy, accessed 9 July 2014.
41 Interview with Thomas Miller, Washington, 15 April 2010.
42 Among tens of works on this theme, the following ones may be cited: Thomas Friedman, "Who lost Turkey," *NYT*, 21 August 1996; Richard Burt, "Are we losing Turkey," *WSJ*, 21 June 1997; "Is the West losing Turkey?" *The Economist*, 19 October 2006; Mark Steyn, "Who lost Turkey," *WT*, 4 June 2010; Bernhard Zand, "How the West is losing Turkey," *Spiegel Online*, 15 June 2010. Available at www.spiegel.de/international/world/the-anatolian-tiger-how-the-west-is-losing-turkey-a-700626.html, accessed 22 August 2012; Rajan Menon and S. Enders Wimbush, "Is the United States losing Turkey?" Hudson Institute, 25 March 2007. Available at www.hudson.org/files/pdf_upload/Turkey%20PDF.pdf, accessed 10 June 2011; Mark Almond, "Losing Turkey," Project Syndicate, 6 June 2008. Available at www.project-syndicate.org/commentary/losing-turkey, accessed 12 February 2011; and Philip Gordon and Ömer Taşpınar, *Winning Turkey: How America, Europe, and Turkey Can Revive a Fading Partnership*, Washington DC: Brookings Institution, 2008.
43 Kostas Ifantis, "Turkey, the US and Greece: Systemic uncertainties and regional prospects," in Mustafa Aydın and Çağrı Erhan (eds.), *Turkish-American Relations: Past, Present and Future*, New York, NY: Routledge, 2004, 107–28, p. 123.
44 Interview with Şükrü Sina Gürel, Istanbul, 9 November 2012.

Index

Aartsen, Jozias van 138
Abernathy/MacGregor Group, Inc. 268
Abkhazia 213n12
Abramowitz, Morton 91–2, 97, 98, 100, 101, 103, 104n16, 106n62
Accession Partnership Document 111, 138, 257
Additional Protocol *see* Ankara Agreement
Adenauer, Konrad 15, 19, 27n55 and 64
Aegean Sea 72, 85, 112, 121, 132, 133, 136, 146, 147
Afghanistan 69, 70, 82, 213n23, 228, 229, 234, 246
Africa 31, 33, 35, 51, 55, 58n3, 165, 217n117, 234, 245, 269
African Union 234
Agenda 2000 122–3, 272
Agnelli, Susanna 114
Ahern, Bertie 181
Ahtisaari, Martti 133, 136, 143, 266
aid: financial 10–12, 15–24, 27n56, 27n57, 34–5, 36, 38, 44, 45, 46, 47, 53, 59n31, 62, 66, 67, 72, 73, 75, 77, 81, 82, 88, 92, 94, 101, 109–110, 112, 130, 134, 140, 150, 164, 165, 177, 179, 194, 200, 204, 210, 211, 212, 228, 234, 235, 259, 262, 275, 297; military 10, 20, 43, 61, 75, 82, 86, 94, 110, 164, 228, 271, 275
Akbulut, Yıldırım 96
AKP 5, 165, 166, 170–2, 176, 182, 183–4, 192, 193, 197, 213n23, 229, 230, 234, 240, 246, 247, 269, 272, 274
Akyol, Nihat 114
Akyüz, Abdullah 167
Albright, Madeline 107–8, 120–1, 125, 127, 128, 130, 131, 137, 138–40, 142, 143, 145, 149, 261, 262, 271; the three Ds of 139

Algeria 51,
Alliance of Civilizations 231
alliances 4, 10, 11, 15, 23, 27n57, 44, 47n3, 54, 57, 67, 68n34, 69, 72, 85, 87, 92–3, 99, 104n13, 138, 139, 174, 185, 197, 204, 230, 231, 236, 244, 258, 259, 260
Alphand, Herve 30
American Farm Bureau Federation 32
American Jewish Committee 204, 267
American Israel Public Affairs Committee 95
American-Turkish Council 192
Amitay, Morris J. 95, 105n32
anarchy 3, 5, 22
Ankara Agreement 29, 36–7, 38n1 and 2, 39n38, 40n39, 45, 46, 55, 57, 58n11, 62, 73, 82, 152n26, 182, 244, 250n41, 256, 262, 272; Additional Protocol to 54, 62, 65, 67, 152n26; Ankara Protocol to 232, 250n41; Provisional Protocol to 39n38, 40n40, 58n11
Ankara Document 198–200
Ankara Protocol *see* Ankara Agreement
Annan, Kofi 133, 195
Annan Plan 155n124, 172, 195–6, 272, 273
Anti-Defamation League 142
Arab states 54, 234, 237, 239–40, 241, 243, 245, 247
Arab League 234, 240, 241
Arab Spring 239–40, 247
Argentina 200
Aristotle 1
Armenia 110, 188, 267, 274
Armenian allegations 82, 87, 95, 97, 142, 143, 188, 243, 267
Armenian lobby *see* lobbies
Ashton, Catherine 232, 238
Assad, Bashar al- 240, 241

Assembly of Turkish American Associations 267
Association Council 36, 40n39, 58n11, 81, 111, 112, 115, 118, 140, 178
Association Council Agreement 123
association relationship with the EU: of African states *see* Yaoundé Convention; of Greece 14, 15, 17, 18, 21, 25n21, 32–3, 46, 55–6, 57, 262, 265; of Turkey 15, 16–19, 21–2, 23, 24, 26n51, 29, 31, 32–3, 34, 35, 36–7, 39n25, 44, 45, 46, 47, 52, 53, 54, 55–6, 57, 62, 65, 67, 244, 256, 259, 262, 264, 265, 268, 272, 273; of other countries 21, 28n74, 51, 53, 55, 105n38
Atatürk, Mustafa Kemal 239
Athens Agreement 29, 39n38, 46, 55, 57, 262
Atherton, Alfred A. 55, 59n24
Atlantic Council 116, 119, 181, 268, 276n2
Audibert, Jacques 233
Australia 31
Austria 25n19, 58n3, 111, 117, 129, 138, 156n165, 184, 187, 207
Azerbaijan 95, 131, 165

Babacan, Ali 193, 194, 229
Bahat, Shulamith 204
Bahçeli, Devlet 166
Baker, James 93, 100, 102, 210, 257
Baku-Tbilisi-Ceyhan pipeline 131, 165
balance of power 4, 23, 37, 47, 57, 67, 76–7, 88, 103, 259, 274
balancing 4, 103
Balkans 97, 120, 123, 139, 149, 167, 209, 228, 229, 230, 234, 244, 270
Balkenende, Jan Peter 206, 207–8
Ball, George 30, 33, 48n11
Baltic region 15
bandwagoning 4, 103, 260
Bangladesh 120
Bär, Dorothee 231
Barkey, Henri 6, 237–9
Barroso, José Manuel 188
Bashir, Omar al- 229
Bayar, Celal 10, 16, 18
Bayrou, François 174
BBC 238
Beckett, Margaret 191
Belgium 13, 17, 18, 70, 73, 82, 84, 95, 96, 98, 111, 112, 117, 119, 121, 124, 126, 127, 131, 138, 139, 140, 146, 166, 168, 170, 174, 179, 180, 181–4, 191, 198, 199, 202, 203, 205, 206, 207, 212, 257, 261, 263, 268
Berger, Sandy 129, 136, 137, 148
Berkley, Shelley 237, 243, 266, 267
Berlin Crisis 34, 37
Berlin Plus agreement 200, 273
Berlusconi, Silvio 182, 212, 227, 245
Bhaskar, Roy 1
Biden, Joe 243
Black Sea 12, 15, 75, 165, 176
Black Wednesday 200
Blair, Tony 129, 137, 138, 140, 141, 147, 162, 166, 182, 187, 198, 203–4, 207, 212
BMENA 165, 180, 186, 209, 211, 213n13, 217n117
Bosnia 93, 119, 228
Bot, Ben 208, 224n299
Boucher, Richard A. 168, 172, 196
Bowles, Chester 14, 264, 265, 277n17
Bozer, Ali 97, 98
Bozkır, Volkan 242
Brazil 228, 229, 235
Brentano, Heinrich von 10, 29
Brezhnev, Léonid 60
Briggs, Ellis O. 32
Brittan, Leon 120, 262
British National Party 244
Broek, Hans van den 121, 126, 262
Brok, Elmar 193
Brookings Institution 268–9
Brzezinski, Zbigniew 70–1, 72, 74, 75, 85
Bulgaria 12, 62
Burns, Bill 232, 243
Burns, Nicholas 120, 121, 133, 187, 262, 271
Burt, Richard 122
Burton, Dan 99, 103, 266
Bush doctrine 164
Bush, George H. W. 89n7, 91–107, 108, 111, 117, 141, 143, 144, 147, 162, 256, 257, 258, 260, 261, 262, 267, 270, 271, 272
Bush, George W. 5, 140, 162–225, 257, 258, 263, 264, 267, 270, 271, 272, 275

Çağaptay, Soner 269
Çağlayan, Zafer 242
Çağlayangil, İhsan Sabri 75
Cahan, John F. 24n14
Callaghan, James 72
Cameron, David 244–5

Canada 5, 13, 19, 60
candidate states 74, 111, 115, 120, 122, 124, 125–38, 141, 146, 149, 154, 168, 174, 179, 186, 198, 200, 203, 215n71, 232, 238, 240, 257, 263, 266
CAP 31, 32
capitulations 15, 23, 25n35, 26n36
Caron, Giuseppe 39n19
Carter doctrine 71, 76
Carter, Jimmy 69–79, 80, 82, 86, 148, 255, 256, 259, 267, 270, 271, 275
Casey, William J. 55
Caspian region 97
Cassell, Lynn 166
Catsimatidis, John 136
Caucasus 96, 229, 230
Cavanaugh, Carey 121
CCT 31, 46, 150, 201
CDA 206, 243
CDU 184, 217n134, 231, 232
CEECs 92, 120, 122, 126, 133
Cem, İsmail 108, 124, 130, 134, 140, 142–3, 150, 198–9, 208
CENTO 15, 17, 21
Central Asia 96, 102, 120, 143, 144, 217n117, 244
Çetin, Hikmet 117, 126, 141
CFSP 96, 106n52, 133, 260
CFT 204, 244
chapters (of Turkey's accession negotiations) 137, 189–92, 197, 211, 227–28, 230, 231, 242, 244, 248, 274
Charlemagne Prize 146
Chechnya 109
Cheney, Dick 177
Chicken War 32, 44
China 128, 147, 192, 201, 208, 240, 261
Chirac, Jacques 118, 125, 126, 136, 138, 162–3, 173, 175, 182, 203–4, 207, 225, 263
CHP 171, 233
Christian Democrats 121, 129, 154n98, 154n100, 184, 206, 232
Christianity 66, 121, 148, 151, 179, 185, 189, 246
Christides, Michael 178
Christopher, Warren 118–19, 262
CIA 66, 79n56, 107, 110
Çiller, Tansu 110, 112, 114, 118, 120, 121, 141, 189
citrus products 50, 51
civilian power Europe 94
clash of civilizations 185, 206, 209, 275

Clerides, Glafcos 137, 196
Cleveland, Harlan 48n11
Clinton, Bill 101, 107–61, 163, 168, 189, 192, 194, 196, 198, 201, 202, 204, 209, 210, 211, 212, 256, 257, 260, 261, 262–3, 264, 265, 267, 270, 271, 272, 275
Clinton, Hillary 229, 2321, 232, 233, 234, 235, 238, 239, 240, 243, 245, 246
Cohen, William 130
Cold War 2, 7, 10, 22, 23, 33, 60, 69, 75, 77, 82, 93, 97, 98, 104n10, 109, 151, 192, 255, 258–60, 270
Common European Home 98
common market 13, 14, 15, 17, 19, 21, 22, 30, 31, 32, 33, 35, 50, 51, 56, 58n3, 64, 66, 112, 119, 149, 263
communism 11, 21, 35, 44, 69, 83, 92–3, 128, 133
Congress (US) 17, 31, 59n31, 61, 62, 69, 70, 75, 94, 95, 97, 99–100, 101, 103, 109, 110, 118, 124, 127, 132, 137–8, 148, 149, 168–9, 183, 187, 188, 233, 237, 243, 265–6, 267, 268, 271, 274; House of Representatives 5, 14, 75, 100, 117, 142, 169, 188, 190, 191, 205, 214n39, 233, 237, 243, 262, 264, 265, 266; Senate 61, 95, 99, 100, 104n10, 265
Conservative Party: of Germany 186; of the UK 204, 244
containment policy 11, 23
Cook, Robin 114, 140, 141
Cook, Steven A. 269
Copenhagen Criteria 120, 125, 131, 135, 154n93, 166, 168, 175, 179, 189, 200, 205
cotton 33, 46, 52
Council on Foreign Relations 269
Council of Ministers see Council of the EU
Council of the EU 33, 34, 64, 65, 70, 87, 96, 97, 99, 103, 119, 133, 154n100, 173, 180, 181, 183, 184, 187, 195, 202, 204, 224n300, 227, 244, 250n41
coups d'État in Turkey 20–1, 75–6, 77, 79n56, 80–7, 90n37, 122, 256, 262, 271
Courtney, Charles Sam 39n19
Courtney, Raymond F. 39n19
Couve de Murville, Maurice 49
Cowe, Brian 203
Cox, Pat 174
CSCE 60, 112

Index

CSU 231
Cuban Missile Crisis 34, 37
customs union 32; between Greece and the EEC 18; between Turkey and the EEC 6, 18, 33, 37, 54, 68n28, 79n49, 100, 101, 111–21, 123, 130, 140, 141, 146–50, 152n26, 152n27, 159n234, 159n253, 183, 201–2, 227, 250n41, 257, 261, 262, 263, 266, 267, 268, 271–2, 274; proposed between Turkey and the US 149
Cyprus: EU membership of 134, 173, 196; extension of the Ankara Agreement to 181–3, 190, 196–7; intercommunal clashes in 41–4; referenda in 180, 195–7; Turkey's military operation in 56, 63–5

D-8 120, 122
Daunt, Timothy 86
Davos crisis 234, 249n18
Davutoğlu, Ahmet 228–30, 234, 243, 245
De Gaulle, Charles 30, 44, 49–50, 51, 91, 244
Defense Policy Board Advisory Committee 213n21
Delors, Jacques 93, 154n100, 262
Demirel, Süleyman 60–1, 62, 66, 68n31, 73, 74, 75 79n34, 96, 108, 120, 135–6, 141, 150
democratization 76, 81, 85, 87, 118–9 138, 173, 175, 211, 260
Democrats 14, 118, 264
Denktaş, Rauf 124, 195
Denmark 25n19, 51, 52, 167, 195, 202, 207, 230
DEP 109
Department of Agriculture 31, 45, 52, 265
Department of Commerce 63
Department of Defence 66
Department of State 12, 13, 14, 16, 21, 25n20, 25n21, 29, 30, 31, 32, 34, 39n19, 42, 44, 45, 52, 57, 68n14, 100, 103, 113, 115, 120, 124, 126, 128, 131, 138, 142, 149, 166, 168, 172, 182, 183, 184, 186, 193, 214n36, 242, 262, 265, 272
dependence 3, 23, 77, 88, 259
DHKP-C 202, 212, 257
Dijk, Jan Jacob van 206
Dillon, C. Douglas 16, 17, 18, 19, 20, 31, 262
Dobbins, James 137
Dolmabahçe Palace 91, 102, 162

domestic politics 1, 2, 3, 5, 11, 23, 37, 57, 74, 75, 76, 77, 84, 87, 100, 102, 103, 120, 129, 142, 168, 176, 192, 194, 197, 203, 209, 211, 233, 238, 239, 247, 257, 258, 259, 270, 274
double-taxation 124, 126, 142
Dulles, John F. 10, 11, 13, 15, 16, 23

earthquake in Turkey in 1999 108, 130, 149
East 20, 102, 144, 148, 151, 232, 236, 240, 270, 272
Eberle, William D. 55
Edelman, Eric S. 133, 137, 158n196, 181, 182, 183–4, 187, 189, 262
EEC *see the relevant entries*
EFTA 14, 25n19, 53
Egypt 14, 51, 89, 120, 144, 239, 241
Eisenhower, Dwight D. 7, 10–28, 29, 31, 37, 38, 77, 108, 256, 259, 264, 270, 273, 275
Eisenhower doctrine 11–12
Eisenhower, John S. D. 27n57
Eizenstat, Stuart 119, 261, 262
Elekdağ, Şükrü 83, 233
Élysée Palace 225–6
embargo: on China 208; on Iraq 93; on Northern Cyprus 190; on Turkey 61–2, 66–7, 70–3, 75, 76–7, 77n6, 110, 271
energy 95, 97, 102, 150, 165, 229, 230
enhanced partnership 189
enlargement: of the EU 1–2, 51, 115, 120, 134, 140, 173, 174, 193, 230; of NATO 120–1, 125
enosis 41, 44, 48n7
epistemic fallacy 1–2
EPU 15–6
Erbakan, Necmettin 68n31, 110, 120, 121
Erdoğan, Recep Tayyip 5, 8n25, 163, 171–4, 176–7, 180–95, 203–7, 213n23, 215n89, 228, 229, 230, 231, 234–6, 239, 241–2, 243, 244, 248, 249n18, 274
Erhard, Ludwig 16, 17, 33
Eric M. Warburg Prize 192
Erkin, Feridun Cemal 33, 42, 44
Erkmen, Hayrettin 73, 89n31
ESDI 138–9, 194
ESDP 198–9, 210, 263, 273
EU *see the relevant entries*
EU-US Summits 118, 119, 180, 181, 193, 230, 261, 262
EUR 14, 31, 39, 55, 57, 58n24, 68n14, 100, 103, 106, 182, 187, 193, 199, 207, 220n186, 231, 236, 265, 269, 272

EURATOM 13, 19, 96
L'Europe des patries 30
European Coal and Steel Community 96
European Commission 16, 18, 39n19, 40n39, 53, 66, 73, 84, 93, 97, 98, 111, 118, 119, 120, 121, 122, 124, 126, 128, 131, 134–5, 138, 154n100, 170, 173–5, 179, 183–4, 188, 190, 200, 214n36, 227–8, 230, 257, 262–3
European Conference 126, 128, 156n137
European Council/Meetings of the Heads of State or Government: Brussels (2002) 170, 212, 257; Brussels (2004) 175, 180–5, 200, 207, 208, 263, 268; Brussels (2007) 191; Cardiff (1998) 141; Copenhagen (1997) 154n93; Copenhagen (2002) 7, 163, 169, 175, 178, 195, 200, 203, 258; Essen (1994) 112; The Hague (1969) 51; Helsinki (1999) 111, 128–38, 141, 143, 147; Laeken (2001) 199; Luxembourg (1997) 111, 119–27; Maastricht (1991) 96; Nice (2000) 138; Thessaloniki (2003) 179
European Defense Agency 230, 233
European Free Market 14
European Investment Bank 44
European Parliament 81, 82, 84, 87, 88, 98–9, 111, 117, 118–19, 140–141, 153n54, 154n98, 159n234, 167, 174, 193, 228, 231, 262, 266, 274
European People's Party 121
European Political Cooperation 99, 106n52
Evren, Kenan 75, 80–2, 83, 85–6, 98, 139, 198
Eyskens, Mark 96

Fabius, Laurent 245
FDP 232
Feith, Douglas 95
Ferber, Markus 231
figs 35, 52
Fillon, François 225
Finland 14, 60–2, 75, 111, 128–38, 140, 141, 143, 147, 149, 150, 158n196, 180, 257, 262–3 266
FIR 72
Fischer, Joschka 129, 169–70
five-year development plans of Turkey 45
Fleishman-Hillard, Inc. 277n26
Flournoy, Michele 233
Foldvary, Fred. E. 5

Foley, James 126
Fontaine, Nicole 174
Ford, Gerald 57, 60–8, 76, 77n1, 77n6, 148, 256, 259, 270, 271
Foreign Affairs 269
Foreign Assistance Act 82
foreign policy 2–3, 12, 14, 20, 21, 44, 46, 47, 56, 57, 82, 83, 88, 97, 106n52, 117, 118, 120, 124, 136, 146, 147, 164, 166–7, 171, 205, 228–30, 234–7, 241, 242, 244–5, 247, 248, 256, 259–60, 265, 268, 276, 277n17
Foreign Agricultural Service 32
Fortuyn, Pim 206
Fouchet Plan 30
Fourth Financial Protocol 102
Fourth Infantry Division 164
Fox, Liam 244
Foxman, Abraham H. 142
France 12, 15, 19, 30, 32, 38n4, 44, 49, 50, 51, 63, 64, 70, 72, 91, 103, 112, 114, 116, 117, 118, 119, 120, 137, 138, 146, 162, 167, 173, 174, 176, 178, 181, 182, 184, 190, 191, 193, 204, 206, 207–8, 210, 211, 225–7, 230, 231–3, 243, 244, 245, 261, 269
Frattini, Franco 245
free-trade area 13–4, 16, 25n19; Turkey-Israel 142, 149, 263; proposed between Turkey-US 100, 123–4, 130, 187, 202, 213n21, 257, 263, 265, 266, 272
Fried, Daniel 167, 187, 189, 190, 220n186, 261
Friedman, Milton 5
Friedman, Thomas 236, 254n129

G7 120
G8 129, 140, 186, 213n13
G20 234, 236
Gaddafi, Muammar 241, 248, 274
gains (absolute / relative) 4, 38, 47, 57, 77, 88, 148, 209, 259
games (positive sum / zero-sum) 4, 148
Gates, Robert 235, 236, 237, 241, 245, 254n119
GATT 29, 31, 32, 44, 51, 52, 53, 54
Gaza flotilla raid 234–5, 236–7
Gaza Strip 234–5
Genscher, Hans-Dietrich 84
geopolitics/geostrategy 2, 34, 37, 76, 87, 93, 95, 97, 102, 143, 144, 163, 164, 177, 208, 245, 255, 259, 269–70
Georgia 165, 228
German Marshall Fund 269

Germany 10, 14–24, 20, 27n55, 32–5, 38, 44, 57n3, 64, 67, 68n34, 70–4, 82, 85, 88, 94–5, 97, 100, 103, 111, 112, 114, 117, 122, 123, 124–5 128–30, 133, 137, 138, 141, 146, 149, 167, 169–70, 173, 176, 178, 181, 184–6, 191, 192, 193, 202, 206, 207, 208, 210, 211, 227, 230, 231, 232, 261, 268
Gibbs, Robert 235
Giscard d'Estaing, Valery 72, 138, 179
Gloannec, Anne-Marie Le 6
Gogh, Theo van 206
Gönensay, Emre 114, 120, 142, 154n87, 159n254
González, Felipe 119, 141
Gooijer, Pieter de 183, 207
Gorbachev, Mikhail 82
Gordon, Philip 231–3, 236, 268, 269
Gramm, Phil 123–4, 266
Grand Trianon Palace 49
Gray, Clayland Boyden 190–1
Greater Middle East Initiative *see* BMENA
Greece 11, 14–22, 24n14, 25n21, 29, 32–3, 41–2, 45–6, 48n7, 51, 52, 52, 55–57, 59n3, 62, 63, 65–6, 72–3, 76, 82, 83–4, 85–6, 87, 88, 89n23, 89n31, 94, 95, 96, 111, 112–16, 117, 124, 125, 128–31, 132–3, 138, 140–1, 146–9, 174, 178, 196, 197, 199, 202–3, 209, 256, 259, 260, 262, 263, 265, 270, 271, 273–4
Greens 129
Grossman, Marc 103, 115–7, 119, 127, 132–3, 135, 137, 142, 149, 166, 167–8, 170, 171, 186–7, 194, 196, 203, 262
GSP 62, 67, 202
GTI 12, 14, 25n25
Guadeloupe summit 72, 77
Gül, Abdullah 171, 177, 184, 187, 189, 193, 204, 215n89, 225, 226, 229, 230
Gulf Cooperation Council 234, 240
Gulf War 93–4, 97, 99, 100, 102–3, 104n13, 109, 110, 189, 260
Güneş, Turan 55, 63–4
Gürel, Şükrü Sina 114, 116, 123, 274
Gürsel, Cemal 20–1

Haass, Richard N. 172
Hadley, Stephen 186, 187
Hagel, Chuck 180, 266
Hague, William 204, 244–5
Haig, Alexander 82, 84–85, 88, 262

Halefoğlu, Vahit 87
Halki Theological School 132
Hallstein, Walter 17–8, 262
Hamas 205, 243
Hannay, David 155n124, 199, 203, 261
Hare, Raymond A. 41–4
Harriman, Pamela 120
Harris, David A. 205
Harris, George 28n79, 52, 58n9
Hartman, Arthur A. 55, 58n24, 65
Hastert, Dennis 142
hazelnuts 52
helicopter sale to Turkey 127, 148, 176, 263, 271
Henze, Paul B. 70–2, 74–6, 78n18, 78n19, 79n56, 85, 103
Herter, Christian 18, 262
Heuss, Theodor 10, 29
Hezbollah 205
Hills, Carla Anderson 100
Holbrooke, Richard 113–24, 126, 128, 143, 146, 147, 148, 150, 155n124, 196, 202, 220n213, 261, 263, 273, 274
Holmes, James Howard 113
hood incident 177
Houghton, Amo 118, 133, 264, 266
House of Representatives (US) *see* Congress
Howe, Geoffrey 86
human rights 80, 97, 99, 109–10, 112, 117, 118, 120–2, 125, 127, 129, 131, 132, 138, 144, 146, 148, 149, 154n93, 234, 239, 240, 263, 264, 270–1
Human Rights Watch 240
Hungary 92, 112, 206
Huntington, Samuel 206
Hurd, Douglas 101–2, 114

Iceland 14, 96
ICJ 125, 132–5
ideology 4, 23, 38, 67, 73, 77, 164, 211, 259
İksel, Settar 19, 27n55,
IMF 10, 13, 23, 24n2, 24n14, 72, 74, 77, 131, 165, 185, 200, 201, 211, 212, 259n4, 275
İncirlik Air Base 177, 179
Indonesia 120, 144,
INF Treaty 81, 82,
İnönü, İsmet 41–3
intergovernmentalism 30
International Advisers, Inc. 95

International Development Association 44
Iran 14, 15, 63, 70, 71, 82, 87, 120, 189,
   228, 229, 234, 235, 237, 238, 239, 240,
   243, 246, 247, 268, 270
Iraq 14, 82, 87, 91, 93–4, 100, 102, 109,
   110, 128, 162–5, 167–78, 179, 185,
   189, 192, 201, 206, 208–11, 228–9,
   240, 243, 270
Iraq crisis 175–8
Iraq War 164, 167, 170–8, 179, 201,
   206, 209
Ireland 51, 52, 181, 207
Irmak, Sadi 66
Irwin, John N. 53
ISAF 164, 228
Islam 66, 75, 96, 145, 148, 151, 163, 170,
   185, 188, 193, 203, 204, 206, 230, 241,
   243, 245, 246, 276n11
Israel 51, 53, 55, 58n3, 90n31, 95–6, 101,
   103, 105n29, 141–3, 145, 148, 149, 150,
   201, 204–5, 212, 229, 234–7, 243, 247,
   248, 253n102, 262, 263, 264, 266–7,
   269, 275–6
Istanbul Declaration 201
Italy 18, 24, 44, 95, 96, 114, 121, 124, 125,
   130, 138, 146, 167, 174, 182, 215n71,
   227, 244, 245, 248, 275

Jeffrey, James F. 133, 243, 262
Jenkins, Roy 73
Johnson letter 43–4, 56
Johnson, Lyndon B. 41–8, 56, 255, 256,
   259, 270
Jones, G. Lewis 21
Jones, Owen T. 12
Jordan 201
Juncker, Jean-Claude 128
Jupiter missiles 17, 34
Juppe, Alain 114, 117
Justice and Home Affairs 96

Karamanlis, Konstantinos 66, 68n34
Karayalçın, Murat 112, 114–15
Katzenbach, Nicholas deB. 265
Kekkonen, Urho 60
Kelly, Tom 203
Kemalism 73, 184
Kennedy, John F. 24n5, 29–40, 44, 45, 46,
   256, 259, 266, 270, 277n17
Kennedy, Laura 182
Khalilzad, Zalmay 127
Khrushchev, Nikita 20, 22
Kışlalı, Mehmet Ali 47n3

Kinkel, Klaus 114, 117, 122, 123
Kirk, Mark 5, 266
Kirkuk-Yumurtalık pipeline 93
Kissinger, Henry A. 51, 52, 53, 54–6, 57,
   60, 61, 63–5, 68n19, 265,
Kohl, Helmut 85, 112, 121, 122, 125, 128,
   129, 154n100, 261, 263
Kok, Wim 154n100
Koliopoulos, Constantinos 6
Komer, Robert W. 31
Korea 11, 80, 234,
Kostopoulos, Sotiris 98–9
Kosygin, Alexei 44, 62
Kouchner, Bernard 244
Kozyrev, Andrey 92
Krause, Lawrance B. 45–6, 268
Kurds 109, 110, 112, 149, 230, 237, 239,
   240, 271
Kuwait 93–4, 110, 210
Kyoto Protocol 234
Kyprianou, Markos 228

Labor Party: of the Netherlands 154n100;
   of the UK 140
Lahr, Rolf Otto 19
Lamy, Pascal 174
Lantos, Tom 168–9, 205, 266, 268
Larcher, Gérard 225
Larson, Alan 202
Latin America 33, 37, 234
Laurence, Peter 86
LDCs 16, 31, 38, 259
Lebanon 51, 205, 229, 239
Leigh, Michael 203
Levitte, Jean-David 231–2
Library of Congress 75
Libya 239, 241
Lidington, David 245
Lieberman, Joe 180, 266
Lipponen, Paavo 133, 134, 136, 264
Livingston Group 268, 277n27
lobbies/lobbying 37, 86, 95, 141, 167,
   168, 191, 196, 201, 245, 260–4 266–8;
   agriculture 31, 37, 57, 259, 266;
   Armenian 94, 100, 101, 103, 137, 165,
   233, 267; Greek 70, 94, 99–100, 101,
   103, 129, 130, 141, 148, 149, 183, 267;
   Jewish 95–6, 101, 143, 204, 205, 212,
   243; textile 142, 150, 201, 211,
   266, 267
Logan, David 140
Luns, Joseph 72, 89n31
Luxembourg 6, 99, 111, 119

Maastricht Criteria 189
Maastricht Treaty 94, 96
Macomber, Jr., William B. 59
Makarios III 41, 60, 61
Malaysia 120
Malta 51, 200, 263
Marjolin, Robert 16–7, 262
Marshall Plan 18, 31, 122
Mashaal, Khaled 205
McClellan, Scott 182, 186
Mearsheimer, John 104n10, 105n32
Mediterranean 12, 51, 53, 63, 87, 205, 240
Menderes, Adnan 11, 15, 16, 17, 18, 20, 21, 23
Menemencioğlu, Turgut 29–30, 42
Menendez, Robert 183, 266
Merkel, Angela 184, 185, 186, 191, 217n134, 227
Mersin crisis 83–4, 88
Metal Storm 192
Mexico 5, 162, 163, 170, 173, 179, 193, 231
Michel, Louis 179
Michelis, Gianni de 96, 100
Middle East 11, 12, 76–77, 82, 93, 95, 97, 99, 102, 140, 142, 143, 144, 148, 165, 167, 178, 180, 186, 189, 209, 211, 217n117, 228, 229, 230, 244, 245, 247, 264, 266, 270, 272
Middle East Newsline 241, 274
Mierlo, Hans van 120
Miliband, David 244
Miller, Thomas 114, 116, 123, 128, 269
Miraillet, Michel 233
Mitterrand, François 112
Monti, Mario 245
Morgan, Bob 69
Morocco 51, 57n3, 239
Mortimer, Edward 87
Mumcu, Uğur 110
Murville, Couve de 49
Muskie, Edmund 76

NAC 69, 74, 80, 198, 200
NAFTA 5, 174, 213n21
Napolitano, Giorgio 245
Nationalist Movement Party 166
NATO 11, 14–15, 18, 21, 30, 33, 43, 44, 47n3, 49, 54, 55, 56, 61, 64, 65, 69, 70, 71, 72, 73–5, 76–7, 80, 82, 84, 85–6, 87–8, 92, 93–6, 99, 104n10, 109, 120, 121, 125, 127, 138, 139–40, 145, 147, 148, 162, 163, 164, 169, 174, 181, 187, 198–200, 203, 205, 206, 209, 212, 230, 231, 232, 233, 236, 238, 241, 243, 248, 256, 258, 261, 263, 273, 274
NEA 14, 21, 55, 57, 265
Near East 14, 23, 58n9, 259
negotiation framework 184, 189
neo-conservativism 264
neo-Ottomanism 239
neorealism 2–5, 8n6, 22–4, 37–8, 47, 57, 67, 76–7, 88, 103, 147, 148, 151, 209, 211, 258, 259, 260, 264
Netanyahu, Benjamin 105n29,
Netherlands 32, 51, 64, 120, 138, 139, 154n100, 182, 183, 202, 205–8, 212, 241, 243, 245, 248, 275
New Atlanticism 93
New Transatlantic Agenda 119
Nicolai, Arzo 183
NIE 11, 20
Nigeria 120
Niles, Thomas 115
Nine, the 70
Nixon, Richard 37, 47, 49–59, 77, 256, 259, 266
Noël, Emile 66
North Atlantic Assembly 26n50
North Korea 234
Norway 25n19, 51, 52, 73, 96
NSC 11, 15, 21, 31, 70, 78n22, 79n56
nuclear energy/weapons 11, 23, 44, 49, 73, 81, 150, 192, 229, 235, 266
Nuland, Victoria 242

Obama, Barack 7, 225–54, 256, 258, 267, 270, 272, 275, 276
OCB 11–4
OECD 35, 38, 72, 74, 242, 259
OEEC 10, 13, 14, 16, 17, 19, 23, 24n2, 24n14, 25n19, 27n55
Öniş, Ziya 6
Operation Desert Storm 210
Operation Northern Watch 110, 179
Operation Provide Comfort 110
opium poppy 56–7, 61–2, 67
Organization of the Islamic Conference 145
OSCE 107, 110
Ottomans 15, 25n35, 91, 144, 162, 188, 239, 274
Outer Seven, the 13–4, 25n19
Özal, Turgut 81, 83–4, 86, 91, 94–5, 96–8, 100, 102, 189, 270
Özilhan, Tuncay 167

Pakistan 31, 34, 120, 144, 229, 246
Palestine 229, 246
Pallone, Frank 190, 266
Pangalos, Theodoros 87, 130
Papadopoulos, Tassos 182
Papandreou, Andreas 86, 112
Papandreou, George 130, 132, 138, 149, 170, 199
Papoulias, Karolos 112, 117
Parris, Mark R. 126, 133, 140, 164–5, 262
Party for Freedom 244
Pascoe, Lynn 199
Patriot missiles 206
Pax Americana 97
Patton Boggs 201
Pearson, W. Robert 169, 172, 200, 210
Pell, Claiborne 99, 101, 266
Pence, Mike 237, 267
Peres, Shimon 141–2, 229, 234, 249n18
Perle, Richard 95, 105n29, 167, 201, 213n21, 265
Persian Gulf 71, 76, 87, 93–5, 97, 99, 100, 102, 103, 108, 109, 110, 189, 234, 240, 260
Persson, Göran 174
PKK 109, 165, 176, 177, 202, 212, 230, 257, 271
Plassnik, Ursula 187
Podgorny, Nikolaï 44
Poland 82, 92, 185
polarity 4, 23, 259
Polatkan, Hasan 12, 17
Pompidou, Georges 50–1
Poos, Jacques 99
Portugal 25n19, 82, 174
Posselt, Bernd 231
Powell, Colin L. 169, 170, 172, 173, 177, 180, 181, 198, 199, 210
power politics 4, 23, 37, 47, 57, 67, 76, 77, 88, 103, 259
pre-accession strategy 135, 179
privileged partnership 184–7, 207, 211, 231, 248, 257, 258
Prodi, Romano 121, 136, 138, 179, 180, 181, 245, 263
Progress Reports 135, 170, 201, 242
Provisional Protocol *see* Ankara Agreement
PTAs 50, 202, 263
Putin, Vladimir 184

QIZs 142, 150, 201, 266,
quotas 33, 36, 45, 58n11, 124, 131, 142, 150, 157n177, 165, 196, 201, 243, 266,

raisins 35
Rallis, George 86,
Ralston, Joseph 168
Ramer, Bruce M. 204
RAND Corporation 103, 127
Randall, Clarence B. 19
Rangel, Charlie 61–2,
Rasmussen, Anders Fogh 163, 173, 195, 230, 233, 248, 263, 273, 274
Reagan, Ronald 7, 77, 80–90, 91, 103, 108, 122, 256, 275
Realpolitik 255
Reeker, Philip T. 130
referenda: in Turkey 81; in Cyprus 180, 196
Reform Treaty 191
Regular Reports for Turkey 131, 201
Rehn, Olli 183, 230
Reliant Mermaid exercises 142
Republicans 5, 14, 118, 123, 264
reverse preferences 51
Rey, Jean 18, 53, 262
Rice, Condoleezza 172, 182, 185–9, 192–3, 194, 210
Rodman, Peter 68n19
Rogers, Bernard W. 85–6, 139, 198
Roj TV 230
Roth, Claudia 119
RRF 139, 169, 199
Rubin, James 124, 149
rule of law 154n93, 163, 237
Rumsfeld, Donald 198, 203
Rusk, Dean 30, 33, 34, 42, 48n11
Russel, Mark 86
Russia 12, 92, 119, 165, 184, 192, 213n12, 228, 229, 240, 244

Saddam Hussein 110, 171, 177, 198
Sailer, Steve 276n11
St. Malo declaration 138
Santer, Jacques 118, 124, 262
Saraçoğlu, Tevfik 66
Sarbanes, Paul 99, 101, 266
Sarkozy, Nicolas 185, 190, 191, 225–7, 230, 231, 233, 241
Sarper, Selim 20
Saudi Arabia 239, 240, 241
Sauvagnargues, Jean 63
Sayarı, Sabri 6

Schäuble, Wolfgang 184, 186
Schaetzel, Robert J. 50
Scharping, Rudolf 141
Scheffer, Jaap de Hoop 162
Schiff, Adam 187–8, 266, 267, 274
Schifter, Richard 125
Schmidt, Helmut 72
Schnabel, Rockwell Anthony 181
Schröder, Gerhard 129–30, 136, 169, 173, 175, 185, 203, 206, 207
Schüssel, Wolfgang 187
Scowcroft, Brent 277n23
SECI 125, 149, 263
Secularism 96, 101, 121, 138, 145, 163, 166, 184, 188, 193, 197, 203, 246, 269
Senate (US) *see* Congress
September 11 attacks 148, 164, 170, 202, 206, 209
Serbia 228
Sezer, Ahmet Necdet 107–8, 137–8, 163, 169, 225
Shattuck, John 127
Shia 239
Shultz, George P. 54
Simitis, Costas 132–4, 136–7, 141, 180
Simonet, Jacques 180
Sisco, Joseph 48n11
Six, the 14, 18, 33
SLG meetings 168, 261
Slovenia 193
Sobel, Clifford 207
Socialist International 141
Solana, Javier 133–7, 149, 195
Solarz, Stephen 99, 103, 188, 265
Soto, Álvaro de 180, 195
South Ossetia 213n12
Spain 51, 52, 53, 55, 57n3, 67n5, 82, 119, 138, 167, 174, 205, 241
Spain, James W. 59n31
SPD 129, 231
Spiers, Ronald I. 86
state (as an international actor) 3, 23, 67, 77, 88, 103, 147, 211, 259
strategic partnership 126, 168, 189, 211, 216n114
strategic vision document 189
Strausz-Hupe, Robert 84
Straw, Jack 187, 199, 203–4
Sudan 229
Sunnis 177, 184
survival 3, 23
Swartbol, Rob 207
Switzerland 25, 125
Syria 189, 228, 229, 240, 241, 243, 246, 270

Talbott, Strobe 122, 271
Tan, Namık 233–4
tariffs 21, 32, 33, 35, 36, 39n38, 45, 46, 50, 51, 54, 62, 65, 67, 77, 111, 142, 150, 152n26, 202
Taşhan, Seyfi 192
Taşpınar, Ömer 6, 268
teritorial waters 72, 132, 176
terrorism 82, 109, 119, 164, 194, 202, 206, 212, 229, 234, 243, 257, 270
Terzi, Giulio 245
textile products 112, 124, 131, 137, 142, 150, 176, 201, 211, 266
Thatcher, Margaret 86
third force (Europe as a) 13, 23, 30
Thorn, Gaston 76, 84, 88, 262
tobacco 32–3, 35, 36, 39n38, 45, 46, 52, 255, 266
Tocci, Nathalie 6
Torumtay, Necip 97
Trade Act of 1974 62
trade agreements 5, 35, 50, 52, 57n3, 100, 123–4, 130, 187, 202, 257, 265, 266
Trade Expansion Act 31
Transatlantic Legislators' Dialogue 237
Treaty on Conventional Armed Forces in Europe 83
TRNC 101, 114, 115, 123–4, 128, 134, 146, 194–5, 272
TRT 91, 136
Truman, Harry S. 10
Tsilas, Loucas 113, 115
Tunisia 21, 51, 239
Turkey: abolishing death penalty in 166; application of, for associate membership 16–7; application of, for full-membership 82; candidacy of 136; domestic politics in 74, 84, 87, 100, 102, 120, 129, 176, 194, 197, 247, 270; Europeanness of 53, 55–6, 57, 63, 102, 270, 272; harmonization packages of 166, 168, 197, 205, 164; reforming criminal code of 166
Turkic states 96, 97, 102
Turkish-American Business Council 83, 267
Turkish Season 225
Türkeş, Alpaslan 68n31
Türkmen, İlter 29–30, 41, 76, 82, 86, 90n37
TÜSİAD 167, 267
Tüzmen, Kürşat 229

UN 33, 123, 125, 133, 135, 137, 142, 148, 164, 172, 194, 195, 235–6
UNCTAD 52
Union for the Mediterranean 240
United Kingdom 14, 25n19, 30–1, 35, 38, 44, 47n3, 49, 50, 51, 52, 56, 64, 65, 67, 72, 73, 82, 86–7, 88, 90n37, 97, 101, 103, 112, 114, 117, 126, 137, 138, 140–1, 150, 155n124, 162, 166, 167, 174, 181, 182, 187, 191, 198–9, 202–4, 206, 207, 208, 212, 244–5, 248, 259, 262, 275
Ürgüplü, Suat H. 10, 44
US *see the relevant entries*
US-France Strategic Dialogue 232–3
USSR 11–2, 14, 18, 20, 21, 22–3, 30, 33–4, 35, 36, 38, 44, 46, 60, 62, 75, 76, 81, 82, 86, 87, 92, 96, 104n10, 109, 258, 270

Valley of the Wolves: Iraq 192
Vatican 179
Verheugen, Günter 134, 136, 163, 166, 174, 178–9, 258, 263
Vershbow, Alexander 233
Vietnam War 54
Vural, Volkan 215n79

Waltz, Kenneth 2, 8n6, 104n10, 276n3
Warren, Fletcher 16, 18, 20, 21
Warsaw Pact 92, 109
Washington Institute for Near East Policy 269
Washington Political Action Committee 95
Watergate scandal 56, 265
Welfare Party 110
West, the 5, 10, 11–2, 20, 21, 22, 23–4, 35, 36, 37, 47, 47n3, 53, 56, 64, 65, 66, 67, 71, 73–4, 76, 82, 87, 89n31, 94, 99, 120, 121, 125, 144, 145, 148–51, 163, 170, 171, 184, 192, 197, 232, 236–7, 240, 243, 246, 247, 258, 259, 269, 270, 272, 278n42
Westerwelle, Guido 232, 233
Westmacott, Peter 181, 187, 189, 203, 204
Weston, Thomas 168, 195, 199
WEU 91, 96, 99
Wexler, Robert 168–9, 191, 266, 268
White House 5, 27n57, 49, 50, 69, 73, 80, 82, 98, 129, 139, 144, 170, 172, 180, 182, 186, 188, 193, 209, 235
Whitfield, Ed 118, 168–9, 266, 268
Wikileaks 182–3, 194, 206, 207, 212, 231–3, 243, 248
Wilders, Geert 243–4
Wilson, Ross 188
Wolfowitz, Paul 167, 168, 170, 171, 172, 175, 177, 179, 194, 203, 209
World Bank 27n55, 125, 165
Wörner, Manfred 93, 96
WTO 201

Yaoundé Convention 35–6, 52, 56
Year of Europe 53, 54–5
Yeşilada, Birol 6, 8n7
Yılmaz, Mesut 91, 96–7, 108, 126–8, 140, 142, 144, 150
Yılmaz, Şuhnaz 6
Yom Kippur War 54
Yugoslavia 15, 51, 109
Yüksel, Ali Sait 92

Zemin, Jiang 128, 147, 261
Zhivkov, Todor 62
Ziyal, Uğur 168
Zoellick, Robert 100, 186, 265
Zorlu, Fatin Rüştü 15, 16, 17, 18, 19, 23, 27, 83